U.S. Government Printing Office

Style Manual

An official guide to the form and style of Federal Government printing

2008

GPO
U.S. GOVERNMENT PRINTING OFFICE
Keeping America Informed | www.gpo.gov

Production and Distribution Notes

This publication was typeset electronically using Helvetica and Minion Pro typefaces. It was printed using vegetable oil-based ink on recycled paper containing 30% post consumer waste.

The GPO STYLE MANUAL will be distributed to libraries in the Federal Depository Library Program. To find a depository library near you, please go to the Federal depository library directory at http://catalog.gpo.gov/fdlpdir/public.jsp.

The electronic text of this publication is available for public use free of charge at http://www.gpoaccess.gov/stylemanual/index.html.

For sale by the Superintendent of Documents, U.S. Government Printing Office
Internet: bookstore.gpo.gov   Phone: toll free (866) 512-1800;   DC area (202) 512-1800
Fax: (202) 512-2104 Mail: Stop IDCC, Washington, DC 20402-0001

ISBN 978-0-16-081811-0 (Cloth)

THE UNITED STATES GOVERNMENT PRINTING OFFICE STYLE MANUAL
IS PUBLISHED UNDER THE DIRECTION AND AUTHORITY OF

THE PUBLIC PRINTER OF THE UNITED STATES
Robert C. Tapella

———————

UNITED STATES GOVERNMENT PRINTING OFFICE
STYLE BOARD
M. Michael Abramson, *Chairman*

Ernest G. Baldwin	Kevin M. Lane
James T. Cameron	Barbara Day Prophet
Tony N. Gilbert	Margaret V. Ross
Michele Y. Harris	Andrew M. Sherman
Yalanda Johnson	Pamela S. Williams

———————

Ex officio
Olivier A. Girod, *Managing Director, Plant Operations*
John W. Crawford, *Production Manager, Plant Operations*
Dannie E. Young, *Superintendent, Pre-Press Division*

M. Michael Abramson	Terence D. Collins	Kenneth C. Puzey
Foreperson	*Foreperson*	*Foreperson*
Proof and Copy Markup Section	*Proof and Copy Markup Section*	*Proof and Copy Markup Section*
Shift 1	*Shift 2*	*Shift 3*

———————

JOINT COMMITTEE ON PRINTING
Representative Robert A. Brady, *Chairman*
Senator Dianne Feinstein, *Vice Chairman*

Representative Michael E. Capuano	Senator Daniel K. Inouye
Representative Susan A. Davis	Senator Patty Murray
Representative Vernon J. Ehlers	Senator Robert F. Bennett
Representative Kevin McCarthy	Senator Saxby Chambliss

———————

Previous printings of the GPO Style Manual: 1894, 1898, 1900, 1903, 1908, 1909, 1911, 1912, 1914, 1917, 1922, 1923, 1924, 1926, 1928, 1929, 1933, 1934, 1935, 1937, 1939, 1945, 1953, 1959, 1962, 1967, 1973, 1984, 2000

III

EXTRACT FROM THE PUBLIC PRINTING LAW

(TITLE 44, U.S.C.)

§ 1105. Form and style of work for departments

The Public Printer shall determine the form and style in which the printing or binding ordered by a department is executed, and the material and the size of type used, having proper regard to economy, workmanship, and the purposes for which the work is needed.

(Pub. L. 90–620, Oct. 22, 1968, 82 Stat. 1261.)

HISTORICAL AND REVISION NOTES

Based on 44 U.S. Code, 1964 ed., § 216 (Jan. 12, 1895, ch. 23, § 51, 28 Stat. 608).

About This Manual

By act of Congress the Public Printer is authorized to determine the form and style of Government printing. The GPO STYLE MANUAL is the product of many years of public printing experience, and its rules are based on principles of good usage and custom in the printing trade.

Editors and writers whose disciplines have taught them aspects of style different from rules followed in this MANUAL will appreciate the difficulty of establishing a single standard. The GPO STYLE MANUAL has served Federal printers since 1894, and with this 30th edition, the traditions of printing and graphic arts are carried forward in the 21st century.

Essentially, the GPO STYLE MANUAL is a standardization device designed to achieve uniform word and type treatment, and it aims for economy of word use. Such rules as are laid down for the submission of copy to GPO point to the most economical manner for the preparation and typesetting of manuscript. Following such rules eliminates additional chargeable processing by GPO.

It should be remembered that the GPO STYLE MANUAL is primarily a GPO printer's stylebook. Easy rules of grammar cannot be prescribed, for it is assumed that editors are versed in correct expression. Likewise, decisions on design and makeup are best determined by the individual publisher to meet the needs of the intended audience. As a printer's book, this MANUAL necessarily uses terms that are obvious to those skilled in the graphic arts.

Users of the GPO STYLE MANUAL should consider it as a general guide. Its rules cannot be regarded as rigid, for the printed word assumes many shapes and variations in type presentation. An effort has been made to provide complete coverage of those elements that enter into the translation of manuscript into type.

The GPO Style Board made significant revisions to update this edition of the GPO STYLE MANUAL. The changes include redesigning the format to make it more modern and easier to read; replacing "What is *GPO Access?*" with "GPO's Online Initiatives"; removing the atomic weights column from the Chemical Symbols table; expanding and updating time zone abbreviations;

listing additional entries to the Post Office abbreviations; extensively reviewing the capitalization chapter to remove outdated entries and include new ones; realigning the abbreviations lists to create a new list of technical abbreviations and initialisms; updating old and adding new tables to the Useful Tables chapter; expanding military titles; creating new sample pages for the Reports and Hearings chapter; providing many URLs as references; and including many suggestions by users.

Comments and suggestions from users of the GPO STYLE MANUAL are invited. All such correspondence should be addressed as follows:

GPO Style Board

Mail Stop PDE

U.S. Government Printing Office

732 North Capitol Street, NW.

Washington, DC 20401

email address: gpostyle@gpo.gov

For the purposes of the GPO STYLE MANUAL, printed examples throughout are to be considered the same as the printed rules.

Acknowledgments

The GPO Style Board would like to thank the following people for assistance in the production of this edition of the GPO STYLE MANUAL:

Stanley P. Anderson, Editor, U.S. Department of Agriculture, Natural Resources Conservation Service, National Soil Survey Center, Lincoln, Nebraska, for the new soil orders in the capitalization chapter.

Molly N. Cameron, for technical advice on the Index.

Robert W. Dahl, Cadastral Surveyor, U.S. Department of the Interior, Bureau of Land Management, Minerals & Realty Management Directorate, Division of Lands, Realty & Cadastral Survey (WO–350), for his contribution of the Principal Meridians and Base Lines of the United States tables.

Cynthia L. Etkin, Program Planning Specialist, Library Services and Content Management, Government Printing Office, for her technical advice on the ANSI/NISO standards for publications.

Robert R. Finch, Mark E. Rockwell, Michele L. Spiro, Operations Directorate, Document Automation and Production Service (DAPS), Defense Logistics Agency, for their contribution to the list of military ranks.

Dean Gardei, Brand/Web Manager, Government Printing Office, for the design of the cover and title page.

Jeremy Gelb, Pre-Press Specialist, Government Printing Office, for technical assistance in the production of this MANUAL.

Geography Division, U.S. Census Bureau, for supplying the cities list.

Robert McArtor, past Chairman of the GPO Style Board and U.S. Board on Geographic Names, who acted as an adviser to the present GPO Style Board.

Joanne Petrie, Office of the General Counsel, U.S. Department of Transportation, and Andrew Novick, National Institute of Standards and Technology, for their assistance with time zone abbreviations.

Betty R. Smith, composition system operator, Government Printing Office, for technical assistance in the production of this MANUAL.

Douglas E. Smith, Sr., Internal Printing Officer, Government Printing Office, for preproduction planning and administrative assistance.

Janice Sterling, Director, Creative Services, and Marco Marchegiani, Graphic Designer, Government Printing Office, for development and production of the new design.

Marcia Thompson, Director, Congressional Record Index Office, Government Printing Office, for revisions to the pages relating to the Congressional Record Index.

Employees of the Proof and Copy Markup Section of the Government Printing Office, for their contributions during the production process.

Current users who have contributed many ideas and suggestions that were incorporated into this edition of the GPO STYLE MANUAL.

GPO's Online Initiatives

Printing continues to serve an important purpose in the Federal Government. Congressional documents, official reports, pamphlets, books, regulations and statutes, passports, tax and census forms, statistical data, and more—in printed form these documents represent a major avenue of communication and information transaction between the Government and the public. In the 21st century, the Government Printing Office (GPO) is committed to providing printed information products for Congress, Federal agencies, and the courts as efficiently, creatively, and cost-effectively as the most modern technology will allow.

With the advent of the electronic information age, GPO has also assumed the responsibility for providing public access to the online versions of most of the official documents it prints, as well as—to the greatest extent possible—the online versions of Government publications that are not printed but are otherwise made available on other Federal Web sites. GPO recognizes that a Federal author today often begins the content creation process at a personal computer, and frequently publishes the final document on the Web, without creating a print version that will make its way to a user's hands or a library's shelves. Many Government publications are now born digital and published to the Web, with few if any copies printed for traditional public access via bookstores or libraries.

To accommodate this transition in Federal publishing strategies while preserving the core responsibility for ensuring public access to Government publications, in 1993 Congress enacted Public Law 103–40, the Government Printing Office Electronic Information Access Enhancement Act, which required GPO to establish online access to key Government publications and provide a system of storage to ensure permanent public access to the information they contain. Since then, the number of publications featured by the resulting Web site, *GPO Access*, at www.gpoaccess.gov, has grown exponentially, as has its use by the public. A decade later the National Archives and Records Administration formally recognized GPO as an affiliated archive for the digital content on the *GPO Access* site.

To meet continued public demand for online access to Government publications, provide for an increased range of search and retrieval options, and ensure the preservation of official Government information content in the 21st century, in 2004 GPO embarked on the construction of a more comprehensive online capability, called GPO's Federal Digital System, or FDsys. Scheduled to become available for public use in late 2008, the new system will serve as GPO's digital platform for the production, storage, and dissemination of official Government publications for the years to come.

GPO Access

Opened to the public in 1994, the *GPO Access* Web site was GPO's entrance into the digital age. *GPO Access* provides free electronic access to a wealth of important information products produced by the Federal Government. The information provided is the official published version, and information retrieved from *GPO Access* can be used without restriction unless specifically noted. This free service is funded through annual appropriations provided to GPO's Federal Depository Library Program.

Under the *GPO Access* legislation, the Superintendent of Documents, under the direction of the Public Printer, is required to: (1) Maintain an electronic directory of Federal electronic information; (2) provide a system of online access to the Congressional Record, the Federal Register, and other appropriate publications as determined by the Superintendent of Documents; (3) operate an electronic storage facility for Federal electronic information; and (4) maintain the Federal Bulletin Board, which was then already in existence.

GPO Access services

GPO Access services are designed to meet the needs of a variety of users. *GPO Access* consists of content and links, including official, full-text information from the three branches of the Federal Government. Databases are updated based on their print equivalent and generally date back to 1994.

Users can find information on the Federal Depository Library Program, which provides no-fee public access to publications disseminated by GPO, regardless of format. *GPO Access* enables users to locate a depository library in their area.

Users may also locate and order publications available for sale through GPO's Publication and Information Sales Program. Orders may be placed online securely through the U.S. Government Bookstore at http://bookstore.gpo. gov.

Ben's Guide to the U.S. Government provides learning tools for K–12 students, parents, and educators. The site provides age-specific explanations about how the Federal Government works, explains the use of the primary source materials available on *GPO Access*, and explains GPO's role in the Federal Government.

Users needing assistance with *GPO Access* or other dissemination services may direct inquiries to the GPO Contact Center specialists available by email (contactcenter@gpo.gov), telephone (1–866–512–1800), or fax (202–512–2104).

Authentication of digital documents

The increasing use of electronic documents poses a special challenge in verifying authenticity, because digital technology makes such documents easy to alter or copy in unauthorized or illegitimate ways.

To help meet this challenge, GPO has implemented digital signatures on certain electronic documents in *GPO Access* that not only establish GPO as the trusted information disseminator, but also provide the assurance that an electronic document has not been altered since GPO disseminated it.

In early 2008, GPO authenticated the first-ever online Federal budget by digital signature. The visible digital signatures on online PDF documents serve the same purpose as handwritten signatures or traditional wax seals on printed documents. The digital signature verifies document integrity and authenticity for online Federal documents, disseminated by GPO, at no cost to the customer.

GPO's Federal Digital System (FDsys)

A critical part of GPO's mission of *Keeping America Informed* is ensuring permanent access to published Government documents. GPO is developing a comprehensive digital content system capable of managing all known Federal Government documents within the scope of GPO's Federal Depository Library Program and other information dissemination programs. GPO's Federal Digital System (FDsys) is an integrated content management system which incorporates state-of-the-art technology for document authentication and digital preservation. FDsys supports GPO's transformation from a print-based environment to a content-based environment, in which digital content is created, submitted, preserved, authenticated, managed, and delivered upon request. The design of FDsys is based on the Reference Model for an Open Archival Information System (OAIS) (ISO 14721:2003), which describes a generalized structure for storing, preserving, and providing access to digital content over time.

FDsys will automate content life-cycle processes and make it easier to deliver digital content in formats suited to customers' needs. FDsys will allow Federal content creators to submit content for preservation, authentication, and delivery to users. Content entered into the system will be cataloged according to GPO and library standards, and will be available on the World Wide Web for searching and viewing, downloading and printing, as document masters for conventional and on-demand printing, or by other dissemination methods. Content may include text and associated graphics, video, audio, and other forms that emerge.

FDsys capabilities will be deployed in a series of releases. An internal proof-of-concept release of FDsys was completed in September 2007 to support the last stage of testing. FDsys is scheduled to become available to agencies and the public in early 2009, beginning a process of incremental releases. Each release will add functionality to the previous one. The first public release will provide FDsys core capabilities, including such foundational elements as system infrastructure and security, and a digital repository that conforms to the OAIS reference model and enables the management of content and metadata. This release will replace the familiar Wide Area Information Server (WAIS)-based *GPO Access*, in use since 1994, with enhanced search and retrieval functionality.

For a comprehensive discussion of system capabilities by release, see the FDsys documentation at http://www.gpo.gov/projects/fdsys_documents.htm.

Information

The rules of grammar, spelling, punctuation, and related matters, as stated in this MANUAL, will serve well when preparing documents for electronic dissemination. Most of the documents currently available via *GPO Access* are derived from databases used in the printing of Government publications. However, as electronic dissemination of Government information continues to grow, the rules as stated in this MANUAL will continue to be the GPO's standard for all document preparation, electronic or otherwise.

Contents

1. Advice to Authors and Editors

The GPO STYLE MANUAL is intended to facilitate Government printing. Careful observance of the following suggestions will aid in expediting your publication and also reduce printing costs.

1.1. Making changes after submission of copy delays the production of the publication and adds to the expense of the work; therefore, copy must be carefully edited before being submitted to the Government Printing Office.

1.2. Legible copy, not faint reproductions, must be furnished.

1.3. Copy should be on one side only with each sheet numbered consecutively. If both sides of copy are to be used, a duplicate set of copy must be furnished.

1.4. To avoid unnecessary expense, it is advisable to have each page begin with a new paragraph.

1.5. Proper names, signatures, figures, foreign words, and technical terms should be written plainly.

1.6. Chemical symbols, such as Al, Cl, Tl are sometimes mistaken for A1, C1, T1. Editors must indicate whether the second character is a letter or a figure.

1.7. Footnote reference marks in text and tables should be arranged consecutively from left to right across each page of copy.

1.8. Photographs, drawings, and legends being used for illustrations should be placed in the manuscript where they are to appear in the publication. They should be on individual sheets, as they are handled separately during typesetting.

1.9. If a publication is composed of several parts, a scheme of the desired arrangement must accompany the first installment of copy.

1.10. To reduce the possibility of costly blank pages, avoid use of new odd pages and halftitles whenever possible. Generally these refinements should be limited to quality bookwork.

1.11.   Samples should be furnished if possible. They should be plainly marked showing the desired type, size of type page, illustrations if any, paper, trim, lettering, and binding.

1.12.   In looseleaf or perforated-on-fold work, indicate folio sequence, including blank pages, by circling in blue. Begin with first text page (title). Do not folio separate covers or dividers.

1.13.   Indicate on copy if separate or self-cover. When reverse printing in whole or in part is required, indicate if solid or tone.

1.14.   Avoid use of oversize fold-ins wherever possible. This can be done by splitting a would-be fold-in and arranging the material to appear as facing pages in the text. Where fold-ins are numerous and cannot be split, consideration should be given to folding and inserting these into an envelope pasted to the inside back cover.

1.15.   Every effort should be made to keep complete jobs of over 4 pages to signatures (folded units) of 8, 12, 16, 24, or 32 pages. Where possible, avoid having more than two blank pages at the end.

1.16.   Indicate alternative choice of paper on the requisition. Where possible, confine choice of paper to general use items carried in inventory as shown in the GPO Paper Catalog.

1.17.   If nonstandard trim sizes and/or type areas are used, indicate head and back margins. Otherwise, GPO will determine the margins.

1.18.   Customers should submit copy for running heads and indicate the numbering sequence for folios, including the preliminary pages.

1.19.   Corrections should be made on first proofs returned, as later proofs are intended for verification only. All corrections must be indicated on the "R" (revise) set of proofs, and only that set should be returned to GPO.

1.20.   Corrections should be marked in the margins of a proof opposite the indicated errors, not by writing over the print or between the lines. All queries on proofs must be answered.

1.21.   The following GPO publications relate to material included in this MANUAL. They may be purchased from the Superintendent of Documents, Government Printing Office, Washington, DC 20402.

Word Division: Supplement to the United States Government Printing Office Style Manual

This publication serves as a quick reference guide for finding correct word divisions, as well as a spelling and pronunciation guide. In addition to the list of words with divisions, it also contains wordbreak rules and line-ending rules. Prepared especially for GPO printers and proofreaders, this supplement is equally useful for keyboarding. 1987.

Government Paper Specifications

The purpose of these standards is to achieve compliance with relevant statutes regarding printing papers; address environmental, workplace safety, and paper longevity issues; and achieve maximum savings in the Government's paper purchases. 2008.

GPO Paper Samples

This publication is a supplement to Government Paper Specification Standards. It includes samples of papers used by GPO. Used as a planning aid and guide in selecting an adequate grade, weight, and color of paper for a job of printing. 2008.

For the latest information about the availability of these and other such publications, go to: http://bookstore.gpo.gov.

1.22. Corrections made to proofs should be indicated as follows:

⊙	Insert period	*rom*.	Roman type
⋏	Insert comma	*caps.*	Caps—used in margin
:	Insert colon	≡	Caps—used in text
;	Insert semicolon	*c+sc*	Caps & small caps—used in margin
?	Insert question mark	≊	Caps & small caps—used in text
!	Insert exclamation mark	*l.c.*	Lowercase—used in margin
=/	Insert hyphen	/	Used in text to show deletion or substitution
⩓	Insert apostrophe		
⩔⩔	Insert quotation marks	ℓ	Delete
⊹	Insert 1-en dash	ℨ	Delete and close up
⊹	Insert 1-em dash	*w.f.*	Wrong font
#	Insert space	⊂	Close up
ld>	Insert ( ) points of space	⊐	Move right
shill	Insert shilling	⊏	Move left
⋁	Superior	⊓	Move up
⋀	Inferior	⊔	Move down
(/)	Parentheses	‖	Align vertically
[/]	Brackets	=	Align horizontally
☐	Indent 1 em	⊐⊏	Center horizontally
☐☐	Indent 2 ems	⊓	Center vertically
¶	Paragraph	*eq.#*	Equalize space—used in margin
no ¶	No paragraph	⋁⋁⋁	Equalize space—used in text
tr	Transpose[1]—used in margin	....	Let it stand—used in text
∼	Transpose[2]—used in text	*stet.*	Let it stand—used in margin
sp	Spell out	⊗	Letter(s) not clear
ital	Italic—used in margin	*run over*	Carry over to next line
___	Italic—used in text	*run back*	Carry back to preceding line
b.f.	Boldface—used in margin	*out, see copy*	Something omitted—see copy
∼∼∼	Boldface—used in text	*9/?*	Question to author to delete[3]
s.c.	Small caps—used in margin	∧	Caret—General indicator used to mark position of error.
≡≡≡	Small caps—used in text		

[1] In lieu of the traditional mark "tr" used to indicate letter or number transpositions, the striking out of the incorrect letters or numbers and the placement of the correct matter in the margin of the proof is the preferred method of indicating transposition corrections.

[2] Corrections involving more than two characters should be marked by striking out the entire word or number and placing the correct form in the margin. This mark should be reserved to show transposition of words.

[3] The form of any query carried should be such that an answer may be given simply by crossing out the complete query if a negative decision is made or the right-hand (question mark) portion to indicate an affirmative answer.

TYPOGRAPHICAL ERRORS

reset 8pt. C & SC

It does not appear that the earliest printers had any method of correcting errors before the form was on the press. The learned correctors of the first two centuries of printing were not proofreaders in our sense, they were rather what we should term office editors. Their labors were chiefly to see that the proof corresponded to the copy, but that the printed page was correct in its latinity—that the words were there, and that the sense was right. They cared but little about orthography, bad letters, or purely printers' errors, and when the text seemed to them wrong they consulted fresh authorities or altered it on their own responsibility. Good proofs, in the modern sense, were impossible until professional readers were employed—men who had first a printer's education, and then spent many years in the correction of proof. The orthography of English, which for the past century has undergone little change, was very fluctuating until after the publication of Johnson's Dictionary, and capitals, which have been used with considerable regularity for the past 80 years, were previously used on the hit or miss plan. The approach to regularity, so far as we have, may be attributed to the growth of a class of professional proofreaders, and it is to them that we owe the correctness of modern printing. More errors have been found in the Bible than in any other one work. For many generations it was frequently the case that Bibles were brought out stealthily, from fear of governmental interference. They were frequently printed from imperfect texts, and were often modified to meet the views of those who published them. The story is related that a certain woman in Germany, who was the wife of a printer, had become disgusted with the continual assertions of the superiority of man over woman which she had heard, hurried into the composing room while her husband was at supper and altered a sentence in the Bible, which he was printing, so that it read Narr instead of Herr, thus making the verse read "And he shall be thy fool" instead of "And he shall be thy lord." The word not was omitted by Barker, the king's printer in England in 1632, in printing the seventh commandment. He was fined £3000 on this account.

NOTE.—The system of marking proofs can be made easier by the use of an imaginary vertical line through the center of the type area. The placement of corrections in the left-hand margin for those errors found in the left-hand portion of the proof and in the right-hand margin for right-side errors prevents overcrowding of marks and facilitates corrections.

2. General Instructions

Job planning

2.1. The use of computers has dramatically altered every phase of the printing industry beginning with the basic planning of each new job. New publications are evaluated by application specialists who review their requirements and design the necessary formats. Each format is made to conform exactly to the copy's specifications for page dimensions, line length, indentions, typefaces, etc. Upon completion, sample pages are produced and submitted to the customer. At this time, customer agencies are requested to indicate precise details of any style changes because this set of pages serves as a guide for the copy preparer, the beginning of actual production.

2.2. In recent years, changes in the needs of the library community have led to a move toward uniform treatment of the component parts of publications. In developing standards to guide publishers of Government documents, consideration has been given to the changing needs of those who seek to produce, reference, index, abstract, store, search, and retrieve data. Certain identifying elements shall be printed on all publications in accordance with this MANUAL and with standards developed by the (ANSI) American National Standards Institute.

Publications such as books and pamphlets should contain:
(a) Title and other title information;
(b) Name of department issuing or creating publication;
(c) Name of author(s) and editor(s) (department or individual);
(d) Date of issuance;
(e) Availability (publisher, printer, or other source and address);
(f) Superintendent of Documents classification and stock numbers if applicable; and
(g) The ISBN (International Standard Book Number).

(See ANSI Standard Z39.15, Title Leaves of a Book.)

Reports of a scientific or technical nature should contain:
(a) Title and other title information;
(b) Report number;

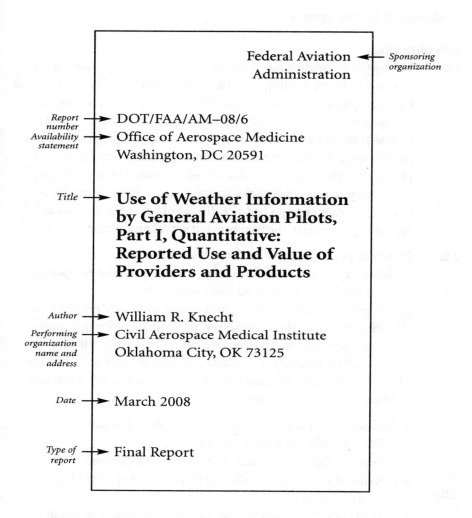

Sponsoring organization → Federal Aviation Administration

Report number → DOT/FAA/AM–08/6

Availability statement → Office of Aerospace Medicine
Washington, DC 20591

Title → **Use of Weather Information by General Aviation Pilots, Part I, Quantitative: Reported Use and Value of Providers and Products**

Author → William R. Knecht

Performing organization name and address → Civil Aerospace Medical Institute
Oklahoma City, OK 73125

Date → March 2008

Type of report → Final Report

Notes:

(1) This sample report cover is reduced in size.

(2) In this sample, items are justified left. Other cover designs and typefaces are acceptable.

(3) This sample page was prepared according to the guidelines of the American National Standards Institute, 25 West 43d St., New York, NY 10036. Users of ANSI standards are cautioned that all standards are reviewed periodically and subject to revision.

(c) Author(s);
(d) Performing organization;
(e) Sponsoring department;
(f) Date of issuance;
(g) Type of report and period covered;
(h) Availability (publisher, printer, or other source and address); and
(i) Superintendent of Documents classification and stock numbers if applicable.

(See ANSI/NISO Standard Z39.18—1995, Scientific and Technical Reports—Elements, Organization, and Design.)

Journals, magazines, periodicals, and similar publications should contain:
(a) Title and other title information;
(b) Volume and issue numbers;
(c) Date of issue;
(d) Publishing or sponsoring department;
(e) Availability (publisher, printer, or other source and address);
(f) International Standard Serial Number; and
(g) Superintendent of Documents classification and stock numbers if applicable.

(See ANSI Standard Z39.1, American Standard Reference Data and Arrangement of Periodicals.)

Makeup

2.3.   The design and makeup of a publication is the responsibility of the publisher. However, when the following elements occur in Government publications, they generally appear in the sequence listed below. The designation "new odd page" generally refers to bookwork and is not required in most pamphlet- and magazine-type publications.

(a) *Frontispiece*, faces title page.

(b) *False title* (frontispiece, if any, on back).

(c) *Title page* (new odd page).

(d) *Back of title*, blank, but frequently carries such useful bibliographic information as list of board members, congressional resolution authorizing publication, note of editions and printings, GPO imprint if departmental imprint appears on title page, sales notice, etc.

(e) *Letter of transmittal* (new odd page).

(f) *Foreword*, differs from a preface in that it is an introductory note written as an endorsement by a person other than the author (new odd page). An introduction differs from a foreword or a preface in that it is the initial part of the text; if the book is divided into chapters, it should be the first chapter.

(g) *Preface*, by author (new odd page).

(h) *Acknowledgments* (if not part of preface) (new odd page).

(i) *Contents* (new odd page), immediately followed by list of illustrations and list of tables, as parts of contents.

(j) *Text*, begins with page 1 (if halftitle is used, begins with p. 3).

(k) *Glossary* (new odd page).

(l) *Bibliography* (new odd page).

(m) *Appendix* (new odd page).

(n) *Index* (new odd page).

2.4.   Preliminary pages use small-cap Roman numerals. Pages in the back of the book (index, etc.), use lowercase Roman numerals.

2.5.   Booklets of 32 pages or less can be printed more economically with a self-cover. A table of contents, title page, foreword, preface, etc., is not usually necessary with so few pages. If some of this preliminary matter is necessary, it is more practical if combined; i.e., contents on cover; contents, title, and foreword on cover 2, etc.

2.6.   Widow lines (lines less than full width of measure) at top of pages are to be avoided, if possible, but are permitted if absolutely necessary to maintain uniform makeup and page depth. Rewording to fill the line is a preferred alternative.

2.7. Paragraphs may start on the last line of a page whenever necessary. If it is found necessary to make a short page, the facing page should be of approximate equal depth.

2.8. A blank space or sink of 6 picas should be placed at the head of each new odd or even page of 46-pica or greater depth; pages with a depth of from 36 to 45 picas, inclusive, will carry a 5-pica sink; pages less than 36 picas, 4 picas.

2.9. When top centered folios are used, the folio on a new page is set 2 points smaller than the top folios. They are centered at the bottom and enclosed in parentheses.

2.10. Where running heads with folios are used, heads are included in overall page depth. However, first pages of chapters and pages with bottom folios do not include the folios as part of the overall page depth.

2.11. Jobs that have both running heads and bottom folios or just bottom folios will align all of the page numbers on the bottom in the margin, including those on preliminary pages. If at all possible avoid use of running heads in conjunction with bottom folios.

2.12. Contents, list of illustrations, preface, or any other matter that makes a page in itself will retain normal 6-pica sink.

2.13. Footnote references are repeated in boxheads or in continued lines over tables, unless special orders are given not to do so.

2.14. When a table continues, its headnote is repeated without the word *Continued*.

2.15. A landscape or broadside table that continues from an even to an odd page must be positioned to read through the center (gutter) of the publication when its size is not sufficient to fill both pages.

2.16. A broadside table of less than page width will center on the page.

2.17. Centerheads, whether in boldface, caps, caps and small caps, small caps, or italic, should have more space above than below. Uniform spacing should be maintained throughout the page.

2.18.   In making up a page of two or more columns, text preceding a page-width illustration will be divided equally into the appropriate number of columns above the illustration.

2.19.   Two or more short footnotes may be combined into one line, with 2 ems of space between.

> [1] Preliminary.   [2] Including imported cases.   [3] Imported.

2.20.   All backstrips should read down (from top to bottom).

Copy preparation

2.21.   At the beginning of each job the proper formats must be plainly marked. New Odd or New Page, Preliminary, Cover, Title, or Back Title should also be plainly indicated.

2.22.   Copy preparers must mark those things not readily understood when reading the manuscript. They must also mark the correct element identifier code for each data element, as well as indicate other matters of style necessary to give the publication good typographic appearance.

2.23.   Preparers must indicate the proper subformat at the beginning of each extension, verify folio numbers, and plainly indicate references, footnotes, cut-ins, etc. Unless otherwise marked, text matter will be set in 10-point solid and tables in 7 point. In tables utilizing down rules, unless a specific weight is requested by the customer, hairline rules will be used. (See rule 13.3.)

2.24.   Quoted or extract matter and lists should be set smaller than text with space above and below. Quotation marks at the beginning and end of paragraphs should be omitted. If the same type size is used, quoted matter should be indented 2 ems on both sides with space top and bottom, and initial and closing quotes should be omitted.

Capitalization

2.25.   Unusual use of capital and lowercase letters should be indicated by the customer to guarantee correct usage.

Datelines, addresses, and signatures

2.26. Copy preparers must mark caps, small caps, italic, abbreviations, indentions, and line breaks where necessary. (For more detailed instructions, see Chapter 16 "Datelines, Addresses, and Signatures.")

Decimals and common fractions

2.27. In figure columns containing both decimals and common fractions, such decimals and/or fractions will not be aligned. The columns will be set flush right.

"Et cetera," "etc.," and "and so forth"

2.28. In printing a speaker's language, the words *and so forth* or *et cetera* are preferred, but in "FIC & punc." matter *etc.*, is acceptable. If a quoted extract is set in type smaller than that of the preceding text and the speaker has summed up the remainder of the quotation with the words *and so forth* or *et cetera*, these words should be placed at the beginning of the next line, flush and lowercase, and an em dash should be used at the end of the extract.

Folioing and stamping copy

2.29. Folio numbers should be placed in the upper right corner, preferably half an inch from the top.

Headings

2.30. The element identifier codes to be used for all headings must be marked. Caps, caps and small caps, small caps, caps and lowercase, lowercase first up (first word and proper nouns capitalized), or italic must be prepared. (See rule 3.49.)

Pickup

2.31. The jacket number of a job from which matter is to be picked up must be indicated. New matter and pickup matter should conform in style.

Sidenotes and cut-in notes

2.32. Sidenotes and cut-in notes are set each line flush left and ragged right, unless otherwise prepared, and are always set solid. Sidenotes are usually set in 6 point, 4½ picas wide. Footnotes to sidenotes and text should be set 21½ picas.

> SEC. 920. Abuse of the rule.
>
> An alleged violation of the rule relating to admission to the floor presents a question of privilege (III, 2624, 2625; VI, 579), but not a higher question of privilege than an election case (III, 2626). In one case where an ex-Member was abusing the privilege * * *.

Signs, symbols, etc.

2.33. All signs, symbols, dashes, superiors, etc., must be plainly marked. Names of Greek letters must be indicated, as they are frequently mistaken for italic or symbols.

2.34. Some typesetting systems produce characters that look the same as figures. A lowercase l resembles a figure 1 and a capital O looks like a figure 0. Questionable characters will be printed as figures unless otherwise marked.

Letters illustrating shape and form

2.35. Capital letters of the text face will be used to illustrate shape and form, as U-shape(d), A-frame, T-bone, and I-beam.

2.36. Plurals are formed by adding an apostrophe and the letter s to letters illustrating shape and form, such as T's and Y's. *Golf tee(s)* should be spelled, as shape is not indicated.

2.37. A capital letter is used in *U-boat*, *V–8*, and other expressions which have no reference to shape or form.

Fol. lit. and FIC & punc.

2.38. After submittal to GPO, manuscript copy is rubber-stamped "Fol. lit." or "FIC & punc." The difference between these two typesetting instructions is explained thus:

> Copy is followed when stamped "Fol. lit." (follow literally). Copy authorized to be marked "Fol. lit." must be thoroughly prepared by the requisitioning agency as to capitalization, punctuation (including

compounding), abbreviations, signs, symbols, figures, and italic. Such copy, including even obvious errors, will be followed. The lack of preparation on copy so designated shall, in itself, constitute preparation. "Fol. lit." does not include size and style of type or spacing.

Obvious errors are corrected in copy marked "FIC & punc." (follow, including capitalization and punctuation).

2.39. In congressional hearings, the name of the interrogator or witness who continues speaking is repeated following a head set in boldface, a paragraph enclosed in parentheses, and a paragraph enclosed in brackets.

In a head set in boldface, the title "Mr." is not used, and "the Honorable" preceding a name is shortened to "Hon." Street addresses are also deleted. Example: "Statement of Hon. John P. Blank, Member, American Bar Association, Washington, DC."

2.40. Paragraph or section numbers (or letters) followed by figures or letters in parentheses will close up, as "section 7(B)(1)(*a*)," "paragraph 23(*a*)," "paragraph b(7)," "paragraph (*a*)(2)"; *but* "section 9(a) (*1*) and (*2*)", "section 7 *a* and *b*". In case of an unavoidable break, division will be made after elements in parentheses, and no hyphen is used.

2.41. *Bill style.*—Bill copy will be followed as supplied. Bills will be treated as "FIC & punc." This data is transmitted to the GPO via fiber optic transmission with element identifier codes in place. Therefore, it is not cost effective to prepare the manuscript as per the GPO STYLE MANUAL and update the data once it is in type form.

2.42. Copy preparer's instructions, which accompany each job, are written to cover the general style and certain peculiarities or deviations from style. These instructions must be followed.

Abbreviations
2.43. In marking abbreviations to be spelled, preparers must show what the spelled form should be, unless the abbreviations are common and not susceptible to more than one construction. An unfamiliar abbreviation, with spelled-out form unavailable, is not changed.

Type composition

2.44. Operators and revisers must study carefully the rules governing composition.

2.45. In correcting pickup matter, the operator must indicate plainly on the proof what portion, if any, was actually reset.

2.46. Every precaution must be taken to prevent the soiling of proofs, as it is necessary for the reviser to see clearly every mark on the margin of a proof after it has been corrected.

2.47. Corrections of queries intended for the author are not to be made. Such queries, however, are not to be carried on jobs going directly to press.

Leading and spacing

2.48. Spacing of text is governed by the leading, narrow spacing being more desirable in solid than in leaded matter.

2.49. A single justified word space will be used between sentences. This applies to all types of composition.

2.50. Center or flush heads set in caps, caps and small caps, small caps, or boldface are keyed with regular justified spaces between words.

2.51. Centerheads are set apart from the text by the use of spacing. The amount of space varies with each publication. However, more space is always inserted above a heading than below. In 10-point type, the spacing would be 10 points over and 8 points under a heading; in 8- and 6-point type, the spacing would be 8 points above and 6 points below.

2.52. Solid matter (text) is defined as those lines set without horizontal space between them. Leaded text is defined as lines separated by 1 or 2 points of space.

2.53. Unless otherwise marked, flush heads are separated from text by 4 points of space above and 2 points of space below in solid matter, and by 6 points of space above and 4 points of space below in leaded matter.

2.54. Full-measure numbered or lettered paragraphs and quoted extracts are not separated by space from adjoining matter.

2.55. Extracts which are set off from the text by smaller type or are indented on both sides or indented 3 ems on the left side (courtwork only) are separated by 6 points of space in leaded matter and by 4 points of space in solid matter.

2.56. Extracts set solid in leaded matter are separated from the text by 6 points.

2.57. Flush lines following extracts are separated by 6 points of space in leaded matter and by 4 points in solid matter.

2.58. Footnotes are leaded if the text is leaded, and are solid if the text is solid.

2.59. Legends are leaded if the text is leaded, and solid if the text is solid. Leaderwork is separated from text by 4 points above and 4 points below.

Indentions

2.60. In measures less than 30 picas, the paragraph indention is 1 em. Paragraph indentions in cut-in matter are 3 ems, overs are 2 ems. Datelines and signatures are indented in multiples of 2 ems. Addresses are set flush left.

2.61. In matter set 30 picas or wider, the paragraph indention is 2 ems. Paragraph indentions in cut-in matter are 6 ems, overs are 4 ems. Datelines and signatures are indented in multiples of 2 ems. Addresses are set flush left.

2.62. In measures less than 30 picas, overruns in hanging indentions are 1 em more than the first line, except that to avoid conflict with a following indention (for example, of a subentry or paragraph), the overrun indention is made 1 em more than the following line.

2.63. In matter set 30 picas or wider, overruns in hanging indentions are 2 ems more than the first line, except that to avoid conflict with a following indention (for example, of a subentry or paragraph), the overrun indention is made 2 ems more than the following line.

2.64.   Indention of matter set in smaller type should be the same, in points, as that of adjoining main-text indented matter.

2.65.   Two-line centerheads are centered, but heads of three or more lines are set with a hanging indention.

2.66.   Overs in flush heads are indented 2 ems in measures less than 30 picas, and 3 ems in wider measures.

Legends for illustrations

2.67.   It is preferred that legends and explanatory data consisting of one or two lines are set centered, while those with more than two lines are set with a hanging indention. Legends are set full measure regardless of the width of the illustration. Paragraph style is acceptable.

2.68.   Legend lines for illustrations which appear broad or turn page (landscape) should be printed to read up; an even-page legend should be on the inside margin and an odd-page legend on the outside margin.

2.69.   Unless otherwise indicated, legends for illustrations are set in 8-point roman, lowercase.

2.70.   Periods are used after legends and explanatory remarks beneath illustrations. However, legends without descriptive language do not use a period. (See rule 8.112.)

2.71.   At the beginning of a legend or standing alone, *Figure* preceding the identifying number or letter is set in caps and small caps and is not abbreviated.

> FIGURE 5, *not* FIG. 5   FIGURE A, *not* FIG. A

2.72.   If a chart carries both a legend and footnotes, the legend is placed above the chart.

2.73.   Letter symbols used in legends for illustrations are set in lowercase italic without periods.

Proofreading

2.74.   All special instructions, layouts, and style sheets must be included with the first installment of each job.

2.75. If the proofreader detects inconsistent or erroneous statements, it is his or her responsibility to query them.

2.76. If the grammatical construction of a sentence or clause is questioned by a proofreader and it seems desirable to change the form, he or she must indicate the proposed correction, add a query mark, and enclose all in a circle.

2.77. All queries appearing on the copy must be carried to the author's set of proofs.

2.78. Proofs that are illegible or are in any manner defective must be called to the attention of the deskperson.

2.79. The manner in which correction marks are made on a proof is of considerable importance. Straggling, unsymmetrical characters, disconnected marks placed in the margin above or below the lines to which they relate, irregular lines leading from an incorrect letter or word to a correction, large marks, marks made with a blunt pencil, indistinct marks, and frequent use of the eraser to obliterate marks hastily or incorrectly made are faults to be avoided.

2.80. In reading proof of wide tables, the proofreader should place the correction as near as possible to the error. The transposition mark should not be used in little-known words or in figures. It is better to cancel the letters or figures and write them in the margin in the order in which they are to appear.

2.81. To assure proper placement of footnotes, the proofreader and reviser must draw a ring around footnote references on the proofs, then check off each corresponding footnote number.

2.82. Proofreaders must not make important changes in indentions or tables without consulting the referee.

2.83. The marks of the copy preparer will be followed, as he or she is in a position to know more about the peculiarities of a job than one who reads but a small portion of it.

2.84. Any mark which will change the proof from the copy as prepared must be circled in the margin.

2.85. All instructions on copy must be carried on proof by readers.

2.86. Folios of copy must be run by the proofreader and marked on the proof.

2.87. All instructions, comments, and extraneous notes on both copy and proofs which are not intended to be set as part of the text must be circled.

Revising galley proofs

2.88. The importance of revising proofs cannot be overemphasized. Although a reviser is not expected to read proof, it is not enough to follow the marks found on the proof. He or she should be alert to detect errors and inconsistencies and must see that all corrections have been properly made and that words or lines have not been transposed or eliminated in making the corrections.

2.89. A reviser must not remodel the punctuation of the proofreaders or make any important changes. If an important change should be made, the reviser must submit the proposed change to the supervisor for a decision.

2.90. In the body of the work, new pages must be properly indicated on the proof. (For new page information, see rule 2.3 "Makeup.")

2.91. All instructions and queries on proofs must be transferred to the revised set of proofs.

Revising page proofs

2.92. Page revising requires great diligence and care. The reviser must see that the rules governing the instructions of previous workers have been followed.

2.93. The reviser is responsible for marking all bleed and off-center pages.

2.94. A blank page must be indicated at the bottom of the preceding page.

2.95. Special care must be exercised in revising corrected matter. If it appears that a correction has not been made, the reviser should carefully examine each line on the page to see if the correction was inserted in the wrong place.

2.96. The following rules must be carefully observed:

(a) See that the proof is clean and clear; request another if necessary.

(b) Verify that the galley proofs are in order and that the data on the galleys runs in properly to facilitate continuous makeup.

(c) Make sure that different sets of proofs of the same job are correctly marked in series ("R," "2R," "3R," etc.); where a sheet is stamped "Another proof," carry the same designating "R" on the corresponding clean proof. Advance the "R," "2R," "3R," etc., on each set of page proofs returned from the originating office.

(d) Run the page folios, make sure they are consecutive and that the running heads, if used, are correct. Check connection pages. Verify correct sequence for footnote references and placement. It is imperative that footnotes appear or begin on the same page as their reference, unless style dictates that all footnotes are to appear together in one location.

(e) Watch for dropouts, doublets, and transpositions.

(f) Legend lines of full-page illustrations that appear broad should be printed to read up—the even-page legend on the binding or inside margin and the odd-page legend on the outside margin.

(g) If a footnote is eliminated, do not renumber the footnotes; change footnote to read "Footnote eliminated."

2.97. If a footnote is added in proof, use the preceding number with a superior letter added, as [15a].

2.98. Where a table with footnotes falls at the bottom of a page containing footnotes to text, print the table footnotes above the text footnotes, separated by a rule 50 points long, flush left, with spacing on each side of the rule. (See also rule 13.77.)

Press revising

2.99. Press revising calls for the exercise of utmost care. The press reviser must be thoroughly familiar with the style and makeup of Government publications. He or she is required to OK all forms that go to press—bookwork, covers, jobwork, etc.—and must see that all queries are answered. A knowledge of the bindery operations required to complete a book or job and familiarity with all types of imposition, folds, etc., is helpful. The reviser must be capable of ascertaining the proper head, back, and side margins for all work, to ensure proper trimming of the completed job.

2.100. Although speed is essential when forms reach the press reviser, accuracy is still paramount and must not be sacrificed.

Signature marks, etc.

2.101. Unless otherwise indicated, signature marks are set in 6-point lowercase and indented 3 ems.

2.102. Figures indicating the year should follow the jacket number in signature marks:

125–327—08——4   116–529—08—vol. 1——3
116–529—08—pt. 5——3

2.103. When the allmark (○) and signature or the imprint and signature appear on same page, the signature line is placed below the allmark or imprint. (See rule 2.117.)

2.104. The allmark is placed below the page, bulletin, or circular number but above the signature line, if both appear on the same page.

2.105. Imprints and signature lines appearing on short pages of text are placed at the bottom of the page.

2.106. On a congressional job reprinted because of change, the House and Senate have approved the following styles:

House of Representatives: Senate:
★17–234—08——2   17–235—08——2 ★(Star Print)

2.107. The following forms are used for signature marks in House and Senate documents and reports printed on session jackets:

H. Doc. 73, 08–1——2	S. Doc. 57, 08–1——2
S. Doc. 57, 08–2, pt. 1——2	S. Doc. 57, 08–2, vol. 1——2
H. Rept. 120, 08–2——8	S. Rept. 100, 08–2——9

2.108. In a document or report printed on other than a session jacket, use the jacket number, year, and signature number only, omitting the document or report number. (See rule 2.102.)

2.109. For pasters, the jacket number, the year, and the page to be faced by the paster are used as follows (note punctuation):

12–344——08 (Face p. 10)

2.110. On a paster facing an even page, the marks are placed on the lower right-hand side; on a paster facing an odd page, the marks are placed on the lower left-hand side.

2.111. If more than one paster faces the same page, each is numbered as follows:

12–344——08 (Face p. 19) No. 1
12–344——08 (Face p. 19) No. 2

2.112. When a paster follows the text, the allmark is placed on the last page of the text and never on the paster.

Reprints

2.113. To aid bibliographic identification of reprints or revisions, the dates of the original edition and of reprint or revision should be supplied by the author on the title page or in some other suitable place. Thus:

First edition July 1990	Original edition May 1990
Reprinted July 1995	Reprinted May 1995
First printed June 1990	Revised July 1997
Revised June 1995	

2.114. The year in the imprint on cover, title page, or elsewhere is not changed from that in the original print, nor are the signatures changed, unless other mends are necessary.

Imprints

2.115.   Unless otherwise stipulated, the GPO imprint must appear on all printed matter, with the exception of certain classified work.

2.116.   The full GPO imprint is used on the title page of a congressional speech.

2.117.   The imprint and allmark are not used together on any page; if one is used, the other is omitted.

2.118.   The imprint is not used on a halftitle or on any page of a cover, with the exception of congressional hearings.

2.119.   If there is a title page, the imprint is placed on the title page; but if there is no title page, or if the title page is entirely an illustration, the imprint is placed on the last page of the text 4 ems from flush right and below the bottom folio.

2.120.   The GPO logo is used only on GPO publications. If it is printed on page ii, the full imprint is used on the title page; if it is printed on the title page, use the half imprint only, thus—Washington : 2008.

Sales notices

2.121.   The use of sales notices is discouraged.

2.122.   If there is a cover but no title page, the sales notice is printed on the cover. Unless otherwise indicated, if there is a title page, with or without a cover, the sales notice is printed at the bottom of the title page below a cross rule. If there is no cover or title page, the sales notice is printed at the end of the text, below the imprint, and the two are separated by a cross rule.

Imprint variations

2.123.   This is one style of an imprint that can appear on the title page.

For sale by the Superintendent of Documents, U.S. Government Printing Office
• Internet: bookstore.gpo.gov • Phone: Toll Free 866–512–1800
• DC area 202–512–1800 • Fax: 202–512–2104
• Mail: Stop SSOP, Washington, DC 20402–0001
• www.gpoaccess.gov

2.124.   In the event that a title page is not used, the imprint is printed on the last page and positioned flush left below the text.

> For sale by the Superintendent of Documents, U.S. Government Printing Office
> • Internet: bookstore.gpo.gov • Phone: toll free 866–512–1800
> • DC area 202–512–1800 • Fax: 202–512–2250
> • Mail: Stop SSOP, Washington, DC 20402–0001
> • www.gpoaccess.gov

2.125.   Outside-purchase publications are identified by an open star at the beginning of the imprint line. These lines are positioned 4 ems from the right margin.

> ☆ U.S. GOVERNMENT PRINTING OFFICE: 2008—456–789

2.126.   Publications purchased outside which are reprinted by the GPO use an em dash in lieu of the open star.

> —U.S. GOVERNMENT PRINTING OFFICE: 2008—456–789

2.127.   Jobs set on outside purchase but printed by the GPO use an asterisk in lieu of the open star.

> *U.S. GOVERNMENT PRINTING OFFICE: 2008—456–789

2.128.   Publications produced from camera copy supplied to the GPO are identified by *cc* printed at the end of the line.

> U.S. GOVERNMENT PRINTING OFFICE: 2008—123–456–cc

Franking

2.129.   The franking (mailing) privilege on covers for Government publications should be at least 1⅛ inches from the trim.

Bibliographies or references

2.130.   There are many styles available to bibliographers, for there are many classes of documents. A Government bulletin citation, according to one authority, would be treated as follows:

> Author's name (if the article is signed); title of article (in quotation marks); the publication (usually in italic), with correct references to volume, number, series, pages, date, and publisher (U.S. Govt. Print. Off.).

Therefore the example would read:

> U.S. Department of the Interior, "Highlights in history of forest and related natural source conservation," *Conservation Bulletin*, No. 41 (serial number not italic), Washington, U.S. Dept. of the Interior (*or* U.S. Govt. Print. Off.), 1997. 1 p. (*or* p. 1).

Another Government periodical citation would read as follows:

> Reese, Herbert Harshman, "How To Select a Sound Horse," *Farmers' Bulletin*, No. 779, pp. 1–26 (1926), U.S. Dept. of Agriculture.

Clarity may be maintained by capitalizing each word in book titles, but only the first word in the title of articles.

Other examples are:

> Preston W. Slosson, *The Great Crusade And After: 1914–1928* (New York: Macmillan, 1940)
>
> Edward B. Rosa, "The economic importance of the scientific work of the government," *J. Wash. Acad. Sci.* 10, 342 (1920)

or:

> Preston W. Slosson, The Great Crusade and After: 1914–1928 (New York: Macmillan, 1940)
>
> Edward B. Rosa, "The Economic Importance of the Scientific Work of the Government," J. Wash. Acad. Sci. 10, 342 (1920)

Note that the principal words in both book titles and titles of articles are capitalized. Consistency is more important in bibliographic style than the style itself.

The science of bibliography is covered in many texts, and the following references are available for study:

> Better Report Writing, by Willis H. Waldo. Reinhold Publishing Corp., New York, 1965.
>
> Macmillan Handbook of English, by Robert F. Wilson. Macmillan Co., New York, 1982.
>
> The Chicago Manual of Style, University of Chicago Press, Chicago, 2003.
>
> Words Into Type, Prentice-Hall, New York, 1974.

3. Capitalization Rules

(See also Chapter 4 "Capitalization Examples" and Chapter 9 "Abbreviations and Letter Symbols")

3.1. It is impossible to give rules that will cover every conceivable problem in capitalization; but by considering the purpose to be served and the underlying principles, it is possible to attain a considerable degree of uniformity. The list of approved forms given in Chapter 4 will serve as a guide. Obviously such a list cannot be complete. The correct usage with respect to any term not included can be determined by analogy or by application of the rules.

Proper names

3.2. Proper names are capitalized.

Rome	John Macadam	Italy
Brussels	Macadam family	Anglo-Saxon

Derivatives of proper names

3.3. Derivatives of proper names used with a proper meaning are capitalized.

Roman (of Rome)	Johannean	Italian

3.4. Derivatives of proper names used with acquired independent common meaning, or no longer identified with such names, are set lowercased. Since this depends upon general and long-continued usage, a more definite and all-inclusive rule cannot be formulated in advance.

roman (type)	macadam (crushed rock)	italicize
brussels sprouts	watt (electric unit)	anglicize
venetian blinds	plaster of paris	pasteurize

Common nouns and adjectives in proper names

3.5. A common noun or adjective forming an essential part of a proper name is capitalized; the common noun used alone as a substitute for the name of a place or thing is not capitalized.

Massachusetts Avenue; the avenue
Washington Monument; the monument
Statue of Liberty; the statue
Hoover Dam; the dam

> Boston Light; the light
> Modoc National Forest; the national forest
> Panama Canal; the canal
> Soldiers' Home in Holyoke; the soldiers' home
> Johnson House (hotel); Johnson house (residence)
> Crow Reservation; the reservation
> Cape of Good Hope; the cape
> Jersey City
> Washington City
> *but* city of Washington; the city
> Cook County; the county
> Great Lakes; the lakes
> Lake of the Woods; the lake
> North Platte River; the river
> Lower California
> *but* lower Mississippi
> Charles the First; Charles I
> Seventeenth Census; the 1960 census

3.6.   If a common noun or adjective forming an essential part of a name becomes separated from the rest of the name by an intervening common noun or adjective, the entire expression is no longer a proper noun and is therefore not capitalized.

> Union Station: union passenger station
> Eastern States: eastern farming States
> United States popularly elected government

3.7.   A common noun used alone as a well-known short form of a specific proper name is capitalized.

> the Capitol building in Washington, DC; *but* State capitol building
> the Channel (English Channel)
> the Chunnel (tunnel below English Channel)
> the District (District of Columbia)

3.8.   The plural form of a common noun capitalized as part of a proper name is also capitalized.

> Seventh and I Streets
> Lakes Erie and Ontario
> Potomac and James Rivers
> State and Treasury Departments
> British, French, and United States Governments
> Presidents Washington and Adams

3.9.   A common noun used with a date, number, or letter, merely to denote time or sequence, or for the purpose of reference, record, or temporary convenience, does not form a proper name and is therefore not capitalized. (See also rule 3.38.)

abstract B	figure 7	room A722
act of 1928	first district (not	rule 8
amendment 5	congressional)	schedule K
apartment 2	flight 007	section 3
appendix C	graph 8	signature 4
article 1	group 7	spring 1926
book II	history 301	station 27
chapter III	mile 7.5	table 4
chart B	page 2	title IV
class I	paragraph 4	treaty of 1919
collection 6	part I	volume X
column 2	phase 3	war of 1914
drawing 6	plate IV	ward 2
exhibit D	region 3	

3.10. The following terms are lowercased, even with a name or number.

aqueduct	irrigation project	shipway
breakwater	jetty	slip
buoy	levee	spillway
chute	lock	turnpike
dike	pier	watershed
dock	reclamation project	weir
drydock	ship canal	wharf

Definite article in proper place names

3.11. To achieve greater distinction or to adhere to the authorized form, the word *the* (or its equivalent in a foreign language) is capitalized when used as a part of an official name or title. When such name or title is used adjectively, *the* is not capitalized, nor is *the* supplied at any time when not in copy.

> *British Consul* v. *The Mermaid* (title of legal case)
> The Dalles (OR); The Weirs (NH); *but* the Dalles region; the Weirs streets
> The Hague; *but* the Hague Court; the Second Hague Conference
> El Salvador; Las Cruces; L'Esterel
> The National Mall; The Mall (Washington, DC only)
> The Gambia
> *but* the Congo, the Sudan, the Netherlands

3.12. In common practice, rule 3.11 is disregarded in references to newspapers, periodicals, vessels, airships, trains, firm names, etc.

the Washington Post	the *U–3*
the Times	the *Los Angeles*
the Atlantic Monthly	the Federal Express
the *Mermaid*	the National Photo Co.

Particles in names of persons

3.13. In foreign names such particles as *d', da, de, della, den, du, van,* and *von* are capitalized unless preceded by a forename or title. Individual usage, if ascertainable, should be followed.

Da Ponte; Cardinal da Ponte
Den Uyl; Johannes den Uyl; Prime Minister den Uyl
Du Pont; E.I. du Pont de Nemours & Co.
Van Rensselaer; Stephen van Rensselaer
Von Braun; Dr. Wernher von Braun
but d'Orbigny; Alcide d'Orbigny; de la Madrid; Miguel de la Madrid

3.14. In anglicized names such particles are usually capitalized, even if preceded by a forename or title, but individual usage, if ascertainable, should be followed.

Justice Van Devanter; Reginald De Koven
Thomas De Quincey; William De Morgan
Henry van Dyke (his usage)
Samuel F. Du Pont (his usage); Irénée du Pont

3.15. If copy is not clear as to the form of such a name (for example, *La Forge* or *Laforge*), the two-word form should be used.

De Kalb County (AL, GA, IL, IN)
but DeKalb County (TN)

3.16. In names set in capitals, *de, von,* etc., are also capitalized.

Names of organized bodies

3.17. The full names of existing or proposed organized bodies and their shortened names are capitalized; other substitutes, which are most often regarded as common nouns, are capitalized only in certain specified instances to indicate preeminence or distinction.

National governmental units:

U.S. Congress: 110th Congress; the Congress; Congress; the Senate; the House; Committee of the Whole, the Committee; *but* committee (all other congressional committees)

Department of Agriculture: the Department; Division of Publications, the Division; similarly all major departmental units; *but* legislative, executive, and judicial departments

Bureau of the Census: the Census Bureau, the Bureau; *but* the agency

Environmental Protection Agency: the Agency

Geological Survey: the Survey

Government Printing Office: the Printing Office, the Office

American Embassy, British Embassy: the Embassy; *but* the consulate; the consulate general

Treasury of the United States: General Treasury; National Treasury; Public Treasury; the Treasury; Treasury notes; New York Subtreasury, the subtreasury

Department of Defense: Military Establishment; Armed Forces; All-Volunteer Forces; *but* armed services

U.S. Army: the Army; All-Volunteer Army; the Infantry; 81st Regiment; Army Establishment; the Army Band; Army officer; Regular Army officer; Reserve officer; Volunteer officer; *but* army shoe; Grant's army; Robinson's brigade; the brigade; the corps; the regiment; infantryman

U.S. Navy: the Navy; the Marine Corps; Navy (Naval) Establishment; Navy officer; *but* naval shipyard; naval officer; naval station

U.S. Air Force: the Air Force

U.S. Coast Guard: the Coast Guard

French Ministry of Foreign Affairs; the Ministry; French Army; British Navy

International organizations:

United Nations: the Council; the Assembly; the Secretariat

Permanent Court of Arbitration: the Court; the Tribunal (only in the proceedings of a specific arbitration tribunal)

Hague Peace Conference of 1907: the Hague Conference; the Peace Conference; the Conference

Common-noun substitutes:

Virginia General Assembly: the assembly

California State Highway Commission: Highway Commission of California; the highway commission; the commission

Montgomery County Board of Health: the Board of Health, Montgomery County; the board of health; the board

Common Council of the City of Pittsburgh: the common council; the council

Buffalo Consumers' League: the consumers' league; the league

Republican Party: the party

Southern Railroad Co.: the Southern Railroad; Southern Co.; Southern Road; the railroad company; the company
Riggs National Bank: the Riggs Bank; the bank
Metropolitan Club: the club
Yale School of Law: Yale University School of Law; School of Law, Yale University; school of law

3.18. The names of members and adherents of organized bodies are capitalized to distinguish them from the same words used merely in a descriptive sense.

a Representative (U.S.)	a Shriner	a Boy Scout
a Republican	a Socialist	a Knight (K.C., K.P., etc.)
an Elk	an Odd Fellow	
a Federalist	a Communist	

Names of countries, domains, and administrative divisions

3.19. The official designations of countries, national domains, and their principal administrative divisions are capitalized only if used as part of proper names, as proper names, or as proper adjectives. (See Chapter 17, Principal Foreign Countries table.)

United States: the Republic; the Nation; the Union; the Government; also Federal, Federal Government; *but* republic (when not referring specifically to one such entity); republican (in general sense); a nation devoted to peace

New York State: the State, a State (a definite political subdivision of first rank); State of Veracruz; Balkan States; six States of Australia; State rights; *but* state (referring to a federal government, the body politic); foreign states; church and state; statehood; state's evidence

Territory (Canada): Yukon, Northwest Territories; the Territory(ies), Territorial; but territory of American Samoa, Guam, Virgin Islands

Dominion of Canada: the Dominion; but dominion (in general sense)

Ontario Province, Province of Ontario: the Province, Provincial; but province, provincial (in general sense)

3.20. The similar designations *commonwealth, confederation (federal), government, nation (national), powers, republic,* etc., are capitalized only if used as part of proper names, as proper names, or as proper adjectives.

British Commonwealth, Commonwealth of Virginia: the Commonwealth; *but* a commonwealth government (general sense)

Swiss Confederation: the Confederation; the Federal Council; the Federal
  Government; *but* confederation, federal (in general sense)
French Government: the Government; French and Italian Governments: the
  Governments; *but* government (in general sense); the Churchill govern-
  ment; European governments
Cherokee Nation: the nation; *but* Greek nation; American nations
National Government (of any specific nation); *but* national customs
Allied Powers, Allies (in World Wars I and II); *but* our allies, weaker allies;
  Central Powers (in World War I); *but* the powers; European powers
Republic of South Africa: the Republic; *but* republic (in general sense)

Names of regions, localities, and geographic features

3.21.   A descriptive term used to denote a definite region, locality, or geographic feature is a proper name and is therefore capitalized; also
for temporary distinction a coined name of a region is capitalized.

the North Atlantic States	Middle East
the Gulf States	Middle Eastern
the Central States	Mideast
the Pacific Coast States	Mideastern (Asia)
the Lake States	Near East (Balkans, etc.)
East North Central States	the Promised Land
Eastern North Central States	the Continent (continental Europe)
Far Western States	the Western Hemisphere
Eastern United States	the North Pole
the West	the North and South Poles
the Midwest	the Temperate Zone
the Middle West	the Torrid Zone
the Far West	the East Side
the Eastern Shore (Chesapeake Bay)	Lower East Side (sections of
the Badlands (SD and NE)	a city)
the Continental Divide	Western Europe, Central Europe)
Deep South	(political entities)
Midsouth	
the Far East	*but*
Far Eastern	lower 48 (States)
the East	the Northeast corridor

3.22.   A descriptive term used to denote mere direction or position is not
a proper name and is therefore not capitalized.

north; south; east; west
northerly; northern; northward
eastern; oriental; occidental

east Pennsylvania
southern California
northern Virginia
west Florida; but West Florida (1763–1819)
eastern region; western region
north-central region
east coast; eastern seaboard
northern Italy
southern France
but East Germany; West Germany (former political entities)

Names of calendar divisions

3.23. The names of calendar divisions are capitalized.

January; February; March; etc.
Monday; Tuesday; Wednesday; etc.
but spring; summer; autumn (fall); winter

Names of holidays, etc.

3.24. The names of holidays and ecclesiastic feast and fast days are capitalized.

April Fools' Day	Independence Day
Arbor Day	Labor Day
Armed Forces Day	Lincoln's Birthday
Birthday of Martin Luther	Memorial Day (also
King, Jr.	Decoration Day)
Christmas Day, Eve	Mother's Day
Columbus Day	New Year's Day, Eve
Father's Day	Presidents Day
Feast of the Passover; the Passover	Ramadan
Flag Day	Rosh Hashanah
Fourth of July; the Fourth	St. Valentine's Day
Halloween	Thanksgiving Day
Hanukkah	Washington's Birthday
Hogmanay	Yom Kippur
Inauguration Day (Federal)	*but* election day, primary day

Trade names and trademarks

3.25. Trade names, variety names, and names of market grades and brands are capitalized. Some trade names have come into usage as generic terms (e.g., cellophane, thermos, and aspirin); when reference is being made to the formal company or specific product name, capitalization should be used. (See Chapter 4 "Capitalization Examples" trade names and trademarks.)

> Choice lamb (market grade)   Xerox (the company)
> Red Radiance rose (variety)   *but* photocopy (the process)

Scientific names

3.26. The name of a phylum, class, order, family, or genus is capitalized. The name of a species is not capitalized, even though derived from a proper name. (See rule 11.9.)

> Arthropoda (phylum), Crustacea (class), Hypoparia (order), Agnostidae (family), *Agnostus* (genus)
> *Agnostus canadensis; Aconitum wilsoni; Epigaea repens* (genus and species)

3.27. In scientific descriptions coined terms derived from proper names are not capitalized.

> aviculoid   menodontine

3.28. Any plural formed by adding *s* to a Latin generic name is capitalized.

> Rhynchonellas   Spirifers

3.29. In soil science the 12 soil orders are capitalized. (See Chapter 4 "Capitalization Examples" soil orders.)

> Alfisols   Andisols   Aridisols

3.30. Capitalize the names of the celestial bodies as well as the planets.

> Sun   Earth   Venus
> Moon   Mercury   Mars
> Jupiter   Uranus   *but* the moons of Jupiter
> Saturn   Neptune

Historical or political events

3.31.   Names of historical or political events used as a proper name are capitalized.

Battle of Bunker Hill	Middle Ages	Revolution, the
Christian Era	New Deal	American, 1775
D-day	New Federalism	English, 1688
Dust Bowl	New Frontier	French, 1789
Fall of Rome	Prohibition	Russian, 1917
Great Depression	Restoration, the	V–E Day
Great Society	Reformation	War of 1812
Holocaust, the	Renaissance	War on Poverty

but Korean war; cold war; Vietnam war; gulf war

Personification

3.32.   A vivid personification is capitalized.

The Chair recognizes the gentlewoman from New York;
but I spoke with the chair yesterday.
For Nature wields her scepter mercilessly.
All are architects of Fate,
　　Working in these walls of Time.

Religious terms

3.33.   Words denoting the Deity except *who, whose,* and *whom;* names for the Bible and other sacred writings and their parts; names of confessions of faith and of religious bodies and their adherents; and words specifically denoting Satan are all capitalized.

Heavenly Father; the Almighty; Lord; Thee; Thou; He; Him; *but* himself; You, Your; Thy, Thine; [God's] fatherhood

Mass; red Mass; Communion

Divine Father; *but* divine providence; divine guidance; divine service

Son of Man; Jesus' sonship; the Messiah; *but* a messiah; messiahship; messianic; messianize; christology; christological

Bible, Holy Scriptures, Scriptures, Word; Koran; *also* Biblical; Scriptural; Koranic

New Testament; Ten Commandments

Gospel (memoir of Christ); *but* gospel music

Apostles' Creed; Augsburg Confession; Thirty-nine Articles

Episcopal Church; an Episcopalian; Catholicism; a Protestant

Christian; *also* Christendom; Christianity; Christianize

Black Friars; Brother(s); King's Daughters; Daughter(s); Ursuline Sisters; Sister(s)

Satan; the Devil; *but* a devil; the devils; devil's advocate

Titles of persons

3.34. Civil, religious, military, and professional titles, as well as those of nobility, immediately preceding a name are capitalized.

President Bush	Dr. Bellinger
Queen Elizabeth II	Nurse Joyce Norton
Ambassador Acton	Professor Leverett
Lieutenant Fowler	Examiner Jones (law)
Chairman Williams	Vice-Presidential candidate Smith

but baseball player Ripken; maintenance man Flow; foreman Collins

3.35. To indicate preeminence or distinction in certain specified instances, a common-noun title immediately following the name of a person or used alone as a substitute for it is capitalized.

Title of a head or assistant head of state:

> George W. Bush, President of the United States: the President; the President-elect; the Executive; the Chief Magistrate; the Commander in Chief; ex-President Clinton; former President Truman; *similarly* the Vice President; the Vice-President-elect; ex-Vice-President Gore

> Tim Kaine, Governor of Virginia: the Governor of Virginia; the Governor; *similarly* the Lieutenant Governor; *but* secretary of state of Idaho; attorney general of Maine

Title of a head or assistant head of an existing or a proposed National governmental unit:

> Condoleezza Rice, Secretary of State: the Secretary; *similarly* the Acting Secretary; the Under Secretary; the Assistant Secretary; the Director; the Chief or Assistant Chief; the Chief Clerk; *but* Secretaries of the military departments; secretaryship

Titles of the military:

> General of the Army(ies): United States only; Supreme Allied Commander; Admiral Michael Mullen, Chairman, Joint Chiefs of Staff; Joint Chiefs of Staff; Chief of Staff, U.S. Air Force; the Chief of Staff; *but* the commanding general; general (military title standing alone not capitalized)

Titles of members of diplomatic corps:

> Walter S. Gifford, Ambassador Extraordinary and Plenipotentiary: the American Ambassador; the British Ambassador; the Ambassador; the Senior Ambassador; His Excellency; *similarly* the Envoy Extraordinary and Minister Plenipotentiary; the Envoy; the Minister; the Chargé d'Affaires; the Chargé; Ambassador at Large; Minister Without Portfolio; *but* the consul general; the consul; the attaché

Title of a ruler or prince:

> Elizabeth II, Queen of England: the Queen; the Crown; Her Most Gracious Majesty; Her Majesty; *similarly* the Emperor; the Sultan

Charles, Prince of Wales: the Prince; His Royal Highness
Titles not capitalized:
> Charles F. Hughes, rear admiral, U.S. Navy: the rear admiral
> Steven Knapp, president of The George Washington University: the president
> C.H. Eckles, professor of dairy husbandry: the professor
> Barbara Prophet, chairwoman of the committee; the chairman; the chairperson; the chair

3.36. In formal lists of delegates and representatives of governments, all titles and descriptive designations immediately following the names should be capitalized if any one is capitalized.

3.37. A title in the second person is capitalized.

Your Excellency	Mr. Chairman	*but* not salutations:
Your Highness	Madam Chairman	my dear General
Your Honor	Mr. Secretary	my dear sir

Titles of publications, papers, documents, acts, laws, etc.

3.38. In the full or short English titles of periodicals, series of publications, annual reports, historic documents, and works of art, the first word and all important words are capitalized.

> Statutes at Large; Revised Statutes; District Code; Bancroft's History; Journal (House or Senate) (short titles); *but* the code; the statutes
> Atlantic Charter; Balfour Declaration; *but* British white paper
> Chicago's American; *but* Chicago American Publishing Co.
> Reader's Digest; *but* New York Times Magazine; Newsweek magazine
> Monograph 55; Research Paper 123; Bulletin 420; Circular A; Article 15: Uniform Code of Military Justice; Senate Document 70; House Resolution 45; Presidential Proclamation No. 24; Executive Order No. 24; Royal Decree No. 24; Public Law 89–1; Private and Union Calendars; Calendar No. 80; Calendar Wednesday; Committee Print No. 32, committee print; *but* Senate bill 416; House bill 61; Congressional Record
> Annual Report of the Public Printer, 2007; *but* seventh annual report, 19th annual report
> Declaration of Independence; the Declaration
> Constitution (United States or with name of country); constitutional; *but* New York State constitution: first amendment, 12th amendment
> Kellogg Pact; North Atlantic Pact; Atlantic Pact; Treaty of Versailles; Jay Treaty; *but* treaty of peace, the treaty (descriptive designations); treaty of 1919
> *United States* v. *Four Hundred Twenty-two Casks of Wine* (law)
> American Gothic, Nighthawks (paintings)

3.39. All principal words are capitalized in titles of addresses, articles, books, captions, chapter and part headings, editorials, essays, headings, headlines, motion pictures and plays (including television and radio programs), papers, short poems, reports, songs, subheadings, subjects, and themes. The foregoing are also quoted.

3.40. In the short or popular titles of acts (Federal, State, or foreign) the first word and all important words are capitalized.

> Revenue Act; Walsh-Healey Act; Freedom of Information Act; Classification Act; *but* the act; Harrison narcotic law; Harrison narcotic bill; interstate commerce law; sunset law

3.41. The capitalization of the titles of books, etc., written in a foreign language is to conform to the national practice in that language.

First words

3.42. The first word of a sentence, of an independent clause or phrase, of a direct quotation, of a formally introduced series of items or phrases following a comma or colon, or of a line of poetry, is capitalized.

> The question is, Shall the bill pass?
> He asked, "And where are you going?"
> The vote was as follows: In the affirmative, 23; in the negative, 11; not voting, 3.
> Lives of great men all remind us
> We can make our lives sublime.

3.43. The first word of a fragmentary quotation is not capitalized.

> She objected "to the phraseology, not to the ideas."

3.44. The first word following a colon, an exclamation point, or a question mark is not capitalized if the matter following is merely a supplementary remark making the meaning clearer.

> Revolutions are not made: they come.
> Intelligence is not replaced by mechanism: even the televox must be guided by its master's voice.
> But two months dead! nay, not so much; not two.
> What is this? Your knees to me? to your corrected son?

3.45. The first word following *Whereas* in resolutions, contracts, etc., is not capitalized; the first word following an enacting or resolving clause is capitalized.

> Whereas the Constitution provides * * *; and
> Whereas, moreover, * * *: Therefore be it
> Whereas the Senate provided for the * * *: Now, therefore, be it
> *Resolved,* That * * *; and be it further
> *Resolved (jointly),* That * * *
> *Resolved by the House of Representatives (the Senate concurring),* That * * *. (Concurrent resolution, Federal Government.)
> *Resolved by the Senate of Oklahoma (the House of Representatives concurring therein),* That * * *. (Concurrent resolution, using name of State.)
> *Resolved by the senate (the house of representatives concurring therein),* That * * *. (Concurrent resolution, not using name of State.)
> *Resolved by the Assembly and Senate of the State of California (jointly),* That * * *. (Joint resolution, using name of State.)
> *Resolved by the Washington Board of Trade,* That * * *
> *Provided,* That * * *
> *Provided further,* That * * *
> *Provided, however,* That * * *
> *And provided further,* That * * *
> *Ordered,* That * * *
> *Be it enacted,* That * * *

Center and side heads

3.46. Unless otherwise marked, centerheads are set in capitals, and sideheads are set in lowercase and only the first word and proper names are capitalized. In centerheads making two lines, wordbreaks should be avoided. The first line should be centered and set as full as possible.

3.47. In heads set in caps, a small-cap *c* or *ac,* if available, is used in such names as *McLean* or *MacLeod*; otherwise a lowercase *c* or *ac* is used. In heads set in small caps, a thin space is used after the *c* or the *ac.*

3.48. In such names as *LeRoy, DeHostis, LaFollette,* etc. (one-word forms only), set in caps, the second letter of the particle is made a small cap, if available; otherwise lowercase is used. In heads set in small caps, a thin space is used. (See rule 3.15.)

3.49. In matter set in caps and small caps or caps and lowercase, capitalize all principal words, including parts of compounds which would be capitalized standing alone. The articles *a, an,* and *the;* the prepositions *at, by, for, in, of, on, to,* and *up;* the conjunctions *and, as, but, if, or,* and *nor;* and the second element of a compound numeral are not capitalized. (See also rule 8.129.)

> World en Route to All-Out War
> Curfew To Be Set for 10 o'Clock
> Man Hit With 2-Inch Pipe
> No-Par-Value Stock for Sale
> Yankees May Be Winners in Zig-Zag Race
> Ex-Senator Is To Be Admitted
> Notice of Filing and Order on Exemption From Requirements
> *but* Building on Twenty-first Street (if spelled)
> One Hundred Twenty-three Years (if spelled)
> Only One-tenth of Shipping Was Idle
> Many 35-Millimeter Films in Production
> Built-Up Stockpiles Are Necessary (*Up* is an adverb here)
> His Per Diem Was Increased (*Per Diem* is used as a noun here); Lower Taxes
> per Person (*per* is a preposition here)

3.50. If a normally lowercased short word is used in juxtaposition with a capitalized word of like significance, it should also be capitalized.

> Buildings In and Near the Minneapolis Mall

3.51. In a heading set in caps and lowercase or in caps and small caps, a normally lowercased last word, if it is the only lowercased word in the heading, should also be capitalized.

> All Returns Are In

3.52. The first element of an infinitive is capitalized.

> Controls To Be Applied
> *but* Aid Sent to Disaster Area

3.53. In matter set in caps and small caps, such abbreviations as *etc., et al.,* and *p.m.* are set in small caps; in matter set in caps and lowercase, these abbreviations are set in lowercase.

> PLANES, GUNS, SHIPS, ETC.   IN RE THE 8 P.M. MEETING
> Planes, Guns, Ships, etc.   In re the 8 p.m. Meeting
> JAMES BROS. ET AL. (no comma)
> James Bros. et al.

3.54.   Paragraph series letters in parentheses appearing in heads set in caps, caps and small caps, small caps, or in caps and lowercase are to be set as in copy.

SECTION 1.580(f)(1)

Addresses, salutations, and signatures

3.55.   The first word and all principal words in addresses, salutations, and signatures are capitalized. See Chapter 16 "Datelines, Addresses, and Signatures."

Interjections

3.56.   The interjection "O" is always capitalized. Interjections within a sentence are not capitalized.

> Sail on, O Ship of State!
> For lo! the days are hastening on.
> But, oh, how fortunate!

Historic or documentary accuracy

3.57.   Where historic, documentary, technical, or scientific accuracy is required, capitalization and other features of style of the original text should be followed.

4. Capitalization Examples

A

A-bomb
abstract B, 1, etc.
Academy:
  Air Force; the Academy
  Andover; the academy
  Coast Guard; the Academy
  Merchant Marine; the Academy
  Military; the Academy
  National Academy of Sciences; the
    Academy of Sciences; the academy
  Naval; the Academy
  but service academies
accord, Paris peace (*see* Agreement)
accords, Helsinki
Act (Federal, State, or foreign), short or
    popular title or with number; the act:
  Appropriations
  Classification
  Clear Skies
  Economy
  Flood Control
  Military Selective Service
  No Child Left Behind
  Organic Act of Virgin Islands
  Panama Canal
  PATRIOT
  Revenue
  Sarbanes-Oxley
  Stockpiling
  Tariff
  Trademark
  Walsh-Healey Act; *but* Walsh-Healey
    law (or bill)
act, labor-management relations
Acting, if part of capitalized title
Active Duty
Adjutant General, the (*see* The)

Administration, with name; capitalized
    standing alone if Federal unit:
  Farmers Home
  Food and Drug
  Maritime
  Transportation Security
  but Bush administration;
    administration bill, policy, etc.
Administrative Law Judge Davis; Judge
    Davis; an administrative law judge
Admiralty, British, etc.
Admiralty, Lord of the
Adobe Acrobat Reader
Adviser, Legal (Department of State)
Africa:
  east
  East Coast
  north
  South
  South-West (Territory of)
  West Coast
African-American (*see* Black; Negro)
Agency, if part of name; capitalized
    standing alone if referring to
    Federal unit:
  Central Intelligence; the Agency
  Chippewa (Indian); the agency
agent orange
Age(s):
  Age of Discovery
  Dark Ages
  Elizabethan Age
  Golden Age (of Pericles only)
  Middle Ages
  but atomic age; Cambrian age; copper
    age; ice age; missile age; rocket age;
    space age; stone age; etc.
Agreement, with name; the agreement:
  General Agreement on Tariffs and
    Trade (GATT); the general agreement

International Wheat Agreement; the
wheat agreement; the coffee agreement
North American Free-Trade
    Agreement (NAFTA)
Status of Forces; *but* status-of-forces
    agreements
United States-Canada Free-Trade
    Agreement; the free-trade agreement
but the Geneva agreement; the Potsdam
    agreement; Paris peace agreement
Air Force:
    Air National Guard (*see* National)
    Base (with name); Air Force base (*see*
        Base; Station)
    Civil Air Patrol; Civil Patrol; the patrol
    Command (*see* Command)
    One (Presidential plane)
    Reserve
    Reserve Officers' Training Corps
Airport: La Guardia; Reagan National;
    the airport
Al Jazeera
Alaska Native (collective term for Aleuts,
    Eskimos, Inuits, and Indians of
    Alaska):
    the Native; *but* Ohio native, a
        native of Alaska, etc.
Alliance, Farmers', etc.; the alliance
alliances and coalitions (*see also* powers):
    Allied Powers; the powers (World
        Wars I and II)
    Atlantic alliance
    Axis, the; Axis Powers; the powers
    Benelux (Belgium, Netherlands,
        Luxembourg)
    Big Four (European); of the Pacific
    Big Three
    Central Powers; the powers (World
        War I)
    Coalition of the Willing
    European Economic Community
    Fritalux (France, Italy, Benelux
        countries)

North Atlantic Treaty Organization
    (*see* Organization)
Western Powers
Allied (World Wars I and II):
    armies
    Governments
    Nations
    peoples
    Powers; the powers; *but* European
        powers
    Supreme Allied Commander
Allies, the (World Wars I and II); *also*
    members of Western bloc (political
    entity); *but* our allies; weaker allies,
    etc.
Al Qaeda
Alzheimer's disease
Ambassador:
    British, etc.; the Ambassador; the
        Senior Ambassador; His Excellency
    Extraordinary and Plenipotentiary;
        the Ambassador; Ambassador at
    Large; an ambassador
amendment:
    Baker amendment
    Social Security Amendments of 1983;
        1983 amendments; the Social Security
        amendments; the amendments
    to the Constitution (U.S.); *but* First
        Amendment, 14th Amendment, etc.;
        the Amendment
American:
    Federation of Labor and Congress of
        Industrial Organizations (AFL–CIO);
        the federation
    Gold Star Mothers, Inc.; Gold Star
        Mothers; a Mother
    Legion (*see* Legion)
    National Red Cross; the Red Cross
    Veterans of World War II (AMVETS)
    War Mothers; a Mother
AmeriCorps Program
Amtrak (National Railroad Passenger
    Corporation)

Ancient Free and Accepted Masons; a
    Mason; a Freemason
Annex, if part of name of building; the
    annex
Antarctic Ocean (*see* Arctic; Ocean)
appendix 1, A, II, etc.; the appendix; *but*
    Appendix II, when part of title:
    Appendix II:[1] Education Directory
appropriation bill (*see also* bill):
    deficiency
    Department of Agriculture
    for any governmental unit
    independent offices
aquaculture; acquiculture
Arab States
Arabic numerals
Arboretum, National; the Arboretum
Archipelago, Philippine, etc.; the
    archipelago
Architect of the Capitol; the Architect
Archivist of the United States; the Archivist
Arctic:
    Circle
    Current (*see* Current)
    Ocean
    zone
    but subarctic
arctic (descriptive adjective):
    clothing
    conditions
    fox
    grass
    night
    seas
Area, if part of name; the area:
    Cape Hatteras Recreational
    White Pass Recreation; etc.
    but area 2; free trade area; Metropolitan
        Washington area; bay area;
        nonsmoking area
Arlington:
    Memorial Amphitheater; the Memorial

Amphitheater; the amphitheater
Memorial Bridge (*see* Bridge)
National Cemetery (*see* Cemetery)
Arm, Infantry, etc. (military); the arm
Armed Forces (synonym for overall
    Military Establishment):
British
    Retirement Home (AFRT)
    of the United States
armed services
armistice
Armory, Springfield, etc.; the armory
Army, American or foreign, if part of name;
    capitalized standing alone only if
    referring to U.S. Army:
    Active; Active-Duty
    Adjutant General, the
    All-Volunteer
    Band (*see* Band)
    branches; Gordon Highlanders; Royal
        Guards; etc.
    Brigade, 1st, etc.; the brigade;
        Robinson's brigade
    Command (*see* Command)
    Command and General Staff College
        (*see* College)
    Company A; A Company; the company
    Confederate (referring to Southern
        Confederacy); the Confederates
    Continental; Continentals
    Corps, Reserve (*see* Corps)
    District of Washington (military); the
        district
    Division, 1st, etc.; the division
    Engineers (the Corps of Engineers); the
        Engineers; *but* Army engineer
    Establishment
    Field Establishment
    Field Forces (*see* Forces)
    Finance Department; the Department
    1st, etc.
    General of the Army; *but* the general

---

[1] The colon is preferred; a dash is permissible;
but a comma is too weak.

General Staff; the Staff
Headquarters, 1st Regiment
Headquarters of the; the headquarters
Regiment, 1st, etc.; the regiment
Regular Army officer; a Regular
Revolutionary (American, British,
    French, etc.)
service
Surgeon General, the (*see* Surgeon
    General)
Volunteer; the Volunteers; a Volunteer
army:
    Lee's army; *but* Clark's 5th Army
    mobile
    mule, shoe, etc.
    of occupation; occupation army
    Red
Arsenal, Rock Island, etc.; the arsenal
article 15; *but* Article 15, when part of title:
    Article 15: Uniform Code of
    Military Justice
Articles:
    of Confederation (U.S.)
    of Impeachment; the articles
Asian (*see* Orient, the; oriental)
Assembly (*see* United Nations)
Assembly of New York; the assembly (*see*
    also Legislative Assembly)
Assistant, if part of capitalized title; the
    assistant
assistant, Presidential (*see* Presidential)
Assistant Secretary (*see* Secretary)
Associate Justice (*see* Supreme Court)
Association, if part of name; capitalized
    standing alone if referring to
    Federal unit:
    American Association for the
        Advancement of Science; the
        association
    Federal National Mortgage (Fannie
        Mae); the Association
    Young Women's Christian; the
        association

Astrophysical Observatory (*see*
    Observatory)
Atlantic (*see also* Pacific):
    Charter (*see* Charter)
    coast
    Coast States
    community
    Destroyer Flotilla; the destroyer flotilla;
        the flotilla
    Fleet (*see* Fleet)
    mid-Atlantic
    North
    seaboard
    slope
    South
    time, standard time (*see* time)
    but cisatlantic; transatlantic
Attorney General (U.S. or foreign country);
    but attorney general of Maine, etc.
attorney, U.S.
Authority, capitalized standing alone if
    referring to Federal unit:
    National Shipping; the Authority
    Port Authority of New York and New
        Jersey; the port authority; the
        authority
    St. Lawrence Seaway Authority of
        Canada; the authority
    Tennessee Valley; the Authority
Auto Train (Amtrak)
autumn
Avenue, Constitution, etc.; the avenue
Award:
    Academy
    Distinguished Service
    Merit
    Mother of the Year
    the award (*see also* decorations, etc.)
Axis, the (*see* alliances)
Ayatollah; an ayatollah

B
Badlands (SD and NE)
Balkan States (*see* States)

Baltic States (*see* States)
Band, if part of name; the band:
  Army, Marine, Navy
  Eastern, etc. (of Cherokee Indians)
Bank, if part of name; the bank; capitalized
  standing alone if referring to
  international bank:
  Export-Import Bank of the United States;
    Ex-Im Bank; the Bank
  Farm Loan Bank of Dallas; Dallas Farm
    Loan Bank; farm loan bank; farm loan
    bank at Dallas
  Farmers & Mechanics, etc.
  Federal Land Bank of Louisville;
    Louisville Federal Land Bank; land
    bank at Louisville; Federal land bank
  Federal Reserve Bank of New York;
    Richmond Federal Reserve Bank;
    but Reserve bank at Richmond;
    Federal Reserve bank; Reserve
    bank; Reserve city
  First National, etc.
  German Central; the Bank
  International Bank for Reconstruction
    and Development; the Bank
  but blood bank, central reserve, soil bank
Bar, if part of name; Maryland (State) Bar
  Association; Maryland (State) bar; the
  State bar; the bar association
Barracks, if part of name; the barracks:
  Carlisle
  Disciplinary (Leavenworth)
  Marine (District of Columbia)
  but A barracks; barracks A; etc.
Base, Andrews Air Force; Air Force base;
  the base (*see also* Naval); *but* Sandia
  Base
Basin (*see* geographic terms)
Battery, the (New York City)
Battle, if part of name; the battle:
  of Gettysburg; *but* battle at Gettysburg;
    etc.
  of the Bulge; of the Marne; of the
    Wilderness; of Waterloo; etc.

battlefield, Bull Run, etc.
battleground, Manassas, etc.
Bay, San Francisco Bay area; the bay area
Belt, if part of name; the belt:
  Bible
  Farm
  Rust
  Sun
  but money belt
Beltway, capitalized with name; the beltway
Bench (*see* Supreme Bench)
Benelux (*see* alliances)
Bible; Biblical; Scriptures; Ten
  Commandments; etc. (*see also* book)
bicentennial
bill, Kiess; Senate bill 217; House bill 31 (*see*
  also appropriation bill)
Bill of Rights (historic document); *but* GI
  bill of rights
Bizonia; bizonal; bizone
Black (*see* African-American; Negro)
Black Caucus (*see* Congressional)
bloc (*see* Western)
block (grants)
Bluegrass region, etc.
B'nai B'rith
Board, if part of name; capitalized standing
  alone only if referring to Federal or
  international board:
  Employees' Compensation Appeals
  Federal Reserve (*see* Federal)
  Military Production and Supply
    (NATO)
  National Labor Relations
  of Directors (Federal unit); *but* board of
    directors (nongovernmental)
  of Health of Montgomery County;
    Montgomery County Board of Health;
    the board of health; the board
  of Regents (Smithsonian)
  of Visitors (Military and Naval
    Academies)
  on Geographic Names
  Railroad Retirement

bond:
  Government
  savings
  series EE
  Treasury
book:
  books of the Bible
  First Book of Samuel; etc.
  Good Book (synonym for Bible)
book 1, I, etc.; *but* Book 1, when part of title:
  Book 1: The Golden Legend
Boolean:
  logic
  operator
  search
border, United States-Mexican
Borough, if part of name: Borough of the
  Bronx; the borough
Botanic Garden (National); the garden (not
  Botanical Gardens)
Bowl, Dust, Rose, Super, etc.; the bowl
Boy Scouts (the organization); a Boy Scout;
  a Scout; Scouting; Eagle Scout;
  Explorer Scout
Branch, if part of name; capitalized
  standing alone only if referring to a
  Federal unit:
  Accounts
  Public Buildings
  but executive, judicial, or legislative
  branch
Bridge, if part of name; the bridge:
  Arlington Memorial; Memorial;
  Francis Scott Key; Key
  but Baltimore & Ohio Railroad bridge
Brother(s) (adherent of religious order)
budget:
  department
  estimate
  Federal
  message
  performance-type
  President's

Budget of the United States Government,
  the Budget (publication)
Building, if part of name; the building:
  Capitol (*see* Capitol Building)
  Colorado
  House (or Senate) Office
  Investment
  New House (or Senate) Office
  Old House Office
  Pentagon
  the National Archives; the Archives
  Treasury; Treasury Annex
Bulletin 420; Farmers' Bulletin No. 420
Bureau, if part of name; capitalized
  standing alone if referring to Federal
  or international unit:
  of Customs (name changed to U.S.
  Customs and Border Protection)
  of Engraving and Printing
  of Indian Affairs

C

C-SPAN
Cabinet, American or foreign, if part of
  name or standing alone (*see also*
  foreign cabinets):
  British Cabinet; the Cabinet
  the President's Cabinet; the Cabinet;
  Cabinet officer, member
Calendar, if part of name; the calendar:
  Consent; etc.
  House
  No. 99; Calendars Nos. 1 and 2
  of Bills and Resolutions
  Private
  Senate
  Unanimous Consent
  Union
  Wednesday (legislative)
Cambrian age (*see* Ages)
Camp Lejeune; David, etc.; the camp
Canal, with name; the canal:
  Cross-Florida Barge

Isthmian
Panama
Cape (see geographic terms)
Capital, Capital City, National Capital
   (Washington, DC); but the capital
   (State)
Capitol Building (with State name); the
   capitol
Capitol, the (Washington, DC):
   Architect of
   Building
   caucus room
   Chamber
   Cloakroom
   dome
   Grounds
   Halls (House and Senate)
   Halls of Congress
   Hill; the Hill
   Police (see Police)
   Power Plant
   Prayer Room
   Press Gallery, etc.
   rotunda
   Senate wing
   stationery room
   Statuary Hall
   the well (House or Senate)
   west front
catch-22
Caucasian (see White)
caucus: Republican; but Congressional
   Black Caucus (incorporated name);
   Sun Belt Caucus
CD–ROM
Cemetery, if part of name: Arlington
   National; the cemetery
Census:
   Twenty-third Decennial (title);
     Twenty-third (title); the census
   2000 census
   2000 Census of Agriculture; the census
     of agriculture; the census

the 23d and subsequent decennial
   censuses
Center, if part of name; the Center
   (Federal); the center (non-Federal):
   Agricultural Research, etc.; the Center
   (Federal)
   Kennedy Center for the Performing
     Arts; the Kennedy Center; the
     Center (Federal)
   the Lincoln Center; the center (non-
     Federal)
central Asia, etc.
Central America
Central Europe
Central States
central time (see time)
century, first, 21st, etc.
Chair, the, if personified
Chairman, Chairwoman, Chair:
   of the Board of Directors; the
     Chairman (Federal); but chairman of
     the board of directors (non-Federal)
   of the Committee of the Whole House;
     the Chairman
   of the Federal Trade Commission; the
     Chairman
   Vice
chairman, chairwoman, chair
   (congressional):
   of the Appropriations Committee
   of the Subcommittee on Banking
   but Chairman Davis, Chairwoman
     Landrieu
Chamber of Commerce; the chamber:
   of Ada; Ada Chamber of Commerce;
     the chamber of commerce
   of the United States; U.S. Chamber of
     Commerce; the chamber of
     commerce; national chamber
Chamber, the (Senate or House)
channel 3 (TV); the channel
Chaplain (House or Senate); but Navy
   chaplain

chapter 5, II, etc.; *but* Chapter 5, when
  part of title: Chapter 5: Research and
  Development; Washington chapter,
  Red Cross
Chargé d'Affaires, British, etc.; the Chargé
  d'Affaires; the Chargé
chart 2, A, II, etc.; *but* Chart 2, when part of
  legend: Chart 2.—Army strength
Charter, capitalized with name; the charter:
  Atlantic
  United Nations
cheese: Camembert, Cheddar, Parmesan,
  Provolone, Roquefort, etc.
Chief, if referring to head of Federal unit;
  the Chief:
  Clerk
  Forester (*see* Forester)
  Intelligence Office
  Judge
  Justice (U.S. Supreme Court); *but* chief
    justice (of a State)
  Magistrate (the President)
  of Division of Publications
  of Engineers (Army)
  of Naval Operations
  of Staff
Christian; Christendom; Christianity;
  Christianize; *but* christen
church and state
church calendar:
  Christmas
  Easter
  Lent
  Pentecost (Whitsuntide)
Church, if part of name of organization or
  building
Circle, if part of name; the circle:
  Arctic
  Logan
  but great circle
Circular 420
cities, sections of, official or popular names:
  East Side
  French Quarter (New Orleans)

Latin Quarter (Paris)
North End
Northwest Washington, etc. (District
  of Columbia); the Northwest; *but*
  northwest (directional)
the Loop (Chicago)
City, if part of corporate or popular name;
  the city:
  Kansas City; the two Kansas Citys
  Mexico City
  New York City; *but* city of New York
  Twin Cities
  Washington City; *but* city of Washington
  Windy City (Chicago)
  but Reserve city (*see* Bank)
civil action No. 46
civil defense
Civil War (*see* War)
Clan, if part of tribal name; Clan
  MacArthur; the clan
class 2, A, II, etc.; *but* Class 2 when part of
  title: Class 2: Leather Products
Clerk, the, of the House of Representatives;
  of the Supreme Court of the United
  States
clerk, the, of the Senate
client
client/server
coal sizes: pea, barley, buckwheat, stove, etc.
coalition; coalition force; coalition
  members, etc.
coast: Atlantic, east, gulf, west, etc.
Coast Guard, U.S.; the Coast Guard;
  Coastguardsman Smith; *but* a
  coastguardsman; a guardsman;
  Reserve
Coastal Plain (Atlantic and Gulf)
Code (in shortened title of a publication);
  the code:
  District
  Federal Criminal
  Internal Revenue (*also* Tax Code)
  International (signal)
  of Federal Regulations

Penal; Criminal; etc.
Pennsylvania State
Radio
Television
Uniform Code of Military Justice
United States
ZIP Code (copyrighted)
but civil code; flag code; Morse code
codel (congressional delegation)
collection, Brady, etc.; the collection
collector of customs
College, if part of name; the college:
   Armed Forces Staff
   Command and General Staff
   Gettysburg
   National War
   of Bishops
   but electoral college
college degrees: bachelor of arts, master's,
   etc.
Colonials (American Colonial Army); *but*
   colonial times, etc.
Colonies, the:
   Thirteen
   Thirteen American
   Thirteen Original
   but 13 separate Colonies
colonists, the
Command, capitalize with name; the
   command:
   Air Force Materiel
   Army
   Central (CENCOM)
   Naval Space
   Zone of Interior
Commandant, the (Coast Guard or Marine
   Corps only)
Commandos, the; Commando raid; a
   commando
Commission (if part of name; capitalized
   standing alone if referring to Federal
   or international commission):
   International Boundary, United States
   and Canada

   of Fine Arts
   Public Buildings
Commissioner, if referring to Federal or
   international commission; the
   Commissioner:
   Land Bank; *but* land bank
   commissioner loans
   of Customs and Border Protection
   U.S. (International Boundary
   Commission, etc.)
   but a U.S. commissioner
Committee (or Subcommittee) (if part of
   name; the Committee, if referring to
   international or noncongressional
   Federal committee or to the
   Committee of the Whole, the
   Committee of the Whole House, or
   the Committee of the Whole House on
   the state of the Union):
   American Medical Association
   Committee on Education; the
   committee on education; the
   committee
   Appropriations, etc.; the committee;
   Subcommittee on Appropriations; the
   subcommittee; subcommittee of the
   Appropriations Committee
   Democratic National; the national
   committee; the committee;
   Democratic national committeeman
   Democratic policy committee; the
   committee
   Joint Committee on Printing; the Joint
   Committee; the committee; *but* a joint
   committee
   of Defense Ministers (NATO); the
   Committee (*see also* Organization,
   North Atlantic Treaty)
   of One Hundred, etc.; the committee
   on Finance; the committee
   President's Advisory Committee on
   Management; the Committee
   Republican National; the national
   committee; the committee;

Republican national committeeman
Republican policy committee; the
   committee
Senate policy committee
Subcommittee on Immigration; the
   subcommittee
but Baker committee
ad hoc committee
conference committee
Committee Print No. 32; Committee Prints
   Nos. 8 and 9; committee print
Common Cause
Commonwealth:
   British Commonwealth; the
      Commonwealth
   of Australia
   of Kentucky
   of Massachusetts
   of Pennsylvania
   of Virginia
Communist Party; a Communist
compact, U.S. marine fisheries, etc.; the
   compact
Company, if part of name; capitalized
      standing alone if referring to unit of
      Federal Government:
   Panama Canal Railway Company; the
      Company
   Procter & Gamble Co.; the company
Comptroller of the Currency; the
   Comptroller
Comptroller General (U.S.); the
   Comptroller
Comsat
Concord
Confederacy (of the South)
Confederate:
   Army
   flag
   Government
   soldier
   States
Confederation, Articles of

Conference, if referring to governmental
      (U.S.) or international conference:
   Bretton Woods; the Conference
   Judicial Conference of the United
      States; U.S. Judicial Conference;
      Judicial Conference; the Conference
   Tenth Annual Conference of the
      United Methodist Churches; the
      conference
Congress (convention), if part of name;
      capitalized standing alone if referring
      to international congress:
   Library of
   of Industrial Organizations
   of Parents and Teachers, National; the
      congress
Congress (legislature), if referring to
      national congress:
   of Bolivia, etc.; the Congress
   of the United States; First, Second,
      10th, 103d, etc.; the Congress
Congressional:
   Black Caucus; the Black Caucus; the
   caucus
   Directory, the directory
   District, First, 10th, etc.; the First
      District; the congressional district; the
      district
   Medal of Honor (*see* decorations)
   but congressional action, committee, etc.
Congressman; Congresswoman;
      Congressman at Large; Member of
      Congress; Member; membership
Conservative Party; a Conservative
Constitution, with name of country;
      capitalized standing alone when
      referring to a specific national
      constitution; *but* New York State
      Constitution; the constitution
constitutional
consul, British, general, etc.
consulate, British, etc.

Consumer Price Index (official title); the
price index; the index; *but* a
consumers' price index (descriptive)
Continent, only if following name;
North American Continent; the
continent; *but* the Continent
(continental Europe)
Continental:
Army; the Army
Congress; the Congress
Divide (*see* Divide)
Outer Continental Shelf
Shelf; the shelf; a continental shelf
continental Europe, United States, etc.
Continentals (Revolutionary soldiers)
Convention, governmental (U.S.),
international, or national political;
the convention:
89th National Convention of the
American Legion
Constitutional (United States, 1787);
the Convention
Democratic National; Democratic
Genocide (international)
on International Civil Aviation
Republican National; Republican
Universal Postal Union; Postal Union
also International Postal; Warsaw
copper age (*see* Ages)
Corporation, if part of name; the
Corporation, if referring to unit of
Federal Government:
Commodity Credit
Federal Deposit Insurance
National Railroad Passenger (Amtrak)
Rand Corp.; the corporation
St. Lawrence Seaway Development
Union Carbide Corp.; the corporation
Virgin Islands
Corps, if part of name; the corps, all other
uses:
Adjutant General's
Army Reserve

Chemical
diplomatic
Finance
Foreign Service Officer (*see* Foreign
Service)
Job
Judge Advocate General's
Marine (*see* Marine Corps)
Medical
Military Police
Nurse
of Cadets (West Point)
of Engineers; Army Engineers; the
Engineers; *but* Army engineer; the
corps
Ordnance
Peace; Peace Corpsman; the corpsman
Quartermaster
Reserve Officers' Training (ROTC)
VII Corps, etc.
Signal
Transportation
Youth
but diplomatic corps
corpsman; hospital corpsman
corridor, Northeast
Council, if part of name; capitalized
standing alone if referring to Federal
or international unit (*see also* United
Nations):
Boston City; the council
Choctaw, etc.; the council
Her Majesty's Privy Council; the Privy
Council; the Council
National Security; the Council
of Foreign Ministers (NATO); the
Council
of the Organization of American States;
the Council
Philadelphia City; the council
counsel; general counsel
County, Prince George's; county of Prince
George's; County Kilkenny, etc.;

Loudoun and Fairfax Counties; the
county
Court (of law) capitalized if part of name;
capitalized standing alone if referring
to the Supreme Court of the United
States, to the Court of Impeachment
(U.S. Senate), or to an international
court:
Circuit Court of the United States for the
Tenth Circuit; Circuit Court for the
Tenth Circuit; the circuit court; the
court; the tenth circuit
Court of Appeals for the State of North
Carolina, etc.; the Tenth Circuit Court
of Appeals; the court of appeals; the
court
Court of Claims; the court
Court of Impeachment, the Senate; the
Court
District Court of the United States for
the Eastern District of Missouri; the
district court; the court
International Court of Justice; the Court
Permanent Court of Arbitration; the
Court
Superior Court of the District of
Columbia; the superior court; the
court
Supreme Court of the United States (*see*
Supreme Court)
Supreme Court of Virginia, etc.; the
supreme court; the court
Tax Court; the court
U.S. Court of Appeals for the District
of Columbia; the court
Covenant, League of Nations; the covenant
Creed, Apostles'; the Creed
Crown, if referring to a ruler; *but* crown
colony, lands, etc.
cruise missile
Current, if part of name; the current:
Arctic
Humboldt

Japan
North Equatorial
customhouse; customs official
czar; czarist

D

Dalai Lama
Dalles, The; *but* the Dalles region
Dark Ages (*see* Ages)
Daughters of the American Revolution;
a Daughter
daylight saving time
Declaration, capitalized with name:
of Independence; the Declaration
of Panama; the declaration
decorations, medals, etc., awarded by
United States or any foreign national
government; the medal, the cross, the
ribbon (*see also* Award):
Air Medal
Bronze Star Medal
Commendation Ribbon
Congressional Medal of Honor
Croix de Guerre
Distinguished Flying Cross
Distinguished Service Cross
Distinguished Service Medal
Good Conduct Medal
Legion of Merit
Medal for Merit
Medal of Freedom
Medal of Honor
Mother of the Year
Purple Heart
Silver Star Medal
Soldier's Medal
Victoria Cross
Victory Medal
but oakleaf cluster
also Carnegie Medal; Olympic Gold
Medal; *but* gold medal
Decree (*see* Executive); Royal Decree
Deep South

Defense Establishment (*see* Establishment)
Deity, words denoting, capitalized
Delegate (U.S. Congress)
Delegates, Virginia House of
delegate (to a conference); the delegate; the
    delegation
Delta, Mississippi River; the delta
Democratic Party; a Democrat
Department, if part of name; capitalized
    standing alone if referring to a Federal
    or international unit:
    of Agriculture
    of the Treasury
    of Veterans Affairs
    Yale University Department of
    Economics; the department of
    economics; the department
Department of New York, American
    Legion
department:
    executive
    judicial
    legislative
Depot, if part of name; the depot (*see also*
    Station)
Depression, Great
Deputy, if part of capitalized title; *but* the
    deputy
derivatives of proper names:

alaska seal (fur)	burley tobacco
angora wool	canada balsam
angstrom unit	(microscopy)
argyle wool	carlsbad twins
artesian well	(petrography)
astrakhan fabric	cashmere shawl
babbitt metal	castile soap
benday process	cesarean section
bologna	chantilly lace
bordeaux	chesterfield coat
bourbon whiskey	china clay
bowie knife	chinese blue
braille	collins (drink)
brazil nut	congo red
brazilwood	cordovan leather
brewer's yeast	coulomb
bristolboard	curie
brussel sprouts	degaussing apparatus
brussels carpet	delftware
bunsen burner	derby hat

diesel engine, dieselize	nelson, half nelson, etc.
dixie cup	neon light
dotted swiss	newton
epsom salt	nissen hut
fedora hat	norfolk jacket
frankfurter	oriental rug
french chalk	oxford shoe
french dressing	panama hat
french-fried potatoes	parianware
fuller's earth	paris green
gargantuan	parkerhouse roll
gauss	pasteurized milk
georgette crepe	persian lamb
german silver	petri dish
gilbert	pharisaic
glauber salt	philistine
gothic type	photostat
graham cracker	pitman arm
herculean task	pitot tube
hessian fly	plaster of paris
holland cloth	prussian blue
hoolamite detector	quisling
hudson seal (fur)	quixotic idea
india ink	quonset hut
india rubber	rembert wheel
italic type	roentgen
jamaica ginger	roman candle
japan varnish	roman cement
jersey fabric	roman type
johnin test	russia leather
joule	russian bath
knickerbocker	rutherford
kraft paper	sanforize
lambert	saratoga chips
leghorn hat	scotch plaid, *but*
levant leather	Scotch tape
levantine silk	(trademark)
lilliputian	shanghai
logan tent	siamese twins
london purple	spanish omelet
lyonnaise potatoes	stillson wrench
macadamized road	surah silk
mach (no period)	swiss cheese
number	timothy grass
madras cloth	turkey red
maginot line	turkish towel
(nonliteral)	utopia, utopian
manila paper	vandyke collar
maraschino cherry	vaseline
mason jar	venetian blind
maxwell	venturi tube
melba toast	victoria (carriage)
mercerized fabric	vienna bread
merino sheep	virginia reel
molotov cocktail	wedgwoodware
morocco leather	wheatstone bridge
morris chair	wilton rug
murphy bed	zeppelin
navy blue	

dial-up
Diet, Japanese (legislative body)
diplomatic corps (*see also* Corps; service)

Director, if referring to head of Federal or
    international unit; the Director:
    District Director of Internal Revenue
    of Fish and Wildlife Service
    of National Geodetic Survey
    of the Mint
    Office of Management and Budget
    but director, board of directors
        (nongovernmental)
Director General of Foreign Service; the
    Director General; the Director
diseases and related terms:
    AIDS (acquired immunodeficiency
        syndrome)
    Alzheimer's disease
    cerebral palsy
    Down syndrome
    German measles
    HIV (human immunodeficiency virus)
    Hodgkin's disease
    Lyme disease
    Marfan's syndrome
    Ménierè's syndrome
    myasthenia gravis
    Parkinson's disease
    Reye's syndrome
    spina bifida
Distinguished Service Medal, etc. (*see*
    decorations)
District, if part of name; the district:
    Alexandria School District No. 4;
        school district No. 4
    Congressional (with number)
    Federal (*see* Federal)
    Los Angeles Water; the water district
    but customs district No. 2; first assembly
        district; public utility district
District of Columbia; the District:
    Anacostia Flats; the flats
    Arlington Memorial Bridge; the
        Memorial Bridge; the bridge
    Children's Hospital; the hospital
    District jail; the jail; DC jail
    Ellipse, the

Mall, The National; The Mall
Mayor (when pertaining to the District
    of Columbia only)
Metropolitan Police; Metropolitan
    policeman; the police
police court
Public Library; the library
Reflecting Pool; the pool
Tidal Basin; the basin
Washington Channel; the channel
Divide, Continental (Rocky Mountains);
    the divide
Divine Father; *but* divine guidance, divine
    providence, divine service
Division, Army, if part of name: 1st Cavalry
    Division; 1st Air Cavalry Division; the
    division
Division, if referring to Federal
    governmental unit; the Division:
    Buick Division; the division; a division
        of General Motors
    Passport; the Division
    but Trinity River division
        (reclamation); the division
Dixie
docket No. 66; dockets Nos. 76 and 77
Doctrine, Monroe; the doctrine; *but*
    Truman, Eisenhower doctrine
doctrine, fairness
Document, if part of name; the document:
    Document No. 130
    Document Numbered One Hundred
        Thirty
draconian
drawing II, A, 3, etc.; *but* Drawing 2 when
    part of title: Drawing 2.—
    Hydroelectric Power Development
Dust Bowl (*see* Bowl)

E
Earth (planet)
East:
    Coast (Africa)
    Middle, Mideast (Asia)

Near (Balkans)
Side of New York
South Central States
the East (section of United States)
east:
  Africa
  coast (U.S.)
  Pennsylvania
Eastern:
  Gulf States
  Middle, Mideastern (Asia)
  North Central States
  Shore (Chesapeake Bay)
  States
  United States
eastern:
  France
  seaboard
  Wisconsin
easterner
EE-bond
electoral college; the electors
Elizabethan Age (*see* Ages)
email (lowercase within a sentence)
Email (uppercase "E" to start a sentence)
Emancipation Proclamation (*see*
  Proclamation)
Embassy, British, etc.; the Embassy
Emperor, Japanese, etc.; the Emperor
Empire, Roman; the empire
Engine Company, Bethesda; engine
  company No. 6; No. 6 engine
company; the company
Engineer officer, etc. (of Engineer Corps);
  the Engineers
Engineers, Chief of (Army)
Engineers, Corps of (*see* Corps)
Envoy Extraordinary and Minister
  Plenipotentiary; the Envoy; the
  Minister
Equator, the; equatorial
Establishment, if part of name; the
  establishment:
  Army

Army Field
Defense
Federal
Military
Naval; *but* naval establishment;
  Naval Establishments Regs
Navy
Postal
Regular
Reserve
Shore
but civil establishment; legislative
  establishment
Estate, Girard (a foundation); the estate
estate, third (the commons); fourth
  (the press); tax; etc.
Eurodollar, euro
Excellency, His, Her; Their Excellencies
Exchange, New York Stock; the stock
  exchange; the exchange
Executive (President of United States):
  Chief
  Decree No. 100; Decree 100; *but*
    Executive decree; direction
  Mansion; the mansion; the White House
  Office; the Office
  Order No. 34; Order 34; *but* Executive
    order
  power
executive:
  agreement
  branch
  communication
  department
  document
  paper
  privilege
exhibit 2, A, II, etc.; *but* Exhibit 2, when
  part of title: Exhibit 2: Capital
  Expenditures, 1935–49
Expedition, Byrd; Lewis and Clark; the
  expedition
Exposition, California-Pacific
  International, etc.; the exposition

F
Fair Deal
Fair, World's, etc.; the fair; Texas State Fair
fall (season)
Falls, Niagara; the falls
Far East, Far Eastern; Far West (U.S.); *but*
    far western
Farm, if part of name; the farm:
    Johnson Farm; *but* Johnson's farm
    San Diego Farm
    Wild Tiger Farm
Fascist; fascism
Father of his Country (Washington)
Fed, the (no period)
Federal (synonym for United States or other
        sovereign power):
    Depository Library Program *but* Federal
        depository library, libraries
    District (Mexico)
    Establishment
    Government (of any national
        government)
    grand jury; the grand jury
    land bank (*see* Bank)
    Register (publication); the Register
    Reserve Board, the Board; *also* Federal
        Reserve System, the System; Federal
        Reserve Board Regulation W, *but*
        regulation W
    but a federal form of government
federally
fellow, fellowship (academic)
Field, Byrd, Stewart, etc.; the field
figure 2, A, II, etc. (illustration); *but* Figure
        2, when part of legend: Figure 2.—
        Market scenes
firewall
firm names:
    ACDelco
    America Online (AOL)
    Bausch & Lomb Inc.
    BP
    Bristol-Myers Squibb
    Carson, Pirie, Scott & Co.

    Coldwell Banker
    Colgate-Palmolive Co.
    Comcast
    Dow Jones & Co., Inc.
    Dun & Bradstreet
    eBay
    E.I. du Pont de Nemours & Co.
    FedEx
    GlaxoSmithKline
    Great Atlantic & Pacific Tea Co. (A&P)
    Hamilton Beach/Proctor Silex, Inc.
    Hartmarx Corp.
    Hewlett-Packard
    Houghton Mifflin Co.
    Ingersoll-Rand Co.
    Intel Corp.
    J.C. Penney Co., Inc.
    Johns-Manville Corp.
    Kennecott Exploration Co.
    Kmart
    Libbey-Owens-Ford Co.
    Macmillan Co.
    Merck & Co., Inc.
    Merrill Lynch
    Microsoft
    Pfizer Inc.
    Phelps Dodge Corp.
    PricewaterhouseCoopers
    Procter & Gamble Co.
    Rand McNally & Co.
    Rolls-Royce
    Sun Microsystems
    3M
    Underwriters Laboratories, Inc.
    US Airways
    Wal-Mart
    Weyerhaeuser Co.
    Xerox Corp.
First Family (Presidential)
First Lady (wife of President)
First World War (*see* War)
flag code
flag, U.S.:
    Old Flag, Old Glory

Stars and Stripes
Star-Spangled Banner
flags, foreign:
 Tricolor (French)
 Union Jack (British)
 United Nations
Fleet, if part of name; the fleet:
 Atlantic
 Channel
 Grand
 High Seas
 Marine Force
 Naval Reserve
 Pacific, etc. (naval)
 6th Fleet, etc.
 U.S.
flex fuel
floor (House or Senate)
flyway; Canadian flyway, etc.
Force(s), if part of name; the force(s):
 Active Forces
 Active-Duty
 Air (*see also* Air Force)
 All-Volunteer
 Armed Forces (synonym for overall
  U.S. Military Establishment)
 Army Field Forces; the Field Forces
 Fleet Marine
 Navy Battle (*see* Navy)
 Navy Scouting (*see* Navy); Reserve Force
 Rapid Deployment
 Task Force 70; the task force; *but* task
  force report
 United Nations Emergency; the
  Emergency Force; the Force; *but*
  United Nations police force
foreign cabinets:
 Minister of Foreign Affairs; Foreign
  Minister; the Minister
 Ministry of Foreign Affairs; the Ministry
 Office of Foreign Missions; the Office
 Minister Plenipotentiary
 Premier
 Prime Minister

Foreign Legion (French); the legion
Foreign Service; the Service:
 officer
 Officer Corps; the corps
 Reserve officer; the Reserve officer
 Reserve Officer Corps; the Reserve
  Corps; the corps
 Staff officer; the Staff officer
 Staff Officer Corps; the Staff Corps; the
  corps
Forest, if part of name; the national forest;
 the forest:
 Angeles National
 Black
 Coconino and Prescott National Forests
 but State and National forests (*see*
  System)
Forester (Chief of Forest Service); the Chief;
 also Chief Forester
form 2, A, II, etc.; *but* Form 2, when part of
 title: Form 1040: Individual Income
 Tax Return; *but* withholding tax form
Fort McHenry, etc.; the fort
Foundation, if part of name; capitalized
 standing alone if referring to Federal
 unit:
 Chemical; the foundation
 Ford; the foundation
 National Science; the Foundation
 Russell Sage; the foundation
Founding Fathers; Founders/Founder (of
 this Nation, Country)
four freedoms
Framers (of the U.S. Constitution; of the
 Bill of Rights)
free world
Frisco (for San Francisco; no apostrophe)
Fritalux (*see* alliances)
Fund, if part of name; capitalized standing
 alone if referring to international or
 United Nations fund:
 Democracy (United Nations); the Fund
 International Monetary; the Fund
 but civil service retirement fund;

highway trust fund; mutual security fund; national service life insurance fund; revolving fund

G

Gadsden Purchase

Gallery of Art, National (*see* National)

Gallup Poll; the poll

GAO (Government Accountability Office)

Geiger counter

General Order No. 14; General Orders No. 14; a general order

General Schedule

gentile

Geographer, the (State Department)

geographic terms (terms, such as those listed below,[2] are capitalized if part of name; are lowercased in general sense (rivers of Virginia and Maryland)):

Archipelago	Cave
Area	Cavern
Arroyo	Channel; *but*
Atoll	Mississippi River
Bank	channel(s)
Bar	Cirque
Basin, Upper (Lower)	Coulee
Colorado River,	Cove
etc. (legal entity);	Crag
but Hansen	Crater
flood-control basin;	Creek
Missouri River	Crossroads
basin (drainage);	Current (ocean
upper Colorado	feature)
River storage project	Cut
Bay	Cutoff
Bayou	Dam
Beach	Delta
Bench	Desert
Bend	Divide
Bight	Dome (not geologic)
Bluff	Draw (stream)
Bog	Dune
Borough (boro)	Escarpment
Bottom	Estuary
Branch (stream)	Falls
Brook	Fault
Butte	Flat(s)
Canal; the canal	Floodway
(Panama)	Ford
Canyon	Forest
Cape	Fork (stream)
Cascade	Gap

Geyser	Park
Glacier	Pass
Glen	Passage
Gorge	Peak
Gulch	Peninsula
Gulf	Plain
Gut	Plateau
Harbor	Point
Head	Pond
Hill	Pool
Hogback	Port (water body)
Hollow	Prairie
Hook	Range (mountain)
Horn	Rapids
Hot Spring	Ravine
Icefield	Reef
Ice Shelf	Reservoir
Inlet	Ridge
Island	River
Isle	Roads (anchorage)
Islet	Rock
Keys (Florida only)	Run (stream)
Knob	Sea
Lagoon	Seaway
Lake	Shoal
Landing	Sink
Ledge	Slough
Lowland	Sound
Marsh	Spit
Massif	Spring
Mesa	Spur
Monument	Strait
Moraine	Stream
Mound	Summit
Mount	Swamp
Mountain	Terrace
Narrows	Thoroughfare
Neck	Trench
Needle	Trough
Notch	Valley
Oasis	Volcano
Ocean	Wash
Oxbow	Waterway
Palisades	Woods

Geological Survey (*see* Survey)

GI bill of rights

Girl Scouts (organization); a Girl Scout; a Scout; Scouting

G-man

Gold Star Mothers (*see* American)

Golden Age (*see* Ages)

Golden Rule

Gospel, if referring to the first four books of the New Testament; *but* gospel music

Government:
  British, etc.; the Government

---

[2] List compiled with cooperation of the U.S. Board on Geographic Names.

department, officials, -owned,
publications, etc. (U.S. Government)
National and State Governments
Printing Office (*see* Office)
U.S.; National; Federal
Government information product
government:
  Churchill
  Communist
  District (of Columbia)
  European governments
  Federal, State, and municipal
    governments
  insular; island
  military
  seat of
  State
  State and Provincial governments
  Territorial
governmental
Governor:
  of Louisiana, etc.; the Governor; a
    Governor; State Governor(s);
    Governors' conference
  of Puerto Rico; the Governor
  of the Federal Reserve Board; the
    Governor
Governor General of Canada; the Governor
  General
GPO Access
grand jury (*see* Federal)
Grange, the (National)
grant, Pell
graph 2, A, II, etc.; *but* Graph 2, when part
  of title: Graph 2.—Production levels
Great:
  Basin
  Depression
  Divide
  Lakes; the lakes; lake(s) traffic
  Plains; *but* southern Great Plains
  Seal (any nation)

Society
War (*see* War)
White Way (New York City)
great circle (navigation)
Greater Los Angeles, Greater New York
gross national product (GNP)
Group:
  G8 (Group of 8) (representatives of the
    eight leading industrial nations)
  Helsinki Monitoring; the group
  Military Advisory Group; the group
  Standing (*see* Organization)
  World Bank
group 2, II, A, etc.; *but* Group 2, when part
  of title: Group II: List of Counties by
  States
Guard, National (*see* National)
guardsman (*see* Coast Guard; National
  Guard)
Gulf:
  Coast States; *but* gulf coast
  of Mexico; the gulf
  States
  Stream; the stream

H
Hall (U.S. Senate or House)
Halls of Congress
H-bomb; H-hour
Headquarters:
  Alaskan Command; the command
    headquarters
  4th Regiment Headquarters; regimental
    headquarters
  32d Division Headquarters; the division
    headquarters
hearing examiner
Heaven (religious); heaven (place)
Heimlich maneuver
hell (place)
Hells (no apostrophe) Canyon
Hemisphere, Eastern; Western; etc.; the
  hemisphere

Hezbollah
High Church
High Commissioner
High Court (*see* Supreme Court)
high definition
High School, if part of name: Western; the
    high school
Highway No. 40; Route 40; State Route 9;
    the highway
Hill (the Capitol)
Hispanic
Holocaust, the (World War II); a holocaust
Holy Scriptures; Holy Writ (Bible)
home page
Hospice, if part of name
Hospital, if part of name; the hospital:
    Howard University
    St. Elizabeths (no apostrophe)
    but naval (marine or Army) hospital
hospital corpsman (*see* corpsman)
House, if part of name:
    Blair
    Johnson house (private residence)
    of Representatives; the House (U.S.)
    Office Building (*see* Building)
    Ohio (State); the house
    but both Houses; lower (or upper)
    House (Congress)
House of Representatives (U.S.), titles of
    officers standing alone capitalized:
    Chairman (Committee of the Whole)
    Chaplain
    Clerk; *but* legislative clerk, etc.
    Doorkeeper
    Official Reporter(s) of Debates
    Parliamentarian
    Postmaster
    post office
    Sergeant at Arms
    Speaker pro tempore
    Speaker; speakership
HUD (Department of Housing and Urban
    Development)

Hudson's Bay Co.
Hurricane Andrew, Katrina, Rita, etc.

I

ice age (*see* Ages)
imam
Independent Party; an Independent
Indians:
    Absentee Shawnee
    Alaska (*see* Native)
    Eastern (or Lower) Band of Cherokee;
        the band
    Five Civilized Tribes; the tribes
    Native Americans
    Shawnee Tribe; the tribe
    Six Nations (Iroquois Confederacy)
Initiative, Caribbean Basin; *but* strategic
    defense initiative
Inquisition, Spanish; the Inquisition
inspector general
Institute, if part of name; capitalized
    standing alone if referring to Federal
    or international organization:
    National Cancer; the Cancer Institute;
        the Institute
    National Institutes of Health; the
        Institutes
    of International Law; the Institute
    Woman's; the institute
Institution, if part of name; capitalized
    standing alone if referring to
    Federal unit:
    Brookings; the institution
    Carnegie; the institution
    Smithsonian; the Institution
insular government; island government
intercoastal waterway (*see* waterway)
interdepartmental
interface
International Court of Justice; the Court
international:
    banks (*see* Bank)
    boundary

dateline
law
Morse code (*see* Code)
Internet, Intranet
Interstate 95; I–95; the interstate
Intracoastal Waterway; the waterway (*see also* waterway)
intrastate
Irish potato
Iron Curtain; the curtain
Islam; Islamic
Isthmian Canal (*see* Canal)
Isthmus of Panama; the isthmus

J

Japan Current (*see* Current)
Java (computer language)
Jersey cattle
Job Corps
Joint Chiefs of Staff; Chiefs of Staff
Joint Committee on Printing (*see* Committee)
Journal clerk; the clerk
Journal (House or Senate)
Judge Advocate General, the
judge; chief judge; circuit judge; district judge; *but* Judge Judy
judiciary, the
Justice; Justice Stevens, etc.

K

kaffiyeh (Arabic headdress)
King of England, etc.; the King
Koran, the; Koranic
Krugerrand

L

Laboratory, if part of name; capitalized standing alone if referring to Federal unit: Forest Products; the Laboratory; *but* laboratory (non-Federal)
Lake: Erie, of the Woods, Great Salt; the lake
Lane, if part of name: Maiden; the lane

Latter-day Saints
law, copyright law; Ohm's, etc.
League, Urban; the league
Legion:
    American; the Legion; a Legionnaire;
    French Foreign; the legion
Legislative Assembly, if part of name:
    of New York; of Puerto Rico, etc.; the
    legislative assembly; the assembly
legislative branch, clerk, session, etc.
Legislature:
    National Legislature (U.S. Congress);
    the Legislature
    Ohio Legislature; Legislature of Ohio;
    the State legislature; the legislature
Letters Patent No. 378,964; *but* patent No. 378,964; letters patent
Liberal Party; a Liberal
Libertarian Party; a Libertarian
Liberty Bell; Liberty ship
Librarian of Congress; the Librarian
Library:
    Army; the library
    Harry S. Truman; the library
    of Congress; the Library
    Hillsborough Public; the library
Lieutenant Governor of Idaho, etc.; the Lieutenant Governor
Light, if part of name; the light:
    Boston
    Buffalo South Pier Light 2; *but* light No. 2; light 2
    but Massachusetts Bay lights
Lighthouse (*see* Light Station)
Lightship, if part of name; the lightship:
    Grays Reef
    North Manitou Shoal
Light Station, if part of name; the light station; the station:
    Minots Ledge
    Watch Hill
Line(s), if part of name; the line(s):
    Greyhound (bus)

Holland-America (steamship)
Maginot (fortification)
line:
    Mason-Dixon line *or* Mason and
      Dixon's line
    State
listserv
Local:
    Columbia Typographical Union,
      Local 101
    International Brotherhood of Electrical
      Workers Local 180; *but* local No. 180
local time, local standard time (*see* time)
locator service
Loop, the (*see* cities)
Louisiana Purchase
Low Church
Lower, if part of name:
    California (Mexico)
    Colorado River Basin
    Egypt
    Peninsula (of Michigan)
lower:
    48 (States)
    House of Congress
    Mississippi

M

Madam:
    Chair
    Chairman
    Chairwoman
Magna Carta
Majesty, His, Her, Your; Their Majesties
Majority Leader Reid; Majority Leader
    Hoyer; *but* the majority leader (U.S.
    Congress)
Mall, The National; The Mall (District of
    Columbia)
Mansion, Executive (*see* Executive)
map 3, A, II, etc.; *but* Map 2, when part of
    title: Map 2.—Railroads of Middle
    Atlantic States

mariculture
Marine Corps; the corps:
    Marines (the corps); *but* marines
      (individuals)
    Reserve; the Reserve
    also a marine; a woman marine; the
      women marines (individuals); soldiers,
      sailors, coastguardsmen, and marines
Maritime Provinces (Canada) (*see* Province)
Marshal (*see* Supreme Court)
marshal (U.S.)
medals (*see* decorations)
Medicaid
MediCal
Medicare Act; Medicare plan
Medicare Plus
Medicare Program
Medigap
Member, if referring to Senator,
    Representative, Delegate, or Resident
    Commissioner of U.S. Congress; *also*
    Member at Large; Member of
    Parliament, etc.; *but* membership;
    member of U.S. congressional
    committee
Memorial:
    Jefferson
    Lincoln
    Vietnam
    WWII
    Korean
    Franklin D. Roosevelt etc.; the memorial
Merchant Marine Reserve; the Reserve;
    but U.S. merchant marine; the
    merchant marine
Metroliner
Metropolitan Washington, etc.; *but*
    Washington metropolitan area
midcontinent region
Middle Ages (*see* Ages)
Middle Atlantic States
Middle East; Mideast; Mideastern; Middle
    Eastern (Asia)

Midwest (section of United States);
    Midwestern States; *but* midwestern
    farmers, etc.
Military Academy (*see* Academy)
Military Establishment (*see* Establishment)
milkshed, Ohio, etc. (region)
millennium
Minister Plenipotentiary; the Minister;
    Minister Without Portfolio (*see also*
    foreign cabinets)
Ministry (*see* foreign cabinets)
Minority Leader McConnell; Minority
    Leader Boehner; *but* the minority
    leader (U.S. Congress)
Mint, Philadelphia, etc.; the mint
minutemen (colonial)
missiles: capitalize such missile names as
    Hellfire, Sparrow, Tomahawk, Scud,
    Trident, etc.; *but* cruise missile, air-to-
    air missile, surface-to-air missile, etc.
Mission, if part of name; the mission:
    Gospel
    but diplomatic mission; military mission;
    Jones mission
Monument:
    Bunker Hill; the monument
    Grounds; the grounds (Washington
        Monument)
    National (*see* National)
    Washington; the monument (District
        of Columbia)
Mountain States
mountain time, mountain standard time
    (*see* time)
Moving Pictures Experts Group (MPEG)
Mr. Chairman; Mr. Secretary; etc.
Mujahedeen
mullah
Museum, capitalize with name; the
    museum:
    Field
    National
    National Air and Space; the Air Museum

National Museum of the American
    Indian

N

Nation (synonym for United States); *but* a
    nation; nationwide; *also* French
    nation, Balkan nations
Nation, Creek; Osage; etc.; the nation
nation, in general, standing alone
National, in conjunction with capitalized
    name:
    Academy of Sciences (*see* Academy)
        and State institutions, etc.
    Archives and Records Administration
    Capital (Washington); the Capital; *but*
        national capital area
    Endowment for the Arts; the
        Endowment
    Gallery of Art; the National Gallery;
        the gallery
    Grange; the Grange
    Guard, Ohio, etc.; Air National; the
        National Guard; the Guard; a
        guardsman; Reserve; *but* a National
        Guard man; National Guardsman
    Institute (*see* Institute)
    Legislature (*see* Legislature)
    Muir Woods National Monument etc.;
        the national monument; the
        monument
    Museum (*see* Museum)
    Naval Medical Center (Bethesda, MD)
    Park, Yellowstone, etc.; Yellowstone Park;
        the national park; the park
    Treasury; the Treasury
    War College
    Woman's Party
    Zoological Park (*see* Zoological)
national:
    agency check (NAC)
    anthem, customs, spirit, etc.
    British, Mexican, etc.
    defense agencies

stockpile
water policy
Native: Alaska; American; *but* Ohio native,
etc. (*see* Alaska)
Naval, if part of name:
Academy (*see* Academy)
Air Station (NAS) Patuxent River;
Pensacola; etc.
Base, Guam Naval; the naval base
Establishment (*see* Establishment)
Observatory (*see* Observatory)
Reserve; the Reserve; a reservist
Reserve Force; the force
Reserve officer; a Reserve officer
Shipyard (if preceding or following name):
Brooklyn Naval Shipyard; Naval
Shipyard, Brooklyn; *but* the naval
shipyard
Volunteer Naval Reserve
War College; the War College; the college
naval, in general sense:
command (*see* Command)
expenditures, maneuvers, officer,
service, stores, etc.
petroleum reserves; *but* Naval
Petroleum Reserve No. 2 (Buena
Vista Hills Naval Reserve); reserve
No. 2
navel orange
Navy, American or foreign, if part of name;
capitalized standing alone only if
referring to U.S. Navy:
Admiral of the; the admiral
Battle Force; the Battle Force; the force
Establishment; the establishment
Hospital Corps; hospital corpsman; the
corps
Regular
Seabees (construction battalion); a
Seabee
navy yard
Nazi; nazism
Near East (Balkans, etc.)

Negro (*see* African-American; Black)
network
New Deal; anti-New Deal
New England States
New Federalism
New Frontier
New World; *but* new world order
North:
Atlantic
Atlantic States
Atlantic Treaty (*see* Treaty)
Atlantic Treaty Organization (NATO)
(*see* Organization)
Equatorial Current (*see* Current)
Korea
Pole
Slope (Alaska)
Star (Polaris)
the North (section of United States)
north:
Africa
Ohio, Virginia, etc.
north-central region, etc.
Northeast corridor
northern Ohio
Northern States
northerner
Northwest Pacific
Northwest Territory (1799)
Northwest, the (section of the United States)
Northwest Washington (*see* cities)
Northwestern:
States
United States
numbers capitalized if spelled out as part of
a name:
Air Force One (Presidential plane)
Charles the First
Committee of One Hundred
Twenty-third Census (*see* Census)

O

Observatory, capitalized with name:
Astrophysical; the Observatory

Lick; the observatory
(nongovernmental)
Naval; the Observatory
Occident, the; occidental
Ocean, if part of name; the ocean:
Antarctic
Arctic
Atlantic
North Atlantic, etc.
Pacific
South Pacific, etc.
Southwest Pacific, etc.
Oceanographer (the Hydrographer), Navy
Office, if referring to unit of Federal
Government; the Office:
Executive
Foreign and Commonwealth (U.K.)
Government Printing; the Printing
Office; the Office
Naval Oceanographic
of Chief of Naval Operations
of General Counsel
of Management and Budget
of Personnel Management
of the Secretary (Defense); Secretary's
Office
Patent and Trademark
but New York regional office (including
branch, division, or section therein);
the regional office; the office
officer:
Army
Marine; *but* naval and marine officers
Navy; Navy and Marine officers
Regular Army; Regular; a Regular
Reserve
Old Dominion (Virginia)
Old South
Old World
Olympic Games; Olympiad; XXIX Olympic
Games
ombudsman, Maryland (State)
online

Operation Iraqi Freedom, Desert Storm
Order of Business No. 56 (congressional
calendar)
Ordnance:
Corps (*see* Corps)
Department; the Department
Organization, if part of name; capitalized
standing alone if referring to
international unit:
International Labour (ILO)
North Atlantic Treaty (NATO):
Chiefs of Staff
Committee of Defense Ministers
Council
Council of Foreign Ministers
Defense Committee
Military Committee
of American States (OAS)
Pact
Regional Planning Group; the Group
Standing Group; the Group
United Nations Educational, Scientific,
and Cultural Organization UNESCO)
Orient, the; oriental (*see* Asian)
Osama bin Laden
Outer Continental Shelf (*see* Continental)

P

Pacific (*see also* Atlantic):
Basin
coast
Coast (or slope) States
Northwest
rim
seaboard
slope
South
States
time, Pacific standard time (*see* time)
but cispacific; transpacific
pan-American games; *but* Pan American
Day
Pan American Union (renamed; *see*
Organization of American States)

Panel, the Federal Service Impasses
(Federal), etc.; the Panel
Panhandle of Texas; Texas Panhandle; the
panhandle; etc.
papers, Woodrow Wilson, etc.; the papers;
but white paper
Parish, Caddo, etc.; *but* parish of Caddo
(Louisiana civil division); the parish
Park, Fairmount, etc.; the park (*see also*
National)
Park Police, U.S.; park policeman
Park, Zoological (*see* Zoological)
Parkway, George Washington Memorial;
the memorial parkway; the parkway
Parliament, Houses of; the Parliament
Parliamentarian (U.S. Senate or House)
part 2, A, II, etc.; *but* Part 2, when part of
title: Part 2: Iron and Steel Industry
Party, if part of name; the party
Pass, Brenner, capitalized if part of name;
the pass
patent (*see* Letters Patent)
Peninsula Upper (Lower) (Michigan); the
peninsula
Penitentiary, Atlanta, etc.; the penitentiary
petrodollar
phase 2; phase I
Philippines, Republic of the
Pilgrim Fathers (1620); the Pilgrims; a
Pilgrim
Place, if part of name: Jefferson Place; the
place
Plains (Great Plains), the
plan:
Colombo
controlled materials
5-year
Marshall (European Recovery Program)
Planetarium, Fels, Hayden; the planetarium
Plant, Picatinny Arsenal; the plant; *but*
United States Steel plant
plate 2, A, II, etc.; *but* Plate 2, when part of
title: Plate 2.—Rural Structures

Plaza, Union Station (Washington, DC);
the plaza
Pledge of Allegiance; the pledge
Pole: North, South; the pole; subpolar
Pole Star (Polaris); polar star
Police, if part of name; the police:
Capitol
Park, U.S.
White House
political action committee (PAC)
political parties and adherents (*see* specific
political party)
Pool, Northwest Power, etc.; the pool
Pope; *but* papal, patriarch, pontiff, primate
Port, if part of name; Port of Norfolk;
Norfolk Port; the port (*see* Authority)
Post Office, Chicago, etc.; the post office
P.O. Box (with number); *but* post office box
(in general sense)
Postmaster General
PostScript; *but* a postscript
Powers, if part of name; the powers (*see
also* alliances):
Allied (World Wars I and II)
Axis (World War I)
Western
but European powers
precinct; first, 10th precinct
Premier (*see* foreign cabinets)
Preserve, Sullys Hill, National Game
Presidency (office of the head of
Government)
President:
of the United States; the Executive; the
Chief Magistrate; the Commander
in Chief; the President-elect; ex-
President; former President; *also*
preceding name
of any other country; the President of
Federal or international unit
but president of the Norfolk Southern
Railroad; president of the Federal
Reserve Bank of New York

Presidential assistant, authority, order,
proclamation, candidate, election,
timber, year, etc.
Prime Minister (*see* foreign cabinets)
Prison, New Jersey State; the prison
Privy Council, Her Majesty's (*see* Council)
Prize, Nobel, Pulitzer, etc.; the prize
Proclamation, Emancipation; Presidential
Proclamation No. 24; Proclamation
No. 24; the proclamation; *but*
Presidential proclamation
Program, if part of name:
European Recovery
Food for Peace
Fulbright
Head Start
Mutual Defense Assistance
Social Security
but universal military training;
government bailout
Progressive Party; a Progressive
Project:
Gutenberg
Manhattan
Vote Smart
Proposition 13
Prosecutor; Special Prosecutor (Federal)
Province, Provincial, if referring to an
administrative subdivision: Ontario
Province; Province of Ontario;
Maritime Provinces (Canada); the
Province
Proving Ground, Aberdeen, etc.; the
proving ground
Public Law; Public Law 110–161, etc.
Public Printer; the Government Printer; the
Printer
public utility district (*see* District)
Pueblo, Santa Clara; the pueblo
Purchase, Gadsden, Louisiana, etc.
Puritan; puritanical
Pyrrhic victory

Q
Quad Cities (Davenport, Rock Island,
Moline, East Moline, and Bettendorf)
query
queue

R
Radio Free Europe/Radio Liberty
Railroad, Alaska; the Railroad
Ranch, King, etc.; the ranch
Range, Cascade, etc. (mountains); the range
Rebellion, if part of name; the rebellion:
Boxer
Whisky
Reconstruction period (post-Civil War)
Red army
Red Cross, American (*see* American)
Reds, the; a Red (political)
Reformatory, Michigan; the reformatory
Refuge, Blackwater National Wildlife, etc.;
Blackwater Refuge; the refuge
region, north-central, etc.; first region, 10th
region; region 7; midcontinent
Regular Army, Navy; a Regular (*see also*
officer)
regulation:
greenhouse gas
W (*see also* Federal Reserve Board)
but Veterans Entitlements Regulations
religious terms:
Baha'i
Baptist
Brahman
Buddhist
Catholic; Catholicism; *but* catholic
(universal)
Christian
Christian Science
Evangelical United Brethren
Hindu; Hinduism
Islam; Islamic
Jewish
Latter-day Saints

Muslim: Shiite; Sikh; Sunni
New Thought
Protestant; Protestantism
Scientology
Seventh-day Adventists
Seventh-Day Baptists
Zoroastrian
Renaissance, the (era)
Report, if part of name (with date or
    number); the annual report; the report:
2007 Report of the Chief of the Forest
    Service
9/11 Commission Report
Annual Report of the Secretary of
    Defense for the year ended
    September 30, 2008
Grace Commission report
President's Economic Report; the
    Economic Report
Railroad Retirement Board Annual
    Report, 2007; *but* annual report of the
    Railroad Retirement Board
Report No. 31
United States Reports (publication)
Reporter, the (U.S. Supreme Court)
Representative; Representative at Large
    (U.S. Congress); U.N.
Republic, capitalized if part of name;
    capitalized standing alone if referring
    to a specific government:
Czech
French
Irish
of Bosnia and Herzegovina
of Panama
of the Philippines
Slovak (Slovakia)
United States
also the American Republics; South
    American Republics; the Latin
    American Republics; the Republics
Republican Party; a Republican

Reservation (forest, military, or Indian), if
    part of name; the reservation:
Hill Military
Standing Rock
Reserve, if part of name; the Reserve (*see
    also* Air Force; Army Corps; Coast
    Guard; Foreign Service; Marine
    Corps; Merchant Marine; Naval;
    National Guard):
Active
Air Force
Army
bank (*see* Bank)
Board, Federal (*see* Federal)
city (*see* Bank)
components
Enlisted
Establishment
Inactive
Naval
officer
Officers' Training Corps
Ready
Retired
Standby
Strategic
Reserves, the; reservist
Resolution, with number; the resolution:
House Joint Resolution 3
Senate Concurrent Resolution 18
War Powers Resolution (short title)
but Tonkin resolution
Revised Statutes (U.S.); Supplement to the
    Revised Statutes; the statutes; Statutes
    at Large (U.S.)
Revolution, Revolutionary (if referring to
    the American, French, or English
    Revolution) (*see also* War)
rim; the Pacific rim
Road, if part of name: Benning; the road
Roman numerals, common nouns used
    with, not capitalized:
book II; chapter II; part II; etc.

but Book II: Modern Types (complete heading); Part XI: Early Thought (complete heading)

Route 66, State Route 9 (highways)

rule 21; rule XXI; *but* Rule 21, when part of title: Rule 21: Renewal of Motion

Rules:
of the House of Representatives; *but* rules of the House; House rule X

Standing Rules of the Senate (publication); *but* rules of the Senate *also* Commission rules

S

Sabbath; Sabbath Day

savings bond (*see* bond)

schedule 2, A, II, etc.; *but* Schedule 2, when part of title; Schedule 2: Open and Prepay Stations

School, if part of name; the school:
any school of U.S. Armed Forces
Hayes
Pawnee Indian
Public School 13; P.S. 13

school district (*see* District)

Scriptures; Holy Scriptures (the Bible)

Seabees (*see* Navy)

seaboard, Atlantic, eastern, etc.

seasons:
autumn (fall)
spring
summer
winter

seaway (*see* geographic terms; Authority; Corporation)

Second World War (*see* War)

Secretariat (*see* United Nations)

Secretaries of the Army and the Navy; *but* Secretaries of the military departments; secretaryship

Secretary, head of national governmental unit:
of Defense; of State; etc.; the Secretary

of State for Foreign Affairs (British); for the Commonwealth, etc.; the Secretary

of the Smithsonian Institution; the Secretary

also the Assistant Secretary; the Executive Secretary

Secretary General; the Secretary General:
Organization of American States
United Nations

section 2, A, II, etc.; *but* Section 2, when part of title: Section 2: Test Construction Theory

Selective Service (*see* Service; System)

Senate (U.S.), titles of officers standing alone capitalized:
Chaplain
Chief Clerk
Doorkeeper
Official Reporter(s)
Parliamentarian
Postmaster
President of the
President pro tempore
Presiding Officer
Secretary
Sergeant at Arms

Senate, Ohio (State); the senate

Senator (U.S. Congress); *but* lowercased if referring to a State senator, unless preceding a name

senatorial

Sergeant at Arms (U.S. Senate or House)

Sermon on the Mount

server

Service, if referring to Federal unit; the Service:
Extension
Federal Mediation and Conciliation
Fish and Wildlife
Foreign (*see* Foreign Service)
Forest
Internal Revenue

Marshals

National Park

Natural Resources Conservation

Postal

Secret (Homeland Security)

Selective (*see also* System); *but* selective
service, in general sense; selective
service classification 1–A, 4–F, etc.

Senior Executive

service:

airmail

Army

city delivery

consular

customs

diplomatic

employment (State)

extension (State)

general delivery

naval

Navy

parcel post

postal field

rural free delivery; rural delivery; free
delivery

special delivery

star route

Shelf, Continental (*see* Continental)

ship of state (unless personified)

Sister(s) (adherent of religious order)

Six Nations (*see* Indians)

Smithsonian Institution (*see* Institution)

Social Security Administration (U.S.),
application, check, number, pension,
trust fund, system, etc.

Socialist Party; a Socialist

Society, if part of name; the society:

American Cancer Society, Inc.

of the Cincinnati

soil bank

soil orders:

Alfisols	Aridisols
Andisols	Entisols

Gelisols	Oxisols
Histosols	Spodosols
Inceptisols	Ultisols
Mollisols	Vertisols

Soldiers' Home; the soldiers' home; (*see*
Armed Forces Retirement Home)

Solicitor for the Department of Labor, etc.;
the Solicitor

Solicitor General (Department of Justice)

Son of Man (Christ)

Sons of the American Revolution
(organization); a Son; a Real Son

South:

American Republics (*see* Republic)

American States

Atlantic

Atlantic States

Deep South (U.S.)

Korea

Midsouth (U.S.)

Pacific

Pole

the South (section of United States);
Southland

Southeast Asia

southern California, southeastern
California, etc.

Southern States

Southern United States

southerner

Southwest, the (section of United States)

space shuttle; the shuttle

space station

Spanish-American War (*see* War)

Speaker of the House of Representatives;
the Speaker

special agent

specialist

Special Order No. 12; Special Orders, No.
12; a special order

Spirit of '76 (painting); *but* spirit of '76 (in
general sense)

Sputnik

Square, Lafayette, etc.; the square

Staff, Foreign Service (*see* Foreign Service);
 Air (U.K.)
standard time (*see* time)
Star of Bethlehem
Star-Spangled Banner (*see* flag)
State:
 Champion
 government
 legislature (*see* Legislature)
 line, Iowa; Ohio-Indiana, etc.
 New York
 of Israel
 of Maryland
 of the Union Message/Address
 of Veracruz
 out-of-State (adjective); *but* out-of-stater
 prison
 Vatican City
state:
 church and
 of the art: state-of-the-art technology
 welfare
 also downstate, instate, multistate,
  statehood, statehouse, stateside,
  statewide, substate, tristate, upstate
State's attorney
state's evidence
states' rights
States:
 Arab
 Balkan
 Baltic
 East North Central
 East South Central
 Eastern; *but* eastern industrial States
 Eastern Gulf
 Eastern North Central, etc.
 Far Western
 Gulf; Gulf Coast
 Lake
 Latin American
 lower 48
 Middle

Middle Atlantic
Middle Western
Midwestern
Mountain
New England
North Atlantic
Northwestern, etc.
Organization of American
Pacific
Pacific Coast
rights
South American
South Atlantic
Southern
the six States of Australia; a foreign state
Thirteen Original; original 13 States
Western; *but* western Gulf; western
 farming States
Station, if part of name; the station; not
 capitalized if referring to surveying
 or similar work:
 Air Force base
 Grand Central
 Naval Air Engineering
 television station WSYR–TV
 Union; Union Depot; the depot
 WAMU station; station WMAL; radio
  station WSM; broadcasting station
  WJSV
station 9; substation A
Statue of Liberty; the statue
Statutes at Large (U.S.) (*see also* Revised
 Statutes)
Stealth: bomber, fighter
Stockpile, Strategic National
stone age (*see* Ages)
storage facility
Stream, Gulf (*see* Gulf; geographic terms)
Street, if part of name; the street:
 I Street (not Eye Street)
 110th Street
 U Street (not You Street)
subcommittee (*see* Committee)

subtropical, subtropic(s) (*see* tropical)
summit meeting; Earth summit
Sun; a sun
Super Bowl
Superfund; the fund
Superintendent, if referring to head of
     Federal unit; the Superintendent:
   of Documents (Government Printing
     Office)
   of the Naval (or Military) Academy
Supplement to the Revised Statutes (*see*
     Revised Statutes)
Supreme Bench; the Bench; *also* High
     Bench; High Tribunal
Supreme Court (U.S.); the Court; *also* High
     Court; titles of officers standing alone
     capitalized:
   Associate Justice
   Chief Justice
   Clerk
   Marshal
   Reporter
   but Ohio Supreme Court; the supreme
     court
Surgeon General, the (Air Force, Army,
     Navy, and Public Health Service)
Survey, if part of name of Federal unit; the
     Survey: Geodetic; Geological
System, if referring to Federal unit; the
     System:
   Federal Home Loan Bank; the System
   Federal Reserve; the System
   National Forest; the System
   National Highway; Interstate Highway;
     the System
   National Park; the System
   National Trails; the System
   National Wild and Scenic Rivers; the
     System
   Regional Metro System; Metro system
   Selective Service (*see also* Service)
   State and National forests
   but Amtrak railway system; Amtrak
     system; the system

   also Federal land bank system

T

table 2, II, A, etc.; *but* Table 2, when part of
     title: Table 2: Degrees of Land
     Deterioration
task force (*see* Force)
Team, USAREUR Technical Assistance,
     etc.; the team
television station (*see* Station)
Telnet
Ten Commandments
Territorial, if referring to a political
     subdivision
Territory:
   Northwest (1799); the territory
   Trust Territory of the Pacific Islands;
   Pacific Islands Trust Territory; the trust
     territory; the territory
   Yukon, Northwest Territories; the
     Territory(ies), Territorial (Canada)
   but territory of: American Samoa, Guam,
     Virgin Islands
The, part of name, capitalized:
   The Dalles; The Gambia; The Hague;
     The Weirs; *but* the Dalles Dam; the
     Dalles region; the Federal Bulletin
     Board; the Hague Conference; the
     Weirs streets
   but the Adjutant General; the National
     Archives; the Archives; the Times; the
     Mermaid; the Federal Express
Third World
Thirteen American Colonies, etc. (*see*
     Colonies)
Thirteen Original States
Thruway, New York State; the thruway
time:
   Alaska, Alaska standard
   Atlantic, Atlantic standard
   central, central standard
   eastern, eastern daylight, eastern daylight
     saving (no *s*), eastern standard
   Greenwich mean time (GMT)

Hawaii-Aleutian standard
local, local standard
mountain, mountain standard
Pacific, Pacific standard
universal
title 2, II, A, etc.; *but* Title 2, when part of
   title: Title 2: General Provisions
Tomb:
   Grant's; the tomb
   of the Unknowns; of the Unknown
     Soldier; Unknown Soldier's Tomb;
     the tomb (*see also* Unknown Soldier)
Tower, Eiffel, etc.; the tower
Township, Union; township of Union
trade names and trademarks:

Blu-Ray	TiVo
Coca-Cola	U-Haul
Dr Pepper	UNIX
Hersheypark	VISA
iPod	WebTV
iTunes	Yahoo!
MasterCard	ZIP Code (Postal)

Trade Representative (U.S.)
transatlantic; transpacific; trans-Siberian,
   etc.; *but* Transjordan; Trans-Alaska
Treasurer, Assistant, of the United States;
   the Assistant Treasurer; *but* assistant
   treasurer at New York, etc.
Treasurer of the United States; the Treasurer
Treasury notes; Treasurys
Treasury, of the United States; General;
   National; Public
Treaty, if part of name; the treaty:
   Jay Treaty
   North Atlantic; North Atlantic Defense
   of Versailles
   but treaty of 1919
triad
tribe (*see* Indians)
Tribunal, standing alone capitalized only in
   minutes and official reports of a
   specific arbitration; *also* High
   Tribunal; the Tribunal (Supreme
   Court)
Tropic of Cancer, of Capricorn; the Tropics

tropical; neotropic, neotropical, sub-
   tropic(s), subtropical
Trust, Power, etc.
trust territory (*see* Territory)
Tunnel, Lincoln, etc.; the tunnel; *but*
   irrigation, railroad, etc., tunnel
Turnpike, Pennsylvania, etc.; the turnpike
Twin Cities (Minneapolis and St. Paul)

U
U-boat
Under Secretary, if referring to officer of
   Federal Government; the Under
   Secretary:
   of Agriculture
   of State
   of the Treasury
Uniform Code of Military Justice (*see* Code)
Union (if part of proper name; capitalized
   standing alone if synonym for United
   States or if referring to international
   unit):
Columbia Typographical
European
Pan American (former name; *see*
   Organization of American States)
Station; *but* union passenger station;
   union freight station
Teamsters Union; the Teamsters; the
   union; *also* the Auto Workers, etc.
Universal Postal; the Postal Union
Western (*see* alliances)
Woman's Christian Temperance
but a painters union; printers union
United Nations:
   Charter; the charter
   Educational, Scientific, and Cultural
   Organization (UNESCO) (*see*
   Organization)
   Food and Agriculture Organization
   (FAO)
   General Assembly; the Assembly

International Children's Emergency
  Fund (UNICEF)
International Court of Justice; the Court
Permanent Court of Arbitration (*see*
  Court)
Secretariat, the
Secretary General
Security Council; the Council
World Employment Conference
World Health Organization (WHO);
  the Organization
universal:
  military training (*see* Program)
  time (*see* time)
University, if part of name: Stanford; the
  university
Unknown Soldier; Unknown of World War
  II; World War II Unknown;
  Unknown of Korea; Korea
  Unknown; the Unknowns (*see also*
  Tomb)
Upper, if part of name:
  Colorado River Basin
  Egypt
  Peninsula (of Michigan)
  but upper House of Congress
U.S.S.R. (former Union of Soviet Socialist
  Republics)

V
Valley, Shenandoah, etc.; the valley; *but* the
  valleys of Virginia and Maryland
V–E Day; V–J Day; V-chip
veteran, World War II; Vietnam
Veterans Affairs, Department of (*see*
  Department)
Vice Chairman, etc. (same as Chairman)
vice consul, British, etc.
Vice President (same as President)
Voice of America; the Voice
volume 2, A, II, etc.; *but* Volume 2, when
  part of title; Volume 2: Five Rivers in
  America's Future

W
War, if part of formal name:
  Between the States
  Civil
  First World War; World War I; World
    War; Great War; Second World War;
    World War II
  for Independence (1776)
  French and Indian (1754–63)
  Mexican
  of 1812
  of the Rebellion; the rebellion
  on Crime
  on Drugs
  on Poverty
  on Terrorism, Global
  Revolutionary; of the Revolution; the
    Revolution
  Seven Years'
  Six-Day (Arab-Israeli)
  Spanish-American
  the two World Wars
  also post-World War II
war, descriptive or undeclared:
  cold, hot
  European
  French and Indian wars
  Indian
  Korean
  Persian Gulf; gulf
  third world; world war III
  Vietnam
  with Mexico
War College, National (*see* College)
War Mothers (*see* American)
ward 1, 2, etc.; first, 11th, etc.
Washington's Farewell Address
water district (*see* District)
waterway, inland, intercoastal, etc.; *but*
  Intracoastal Waterway
Web:
  page
  site

Week, Fire Prevention; etc.
welfare state
West:
  Bank (Jordan)
  Coast (Africa); *but* west coast (U.S.)
  End, etc. (section of city)
  Europe (political entity)
  Far West; Far Western States
  Florida (1763–1819)
  Middle (United States); Midwest
  South Central States, etc.
  the West (section of United States; *also*
    world political entity)
west, western Pennsylvania
Western:
  bloc
  civilization
  countries
  Europe(an) (political entity)
  Hemisphere; the hemisphere
  ideas
  Powers
  States
  United States
  World
  but far western; western farming States
    (U.S.)
westerner
Whip, Majority; Minority
Whisky Rebellion (*see* Rebellion)
White (*see* Caucasian)
White House:
  Blue Room
  East Room
  Oval Office
  Police (*see* Police)
  Red Room
  Rose Garden
  State Dining Room
white paper, British, etc.
Wilderness, capitalized with name; San
  Joaquin Wilderness, CA; the

wilderness; *but* the Wilderness
  (Virginia battlefield)
Wood, if part of name:
  Belleau
  County
  Fort Leonard
World: New, Old, Third; *but* free world
World Bank; the Bank
World Series
World War (*see* War)
World War II veteran
World Wide Web (WWW), the Web

X
x ray (note: no hyphen)

Y
year, calendar, fiscal
Your Excellency; Your Honor; Your
  Majesty; etc.
Youth Corps; the Corps

Z
ZIP Code number; ZIP+4
Z39.50
Zone, if part of name; the zone:
  British (in Germany)
  Canal (Panama)
  Eastern, Western (Germany)
  Frigid
  Hot (infectious area)
  of Interior (*see* Command)
  Temperate, Torrid; the zone
  U.S. Foreign Trade; Foreign
    Trade Zone; *but* the foreign trade
    zone, free trade zone
zone:
  Arctic
  eastern standard time
  no-fly
  polar
  tropical
Zoological Park (National); the zoo;
  the park

5. Spelling

(See also Chapter 7 "Compounding Examples" and Chapter 9 "Abbreviations and Letter Symbols")

5.1. GPO uses Webster's Third New International Dictionary as its guide for the spelling of words not appearing in the GPO STYLE MANUAL. Colloquial and dialect spellings are not used unless required by the subject matter or specially requested. The tendency of some producers of computer-assisted publications to rely on the limited capability of some spell-checking programs adds importance to this list.

Preferred and difficult spellings

5.2. In addition to indicating the preferred forms of words with variant spellings, the list also contains other words frequently misspelled or causing uncertainty. (See also "Word Division," a supplement to the GPO STYLE MANUAL.)

A
abattoir
aberration
abetter
  abettor (law)
abridgment
absorb (take in)
  adsorb (adhesion)
abysmal
a cappella
accede (yield)
  exceed (surpass)
accepter
  acceptor (law)
accessory
accommodate
accordion
accouter
accursed
acetic (acid)
  ascetic (austere)
acknowledgment
acoustic
adapter

adjurer
adjuster
ad nauseam
adviser
  advisor (law)
adz
aegis
aesthetic
affect (influence, v.)
  effect (result,
    finish, n., v.)
afterward(s)
afterword
aging
aid (n., v.)
aide
aide-de-camp
albumen (egg)
  albumin
    (chemistry)
align
allottee
all ready (prepared)
  already (previous)

all right
altogether
  (completely)
all together
  (collectively)
aluminum
ambidextrous
amoeba
ampoule
analog
analogous
anemia
anesthetic
aneurysm
anomalous
anonymous
antediluvian
antibiotics (n.)
  antibiotic (adj.)
anyway (adv.)
anywise (adv.)
appall, -ed, -ing
appareled, -ing
aquatic

aqueduct
archaeology
arrester
artifact
artisan
ascendance, -ant
ascent (rise)
  assent (consent)
assassinate
athenaeum
attester
autogiro
awhile (for some
  time)
  a while (a short
    time)
ax
aye

B
backward
baloney (nonsense)
  bologna (sausage)
bandanna

79

bargainer
  bargainor (law)
baritone
bark (boat)
barreled, -ing
bastille
bathyscaph
battalion
bazaar (event)
bizarre (strange on
  absurd)
behoove
beneficent
benefited, -ing
bettor (wagerer)
beveled, -ing
biased, -ing
blessed
bloc (group)
  block (grants)
blond (masc., fem.)
bluing
born (birth)
  borne (carried)
bouillon (soup)
  bullion (metal)
boulder
bourgeoisie
breach (gap)
  breech (lower part)
brier
briquet, -ted, -ting
Britannia
broadax
bronco
brunet (masc., fem.)
buccaneer
buncombe
bunion
bur
burned
bus, bused, buses,
  busing

butadiene

C
caffeine
calcareous
calcimine
caldron
calendar
calender (paper
  finish)
caliber
caliper
calk (spike)
  caulk (seal)
calligraphy
callus (n.)
  callous (adj.)
calorie
canceled, -ing
cancellation
candor
canister
cannot
canoeing
cantaloupe
canvas (cloth)
  canvass (solicit)
capital (city, money)
  capitol (building)
carabao (sing., pl.)
carat (gem weight)
  caret (omission
    mark)
  karat (gold weight)
carbureted, -ing
carburetor
Caribbean
caroled, -ing
carotene
carrot
cartilage
caster (roller)
  castor (oil)

casual (informal)
  causal (cause)
catalog, -ed, -ing
cataloger
catsup
caviar
caviled, -er, -ing
center
centipede
centrifugal
cesarean
chairmaned
chaise longue
chancellor
channeled, -ing
chaperon
chautauqua
chauvinism
chiffonier
chile con carne
chili (pepper)
chiseled, -ing
chlorophyll
cigarette
citable
cite (quote)
  site (place)
clamor
climactic (climax)
  climatic (climate)
cocaine
coconut
cocoon
coleslaw
colloquy
colossal
combated, -ing
commenter
  commentor (law)
commingle
commiserate
complement
  (complete)

compliment
  (praise)
confectionery
confidant (masc.,
  fem.)
confident (sure)
confirmer
  confirmor (law)
conjurer
connecter
  connector (road)
connoisseur
consecrator
consensus
consignor
consulter
consummate
contradicter
control, -lable, -ling
converter
conveyor
cookie
cornetist
corollary
corvette
councilor (of
  council)
  counselor
    (adviser)
counseled, -ing
cozy
crawfish
creneled, -ing
crystaled, -ing
crystalline
crystallize
cudgeled, -ing
cyclopedia
czar

D
darndest
debarkation
decaffeinated

decalogue
defense
deliverer
    deliveror (law)
demagogue
demarcation
dependent
descendant (n., adj.)
desecrater
desiccate
desuetude
    (suspended)
    destitute (bereft)
detractor
develop, -ment
device (contrivance)
    devise (convey)
dextrous (syllable
    division)
diaeresis
diaeretic
    diuretic (water pill)
diagramed, -ing
diagrammatic
dialed, -ing
dialogue
dialysis
diaphragm
diarrhea
dickey
dietitian
diffuser
dike
dilettante
dinghy (boat)
diphtheria
discreet (prudent)
    discrete (distinct)
disheveled, -ing
disk
dispatch
dissension
distention

distill, -ed, -ing,
    -ment
distributor
diverter
divorcee
doctoral
doctrinaire
doggerel
dossier
doweled, -ing
downward
dreadnought
dreamed
drought
dueled, -ing
duffelbag
dullness
dumfound
dwelt
dyeing (coloring)
    dying (death)

E
eastward
ecstasy
edema
edgewise
electronics (n.)
    electronic (adj.)
eleemosynary
elicit (to draw)
    illicit (illegal)
embarrass
embed
embellish
emboweled, -ing
emboweler
emigrant (go from)
    immigrant (go
    into)
emigree
eminent (famous)
    imminent (soon)
employee

enameled, -ing
encage
encase
encave
enclasp
enclose
enclosure
encumber
encumbrance
encyclopedia
endorse, -ment
endwise
enfeeble
enforce, -ment
engraft
enroll, -ed, -ing,
    -ment
enshade
ensheathe
ensnare
ensure (guarantee)
    insure (protect)
entrench
entrepreneur
entrust
entwine
envelop (v.)
    envelope (n.)
enwrap
eon
epaulet, -ed, -ing
epiglottis
epilogue
equaled, -ing
erysipelas
escallop
escapable
esophagus
etiology
evacuee
evanescent
eviscerate
evocative

exhibitor
exhilarate
exonerate
exorbitant
expellant
exposé (n.,
    exposure)
    expose (v., to lay
    open)
exsiccate
extant (in existence)
    extent (range)
extoll, -ed, -ing
eying
eyrie

F
fantasy
farther (distance)
    further (degree)
favor
fecal
feces
fetal
fetish
fetus
fiber
fiche (microfiche)
filigree
finable
finagle
financier
fjord
flammable (*not*
    inflammable)
flection
fledgling
flexitime
flier
flotage
flotation
fluorescent
focused, -ing

folderal
forbade
forbear (endurance)
　forebear (ancestor)
foresee
forgettable
forgo (relinquish)
　forego (precede)
format, formatted,
　formatting
forswear
fortissimo
forward (ahead)
　foreword (preface)
fricassee
fuchsia
fueler
fulfill, -ed, -ing,
　-ment
fulsome
fungus (n., adj.)
funneled, -ing
furor
fuse (all meanings)
fuselage
fusillade

G

gaiety
gaily
galosh
gamboled, -ing
garrote
gauge
gazetteer
gelatin
genealogy
generalissimo
germane
glamorous
glamour
glycerin
gobbledygook
goodbye

graveled, -ing
gray
grievous
groveled, -ing
gruesome
guarantee (n., v.)
　guaranty (n., law)
guerrilla (warfare)
　gorilla (ape)
guesstimate
guttural
gypsy

H

hallelujah
hara-kiri
harass
harebrained
healthful (for
　health)
healthy (with
　health)
heinous
hemoglobin
hemorrhage
heterogeneous
hiccup
highfalutin
hijack
homeopath
homogeneity
homologue
hors d'oeuvre
hypocrisy
hypotenuse

I

idiosyncrasy
idle (inactive)
　idol (statue)
idyll
imminent (soon)
　eminent (famous)
impaneled, -ing

impasse
imperiled, -ing
impostor
impresario
imprimatur
inculcate
indict (to accuse)
　indite (to compose)
inequity (unfairness)
　iniquity (sin)
inferable
infold
ingenious (skillful)
　ingenuous (simple)
innocuous
innuendo
inoculate
inquire, inquiry
install, -ed, -ing,
　-ment
installation
instill, -ed, -ing
insure (protect)
　ensure (guarantee)
intelligentsia
interceptor
interment (burial)
　internment (jail)
intern
intervener
　intervenor (law)
intransigent (n., adj.)
iridescent
italic

J

jalopy
jalousie
jerry-(built)
　jury-(rigged)
jeweled, -ing, -er
jewelry
judgeship
judgment

jujitsu
juxtaposition

K

karat
kerneled, -ing
kerosene
kidnapped, -ing
kidnapper
kilogram
knapsack
kopek
kumquat

L

labeled, -ing
lacquer
landward
lath (wood)
　lathe (machine)
laureled
leukemia
leveled, -ing
leveler
liable (responsible)
　libel (legal)
liaison
libelant
libeled, -ing
libelee
libeler
license
licenser (issuer)
　licensor (grantor)
licorice
likable
lilliputian
linage (lines)
　lineage (descent)
liquefy
liquor
　liqueur
liter
livable

loath (reluctant)
loathe (detest)
lodestar
lodestone
lodgment
logistics (n.)
logistic (adj.)
louver
luster
lyonnaise

M

madam
Mafia
maim
maize (corn)
maze (labyrinth)
maneuver
manifold
manikin (dwarf)
mannequin (model)
mantel (shelf)
mantle (cloak)
marbleize
marijuana
marshaled, -ing
marshaler
marveled, -ing
marvelous
material (goods)
materiel (military)
meager
medaled, -ing
medalist
medieval
metaled, -ing
metalize
meteorology
(weather)
metrology
(weights and
measures)
meter

mil (¹⁄₁₀₀₀ inch)
mill (¹⁄₁₀₀₀ dollar)
mileage
miliary
(tuberculosis)
milieu
milk cow
millenary (1,000)
millinery (hats)
millennium
minable
missilery
misspell
miter
moccasin
modeled, -ing
modeler
mold
mollusk
molt
moneys
monogramed, -ing
monologue
mortise
movable
mucilage
mucus (n.)
mucous (adj.)
Muslim
mustache

N

naphtha
Navajo
nazism
neophyte
niacin
nickel
niter
nonplused
northward
Novocain
(trademark)

novocaine
(anesthetic)
numskull

O

obbligato
obloquy
ocher
octet
offal
offense
omelet
ophthalmology
opossum
orangutan
orbited, -ing
ordinance (law)
ordnance
(military)
organdy
overseas or oversea

P

pajamas
paleontology
paneled, -ing
paraffin
paralleled, -ing
parallelepiped
parceled, -ing
partisan
pastime
patrol, -led, -ling
peccadillo
pedant (n.)
pedantic (adj.)
peddler
penciled, -ing
pendant (n.)
pendent (u.m.)
percent
peremptory
(decisive)
preemptory
(preference)

perennial
periled, -ing
permittee
perquisite (privilege)
prerequisite
(requirement)
personal (individual)
personnel (staff)
perspective (view)
prospective
(expected)
petaled, -ing
pharaoh
pharmacopeia
phoenix
phlegm
phony
phosphorus (n.)
phosphorous (adj.)
photostated
pickax
picnicking
pipet
plaque
plastics (n.)
plastic (adj.)
pledger
pledgor (law)
plenitude
pliers
plow
poleax
pollination
pommeled, -ing
pontoon
porcelaneous
practice (n., v.)
precedence
(priority)
precedents (usage)
prerogative
pretense
preventive

principal (chief)
  principle
  (proposition)
privilege
proffer
programmatic
programmed, -mer,
  -ming
prologue
promissory
pronunciation
propel, -led, -ling
propellant (n.)
  propellent (adj.)
prophecy (n.)
  prophesy (v.)
ptomaine
pubic (anatomy)
pulmotor
pusillanimous

Q

quarreled, -ing
quartet
quaternary
questionnaire
queue

R

raccoon
racket (all meanings)
rapprochement
rarefy
rarity
ratable
rational (adj.)
  rationale (n.)
rattan
raveled, -ing
reconnaissance
reconnoiter
recyclable
referable
refuse
registrar

reinforce
relater
  relator (law)
remodeler
renaissance
reparable
repellant (n.)
  repellent (adj.)
requester
  requestor (law)
rescission
responder
  (electronics)
responser
  (electronics)
reveled, -er, -ing
rhyme, rhythmic
RIFing, RIFed, RIFs
rivaled, -ing
roweled, -ing
ruble

S

saccharin (n.)
  saccharine (adj.)
sacrilegious
salable
sandaled, -ing
savable
savanna
savior
  Saviour (Christ)
scalloped, -ing
schizophrenia
scion (horticulture)
scurrilous
seismology
selvage (edging)
  salvage (save)
sentineled, -ing
separate (v., adj.)
sepulcher
seriatim
settler
  settlor (law)

sewage (waste)
  sewerage (drain
  system)
sextet
Shakespearean
shellacking
shoveled, -ing
shriveled, -ing
sideward
signaled, -ing
siphon
site (place)
  cite (quote)
sizable
skeptic
skillful
skulduggery
sleight (deft)
  slight (meager)
smolder
sniveled, -ing
snorkel
soliloquy
sometime
  (formerly)
  some time (some
  time ago)
  some times (at
  times)
southward
spacious (space)
  specious
  (deceptive)
specter
spirituous (liquor)
spirochete
spoliation
stationary (fixed)
  stationery (paper)
statue (sculpture)
  stature (height)
  statute (law)
staunch
stenciled, -ing
stenciler

stifling
stratagem
stubbornness
stultify
stupefy
subpoena, -ed
subtlety
succor
sulfur (also
  derivatives)
  sulfanilamide
  sulfureted, -ing
supererogation
surfeit
surreptitious
surveillance
swiveled, -ing
sylvan
synonymous
syrup

T

taboo
tactician
tasseled, -ing
tattoo
taxied, -ing
technique
teetotaler
tercentenary
theater
therefor (for it)
  therefore (for that
  reason)
thiamine
thralldom
thrash (beat)
  thresh (grain)
threshold
tie, tied, tying
timber (wood)
  timbre (tone)
tinseled, -ing
titer
tonsillitis

tormenter
totaled, -ing
toward
toweled, -ing
toxemia
trafficking
trammeled, -ing
tranquilize(r)
tranquillity
transcendent
transferable
transferor
transferred
transonic
transponder
  (electronics)
transshipment
traveled, -ing
traveler
travelogue

triptych
trolley
troop (soldiers)
  troupe (actors)
troweled, -ing
tryptophan
tularemia
tunneled, -ing
tunneler
turquoise
typify
tyrannical
tyro

U

unctuous
unwieldy
upward
uremia
usable

V
vacillate
valance (drape)
  valence
    (chemistry)
veld
veranda
vermilion
vicissitude
victualed, -ing
victualer
vilify
villain
visa, -ed, -ing
vitamin
vitrify
volcanism
voluntarism
votable
vying

W
wainscoting
warranter
  warrantor (law)
warranty
weeviled, -ing
welder
westward
whimsy
whiskey, -s
willful
withe
woeful
woolen
woolly
worshiped, -er, -ing

Anglicized and foreign words

5.3.   Diacritical marks are not used with anglicized words.

A
abaca
aide memoire
a la carte
a la king
a la mode
angstrom
aperitif
applique
apropos
auto(s)-da-fe

B
blase
boutonniere
brassiere

C
cabana
cafe

cafeteria
caique
canape
cause celebre
chateau
cliche
cloisonne
comedienne
comme ci
  comme ca
communique
confrere
consomme
cortege
coulee
coup de grace
coup d'etat
coupe
creme
crepe

crepe de chine
critique
critiquing

D
debacle
debris
debut
debutante
decollete
dejeuner
denouement
depot
dos-a-dos

E
eclair
eclat
ecru
elan

elite
entree
etude

F
facade
faience
faux pas
fete
fiance (masc., fem.)
frappe

G
garcon
glace
grille
gruyere

H
habitue

I
ingenue

J
jardiniere

L
laissez faire
litterateur

M
materiel
matinee
melange
melee
menage
mesalliance
metier

moire

N
naive
naivete
nee

O
opera bouffe
opera comique

P
papier mache
piece de resistance
pleiade
porte cochere
porte lumiere

portiere
pousse cafe
premiere
protege (masc., fem.)
puree

R
rale
recherche
regime
risque
role
rotisserie
roue

S
saute

seance
senor
smorgasbord
soiree
souffle
suede

T
table d'hote
tete-a-tete
tragedienne

V
vicuna
vis-a-vis

5.4.   Foreign words carry the diacritical marks as an essential part of their spelling.

à l'américaine	chargé d'affaires	entrepôt	passé (masc., fem.)
attaché	congé	exposé	pâté
béton	crédit foncier	longéron	père
blessé	crédit mobilier	mañana	piña
calèche	curé	maté	précis
cañada	déjà vu	mère	raisonné
cañon	détente	nacré	résumé
chargé	doña	outré	touché

Plural forms

5.5.   Nouns ending in *o* immediately preceded by a vowel add *s* to form the plural; nouns ending in *o* preceded by a consonant add *es* to form the plural, except as indicated in the following list.

albinos	falsettos	merinos	sextodecimos
armadillos	gauchos	mestizos	sextos
avocados	ghettos	octavos	siroccos
banjos	halos	octodecimos	solos
cantos	indigos	pianos	tangelos
cascos	infernos	piccolos	tobaccos
centos	juntos	pomelos	twos
didos	kimonos	provisos	tyros
duodecimos	lassos	quartos	virtuosos
dynamos	magnetos	salvos	zeros
escudos	mementos		

5.6. When a noun is hyphenated with an adverb or preposition, the plural is formed on the noun.

comings-in	hangers-on	markers-up
fillers-in	listeners-in	passers-by
goings-on	lookers-on	swearers-in

5.7. When neither word is a noun, the plural is formed on the last word.

also-rans	go-betweens	run-ins
come-ons	higher-ups	tie-ins

5.8. In forming the plurals of compound terms, the significant word takes the plural form.

Significant word first:

adjutants general	rights-of-way
aides-de-camp	secretaries general
ambassadors at large	sergeants at arms
attorneys at law	sergeants major
attorneys general	solicitors general
billets-doux	surgeons general
bills of fare	
brothers-in-law	Significant word in middle:
chargés d'affaires	assistant attorneys general
chiefs of staff	assistant chiefs of staff
commanders in chief	assistant comptrollers general
comptrollers general	assistant surgeons general
consuls general	
courts-martial	Significant word last:
crepes suzette	assistant attorneys
daughters-in-law	assistant commissioners
governors general	assistant corporation counsels
grants-in-aid	assistant directors
heirs at law	assistant general counsels
inspectors general	brigadier generals
men-of-war	deputy judges
ministers-designate	deputy sheriffs
mothers-in-law	general counsels
notaries public	judge advocates
pilots-in-command	judge advocate generals
postmasters general	lieutenant colonels
presidents-elect	major generals
prisoners of war	provost marshals
reductions in force	provost marshal generals
	quartermaster generals

trade unions	men employees
under secretaries	secretaries-treasurers
vice chairmen	women aviators

Both words equally significant:	No word significant in itself:
Bulletins Nos. 27 and 28 *not*	forget-me-nots
Bulletin Nos. 27 and 28 *but*	hand-me-downs
Bulletin No. 27 or 28	jack-in-the-pulpits
coats of arms	man-of-the-earths
masters at arms	pick-me-ups
men buyers	will-o'-the-wisps

5.9.   Nouns ending with *ful* form the plural by adding *s* at the end; if it is necessary to express the idea that more than one container was filled, the two elements of the solid compound are printed as separate words and the plural is formed by adding *s* to the noun.

> five bucketfuls of the mixture (one bucket filled five times)
> five buckets full of earth (separate buckets)
> three cupfuls of flour (one cup filled three times)
> three cups full of coffee (separate cups)

5.10.   The following list comprises other words the plurals of which may cause difficulty.

addendum, addenda	cherub, cherubs
adieu, adieus	cicatrix, cicatrices
agendum, agenda	Co., Cos.
alga, algae	coccus, cocci
alumnus, alumni (masc.); alumna, alumnae (fem.)	consortium, consortia
antenna, antennas (antennae, zoology)	corrigendum, corrigenda
	crisis, crises
appendix, appendixes	criterion, criteria
aquarium, aquariums	curriculum, curriculums
automaton, automatons	datum (singular), data (plural, but singular in collective sense)
axis, axes	desideratum, desiderata
bandeau, bandeaux	dilettante, dilettanti
basis, bases	dogma, dogmas
bateau, bateaux	ellipsis, ellipses
beau, beaus	equilibrium, equilibriums (equilibria, scientific)
cactus, cactuses	
calix, calices	erratum, errata
cargo, cargoes	executrix, executrices
chassis (singular and plural)	flambeau, flambeaus

focus, focuses
folium, folia
formula, formulas
forum, forums
fungus, fungi
genius, geniuses
genus, genera
gladiolus (singular and plural)
helix, helices
hypothesis, hypotheses
index, indexes (indices, scientific)
insigne, insignia
italic (singular and plural)
Kansas Citys
lacuna, lacunae
larva, larvae
larynx, larynxes
lens, lenses
lira, lire
locus, loci
madam, mesdames
Marys
matrix, matrices
maximum, maximums
medium, mediums *or* media
memorandum, memorandums
minimum, minimums
minutia, minutiae
monsieur, messieurs
nucleus, nuclei
oasis, oases
octopus, octopuses
opus, opera
parenthesis, parentheses

phenomenon, phenomena
phylum, phyla
plateau, plateaus
podium, podiums
procès-verbal, procès-verbaux
radius, radii
radix, radixes
referendum, referendums
sanatorium, sanatoriums
sanitarium, sanitariums
septum, septa
sequela, sequelae
seraph, seraphs
seta, setae
ski, skis
stadium, stadiums
stimulus, stimuli
stratum, strata
stylus, styluses
syllabus, syllabuses
symposium, symposia
synopsis, synopses
tableau, tableaus
taxi, taxis
terminus, termini
testatrix, testatrices
thesaurus, thesauri
thesis, theses
thorax, thoraxes
vertebra, vertebras (vertebrae, zoology)
virtuoso, virtuosos
vortex, vortexes

Endings "ible" and "able"

5.11.   The following words end in *ible*; other words in this class end in *able*.

abhorrible	appetible	coctible	combustible
accendible	apprehensible	coercible	comestible
accessible	audible	cognoscible	commonsensible
addible	avertible	cohesible	compactible
adducible	bipartible	collapsible	compatible
admissible	circumscriptible	collectible(s)	competible

compossible	distractible	impersuasible	inexpressible
comprehensible	divertible	implausible	infallible
compressible	divestible	impossible	infeasible
conducible	divisible	imprescriptible	inflexible
conductible	docible	imputrescible	infractible
confluxible	edible	inaccessible	infrangible
congestible	educible	inadmissible	infusible
contemptible	effectible	inapprehensible	innascible
controvertible	effervescible	inaudible	inscriptible
conversable (oral)	eligible	incircumscriptible	insensible
conversible	eludible	incoercible	instructible
(convertible)	erodible	incognoscrible	insubmergible
convertible	evasible	incombustible	insuppressible
convincible	eversible	incommiscible	insusceptible
corrigible	evincible	incompatible	intactible
corrodible	exemptible	incomprehensible	intangible
corrosible	exhaustible	incompressible	intelligible
corruptible	exigible	inconcussible	interconvertible
credible	expansible	incontrovertible	interruptible
crucible	explosible	inconvertible	intervisible
cullible	expressible	inconvincible	invendible
decoctible	extensible	incorrigible	invertible
deducible	fallible	incorrodible	invincible
deductible	feasible	incorruptible	invisible
defeasible	fencible	incredible	irascible
defectible	flexible	indefeasible	irreducible
defensible	fluxible	indefectible	irrefrangible
delible	forcible	indefensible	irremissible
deprehensible	frangible	indelible	irreprehensible
depressible	fungible	indeprehensible	irrepressible
descendible	fusible	indestructible	irresistible
destructible	gullible	indigestible	irresponsible
diffrangible	horrible	indiscernible	irreversible
diffusible	ignitible	indivertible	legible
digestible	illegible	indivisible	mandible
dimensible	immersible	indocible	marcescible
discernible	immiscible	inducible	misicible
discerpible	impartible	ineffervescible	negligible
discerptible	impatible	ineligible	nexible
discussible	impedible	ineludible	omissible
dispersible	imperceptible	inevasible	ostensible
dissectible	impermissible	inexhaustible	partible
distensible	imperscriptible	inexpansible	passable (open)

passible (feeling)	reflectible	sensible	transmissible
perceptible	reflexible	sponsible	transvertible
perfectible	refrangible	suasible	tripartible
permissible	remissible	subdivisible	unadmissible
persuasible	renascible	submergible	uncorruptible
pervertible	rendible	submersible	unexhaustible
plausible	reprehensible	subvertible	unexpressible
possible	repressible	suggestible	unintelligible
prehensible	reproducible	supersensible	unresponsible
prescriptible	resistible	suppressible	unsusceptible
producible	responsible	susceptible	vendible
productible	reversible	suspensible	vincible
protrusible	revertible	tangible	visible
putrescible	risible	tensible	vitrescible
receptible	runcible	terrible	
redemptible	sconcible	thurible	
reducible	seducible	traducible	

Endings "ise," "ize," and "yze"

5.12.   A large number of words have the termination *ise, ize,* or *yze*. The letter *l* is followed by *yze* if the word expresses an idea of loosening or separating, as *analyze*; all other words of this class, except those ending with the suffix *wise* and those in the following list, end in *ize*.

advertise	compromise	excise	prise (to force)
advise	demise	exercise	prize (to value)
affranchise	despise	exorcise	reprise
apprise (to inform)	devise	franchise	revise
apprize (to appraise)	disenfranchise	improvise	rise
	disfranchise	incise	supervise
arise	disguise	merchandise	surmise
chastise	emprise	misadvise	surprise
circumcise	enfranchise	mortise	televise
comprise	enterprise	premise	

Endings "cede," "ceed," and "sede"

5.13.   Only one word ends in *sede* (supersede); only three end in *ceed* (exceed, proceed, succeed); all other words of this class end in *cede* (precede, secede, etc.).

Doubled consonants

5.14.   A single consonant following a single vowel and ending in a monosyllable or a final accented syllable is doubled before a suffix beginning with a vowel.

bag, bagging	red, reddish	*but*
format, formatting	rob, robbing	total, totaled, totaling
input, inputting	transfer, transferred	travel, traveled, traveling

5.15.   If the accent in a derivative falls upon an earlier syllable than it does in the root word, the consonant is not doubled.

refer, reference	prefer, preference	infer, inference

Indefinite articles

5.16.   The indefinite article *a* is used before a consonant and an aspirated *h*; *an* is used before a silent *h* and all vowels except *u* pronounced as in *visual* and *o* pronounced as in *one*.

a historic occasion	an herbseller	*but*
a hotel	an hour	an H-U-D directive
a human being	an honor	a HUD directive
a humble man	an onion	
a union	an oyster	

5.17.   When a group of initials begins with *b, c, d, g, j, k, p, q, t, u, v, w, y,* or *z*, each having a consonant sound, the indefinite article *a* is used.

a BLS compilation	a GAO limitation	a WWW search
a CIO finding	a UFO sighting	

5.18.   When a group of initials begins with *a, e, f, h, i, l, m, n, o, r, s,* or *x*, each having a vowel sound, the indefinite article *an* is used.

an AEC report	an NSC (en) proclamation
an FCC (ef) ruling	an RFC (ahr) loan

5.19.   Use of the indefinite article *a* or *an* before a numerical expression is determined by the consonant or vowel sound of the beginning syllable.

an 11-year-old	an VIII (eight) classification
a onetime winner	a IV–F (four ef) category (military draft)
a III (three) group	a 4–H Club

Geographic names

5.20. The spelling of geographic names must conform to the decisions of the U.S. Board on Geographic Names (BGN) (http://geonames. usgs.gov). In the absence of such a decision, the U.S. Directory of Post Offices is to be used.

5.21. If the decisions or the rules of the BGN permit the use of either the local official form or the conventional English form, it is the prerogative of the originating office to select the form which is most suitable for the matter in hand; therefore, in marking copy or reading proof, it is required only to verify the spelling of the particular form used. GPO's preference is for the conventional English form. Copy will be followed as to accents, but these should be consistent throughout the entire job.

Nationalities, etc.

5.22. The table on Demonyms in Chapter 17 "Useful Tables" shows forms to be used for nouns and adjectives denoting nationality.

5.23. In designating the natives of the States, the following forms will be used.

Alabamian	Louisianian	Ohioan
Alaskan	Mainer	Oklahoman
Arizonan	Marylander	Oregonian
Arkansan	Massachusettsan	Pennsylvanian
Californian	Michiganian	Rhode Islander
Coloradan	Minnesotan	South Carolinian
Connecticuter	Mississippian	South Dakotan
Delawarean	Missourian	Tennessean
Floridian	Montanan	Texan
Georgian	Nebraskan	Utahn
Hawaiian	Nevadan	Vermonter
Idahoan	New Hampshirite	Virginian
Illinoisan	New Jerseyan	Washingtonian
Indianian	New Mexican	West Virginian
Iowan	New Yorker	Wisconsinite
Kansan	North Carolinian	Wyomingite
Kentuckian	North Dakotan	

5.24.   Observe the following forms:

African-American
Alaska Native (Aleuts, Eskimos, Indians of Alaska)
Amerindian
Native American (American Indian)
Puerto Rican
Part-Hawaiian (legal status)
but part-Japanese, etc.

Native American words

5.25.   Words, including tribal and other proper names of Indian, Aleut, Hawaiian, and other groups, are to be followed literally as to spelling and the use of spaces, hyphens, etc.

Transliteration

5.26.   In the spelling of nongeographic words transliterated from Chinese, Japanese, or any other language that does not have a Latin alphabet, copy is to be followed literally.

6. Compounding Rules
(See also Chapter 7 "Compounding Examples")

6.1. A compound word is a union of two or more words, either with or without a hyphen. It conveys a unit idea that is not as clearly or quickly conveyed by the component words in unconnected succession. The hyphen is a mark of punctuation that not only unites but separates the component words, and thus facilitates understanding, aids readability, and ensures correct pronunciation. When compound words must be divided at the end of a line, such division should be made leaving prefixes and combining forms of more than one syllable intact.

6.2. In applying the rules in this chapter and in using the list of examples in the following chapter, "Compounding Examples," the fluid nature of our language should be kept in mind. Word forms constantly undergo modification. Two-word forms, which often acquired the hyphen first, frequently bypass the hyphen stage and instantly assume a one-word form.

6.3. The rules, therefore, are somewhat flexible. Exceptions must necessarily be allowed. Current language trends continue to point to closing up certain words which, through either frequent use or widespread dissemination through modern media exposure, have become fixed in the reader's mind as units of thought. The tendency to merge two short words continues to be a natural progression toward better communication.

General rules
6.4. In general, omit the hyphen when words appear in regular order and the omission causes no ambiguity in sense or sound.

banking hours	eye opener	real estate
blood pressure	fellow citizen	rock candy
book value	living costs	training ship
census taker	palm oil	violin teacher
day laborer	patent right	

6.5.   Words are usually combined to express a literal or nonliteral (figurative) unit idea that would not be as clearly expressed in unconnected succession.

afterglow	forget-me-not	right-of-way
bookkeeping	gentleman	whitewash
cupboard	newsprint	

6.6.   A derivative of a compound retains the solid or hyphenated form of the original compound unless otherwise indicated.

coldbloodedness	outlawry	Y-shaped
footnoting	praiseworthiness	
ill-advisedly	railroader	

6.7.   A hyphen is used to avoid doubling a vowel or tripling a consonant, except after the short prefixes *co, de, pre, pro,* and *re,* which are generally printed solid. (See also rules 6.29 and 6.32.)

cooperation	semi-independent	shell-like
deemphasis	brass-smith	hull-less
preexisiting	Inverness-shire	*but*
anti-inflation	thimble-eye	co-occupant
micro-organism	ultra-atomic	cross section

Solid compounds

6.8.   Print solid two nouns that form a third when the compound has only one primary accent, especially when the prefixed noun consists of only one syllable or when one of the elements loses its original accent.

airship	cupboard	footnote
bathroom	dressmaker	locksmith
bookseller	fishmonger	workman

6.9.   Print solid a noun consisting of a short verb and an adverb as its second element, except when the use of the solid form would interfere with comprehension.

blowout	builddown	flareback
breakdown	cooldown	giveaway
hangover	runoff	*but*
holdup	setup	cut-in
makeready	showdown	phase-in
markoff	thowaway	run-in
pickup	tradeoff	sit-in

6.10.   Compounds beginning with the following nouns are usually printed solid.

book	mill	snow
eye	play	way
horse	school	wood
house	shop	work

6.11.   Compounds ending in the following are usually printed solid, especially when the prefixed word consists of one syllable.

berry	keeping	room
bird	land	shop
blossom	light	site
board	like	skin
boat	line	smith
book	load	stone
borne	maid	store
bound	maker	tail
box	making	tight
boy	man	time (not clock)
brained	master	ward
bug	mate	ware
bush	mill	water
cam	mistress	way
craft	monger	wear
field	over	weed
fish	owner	wide
flower	*but* #ownership	wise
fly	person	woman
girl	picker	wood
grower	picking	work
headed	piece	worker
hearted	plane	working
holder	power	worm
hopper	proof	worthy
house	roach	writer
keeper		

6.12. Print solid *any, every, no,* and *some* when combined with *body, thing,* and *where*. When *one* is the second element, print as two words if meaning a single or particular person or thing. To avoid mispronunciation, print *no one* as two words at all times.

anybody	everywhere	somebody
anything	everyone	something
anywhere	nobody	somewhere
anyone	nothing	someone
everybody	nowhere	
everything	no one	

but any one of us may stay; every one of the pilots is responsible; every body was accounted for

6.13. Print compound personal pronouns as one word.

herself	oneself	yourself
himself	ourselves	yourselves
itself	themselves	
myself	thyself	

6.14. Print as one word compass directions consisting of two points, but use a hyphen after the first point when three points are combined.

northeast	north-northeast
southwest	south-southwest

also north-south alignment

Unit modifiers

6.15. Print a hyphen between words, or abbreviations and words, combined to form a unit modifier immediately preceding the word modified, except as indicated in rule 6.16 and elsewhere throughout this chapter. This applies particularly to combinations in which one element is a present or past participle.

agreed-upon standards	Federal-State-local cooperation
Baltimore-Washington road	German-English descent
collective-bargaining talks	guided-missile program
contested-election case	hearing-impaired class
contract-bar rule	high-speed line
cost-of-living increase	large-scale project
drought-stricken area	law-abiding citizen
English-speaking nation	long-term loan
fire-tested material	line-item veto

long-term-payment loan
low-cost housing
lump-sum payment
most-favored-nation clause
multiple-purpose uses
no-par-value stock
one-on-one situation
part-time personnel
rust-resistant covering
service-connected disability
state-of-the-art technology
supply-side economics
tool-and-die maker
up-or-down vote

U.S.-owned property; U.S.-flagship
1-inch diameter; 2-inch-diameter
pipe
a 4-percent increase, the 10-percent
rise

but

4 percent citric acid
4 percent interest. (Note the absence
of an article: *a, an,* or *the.* The
word *of* is understood here.)

6.16. Where meaning is clear and readability is not aided, it is not necessary to use a hyphen to form a temporary or made compound. Restraint should be exercised in forming unnecessary combinations of words used in normal sequence.

atomic energy power
bituminous coal industry
child welfare plan
civil rights case
civil service examination
durable goods industry
flood control study
free enterprise system
ground water levels
high school student
elementary school grade
income tax form
interstate commerce law
land bank loan
land use program
life insurance company
mutual security funds

national defense appropriation
natural gas company
per capita expenditure
Portland cement plant
production credit loan
public at large
public utility plant
real estate tax
small businessman
Social Security pension
soil conservation measures
special delivery mail
parcel post delivery
speech correction class

but no-hyphen rule (readability
aided); *not* no hyphen rule

6.17. Print without a hyphen a compound predicate adjective or predicate noun the second element of which is a present participle.

The duties were price fixing.
The effects were far reaching.

The shale was oil bearing.
The area is used for beet raising.

6.18. Print without a hyphen a compound predicate adjective the second element of which is a past participle. Omit the hyphen in a predicate modifier of comparative or superlative degree.

The area is drought stricken.	This material is fire tested.
The paper is fine grained.	The cars are higher priced.
Moderately fine grained wood.	The reporters are better informed.

6.19. Print without a hyphen a two-word modifier the first element of which is a comparative or superlative.

better drained soil	*but*
best liked books	uppercrust society
higher level decision	lowercase, uppercase type
highest priced apartment	upperclassman
larger sized dress	bestseller (noun)
better paying job	lighter-than-air craft
lower income group	higher-than-market price

6.20. Do not use a hyphen in a two-word unit modifier the first element of which is an adverb ending in *ly*, nor use hyphens in a three-word unit modifier the first two elements of which are adverbs.

eagerly awaited moment	*but*
wholly owned subsidiary	ever-normal granary
unusually well preserved specimen	ever-rising flood
very well defined usage	still-new car
longer than usual lunch period	still-lingering doubt
not too distant future	well-known lawyer
most often heard phrase	well-kept secret

6.21. Proper nouns used as unit modifiers, either in their basic or derived form, retain their original form; but the hyphen is printed when combining forms.

Latin American countries	Seventh-day Adventists
North Carolina roads	*but*
a Mexican-American	Minneapolis-St. Paul region
South American trade	North American-South American
Spanish-American pride	sphere
Winston-Salem festival	French-English descent
African-American program	Washington–Wilkes-Barre route
Anglo-Saxon period	*or* Washington/Wilkes-Barre
Franco-Prussian War	route

6.22.   Do not confuse a modifier with the word it modifies.

elderly clothesman	well-trained schoolteacher
old-clothes man	elementary school teacher
competent shoemaker	preschool children (kindergarten)
wooden-shoe maker	pre-school children (before school)
field canning factory	rezoned wastesite
tomato-canning factory	hazardous-waste site
brave servicemen	
service men and women	*but*
light blue hat (weight)	common stockholder
light-blue hat (color)	stock ownership
average taxpayer	small businessman
income-tax payer	working men and women
American flagship (military)	steam powerplant site
American-flagship	meat packinghouse owner

6.23.   Where two or more hyphenated compounds have a common basic element and this element is omitted in all but the last term, the hyphens are retained.

2- to 3- and 4- to 5-ton trucks
2- by 4-inch boards, *but* boards 2 to 6 inches wide
8-, 10-, and 16-foot boards
6.4-, 3.1-, and 2-percent pay raises
moss- and ivy-covered walls, *not* moss and ivy-covered walls
long- and short-term money rates, *not* long and short-term money rates
but twofold or threefold, *not* two or threefold
goat, sheep, and calf skins, *not* goat, sheep, and calfskins
intrastate and intracity, *not* intra-state and -city
American owned and managed companies
preoperative and postoperative examination

6.24.   Do not use a hyphen in a unit modifier consisting of a foreign phrase.

ante bellum days	ex officio member	per diem employee
bona fide transaction	per capita tax	prima facie evidence

6.25.   Do not print a hyphen in a unit modifier containing a letter or a numeral as its second element.

abstract B pages	class II railroad	point 4 program
article 3 provisions	grade A milk	ward D beds

6.26. Do not use a hyphen in a unit modifier enclosed in quotation marks unless it is normally a hyphenated term, but quotation marks are not to be used in lieu of a hyphen.

"blue sky" law	*but*
"good neighbor" policy	right-to-work law
"tie-in" sale	line-item veto

6.27. Print combination color terms as separate words, but use a hyphen when such color terms are unit modifiers.

bluish green	bluish-green feathers
dark green	iron-gray sink
orange red	silver-gray body

6.28. Do not use a hyphen between independent adjectives preceding a noun.

big gray cat	a fine old southern gentleman

Prefixes, suffixes, and combining forms

6.29. Print solid combining forms and prefixes, except as indicated elsewhere.

*after*birth	*infra*red	*peri*patetic
*Anglo*mania	*inter*view	*plano*convex
*ante*date	*intra*spinal	*poly*nodal
*anti*slavery	*intro*vert	*post*script
*bi*weekly	*iso*metric	*pre*exist
*by*law	*macro*analysis	*pro*consul
*circum*navigation	*meso*thorax	*pseudo*scholastic
*cis*alpine	*meta*genesis	*re*enact
*co*operate	*micro*phone	*retro*spect
*contra*position	*mis*state	*semi*official
*counter*case	*mono*gram	*step*father
*de*energize	*multi*color	*sub*secretary
*demi*tasse	*neo*phyte	*super*market
*ex*communicate	*non*neutral	*thermo*couple
*extra*curricular	*off*set	*trans*onic
*fore*tell	*out*bake	*trans*ship
*heroi*comic	*over*active	*tri*color
*hyper*sensitive	*pan*cosmic	*ultra*violet
*hypo*acid	*para*centric	*un*necessary
*in*bound	*parti*coated	*under*flow

6.30. Print solid combining forms and suffixes, except as indicated elsewhere.

port*able*	geo*graphy*	procure*ment*
cover*age*	man*hood*	inner*most*
oper*ate*	self*ish*	partner*ship*
plebis*cite*	pump*kin*	lone*some*
twenty*fold*	meat*less*	home*stead*
spoon*ful*	out*let*	north*ward*
kilo*gram*	wave*like*	clock*wise*

6.31. Print solid words ending in *like*, but use a hyphen to avoid tripling a consonant or when the first element is a proper name.

lifelike	girllike	Scotland-like
lilylike	bell-like	McArtor-like

6.32. Use a hyphen or hyphens to prevent mispronunciation, to ensure a definite accent on each element of the compound, or to avoid ambiguity.

anti-hog-cholera serum	re-cover (cover again)
co-occurrence	re-creation (create again)
co-op	re-lay (lay again)
mid-decade	re-sorting (sort again)
multi-ply (several plies)	re-treat (treat again)
non-civil-service position	un-ionized
non-tumor-bearing tissue	un-uniformity
pre-midcourse review	
pre-position (before)	*but*
pro-choice	rereferred
pro-life	rereviewed

6.33. Use a hyphen to join duplicated prefixes.

re-redirect	sub-subcommittee	super-superlative

6.34. Print with a hyphen the prefixes *ex, self,* and *quasi.*

ex-governor	quasi-argument
ex-serviceman	quasi-corporation
ex-son-in-law	quasi-young
ex-vice-president	
self-control	*but*
self-educated	selfhood
quasi-academic	selfsame

6.35.   Unless usage demands otherwise, use a hyphen to join a prefix or combining form to a capitalized word. (The hyphen is retained in words of this class set in caps.)

anti-American	non-Federal
pro-British	
un-American	*but*
non-Government	nongovernmental
neo-Nazi	overanglicize
post-World War II	transatlantic
or post-Second World War	

Numerical compounds

6.36.   Print a hyphen between the elements of compound numbers from twenty-one to ninety-nine and in adjective compounds with a numerical first element.

twenty-one	three-and-twenty
twenty-first	two-sided question
6-footer	multimillion-dollar fund
6-foot-11-inch man	10-dollar-per-car tax
24-inch ruler	thirty- (30-) day period
3-week vacation	
8-hour day	*but*
10-minute delay	one hundred twenty-one
20th-century progress	100-odd
3-to-1 ratio	foursome
5-to-4 vote	threescore
.22-caliber cartridge	foursquare
2-cent-per-pound tax	$20 million airfield
four-in-hand tie	second grade children

6.37.   Print without a hyphen a modifier consisting of a possessive noun preceded by a numeral. (See also rule 8.14.)

1 month's layoff	3 weeks' vacation
1 week's pay	1 minute's delay
2 hours' work	*but* a 1-minute delay

6.38. Print a hyphen between the elements of a fraction, but omit it between the numerator and the denominator when the hyphen appears in either or in both.

one-thousandth	twenty-three thirtieths
two-thirds	twenty-one thirty-seconds
two one-thousandths	three-fourths of an inch

6.39. A unit modifier following and reading back to the word or words modified takes a hyphen and is printed in the singular.

motor, alternating-current, 3-phase, 60-cycle, 115-volt
glass jars: 5-gallon, 2-gallon, 1-quart
belts: 2-inch, 1¼-inch, ½-inch, ¼-inch

Civil and military titles

6.40. Do not hyphenate a civil or military title denoting a single office, but print a double title with a hyphen.

ambassador at large	secretary-treasurer
assistant attorney general	sergeant at arms
commander in chief	treasurer-manager
comptroller general	under secretary
Congressman at Large	*but* under-secretaryship
major general	vice president
notary public	*but* vice-presidency
secretary general	

6.41. The adjectives *elect* and *designate,* as the last element of a title, require a hyphen.

President-elect (Federal)	ambassador-designate
Vice-President-elect (Federal)	minister-designate
Secretary of Housing and Urban Development-designate	

Scientific and technical terms

6.42. Do not print a hyphen in scientific terms (names of chemicals, diseases, animals, insects, plants) used as unit modifiers if no hyphen appears in their original form.

carbon monoxide poisoning	whooping cough remedy
guinea pig raising	*but*
hog cholera serum	Russian-olive plantings
methyl bromide solution	Douglas-fir tree
stem rust control	
equivalent uranium content	

6.43. Chemical elements used in combination with figures use a hyphen, except with superior figures.

Freon-12	uranium-235	Sr^{90}
polonium-210	U^{235}	$_{92}U^{234}$

6.44. Note use of hyphens and closeup punctuation in chemical formulas.

9-nitroanthra(1,9,4,10)bis(1)oxathiazone-2,7-bisdioxide
Cr-Ni-Mo
2,4-D

6.45. Print a hyphen between the elements of technical or contrived compound units of measurement.

candela-hour	light-year	work-year
crop-year	passenger-mile	*but* kilowatthour
horsepower-hour	staff-hour	

Improvised compounds

6.46. Print with a hyphen the elements of an improvised compound.

blue-pencil (v.)	George "Pay-As-You-Go" Miller
18-year-old (n., u.m.)	stick-in-the-mud (n.)
know-it-all (n.)	let-George-do-it attitude
know-how (n.)	how-to-be-beautiful course
lick-the-finger-and-test-the-wind	hard-and-fast rule
economics	penny-wise and pound-foolish policy
make-believe (n., u.m.)	first-come-first-served basis
one-man-one-vote principle	*but* a basis of first come, first served
roll-on/roll-off ship	

6.47. Use hyphens in a prepositional-phrase compound noun consisting of three or more words.

		but
cat-o'-nine-tails	man-of-war	
government-in-exile	mother-in-law	heir at law
grant-in-aid	mother-of-pearl	next of kin
jack-in-the-box	patent-in-fee	officer in charge

6.48. When the corresponding noun form is printed as separate words, the verb form is always hyphenated.

cold-shoulder   blue-pencil   cross-brace

6.49. Print a hyphen in a compound formed of repetitive or conflicting terms and in a compound naming the same thing under two aspects.

boogie-woogie	hanky-panky	young-old
comedy-ballet	murder-suicide	*but*
dead-alive	nitty-gritty	bowwow
devil-devil	pitter-patter	dillydally
even-stephen	razzle-dazzle	hubbub
farce-melodrama	walkie-talkie	nitwit
fiddle-faddle	willy-nilly	riffraff

6.50. Use a hyphen in a nonliteral compound expression containing an apostrophe in its first element.

asses'-eyes	bull's-eye	crow's-nest
ass's-foot	cat's-paw	

6.51. Use a hyphen to join a single capital letter to a noun or a participle.

		but
H-bomb	C-section	
I-beam	V-necked	x ray
T-shaped	S-iron	x raying
U-boat	T-square	S turns
C-chip	X-ed out	

6.52. Print idiomatic phrases without hyphens.

come by	insofar as	nowadays
inasmuch as	Monday week	

7. Compounding Examples

7.1. The following examples are based on the rules for compounding found in chapter 6. Obviously, this list or any other list of compound words could not possibly be a complete reference due to sheer volume. However, an analogy of the words listed with like prefixes and suffixes together with an application of the rules will result in easier handling of those compound words not listed.

7.2. In order to keep the list from becoming cumbersome, certain restrictions had to be adopted.

7.3. The listing of hyphenated compounds ending in *ed* was kept to a minimum. The rationale was to provide one or two examples under a keyword rather than needless repetition.

7.4. Similarly, many two-word forms which create no difficulty were omitted.

7.5. Care was exercised to achieve fuller coverage of solid compounds, particularly when the adopted form is different than that of Webster's Third New International Dictionary. This dictionary is GPO's guide for spelling with the exception of those words listed in rule 5.2. It is not GPO's guide to compounding.

7.6. A distinction exists between words used in a literal sense and a non-literal sense. With few exceptions, one-word forms usually express a nonliteral interpretation, while two-word forms invariably convey a literal meaning. For example, a person may have an interesting *sideline* or hobby, but be forced to sit on the *side line* during periods of inactivity.

7.7. Distinction should also be made in the compounding of two words to form an adjective modifier and the use of the same words as a predicate adjective; e.g., "crystal-clear water," *but* "the water is crystal clear"; "fire-tested material," *but* "the material is fire tested."

7.8. Caution should be exercised when distinguishing whether a succession of words is being used as a compound or whether they simply appear together. Consider, for example, "We know *someone* should do it and who that *some one* ought to be."

7.9. For better appearance, it may sometimes be necessary to treat alike words which would have different forms when they appear separately; e.g., *bumblebee* and *queen bee, farmhand* and *ranch hand.* In juxtaposition, these and similar words should be made uniform by being printed as two words. This is only a temporary expedient and does not supersede the list.

7.10. Combining forms and prefixes are usually printed solid. For greater readability, the hyphen is sometimes used to avoid doubling a vowel (*anti-inflation, naso-orbital*); to facilitate a normally capitalized word (*mid-April, non-European*); to assure distinct pronunciation of each element of a compound or ready comprehension of intended meaning (*contra-ion, un-ionized*); or to join a combining form or prefix to a hyphenated compound (*equi-gram-molar, pro-mother-in-law*).

7.11. As nouns and adjectives, *holdup, calldown, layout, makeup,* and similar words should be printed solid. Their *er* derivatives, (*holder-up, caller-down, layer-out,* and *maker-up*) require hyphens. Such compounds as *run-in, run-on,* and *tie-in* resist quick comprehension when solid. They are therefore hyphenated.

7.12. Words spelled alike but pronounced differently, such as *tear-dimmed* and *tearsheet, wind tunnel* and *windup,* are listed under the same keyword.

7.13. Words printed flush in the following list combine with the words which follow to indicate solid or hyphenated compounds. A space-mark (#) appearing before an indented entry indicates a two-word form, but two-word forms appearing in the adjective position usually take a hyphen.

7.14. To indicate word function, several abbreviations have been appended. They are: *adv.,* adverb; *n.,* noun; *v.,* verb; *u.m.,* unit modifier; *pref.,* prefix; *c.f.,* combining form; and *conj.,* conjunction.

A

A
  BC(s) (n.)
  –B–C (u.m.)
  -bomb
  -day
  -flat
  -frame
  -pole
  -sharp

a
  borning, etc.
  foot
  while (adv.)
abdomino (c.f.)
  all one word
able
  -bodied (u.m.)
  -minded (u.m.)
about-face
above
  -cited (u.m.)
  deck
  -found (u.m.)
  -given (u.m.)
  ground (u.m.)
  -mentioned (u.m.)
  -named (u.m.)
  -said (u.m.)
  -water (u.m.)
  -written (u.m.)
absentminded
ace-high (u.m.)
acid
  fast
  -treat (v.)
  works
ack-ack
acre
  -foot
  -inch
actino (c.f.)
  all one word

addle
  brain
  head
  pate
add-on (n., u.m.)
adeno (c.f.)
  all one word
aero (c.f.)
  -otitis
  rest one word
afore
  all one word
after (c.f.)
  all one word
agar-agar
age
  less
  long
  -old (u.m.)
  -stricken (u.m.)
  -weary (u.m.)
agribusiness
ague
  -faced (u.m.)
  -plagued (u.m.)
  -sore (u.m.)
aide-de-camp
air
  bag
  base
  bill
  blast
  -blasted (u.m.)
  blown
  brake
  brush
  burst
  cargo
  -clear (u.m.)
  coach
  -condition (all
    forms)
  -cool (v.)

  -cooled (u.m.)
  course
  crew
  -dried (u.m.)
  -driven (u.m.)
  drome
  drop
  -dry (u.m., v.)
  fare
  -floated (u.m.)
  flow
  foil
  -formed (u.m.)
  frame
  freight
  gap
  glow
  hammer
  head
  hole
  hose
  lane
  lift
  #line (line for air)
  line (aviation)
  liner
  link
  locked
  mail
  mark (v.)
  marker
  mass
  minded
  park
  path
  photo
  port (all
    meanings)
  #raid
  scoop
  ship
  show
  sick

  -slaked (u.m.)
  sleeve
  space
  speed
  stream
  strike
  strip
  #time (radio and
    TV)
  wave
  woman
  worthy
alder-leaved (u.m.)
ale
  cup
  -fed (u.m.)
  glass
alkali#land
all
  -absorbing (u.m.)
  -aged (u.m.)
  -American
  -clear (n., u.m.)
  -fired (u.m.)
  -flotation
    (mining)
  #fours
  #in
  -inclusive (u.m.)
  mark (printing)
  -out (u.m.)
  -possessed (u.m.)
  -round (u.m.)
  spice
  -star (u.m.)
  time (u.m.)
  wise
alleyway
allo (c.f.)
  all one word
almsgiver
along
  ship

shore
side
alpen
  glow
  stock
alpha
  -cellulose
  -iron
  -naphthol
  also-ran (n., u.m.)
alto
  cumulus
  relievo
  stratus
amber
  -clear (u.m.)
  -colored (u.m.)
  -tipped (u.m.)
ambi (c.f.)
  all one word
amidships
amino
  #acid
  as prefix, all one
  word
ampere
  -foot
  -hour
  meter
  -minute
  -second
amphi (pref.)
  all one word
amylo (c.f.)
  all one word
anchor
  hold
  #light
  plate
angel
  cake
  -eyed (u.m.)
  -faced (u.m.)

food
angio (c.f.)
  all one word
angle
  hook
  meter
  wing
  worm
Anglo (c.f.)
  -American, etc.
  rest one word
anhydr(o) (c.f.)
  all one word
ankle
  bone
  -deep (u.m.)
  jack
ant
  eater
  hill
ante (pref.)
  #bellum, etc.
  -Christian, etc.
  #mortem
  mortem
    (nonliteral)
  rest one word
antero (c.f.)
  all one word
anthra (c.f.)
  all one word
anthropo (c.f.)
  all one word
anti (pref.)
  -American, etc.
  -choice
  christ
  god
  -hog-cholera
    (u.m.)
  -icer
  -imperial
  -inflation, etc.

-life
-missile-missile
  (u.m.)
  missile
  personnel
  trust, etc.
  -New#Deal, etc.
  rest one word
antro (c.f.)
  all one word
anvil
  -faced (u.m.)
  -headed (u.m.)
any
  body
  how
  one
  #one (one thing
    or one of
    a group)
  place (adv.)
aorto (c.f.)
  all one word
apo (pref.)
  all one word
apple
  cart
  jack
  #juice
  sauce
  -scented (u.m.)
April-fool (v.)
aqua
  culture
  lung
  marine
  meter
  puncture
  tint
  tone
aquo (c.f.)
  -ion
  rest one word

arc
  -over (n., u.m.)
  -weld (v.)
arch (pref.)
  band
  bishop
  duke
  enemy
  -Protestant
archeo (c.f.)
  all one word
archi (pref.)
  all one word
archo (c.f.)
  all one word
areo (c.f.)
  all one word
aristo (c.f.)
  all one word
arithmo (c.f.)
  all one word
arm
  band
  bone
  chair
  hole
  lift
  pit
  plate
  rack
  rest
  -shaped (u.m.)
armor
  -clad (u.m.)
  -piercing (u.m.)
  plate
  -plated (u.m.)
  smith
arm's-length (u.m.)
arrow
  head
  -leaved (u.m.)
  plate

-shaped (u.m.)
shot
-toothed (u.m.)
arseno (c.f.)
  all one word
art-colored (u.m.)
arterio (c.f.)
  all one word
arthro (c.f.)
  all one word
artillery
  man
  woman
asbestos
  -covered (u.m.)
  -packed (u.m.)
ash
  bin
  can
  -colored (u.m.)
  -free (u.m.)
  -gray (u.m.)
  #heap
  pan
  pile
  pit
  tray
assembly
  #line
  man
  #room
astro (c.f.)
  all one word
attorney#at#law
audio
  frequency
  gram
  meter
  tape
  visual
auri (c.f.)
  -iodide
  rest one word

authorship
auto (c.f.)
  -logon
  matic#backup
  -objective
  -observation
  -omnibus
  -ophthalmoscope
  rest one word
awe
  -bound (u.m.)
  -filled (u.m.)
  -inspired (u.m.)
  some
ax
  -adz
  -grinding (u.m.)
  hammer
  head
  -shaped (u.m.)
axletree
axo (c.f.)
  all one word
azo (c.f.)
  -orange
  -orchil
  -orseilline
  rest one word

B

B-flat
baby
  #boomer
  face (n.)
  #food
  sit (v.)
  sitter
back
  ache
  band
  bite (v.)
  biter
  bone

breaker
cap
chain
charge
-country (u.m.)
cross
date
down (n., u.m.)
drop
face
feed
fill
fire
flap
flash
flow
-focus (v.)
furrow
ground
hand
haul
-in (n., u.m.)
lash
list (v.)
log
lotter
packer (n.)
paddle (v.)
pay
payment
pedal (v.)
plate
rest
road
run
saw
scatter
set
shift
slide
space
spin
spread

staff
stage
stairs
stamp
stay
stitch
stop
strap
-streeter
stretch (n.)
string
strip (book)
stroke
-swath (v.)
swept
swing
tack
talk
tender
tenter
-titrate (v.)
track (v.)
trail
up (n., u.m.)
wall
wash
water
backer
  -down
  -off
  -up
bag
  boy
  -cheeked (u.m.)
  girl
  pipe
  -shaped (u.m.)
baggage
  man
  #rack
  #room
  #train
bailout (n., u.m.)

bake
  oven
  pan
  shop
bald
  faced
  head (n.)
  pate
ball
  field
  #game
  -like
  park (nonliteral)
  #park (literal)
  player
  point (n., u.m.)
  stock
ballot#box
band
  aid
  box
  cutter
  saw
  stand
  string
  -tailed (u.m.)
  wagon
  width
bandy
  ball
  -legged (u.m.)
bangup (n., u.m.)
bank
  book
  note
  #paper
  side (stream)
bantamweight
bar
  #bit
  code
  keeper
  maid

  post
  tender
  -wound (u.m.)
bare
  -armed (u.m.)
  back
  bone
  faced
  foot
  handed
  legged
  necked
  worn
barge-laden (u.m.)
bark
  cutter
  peel
  -tanned (u.m.)
barley
  corn
  mow
  #water
barnstormer
barrel
  head
  -roll (v.)
  -shaped (u.m.)
base
  ball
  ball#bat
  line
  #line (surveying)
  -minded (u.m.)
basi (c.f.)
  all one word
basketball
bas-relief
bat
  blind
  -eyed (u.m.)
  fowl
  wing
batch#file

bath
  mat
  robe
  #towel
  tub
batswing (cloth)
battercake
battle
  ax
  -fallen (u.m.)
  front
  ground
  -scarred (u.m.)
  ship
  stead
  wagon
baud#rate
baybolt
beach
  comber
  head
  wagon
bead
  flush
  roll
beak
  head
  iron
  -shaped (u.m.)
beam
  filling
  -making (u.m.)
bean
  bag
  cod
  -fed (u.m.)
  pole
  pot
  setter
  -shaped (u.m.)
  stalk
bear
  baiting

  herd
  hide
  hound
  off (n., u.m.)
  trap
beater
  -out
  -up
beauty
  -blind (u.m.)
  -clad (u.m.)
  #shop
beaverpelt
bed
  board
  chair
  chamber
  clothes
  cord
  cover
  -fallen (u.m.)
  fast
  fellow
  frame
  lamp
  linen
  pad
  pan
  plate
  post
  quilt
  rail
  #rest
  ridden
  rock
  sheet
  sick
  side
  sore
  space
  spread
  spring
  stand

stead	wether	name (top rank)	#date
straw	**belly**	(n., u.m.)	day
time	ache	**bill**	mark
bee	band	back	place
bread	buster	beetle	right
-eater	button	broker	#year
herd	fed (u.m.)	fold	biscuit-shaped
hive	pinch	head	(u.m.)
keeper	belowstairs	hook	**bismuto** (c.f.)
line	**belt**	poster	*all one word*
way	-driven (u.m.)	sticker	**bit**
beechnut	saw	**billet**	stock
beef	**bench**	-doux	-mapped
eater	fellow	head	**bitter**
#extract	-hardened (u.m.)	billingsgate	-ender
-faced (u.m.)	made (u.m.)	**bio** (c.f.)	head
head	mark (nonliteral)	-aeration	sweet
steak	#mark (surveying)	-osmosis	-tongued (u.m.)
tongue	warmer	*rest one word*	**black**
bees	bentwing (n., u.m.)	birchbark	ball (nonliteral)
wax	**benzo** (c.f.)	**bird**	-bordered (u.m.)
wing	*all one word*	bath	-eyed (u.m.)
beet	berry-brown (u.m.)	bander	guard
field	**best**	cage	jack
#sugar	#man	call	leg
beetle	seller (n.)	catcher	list
-browed (u.m.)	**beta**	#dog (literal)	mail
head	-glucose	dog (nonliteral)	mark
stock	tron	-eyed (u.m.)	#market (n.)
before	**between**	-faced (u.m.)	-market (u.m., v.)
-cited (u.m.)	decks	life	-marketer
hand	whiles	lime	out (n., u.m.)
-mentioned (u.m.)	**bi** (pref.)	lore	plate (printing)
-named (u.m.)	-iliac	mouthed	print
behindhand	*rest one word*	seed	-robed (u.m.)
bell	**big**	shot	#sheep (all
-bottomed (u.m.)	-eared (u.m.)	watcher	meanings)
crank	-eyed (u.m.)	**bird's**	shirted
-crowned (u.m.)	head (ego)	-eye	snake
hanger	horn (sheep)	#nest (literal) (n.)	strap (n.)
hop	-horned (u.m.)	-nest (n., u.m., v.)	-tie (u.m.)
mouthed	-leaguer	**birth**	top
ringer	mouthed	bed	#widow

blast
  hole
  plate
blasto (c.f.)
  all one word
bleach
  ground
  works
blear
  eye
  -eyed (u.m.)
  -witted (u.m.)
blepharo (c.f.)
  all one word
blight-resistant
  (u.m.)
blind
  -bomb (v.)
  -flying (u.m.)
  fold
  -loaded (u.m.)
  #man
  spot
  stitch
  story
blink-eyed (u.m.)
blithe-looking (u.m.)
blitz
  buggy
  krieg
block
  buster
  head
  hole (v.)
  ship
blood
  -alcohol (u.m.)
  bath
  beat
  curdling
  -drenched (u.m.)
  -giving (u.m.)
  guilty

-hot (u.m.)
hound
letting
mobile
-red (u.m.)
ripe
shed
shot
spiller
spot
stain
stock
stream
sucker
thirsty
-warm (u.m.)
bloody
  -nosed (u.m.)
  -red (u.m.)
blossom
  -bordered (u.m.)
  -laden (u.m.)
blow
  back
  by (n., u.m.)
  cock
  down (n., u.m.)
  gun
  hard (n.)
  hole
  iron
  lamp
  off (n., u.m.)
  out (n., u.m.)
  pipe
  spray
  through (u.m.)
  torch
  tube
  up (n., u.m.)
blue
  -annealed (u.m.)
  beard (n.)

blood
bonnet
book (nonliteral)
bottle
coat (n.)
-eyed (u.m.)
gill
grass
-gray (u.m.)
-green (u.m.)
-hot (u.m.)
jack
jacket
nose
-pencil (v.)
point (oyster)
print
stocking
streak (nonliteral)
tongue (n.)
blunder
  buss
  head
blunt
  -edged (u.m.)
  -spoken (u.m.)
boar
  spear
  staff
board
  #foot
  rack
  walk
boat
  builder
  crew
  head
  hook
  house
  loader
  owner
  #people

setter
shop
side
swain
wright
yard
bob
  cat
  sled
  stay
  tail
  white
bobby
  pin
  -soxer
body
  bearer
  bending
  builder
  -centered (u.m.)
  guard
  -mind
  plate
bog
  -eyed (u.m.)
  land
  man
  trot (v.)
boil
  down (n., u.m.)
  off (n., u.m.)
  out (n., u.m.)
  over (n., u.m.)
boiler
  -off
  -out
  plate
  works
boiling#house
bold
  face (printing)
  -spirited (u.m.)

bolt
cutter
head
hole
-shaped (u.m.)
strake
bomb
drop
fall
shell
sight
thrower
-throwing (u.m.)
bone
ache
#ash
black
breaker
-bred (u.m.)
-dry (u.m.)
-eater
-hard (u.m.)
head
lace
meal
set
shaker
-white (u.m.)
boobytrap
boogie-woogie
book
binder
case
dealer
#end
fair
-fed (u.m.)
fold
-learned (u.m.)
-lined (u.m.)
list
lore
lover

mark
mobile
plate
rack
rest
sale
seller
shelf
stack
stall
stamp
stand
stitch
-stitching (u.m.)
-taught (u.m.)
wright
boom
town
truck
boondoggling
boot
black
hose
jack
lace
last
leg
lick
strap
bore
hole
safe
sight
bosom
-deep (u.m.)
-folded (u.m.)
-making (u.m.)
bottle
-fed (u.m.)
neck
-nosed (u.m.)
bottom#land
boughpot

bow
back
bent
grace
head
knot
legged
-necked (u.m.)
pin
shot
sprit
stave
string
wow
box
car
haul
head (printing)
truck
boxer
-off
-up
brachio (c.f.)
all one word
brachy (c.f.)
all one word
brain
cap
child
-cracked (u.m.)
pan
sick
-spun (u.m.)
storm
-tired (u.m.)
wash
brake
drum
head
meter
shoe
brandnew (u.m.)

brandy
-burnt (u.m.)
wine
brass
-armed (u.m.)
-bold (u.m.)
-smith
works
brave
hearted
-looking (u.m.)
-minded (u.m.)
brazen
-browed (u.m.)
face
bread
basket
crumb
earner
fruit
#knife
liner
plate
seller
stuff
#tray
winner
break
away (n., u.m.)
ax
back (n., u.m.)
bone (fever)
#circuit
down (n., u.m.)
-even (u.m.)
fast
fast#room
front
-in (n., u.m.)
neck
off (n., u.m.)
out (n., u.m.)
point

through (n., u.m.)
up (n., u.m.)
wind (n.)
breaker
-down
-off
-up
breast
band
beam
bone
-deep (u.m.)
-fed (u.m.)
feed
-high (u.m.)
hook
mark
piece
pin
plate
plow
rail
rope
work
breath
-blown (u.m.)
-tainted (u.m.)
taking
breech
block
cloth
loader
-loading (u.m.)
lock
pin
plug
sight
breeze
-borne (u.m.)
-lifted (u.m.)
-swept (u.m.)
way
bribe
-free (u.m.)

giver
taker
bric-a-brac
brick
bat
-built (u.m.)
-colored (u.m.)
kiln
layer
liner
mason
-red (u.m.)
setter
work
yard
bride
bed
bowl
cake
chamber
cup
groom
knot
lace
maiden
stake
bridge
builder
head
pot
tree
#wall
work
briefcase
bright
-colored (u.m.)
-eyed (u.m.)
brilliant
-cut (u.m.)
-green (u.m.)
brine-soaked (u.m.)
bringer-up
bristle
cone (u.m.)

-pointed (u.m.)
broad
acre
ax
band (n., u.m.)
-beamed (u.m.)
brim
cast
cloth
head
#jump
leaf (n.)
-leaved (u.m.)
loom
minded
-mouthed (u.m.)
share (n., v.)
sheet (n.)
side
sword
wife
woven
broken
-down (u.m.)
-legged (u.m.)
-mouthed (u.m.)
bromo (c.f.)
all one word
bronchio (c.f.)
all one word
broncho (c.f.)
all one word
broncobuster
bronze
-clad (u.m.)
-covered (u.m.)
-red (u.m.)
broom
#handle
-leaved (u.m.)
-making (u.m.)
stick
brother
-german

hood
-in-law
brow
beat
point
post
brown
back
-eyed (u.m.)
out (n., u.m.)
print
brush
ball
#holder
off (n., u.m.)
-treat (v.)
brusher
-off
-up
buck
eye
-eyed (u.m.)
horn
hound
passer
plate
pot
saw
shot
skinned
stall
stay
stove
tooth
wagon
wash
bucket-shaped
(u.m.)
buff
-tipped (u.m.)
ware
-yellow (u.m.)
bug
bear

bite
-eyed (u.m.)
build
  down (n., u.m.)
  up (n., u.m.)
built
  -in (u.m.)
  -up (u.m.)
  bulb-tee (u.m.)
bulbo (c.f.)
  all one word
bulk
  head
  -pile (v.)
  weigh (v.)
bull
  baiting
  dog
  doze
  -faced (u.m.)
  fight
  frog
  head
  -mouthed (u.m.)
  neck
  nose
  pen
  ring
  #terrier
  toad
  -voiced (u.m.)
  whack
  whip
bullet
  head
  maker
  proof
bull's
  -eye (nonliteral)
  -foot
bumble
  bee
  foot

kite
bung
  hole
  start
burn
  -in (n., u.m.)
  out (n., u.m.)
  up (n., u.m.)
  burned-over (u.m.)
  burner-off
burnt
  -out (u.m.)
  -up (u.m.)
bus
  boy
  #conductor
  driver
  fare
  girl
  line
  load
bush
  beater
  buck
  fighter
  -grown (u.m.)
  hammer
  -leaguer
  ranger
  whacker
  wife
  bustup (n., u.m.)
busy
  body
  -fingered (u.m.)
  head
butt
  -joint (v.)
  saw
  stock
  strap

-weld (v.)
butter
  ball
  -colored (u.m.)
  fat
  fingers
  head
  milk
  mouth
  nut
  print
  -rigged (u.m.)
  scotch
  -smooth (u.m.)
  wife
  -yellow (u.m.)
button
  -eared (u.m.)
  -headed (u.m.)
  hold
  hole
  hook
  mold
  buzzerphone
by
  -and-by
  -the-way (n., u.m.)
  -your-leave (n., u.m.)
  rest one word

C

C
  -sharp
  -star
  -tube
cab
  driver
  fare
  #owner
  stand
  cabbagehead

cabinet
  maker
  making
  cable-laid (u.m.)
caco (c.f.)
  all one word
  cage#bird
cake
  baker
  bread
  -eater
  mixer
  -mixing (u.m.)
  pan
  walk
calci (c.f.)
  all one word
  calk-weld (v.)
call
  back (n., u.m.)
  box
  down (n., u.m.)
  -in (n., u.m.)
  note
  -off (n., u.m.)
  out (n., u.m.)
  -over (n., u.m.)
  up (n., u.m.)
  camshaft
camel
  back (rubber)
  -backed (u.m.)
  driver
  -faced (u.m.)
  camel's-hair (u.m.)
camp
  fire
  ground
  stool
can
  capper
  not
  #opener

canalside
candle
  bomb
  -foot
  holder
  -hour
  lighter
  lit
  -meter
  power
  -shaped (u.m.)
  stand
  stick
  wick
  wright
candystick
cane
  -backed (u.m.)
  brake
  crusher
  cutter
  #sugar
canker
  -eaten (u.m.)
  -mouthed (u.m.)
cannonball
canvas-covered
  (u.m.)
cap
  -flash (v.)
  nut
  screw
  sheaf
  shore
car
  barn
  break
  builder
  fare
  goose
  hop
  jacker
  lot

-mile
owner
pool
port
sick
wash
carbo (c.f.)
  all one word
carbol (c.f.)
  all one word
carcino (c.f.)
  all one word
card
  case
  -index (u.m., v.)
  player
  sharp
  stock
cardio (c.f.)
  -aortic
  rest one word
care
  free
  giver
  -laden (u.m.)
  taker
  -tired (u.m.)
  worn
carpet
  bagger
  beater
  #cleaner
  -cleaning (u.m.)
  -covered (u.m.)
  fitter
  layer
  -smooth (u.m.)
  -sweeping (u.m.)
  weaver
  -weaving (u.m.)
  web
  woven

carpo (c.f.)
  -olecranal
  rest one word
carriage-making
  (u.m.)
carrot
  -colored (u.m.)
  head (nonliteral)
  juice
  top (nonliteral)
carry
  all (n., u.m.)
  around (n., u.m.)
  back (n., u.m.)
  forward (n.)
  -in (n., u.m.)
  out (n., u.m.)
  over (n., u.m.)
cart
  load
  wheel (coin)
  whip
  wright
case
  bearer
  finding
  hammer
  harden
  load
  mated
  worker
caser-in
cashflow
cast
  away (n., u.m.)
  back (n., u.m.)
  -by (u.m.)
  off (n., u.m.)
  out (n., u.m.)
  -ridden (u.m.)
  -weld (v.)
caster
  -off

-out
castlebuilder
  (nonliteral)
cat
  back
  beam
  bird
  call
  -eyed (u.m.)
  face (n.)
  fall
  gut
  head
  hole
  hook
  -ion
  like
  nap
  nip
  -o'-nine-tails
  stitch
  walk
CAT scan
catch
  all (n., u.m.)
  -as-catch-can
  (u.m.)
  cry
  penny
  plate
  up (n., u.m.)
  weight
  word
cater
  corner
  wauling
cat's
  -eye (nonliteral)
  -paw (nonliteral)
cattle
  #boat
  feed
  -raising (u.m.)

yak
cauliflower
-eared (u.m.)
#ware
causeway
cave
dweller
-dwelling (u.m.)
#fish
-in (n., u.m.)
cease-fire (n., u.m.)
cedar-colored (u.m.)
celi (c.f.)
all one word
celio (c.f.)
all one word
cell
cement
-covered (u.m.)
mason
-temper (v.)
census
#taker
-taking
center
#field (sports)
head (printing)
line
most
piece
-second
centi (c.f.)
all one word
centimeter-gram-
second
centri (c.f.)
all one word
centro (c.f.)
all one word
cephalo (c.f.)
all one word
cerato (c.f.)
all one word

cerebro (c.f.)
-ocular
rest one word
certificate holder
cervico (c.f.)
-occipital
-orbicular
rest one word
cess
pipe
pit
pool
chaffcutter
chain
#belt
-driven (u.m.)
#gang
stitch
chair
fast
mender
person
-shaped (u.m.)
warmer
chalk
cutter
line
-white (u.m.)
chamber
maid
woman
changeover
chapfallen
chapelgoing
char
broiler
coal
pit
woman
charge
#book
off (n., u.m.)
out (n., u.m.)

chartbook
chattermark
cheapskate
check
bite
forger
hook
-in (n., u.m.)
list
mark
nut
off (n., u.m.)
out (n., u.m.)
passer (n.)
point
rack
rail
rein
ring
roll
rope
row
sheet
strap
string
up (n., u.m.)
washer
weigher
writer
checker
-in
-off
-out
-up
cheek
bone
strap
cheerleader
cheese
burger
cake
cloth
curd

cutter
head
lip
parer
plate
chemico (c.f.)
all one word
chemo (c.f.)
all one word
cherry
-colored (u.m.)
stone (nonliteral)
#stone (literal)
chestnut
-colored (u.m.)
-red (u.m.)
chicken
bill
-billed (u.m.)
#breast
breasted
#coop
#farm
feed
heart
pox
#yard
chief
#justice
-justiceship
#mate
child
bearing
bed
birth
care
crowing
hood
kind
life
-minded (u.m.)
ridden
wife

chill-cast (u.m., v.)
chin
  band
  -bearded (u.m.)
  -chin
  cloth
  cough
  -high (u.m.)
  rest
  strap
china
  -blue (u.m.)
  #shop
  ware
Chinatown
chipmunk
chiro (c.f.)
  all one word
chisel
  -cut (u.m.)
  -edged (u.m.)
  #maker
chitchat
chitter-chatter
chloro (c.f.)
  all one word
chock
  ablock
  -full (u.m.)
chocolate
  -brown (u.m.)
  -coated (u.m.)
  #maker
choir
  boy
  #master
choke
  bore
  chain
  damp
  out (n., u.m.)
  point
  strap

chole (c.f.)
  all one word
chondro (c.f.)
  -osseous
  rest one word
chop
  -chop
  stick
chowchow
Christ
  -given (u.m.)
  -inspired (u.m.)
  like
chromo (c.f.)
  all one word
chrono (c.f.)
  all one word
chuck
  hole
  plate
  wagon
chucklehead
chunkhead
church
  #choir
  goer
  like
  work
  yard
churn
  -butted (u.m.)
  milk
cigar
  case
  cutter
  -shaped (u.m.)
cigarette
  #holder
  #maker
  -making (u.m.)
cine (c.f.)
  all one word
circuitbreaker

circum (pref.)
  arctic, pacific,
    etc.
  -Saturnal, etc.
  rest one word
cirro (c.f.)
  all one word
cis (pref.)
  alpine
  atlantic
  -trans (u.m.)
  rest one word
city
  -born (u.m.)
  -bred (u.m.)
  folk
  #man
  scape
clam
  bake
  shell
clampdown (n.,
  u.m.)
clap
  net
  trap
clasphook
class
  book
  -conscious (u.m.)
  #consciousness
  #day
  work
claw
  bar
  -footed (u.m.)
  hammer
  hatchet
  -tailed (u.m.)
clay
  bank
  -colored (u.m.)
  pan

  pit
  works
clean
  -cut (u.m.)
  handed
  out (n., u.m.)
  -shaved (u.m.)
  -smelling (u.m.)
  up (n., u.m.)
clear
  cole
  -cut (u.m.)
  cut (forestry) (n.,
    v.)
  -eyed (u.m.)
  headed
  -sighted (u.m.)
  up (n., u.m.)
  wing
clearinghouse
cleft
  -footed (u.m.)
  -graft (v.)
client/server
cliff
  dweller
  -dwelling (u.m.)
  hanger
  side
  top
  -worn (u.m.)
clinch-built (u.m.)
clink-clank
clinker-built (u.m.)
clip
  -clop
  -edged (u.m.)
  sheet
clipper-built (u.m.)
cloak
  -and-dagger (n.,
    u.m.)
  room

clock
  case
  face
  -minded (u.m.)
  setter
  #speed
  watcher
clod
  head
  hopping
  pate
close
  bred
  -connected (u.m.)
  cross
  -cut (u.m.)
  down (n.)
  -fertilize (v.)
  fisted
  handed
  -knit
  minded
  mouthed
  out (n., u.m.)
  up (n., u.m.)
closed
  -circuit (u.m.)
  #end
  #shop
cloth-backed (u.m.)
clothes
  bag
  basket
  brush
  #closet
  horse
  pin
  line
  press
  rack
  #tree
cloud
  base

burst
  cap
  -hidden (u.m.)
clover
  bloom
  leaf
  seed
  sick
club
  #car
  foot
  hand
  haul
  mobile
  ridden
  room
  root
  -shaped (u.m.)
co (pref.)
  -op
  exist, operate, etc.
  processor
  rest one word
coach
  -and-four
  builder
  whip
coal
  bag
  bed
  bin
  -black (u.m.)
  breaker
  #car
  dealer
  digger
  -faced (u.m.)
  hole
  -laden (u.m.)
  #loader
  #mine
  #oil
  pit

rake
  sack (astron. only)
  shed
  ship
  #tar
  #truck
  yard
coastside
coat
  hanger
  rack
  tailed
cob
  head
  meal
  shed
  web
cock
  bill
  brain
  crow
  eye
  fight
  head
  pit
  #robin
  spur
  sure
  -tailed (u.m.)
  up (n., u.m.)
cockleshell
cockscomb
cod
  bank
  fishing
  head
  #liver
  piece
  pitchings
  smack
code
  #name
  -named (u.m.)

coffee
  break
  cake
  -colored (u.m.)
  -growing (u.m.)
  pot
  room
cofferdam
coffin-headed (u.m.)
cogwheel
coin-operated
  (u.m.)
cold
  blooded
  -chisel (v.)
  cuts
  -draw (v.)
  finch
  -flow (v.)
  -forge (v.)
  frame
  -hammer (v.)
  -hammered (u.m.)
  pack
  -press (v.)
  -roll (v.)
  -rolled (u.m.)
  -short (u.m.)
  -shortness
  -shoulder (v.)
  type (printing)
  #war
  #wave
  -work (v.)
cole
  seed
  slaw
coli (c.f.)
  all one word
collar
  bag
  band
  bone

colo (c.f.)
  all one word
color
  bearer
  blind
  #blindness
  fast
  -free (u.m.)
  #line
  type (printing)
    (n.)
  -washed (u.m.)
comb-toothed
    (u.m.)
come
  -along (tool)
  back (n., u.m.)
  -between (n.)
  down (n.)
  -off (n., u.m.)
  -on (n., u.m.)
  -out (n.)
  -outer
  uppance
comic#book
command
  -line
  #prompt
commander#in
    #chief
common
  -carrier
  #law
  place
  #sense (n.)
  sense (u.m.)
  weal
  wealth
companionship
compressed#file
comptime
cone
  -shaped (u.m.)

  speaker
conference#room
Congressman#at
    #Large
contra (pref.)
  -acting
  -approach
  -ion
  rest one word
cook
  book
  off (n., u.m.)
  out (n., u.m.)
  shack
  stove
coolheaded
cooped
  -in (u.m.)
  -up (u.m.)
cop
  #out (v.)
  out (n.)
copper
  -bottomed (u.m.)
  -colored (u.m.)
  head
  -headed (u.m.)
  #mine
  nose
  plate
  -plated (u.m.)
  smith
  works
copy
  cat
  cutter
  desk
  #editor
  fitter
  holding
  reader
  right
  writer

coral
  -beaded (u.m.)
  -red (u.m.)
cork
  -lined (u.m.)
  screw
corn
  bin
  bread
  cake
  cob
  cracker
  crib
  crusher
  cutter
  dodger
  -fed (u.m.)
  husk
  loft
  meal
  #pone
  stalk
  starch
corner
  bind
  post
corpsmember
cost
  #effective (n.)
  -effectiveness
  wise
costo (c.f.)
  all one word
cotton
  -clad (u.m.)
  -covered (u.m.)
  -growing (u.m.)
  #mill
  mouth (snake)
  packer
  picker, ing
  seed
  sick

countdown (n., u.m.)
counter
  #check (banking)
  #septum
  -off
  act, propaganda,
    top, etc.
  *as combining
    form, one
    word*
country
  -born (u.m.)
  -bred (u.m.)
  folk
  people
  side
  wide
county
  #seat
  wide
court
  bred
  -martial
  ship
cousin
  -german
  hood
  -in-law
cover
  alls
  let
  side
  up (n., u.m.)
cow
  barn
  bell
  catcher
  -eyed (u.m.)
  gate
  hand
  herd
  hide
  hitch

lick
path
pen
#pony
pox
puncher
shed
sucker
crab
  cake
  catcher
  eater
  faced
  hole
  meat
  stick
crack
  down (n., u.m.)
  house (slang)
  jaw
  pot
  -the-whip (n., u.m.)
  up (n., u.m.)
cradle
  side
  #snatcher
  song
cranio (c.f.)
  all one word
crank
  case
  -driven (u.m.)
  pin
  pit
  shaft
crapehanger
crashdive (v.)
crawlup (n., u.m.)
crazy
  bone
  cat
cream
  cake

-colored (u.m.)
creditworthiness
creek
  bed
  side
creep
  hole
  mouse
crepe#de#chine
crestfallen
crew
  cut
  member
cribstrap
crime
  fighter
  solver
  wave
crisscross
crook
  all one word
crooked
  -foot (n.)
  -legged (u.m.)
  -nosed (u.m.)
crop
  -bound (u.m.)
  -haired (u.m.)
  head
  mark
  -year
cross
  -appeal
  arm
  band
  bar
  beam
  bearer
  bedded
  belt
  bench
  -bidding
  bill (bird)

#bill (legal)
bind
bolt
bond
bones
bred
breed
-bridge (v.)
-brush (v.)
-carve (v.)
-channel (u.m.)
-check
-claim
-compound (v.)
-connect (v.)
-country (u.m.)
-cultivate (v.)
current
-curve (math.) (n.)
cut
-date (v.)
-drain (v.)
-dye (v.)
-dyeing (n.)
-examine (v.)
-eye (n., u.m.)
-eyed (u.m.)
fall
feed
-fertile (u.m.)
-fertilize (v.)
-fiber (u.m.)
file
fire
flow
foot
-grained (u.m.)
hair
hand
hatch
haul
head
-immunity

-index (u.m.)
-interrogate (v.)
-interrogatory
-invite (v.)
legged
legs
-level (v.)
-license (v.)
lift (v.)
lock
lots
mark
member
patch
path
plow (v.)
-pollinate (v.)
-purpose (n.)
-question
rail
-reaction
-refer (v.)
-reference
road
row
-service
-shaft
-slide
-staff
-sterile
-stitch
-stone
-stratification
-sue (v.)
-surge (v.)
talk
tie
town
track
trail
tree
under (n., u.m.)
-vote

walk
web
wind
word
crow
  bait
  bar
  foot
crownbar
crow's
  -foot (nonliteral)
  -nest (nonliteral)
crybaby
crypto (c.f.)
  -Christian, etc.
  rest one word
crystal
  -clear (u.m.)
  -girded (u.m.)
  -smooth (u.m.)
cubbyhole
cumulo (c.f.)
  all one word
cup
  bearer
  cake
  ful
  head
curb
  side
  stoner
cure-all (n., u.m.)
curly
  head
  locks (n.)
currycomb
cussword
custom
  -built (u.m.)
  -made (u.m.)
  -tailored (u.m.)
cut
  away (n., u.m.)

back (n., u.m.)
  glass
  -in (n., u.m.)
  off (n., u.m.)
  out (n., u.m.)
  rate (u.m.)
  throat
  -toothed (u.m.)
  -under (u.m.)
  -up (n., u.m.)
cutter
  -built (u.m.)
  -down
  head
  -off
  -out
  -rigged (u.m.)
  -up
cuttlebone
cyano (c.f.)
  all one word
cyber
cyclecar
cyclo (c.f.)
  -olefin
  rest one word
cysto (c.f.)
  all one word
cyto (c.f.)
  all one word

D

D
  -day
  -major
  -plus-4-day
dairy
  -fed (u.m.)
  -made (u.m.)
daisy#chain
damp
  proofing
  -stained (u.m.)

damping-off (n., u.m.)
dancehall
danger#line
dare
  -all (n., u.m.)
  devil
  say
dark
  -eyed (u.m.)
  horse (nonliteral)
  room (n.)
  -skinned (u.m.)
dash
  plate
  wheel
data
  bank
  base
  set
date
  lined
  mark
daughter-in-law
dawn
  -gray (u.m.)
  streak
day
  beam
  bed
  break
  -bright (u.m.)
  care
  dawn
  dream
  -fly (aviation) (v.)
  -flying (u.m.)
  going
  lighted
  lit
  long (u.m.)
  mark
  side

star
  -to-day (u.m.)
  worker
de (pref.)
  -air
  icer
  -ink
  -ion
  centralize,
    energize, etc.
  rest one word
dead
  -alive
  beat (n.)
  born
  -burn (v.)
  #center
  -cold (u.m.)
  -dip (v.)
  -drunk (u.m.)
  -ender
  eye (n.)
  -eyed (u.m.)
  fall
  head
  -heated (u.m.)
  -heater
  -heavy (u.m.)
  latch
  #load
  lock
  pan
  -roast (v.)
  weight (n., u.m.)
  wood
death
  bed
  blow
  day
  -divided (u.m.)
  -doom (v.)
  #house
  -struck (u.m.)

trap
watch
-weary (u.m.)
decisionmaking
deckhand
deep
-affected (u.m.)
-cut (u.m.)
-felt (u.m.)
-freeze (u.m., v.)
-frying (u.m.)
going
-grown (u.m.)
-laid (u.m.)
most
mouthed
-rooted (u.m.)
#sea
-seated (u.m.)
-set (u.m.)
-sunk (u.m.)
-voiced (u.m.)
water (u.m.)
deer
drive (n.)
-eyed (u.m.)
food
herd
horn
hound
meat
stalker
stand
tick
dehydr(o) (c.f.)
all one word
demi (pref.)
-Christian, etc.
-incognito
rest one word
dermato (c.f.)
all one word
desk
#room

top (n., u.m.)
dessert
#fork
#knife
spoon
deutero (c.f.)
all one word
devil
-devil
dog (a marine)
-inspired (u.m.)
-ridden (u.m.)
dew
beam
cap
-clad (u.m.)
claw
damp
-drenched (u.m.)
drop
fall
-fed (u.m.)
-laden (u.m.)
lap
point
dextro (c.f.)
all one word
di (pref.)
all one word
dia (pref.)
all one word
dialog#box
dial-up
diamond
back
-backed (u.m.)
-shaped (u.m.)
diazo (c.f.)
-oxide
rest one word
dice
cup
play

die
-away (u.m.)
back
case
-cast (u.m., v.)
caster
-cut (u.m., v.)
cutter
hard (n., u.m.)
head
#proof (philately)
(n.)
setter
sinker
-square (u.m.)
stock
diesel
-driven (u.m.)
-electric (u.m.)
dillydally
dim
-lighted (u.m.)
lit
out (n., u.m.)
diner-out
ding
bat
dong
dining#room
dinitro (c.f.)
#spray
rest one word
dip
-dye (v.)
-grained (u.m.)
head
stick
dipper-in
direct
-connected (u.m.)
-indirect
direction-finding
(u.m.)

dirt
-cheap (u.m.)
fast
-incrusted (u.m.)
plate
dirty
-faced (u.m.)
-minded (u.m.)
#work
dis (pref.)
all one word
dish
cloth
#cover
pan
rack
rag
#towel
washer
disk
#drive
jockey
pack
plow
-shaped (u.m.)
ditch
bank
digger
rider
side
dive
-bomb (v.)
#bomber
do
-all (n., u.m.)
-gooder
-little (n., u.m.)
-nothing (n.,
u.m.)
dock
hand
head
side
worker

dog
bite
-bitten (u.m.)
breeder
cart
catcher
#days
-drawn (u.m.)
-ear (v.)
-eared (u.m.)
face (soldier)
-faced (u.m.)
fall
fight
food
-headed (u.m.)
hole
leg
#owner
race
shore
sled
-tired (u.m.)
tooth
-toothed (u.m.)
trick
trot
watch
-weary (u.m.)
doll
face
-faced (u.m.)
dollyhead
donkey
back
-drawn (u.m.)
-eared (u.m.)
doomsday
door
bed
bell
case
check

frame
head
jamb
keeper
knob
knocker
mat
nail
#opener
plate
post
-shaped (u.m.)
sill
step
stop
dope
fiend
passer
pusher
sheet
dorsi (c.f.)
all one word
dorso (c.f.)
-occipital
rest one word
dot
-matrix
#pitch
double
-barrel (n., u.m.)
-barreled (u.m.)
-bitt (v.)
-breasted (u.m.)
-charge (v.)
check (n., v.)
checked (u.m., v.)
-chinned (u.m.)
-click
cross (nonliteral)
deal (v.)
-decker
dipper
(nonliteral)

-duty (u.m.)
-dye (v.)
-edged (u.m.)
-ender
-entendre
handed
-headed (u.m.)
header
-jointed
-leaded (u.m.)
-quick (u.m.)
-sided
#space (v.)
#take
talk
tone (printing)
tree
-trouble
-up (u.m., v.)
#work
dough
boy
-colored (u.m.)
face
-faced (u.m.)
head
mixer
nut
down
beat
by
cast
check
coast
come
-covered (u.m.)
crier
cry
curved
cut
dale
draft
drag

face
fall
feed
filled
flow
fold
grade
gradient
growth
hanging
haul
hearted
hill
lead
load
lock (n.)
look
most
payment
pour
rate
right
river
rush
shore
side
sitting
slip
slope
-soft (u.m.)
spout
stage
stairs
state
stream
street
stroke
sun (adv., u.m.)
swing
take
throw
thrust
time

town	back	world	kick
trampling	bar	dredge#net	leaf (n., u.m.)
trend	beam	dressup (n., u.m.)	leg
trodden	bench	dressing#room	off (n., u.m.)
turn	bolt	**drift**	out (n., u.m.)
valley	bore	#boat	sonde
weigh	bridge	bolt	stitch
weight	cut	meter	**drug**
wind	down (n., u.m.)	-mining (u.m.)	-addicted (u.m.)
draft	file	#net	mixer
age (allowance)	gate	pin	passer
#age	gear	wind	pusher
-exempt (u.m.)	glove	**drill**	seller
drag	head	case	#user
bar	horse	-like	**drum**
bolt	knife	stock	beat
net	knot	**drip**	fire
pipe	link	cock	head
rope	loom	-drip	stick
saw	net	-dry (u.m., v.)	-up (n., u.m.)
staff	off (n., u.m.)	sheet	**dry**
wire	out (n., u.m.)	stick	-burnt (u.m.)
dragger	pin	**drive**	#cell
-down	plate	away (n., u.m.)	clean
-in	point	belt	-cure (v.)
-out	sheet	bolt	dock
-up	span	by (n., u.m.)	-dye (v.)
dragon	stop	cap	-farm (v.)
-eyed (u.m.)	string	head	farming (n.,
fly	tongs	-in (n., u.m.)	u.m.)
#piece	tube	pipe	gulch
drain	**drawer**	screw	(nonliteral)
cleaner	-down	#shaft	lot
pipe	-in	way	-pack (u.m., v.)
plug	-off	**drop**	-rotted (u.m.)
tile	-out	away (n., u.m.)	-salt (v.)
drainage	**drawing**	bolt	wash
#area	#board	cloth	**duck**
#basin	#room	-down	bill
way	**dream**	-forge (v.)	-billed (u.m.)
draw	-haunted (u.m.)	front	bore
-arch (n.)	land	hammer	#breast
arm	lore	head	foot (tool)

-footed (u.m.)
pin
pond
walk
due
-in (n., u.m.)
out (n., u.m.)
duffelbag
dug
out (n.)
-up (u.m.)
dull
-edged (u.m.)
head
-looking (u.m.)
-witted (u.m.)
dumdum
dumb
bell
head
waiter
dump
car
cart
site
dunderhead
duo (c.f.)
all one word
dust
bag
bin
brush
cloth
-covered (u.m.)
fall
-gray (u.m.)
-laden (u.m.)
pan
storm
duty
bound
-free (u.m.)
dwelling#house

dye
mixer
stuff
works
dys (pref.)
all one word
E
E-minor
e
file
Government
Library
mail
eagle
#eye
-eyed (u.m.)
ear
ache
cap
drop
drum
flap
guard
hole
lap
lobe
mark
#muff
phone
-piercing (u.m.)
plug
ring
screw
shot
sore
splitting
tab
wax
wig
witness
earth
bank
born

-bred (u.m.)
fall
fast
-fed (u.m.)
fill
grubber
#house
kin
lit
mover
nut
quake
-shaking (u.m.)
slide
-stained (u.m.)
wall
east
bound
-central (u.m.)
going
-northeast
#side
-sider
-southeast
Eastertime
easy
going
mark (n.)
-rising (u.m.)
-spoken (u.m.)
eavesdrop
ebbtide
edge
#plane
shot
ways
wise
eel
cake
catcher
fare
pot
pout

skin
spear
egg
beater (all
meanings)
cup
eater
fruit
head (nonliteral)
hot (n.)
nog
plant
-shaped (u.m.)
shell
-white (u.m.)
eight
-angled (u.m.)
#ball
fold
penny (nail)
-ply (u.m.)
score
-wheeler
elbowchair
elder
#brother
-leaved (u.m.)
electro (c.f.)
-optics
-osmosis
-ultrafiltration
rest one word
embryo (c.f.)
all one word
empty
handed
-looking (u.m.)
en
#banc
#gros
#route
encephalo (c.f.)
all one word

end
-all (n., u.m.)
bell
brain
gate
lap
long
-match (v.)
matcher
-measure (v.)
most
-shrink (v.)
ways
ender
-on
-up
endo (c.f.)
all one word
engine
#shop
-sized (u.m.)
work
#worker
#yard
entero (c.f.)
all one word
entry
#book
way
envelope
#holder
#maker
epi (pref.)
all one word
equi (c.f.)
-gram-molar
rest one word
ere
long
now
errorproof
erythro (c.f.)
all one word

even
glow
handed
minded
-numbered (u.m.)
song
-tempered (u.m.)
ever
-abiding (u.m.)
bearing
blooming
-constant (u.m.)
-fertile (u.m.)
glade
going
green
lasting
more
-normal (u.m.)
-present (u.m.)
-ready (u.m.)
sporting (biol.)
which
every
day (n., u.m.)
#day (each day)
how
one (all)
#one (distributive)
#time
evil
doer
#eye
-eyed (u.m.)
-faced (u.m.)
-looking (u.m.)
minded (u.m.)
sayer
speaker
wishing
ex
#cathedra
cathedral

communicate
-Governor
#libris
#officio
#post#facto
#rights
-serviceman
-trader
-vice-president
extra
-alimentary
-American
bold
-Britannic
-condensed (u.m.)
curricular
-fine (u.m.)
hazardous
judicial
-large (u.m.)
-long (u.m.)
marginal
mural
ordinary
polar
-strong (u.m.)
territorial
vascular
eye
#appeal
ball
bank
bar
blink
-blurred (u.m.)
bolt
brow
-conscious (u.m.)
cup
flap
glance
glass
hole

lash
lens
lid
mark
-minded (u.m.)
#opener
peep
pit
point
service
shade
shield
shot
sick
sight
sore
spot
-spotted (u.m.)
stalk
strain
string
tooth
wash
#weariness
wink
witness

F
F
-flat
-horn
-sharp
fable
#book
teller
face
about (n., u.m., v.)
-arbor (v.)
cloth
-harden (v.)
-hardened (u.m.)
lifting
mark

-off (n.)
-on (n., u.m.)
plate
up (n., u.m.)
fact
book
finding
sheet
fade
away (n., u.m.)
-in (n., u.m.)
out (n., u.m.)
fail-safe
faint
heart
-voiced (u.m.)
fair
ground
-lead (n., u.m.)
minded
play
-skinned (u.m.)
#trade
fairy
folk
hood
tale
faithbreaker
fall
away (n., u.m.)
back (n., u.m.)
#guy
-in (n., u.m.)
out (n., u.m.)
-plow (v.)
-sow (v.)
trap
fallow#land
false
-bottomed (u.m.)
#face
-faced (u.m.)
hood

-tongued (u.m.)
fame
-crowned (u.m.)
-thirsty (u.m.)
fan
back
bearer
#belt
fare
fold
foot
-jet
-leaved (u.m.)
marker
-shaped (u.m.)
-tailed (u.m.)
fancy
-free (u.m.)
-loose (u.m.)
-woven (u.m.)
-wrought (u.m.)
far
-aloft (u.m.)
away (n., u.m.)
-borne (u.m.)
-distant (u.m.)
-eastern (u.m.)
-famed (u.m.)
fetched
flung (u.m.)
gone
-off (u.m.)
#out
-reaching (u.m.)
seeing
-seen (u.m.)
-set (u.m.)
sight
farm
-bred (u.m.)
hand
hold
owner

people
place
stead
worker
fashion
-led (u.m.)
#piece (naut.)
#plate
-setting (u.m.)
fast
-anchored (u.m.)
back
-dyed (u.m.)
going
hold
-moving (u.m.)
-read (v.)
-reading (u.m.)
#time (daylight
saving)
fat
back
-bellied (u.m.)
-free (u.m.)
head
-soluble (u.m.)
father
-confessor
-in-law
land
fault
finder
line
slip
faux#pas
fax
-and-voice#
mailbox
#modem
-on-demand
fear
-free (u.m.)
nought

-pursued (u.m.)
-shaken (u.m.)
feather
bed (v.)
bedding
bone
brain
edge
-footed (u.m.)
head
-leaved (u.m.)
stitch
-stitched (u.m.)
-stitching
-tongue (v.)
weight
wing (moth)
fed-up (u.m.)
feeble
-bodied (u.m.)
minded
feed
back (n., u.m.)
bag
bin
box
crusher
cutter
head
lot
mixer
pipe
rack
store
stuff
feeder
-in
-up
fellow
craft
ship
rest two words

felt
cutter
-lined (u.m.)
packer
fenbank
fence
post
#row
fern
-clad (u.m.)
leaf
-leaved (u.m.)
ferro (c.f.)
-carbon-titanium
-uranium
rest one word
ferry
boat
#car
#slip
fever
less
-stricken (u.m.)
trap
-warm (u.m.)
fiber
-faced (u.m.)
glass
#optics
stitch
Fiberglas
(copyright)
fibro (c.f.)
-osteoma
rest one word
fickleminded
fiddle
back
-faddle
head
-shaped (u.m.)
stick
string

field
ball
glass
goal
-strip
fierce
-eyed (u.m.)
-looking (u.m.)
fiery
-flaming (u.m.)
-hot (u.m.)
-red (u.m.)
-tempered (u.m.)
fig
bar
eater
leaf
shell
figure
head
-of-eight (u.m.)
#work (printing)
file
card
-hard (u.m.)
name
setter
-soft (u.m.)
fill
-in (n., u.m.)
out (n., u.m.)
-up (n., u.m.)
filler
cap
-in
-out
-up
film
cutter
goer
going
#paper
slide

strip
-struck (u.m.)
fin
back
-shaped (u.m.)
fine
-cut (u.m., v.)
-draw (v.)
-drawn (u.m.)
-featured (u.m.)
-looking (u.m.)
-set (u.m.)
finger
breadth
-cut (u.m.)
hold
hole
hook
mark
nail
parted
post
print
shell
spin
stall
tip
fire
arm
back (n.)
ball
bell
bolt
bomb
brand
brat
break
brick
-burnt (u.m.)
-clad (u.m.)
coat
cracker
crest

-cure (v.)
damp
#drill
-eater
fall
fang
fighter
guard
-hardened (u.m.)
horse
hose
lit
pit
place
plow
plug
-polish (v.)
power
proof
-red (u.m.)
-resistant (u.m.)
safe
side
spout
trap
truck
wall
warden
firm
-footed (u.m.)
-set (u.m.)
-up (n., u.m.)
first
#aid
-aider
-born (u.m.)
-class (u.m.)
comer
hand (u.m.)
-made (u.m.)
-named (u.m.)
-nighter
-rate (u.m.)

fish
back
bed
-bellied (u.m.)
bolt
bone
bowl
cake
eater
eye
-eyed (u.m.)
fall
#farm
-fed (u.m.)
food
garth
hook
-joint (v.)
kill
#ladder
meal
mouth
plate
pond
pool
pot
pound
trap
weir
works
fisher
folk
man
people
fishyback (n., u.m.)
fit
out (n.)
strip
five
bar
fold
-ply (u.m.)
-pointed (u.m.)

-reeler
score
flag
bearer
pole
post
-raising (u.m.)
ship
-signal (v.)
staff
stick
flame
-colored (u.m.)
-cut (v.)
out (n.)
proof
thrower
flannelmouth
flap
cake
doodle
-eared (u.m.)
jack
flare
back (n., u.m.)
out (n., u.m.)
path
up (n., u.m.)
flash
back (n., u.m.)
bulb
card
cube
gun
lamp
pan
point
flat
back
(bookbinding)
bed (printing)
-bottomed (u.m.)
car

-compound (v.)
fold
foot (n.)
hat
head
iron
nose
out (n., u.m.)
-rolled (u.m.)
sawn
top
-topped (u.m.)
woods
flax
drop
-leaved (u.m.)
-polled (u.m.)
seed
flea
bite
-bitten (u.m.)
trap
fleet
foot
-footed (u.m.)
wing
flesh
brush
hook
-pink (u.m.)
pot
fleur-de-lis
flextime
flight
crew
-hour
path
-test (v.)
flimflam
flip
-flap
-flop
-up (n., u.m.)

flood
cock
flow
gate
lamp
lighting
mark
#plain
tide
wall
water
floor
beam
cloth
head
lamp
mat
mop
#show
space
stain
walker
#wax
-waxing (u.m.)
flophouse
floppy#disk
flour
bag
bin
#mill
sack
#sifter
flow
chart
meter
off (n., u.m.)
sheet
through (n.,
u.m.)
flower
bed
bud
-crowned (u.m.)

#grower
-hung (u.m.)
#piece
pot
-scented (u.m.)
#shop
flue-cure (v.)
fluid
-compressed
(u.m.)
extract (pharm.)
(n.)
glycerate
fluo (c.f.)
all one word
fluoro (c.f.)
all one word
flush
-cut (u.m.)
-decked (u.m.)
-decker
gate
fluvio (c.f.)
all one word
fly
away
back
ball
-bitten (u.m.)
blow
blown
-by-night (n.,
u.m.)
catcher
eater
-fish (v.)
-fisher
-fisherman
#fishing
flap
-free (u.m.)
leaf
paper

sheet
speck
-specked (u.m.)
tier
trap
weight
wheel
winch
flying
#boat
#fish
foam
bow
-crested (u.m.)
-white (u.m.)
fog
bound
bow
dog
eater
-hidden (u.m.)
horn
#light
-ridden (u.m.)
fold
-in
up (n., u.m.)
folk
#dance
lore
song
follow
-on
through (n.,
u.m.)
up (n., u.m.)
follower-up
food
-fasted (u.m.)
-fasting (v.)
packer
store
stuff

foolhardy
foolscap
foot
-and-mouth
(u.m.)
ball
band
bath
blower
board
brake
breadth
bridge
candle
fall
-free (u.m.)
gear
-grain
hill
hold
lambert
licker
light(s)
lining
locker
loose
mark
note
pad
path
pick
plate
-pound
-pound-second
print
race
rail
rest
rope
scald
-second
slogger
sore

stalk
stall
step
stick
stock
stool
-ton
walk
wall
-weary (u.m.)
worn
for (pref.)
all one word
fore
-age
-and-aft (n., u.m.)
-and-after (n.)
-edge
-end
-exercise
word
rest one word
forest
-clad (u.m.)
-covered (u.m.)
#land
side
fork
head
lift
-pronged (u.m.)
tail
-tailed (u.m.)
form
fitting
#work (printing)
forth
coming
right
with
fortune
#hunter
teller

forty-niner
foul
  #line
  -looking (u.m.)
  mouthed
  -spoken (u.m.)
  -tongued (u.m.)
  up (n., u.m.)
fountainhead
four
  -bagger
  -eyed (u.m.)
  flusher
  fold
  -footed (u.m.)
  -in-hand (n., u.m.)
  -masted (u.m.)
  -master
  penny (nail)
  -ply (u.m.)
  score
  some
  square
  -wheeler
fox
  -faced (u.m.)
  hole
  hound
  #hunting
  skinned
  tailed
  trot
fracto (c.f.)
  all one word
frameup (n., u.m.)
free
  booter
  born
  drop
  -for-all (n., u.m.)
  -grown (u.m.)
  hand (drawing)

handed
hold
lance
loader
-minded
masonry
#post
-spoken (u.m.)
standing (u.m.)
thinker
trader
wheel (u.m., v.)
wheeler (n.)
#will (n.)
will (u.m.)
freedom#fighter
freeze
  down (n., u.m.)
  out (n., u.m.)
  up (n., u.m.)
freight
  #house
  -mile
  #room
  #train
fresh
  -looking (u.m.)
  -painted (u.m.)
  water
frog
  belly
  eater
  -eyed (u.m.)
  face
  mouth
  nose
  pond
  tongue
  (medicine)
front
  -end (u.m.)
  -focused (u.m.)
  runner

stall
-wheel (u.m.)
fronto (c.f.)
  -occipital
  -orbital
  rest one word
frost
  bite
  bow
  -free (u.m.)
  -hardy (u.m.)
  -heaving (u.m.)
  -killed (u.m.)
  lamp
  line
fruit
  cake
  #fly
  growing
  #shop
  stalk
frying#pan
fuel
  #line
  #oil
full
  back
  -bellied (u.m.)
  blood
  -bound (u.m.)
  -duplex
  face
  -fashioned (u.m.)
  -flowering (u.m.)
  -grown (u.m.)
  -handed (u.m.)
  -headed (u.m.)
  -lined (u.m.)
  #load
  mouth
  -strength (u.m.)
  -text
  -time (u.m.)

fundraising
funlover
funnel
  form
  -shaped (u.m.)
fur
  -clad (u.m.)
  coat
  -lined (u.m.)
  skin
  -trimmed (u.m.)
fuse
  box
  #gauge
  plug

G

G
  -major
  -man
  -minor
  -sharp
gabfest
gad
  about (n., u.m.)
  fly
gaff-topsail
gag
  -check (v.)
  #order
  root
  #rule
gaugepin
gain
  say
  -sharing (u.m.)
galact(o) (c.f.)
  all one word
gallbladder
galley#proof
  (printing)
galvano (c.f.)
  all one word

game
  bag
  cock
gang -
  boss
  plank
  saw
gapeseed
garnet-brown
  (u.m.)
gas
  bag
  bomb
  -driven (u.m.)
  field
  -fired (u.m.)
  firing
  fitter
  -heated (u.m.)
  -laden (u.m.)
  lamp
  lighted
  line (auto)
  #line (queue)
  lock
  #main
  #mask
  meter
  works
gastro (c.f.)
  -omental
  rest one word
gate
  house
  keeper
  leg (u.m.)
  pin
  post
  tender
  works
gay
  #blade
  cat

  -colored (u.m.)
  #dog
  -looking (u.m.)
gear
  box
  case
  -driven (u.m.)
  fitter
  -operated (u.m.)
  set
  shift
  wheel
gelatin
  -coated (u.m.)
  -making (u.m.)
gelatino (c.f.)
  bromide
  chloride
gem
  cutter
  -set (u.m.)
  #stone
genito (c.f.)
  all one word
gentle
  folk
  -looking (u.m.)
  man
  -mannered (u.m.)
  mouthed
  -spoken (u.m.)
  woman
geo (c.f.)
  all one word
  germ-free (u.m.)
  gerrymander
get
  -at-able
  away (n., u.m.)
  off (n., u.m.)
  -together (n.,
    u.m.)
  up (n., u.m.)

ghost
  -haunted (u.m.)
  write (v.)
giddy
  brain
  head
  -paced (u.m.)
gilt-edge (u.m.)
gin-run (u.m.)
ginger
  #ale
  bread
  -colored (u.m.)
  snap
  spice
give
  -and-take (n.,
    u.m.)
  away (n., u.m.)
glacio (c.f.)
  all one word
glass
  blower
  #ceiling
  cutter
  -eater
  -eyed (u.m.)
  -hard (u.m.)
  house
  works
glauco (c.f.)
  all one word
  glidepath
  globetrotter
glosso (c.f.)
  all one word
glow
  lamp
  meter
gluc(o) (c.f.)
  all one word
glue
  pot

  stock
glycero (c.f.)
  all one word
glyco (c.f.)
  all one word
go
  -ahead (n., u.m.)
  -around (n., u.m.)
  -as-you-please
    (u.m.)
  -back (n., u.m.)
  -between (n.)
  by (n.)
  cart
  -devil (n.)
  -getter
  -getting (n., u.m.)
  -off (n., u.m.)
goal
  post
  #setter
goat
  -bearded (u.m.)
  -drunk (u.m.)
  -eyed (u.m.)
  herd
goat's
  -hair
  -horn
God
  -conscious (u.m.)
  -fearing (u.m.)
  -forsaken (u.m.)
  -given (u.m.)
  head
  -man
  -ordained (u.m.)
  -sent (u.m.)
  -sped (u.m.)
  speed
  -taught (u.m.)
god
  child

daughter	**goose**	-meter	beard (n.)
father	bone	-molecular	-clad (u.m.)
head	bumps	-negative (u.m.)	coat (n.)
hood	-cackle	-positive (u.m.)	-eyed (u.m.)
less	#egg	**grand**	-haired (u.m.)
mother	-eyed (u.m.)	aunt	head
parent	flesh	child, etc.	-headed (u.m.)
send	-footed (u.m.)	stand	out (n., u.m.)
ship	herd	grant-in-aid	**grease**
son	mouth	**grape**	#gun
sonship	neck	fruit	#pit
goggle-eyed (u.m.)	pimples	#juice	proof
goings-on	rump	-leaved (u.m.)	**great**
gold	step	seed	-aunt
beater	wing	stalk	coat
brick (shirker)	**gospel**	vine	-eared (u.m.)
#brick (of real gold)	like	**graph**	-grandchild, etc.
-bright (u.m.)	-true (u.m.)	alloy	-headed (u.m.)
-brown (u.m.)	gourdhead	#paper	heart
digger	**Government**	**grapho** (c.f.)	mouthed
#dust	(U.S. or	*all one word*	**green**
-filled (u.m.)	foreign)	**grass**	back (n., u.m.)
foil	-in-exile	-clad (u.m.)	belt
-inlaid (u.m.)	-owned (u.m.)	-covered (u.m.)	(community)
leaf	wide	cutter	-clad (u.m.)
plate (v.)	governmentwide	flat	-eyed (u.m.)
-plated (u.m.)	(State, city, etc.)	-green (u.m.)	gage (plum)
-plating (u.m.)	**grab**	hop	gill
smithing	-all (n., u.m.)	nut	grocer
-wrought (u.m.)	#bag	plot	horn
golden	hook	roots (nonliteral)	keeper
-fingered (u.m.)	rope	#roots (literal)	-leaved (u.m.)
-headed (u.m.)	**grade**	widow	sand (geology)
good	finder	**grave**	sick
-bye	mark	clothes	stuff
-for-nothing (n.,	**grain**	digger	sward
u.m.)	-cut (u.m.)	side	town
-looker	field	stead	(community)
-looking (u.m.)	-laden (u.m.)	**gravel**	#wood (literal)
-natured (u.m.)	mark	-blind (u.m.)	wood (forest)
#will (kindness)	sick	stone	greyhound
will (salable	**gram**	**gray**	**grid**
asset)	-fast (u.m.)	back (n., u.m.)	iron

lock
griddlecake
grillroom
grip
  sack
  wheel
gross
  -minded (u.m.)
  #weight
ground
  breaking
  hog
  mass
  nut
  path
  plot
  -sluicer
  speed
  #water
  wave
  work
group-connect (v.)
grownup (n., u.m.)
grubstake
guard
  house
  plate
  rail
guest
  chamber
  house
  room
guided-missile
  (u.m.)
guidepost
guider-in
gum
  boil
  chewer
  digger
  drop
  -gum
  lac

-saline (n.)
shoe
gun
  #barrel
  bearer
  blast
  builder
  cotton
  crew
  deck
  fight
  fire
  flint
  lock
  paper
  pit
  play
  point
  powder
  rack
  -rivet (v.)
  runner
  shop
  shot
  -shy (u.m.)
  sight
  stock
  wale
gut
  less
  string
gutter
  blood
  -bred (u.m.)
  snipe
  spout
gymno (c.f.)
  all one word
gyneco (c.f.)
  all one word
gyro
  #horizon
  #mechanism

#pelorus
  plane, compass,
    etc.

H

H
  -bar
  -beam
  -bomb
  -hour
hack
  barrow
  hammer
  log
  saw
hailstorm
hair
  band
  breadth
  brush
  -check (n.)
  cloth
  cut (n.)
  do
  dresser
  -fibered (u.m.)
  lock
  pin
  #ribbon
  space (printing)
  splitting
  spring
  streak
  stroke (printing)
  #trigger
half
  -and-half (n.,
    u.m.)
  -afraid
  -alive
  -angry
  back (football)
  -backed (u.m.)

-baked (u.m.)
-bound (u.m.)
caste
-clear
cock (v.)
cocked
  (nonliteral)
-dark
#day
deck
-decked (u.m.)
-decker
-feed (v.)
hearted
-hourly (u.m.)
-life
#load
-loaded (u.m.)
-mast
-miler
-monthly (u.m.)
-on (n., u.m.)
pace
penny
-ripe
-shy
-sole (v.)
staff
stitch
-strength (u.m.)
title
tone (printing)
track
-true
-truth
-weekly (u.m.)
wit
-witted (u.m.)
-yearly (u.m.)
hallmark
ham
  shackle
  string

hammer
  cloth
  dress (v.)
  -hard (u.m.)
  -harden (v.)
  -hardened (u.m.)
  head
  lock
  #thrower
  toe
  -weld (v.)
  -wrought (u.m.)
hand
  bag
  ball
  bank (v.)
  barrow
  bill
  book
  -bound (u.m.)
  bow
  brake
  breadth
  brush
  -built (u.m.)
  car
  -carry (v.)
  cart
  -carve (v.)
  clap
  clasp
  -clean (v.)
  crank
  cuff
  -cut (v.)
  -embroidered
    (u.m.)
  -fed (v.)
  fold
  grasp
  grenade
  grip
  guard

gun
  -held (u.m.)
  -high (u.m.)
  hold
  hole
  -in-hand (u.m.)
  kerchief
  -knit (v.)
  -knitter
  laid
  -letter (v.)
  lift (truck)
  liner
  made
  -me-down (n.,
    u.m.)
  mix (v.)
  mold (v.)
  mower
  off (n., u.m.)
  out (n., u.m.)
  pick (v.)
  post
  press
  print
  rail
  reading
  saw
  scrape (v.)
  set
  shake
  spade
  spike
  splice
  split
  spring
  spun
  -stamp (v.)
  stand
  stitch
  stroke
  stuff
  -tailored (u.m.)

tap
  tool
  -tooled (u.m.)
  -tooling (u.m.)
  truck
  weave
  wheel
  worked
  woven
  write (v.)
  written
  wrought
  hands#free
  handlebar
hang
  dog
  nail
  net
  out (n., u.m.)
  up (n.)
hanger
  -back
  -on
  -up
happy-go-lucky
hara-kiri
harbor
  master
  side
hard
  -and-fast (u.m.)
  back (beetle)
  -baked (u.m.)
  -bitten (u.m)
  -boiled (u.m.)
  case
  copy (n.)
  core
  #disk
  #drive
  fist (n.)
  handed
  hat (n.)

head
  -hit (u.m.)
  -looking (u.m.)
  mouthed
  nose
  pan
  -pressed (u.m.)
  -set (u.m.)
  #shell (n.)
  ship
  spun
  stand
  tack
  top (auto)
  ware
  -won (u.m.)
  #work
  -working (u.m.)
  wrought
hare
  brain
  foot
  hound
  lip
  -mad (u.m.)
harness-making
  (u.m.)
harum-scarum
harvesttime
has-been (n.)
hashmark
hat
  band
  box
  brim
  brush
  cleaner
  pin
  rack
  rail
  stand
  #tree
hatchback

hatchet-faced (u.m.)
haul
  about (n., u.m.)
  away (n., u.m.)
  back (n.)
have-not (n., u.m.)
haversack
hawk
  bill
  -billed (u.m.)
  head
  -nosed (u.m.)
hawse
  hole
  pipe
hay
  band
  cap
  cart
  cock
  #fever
  field
  fork
  lift
  loft
  market
  mow
  rack
  rake
  rick
  -scented (u.m.)
  seed
  stack
  wire
hazardous
  #waste#site
hazel
  -eyed (u.m.)
  nut
he-man
head
  ache
  achy

band
bander
block
cap
chair
cheese
chute
cloth
count
dress
-ender
first
frame
gate
gear
hunter
lamp
ledge
lighting
liner
lock
long
master
mistress
mold
most
note
-on (u.m.)
phone
plate
post
quarters
rail
reach
rest
ring
rope
set
shake
sill
space
spin
spring

stall
stand
start
stick
stock
stream
strong
waiter
wall
wind
header-up
heal-all (n., u.m.)
heart
  ache
  aching
  beat
  block
  blood
  break
  burn
  deep
  felt
  free (u.m.)
  grief
  heavy
  leaf
  -leaved (u.m.)
  nut
  quake
  seed
  sick
  sore
  string
  struck
  throb
  -throbbing (u.m.)
  -weary (u.m.)
hearth
  rug
  warming
heat
  drops
  #pump

#rash
-resistant (u.m.)
stroke
treat (v.)
-treating (u.m.)
#wave
heaven
  bound
  -inspired (u.m.)
  -sent (u.m.)
heaver
  -off
  -out
  -over
heavy
  back
  -duty (u.m.)
  -eyed (u.m.)
  -footed (u.m.)
  handed
  -looking (u.m.)
  -set (u.m.)
  #water
  weight (n., u.m.)
hecto (c.f.)
  all one word
hedge
  born
  breaker
  hog
  hop
  pig
  row
  #trimmer
heel
  ball
  band
  block
  cap
  fast
  grip
  pad
  path

plate
post
print
ring
stay
strap
tap
helio (c.f.)
  all one word
hell
  bender
  bent
  born
  bound
  bred
  cat
  diver
  dog
  fire
  hole
  hound
  -red (u.m.)
helpmeet
helter-skelter
hemstitch
hema (c.f.)
  all one word
hemato (c.f.)
  all one word
hemi (pref.)
  all one word
hemo (c.f.)
  all one word
hemp
  seed
  string
hen
  bill
  coop
  -feathered (u.m.)
  house
  pecked
  roost

hence
  forth
  forward
hepato (c.f.)
  all one word
hepta (c.f.)
  all one word
here
  about
  after
  at
  by
  from
  in
  inabove
  inafter
  inbefore
  into
  of
  on
  to
  tofore
  under
  unto
  upon
  with
herringbone
hetero (c.f.)
  -ousia, etc.
  rest one word
hexa (c.f.)
  all one word
hi-fi
hide
  -and-seek (n., u.m.)
  away (n., u.m.)
  out (n., u.m.)
high
  ball
  binder
  born
  bred

brow (nonliteral)
  -caliber (u.m.)
  -class (u.m.)
  -density
  flier (n.)
  flying (u.m.)
  -foreheaded (u.m.)
  #frequency
  handed
  -hat (v.)
  jinks
  lander
  #light (literal)
  light (nonlit.)
  -minded (u.m.)
  -power (u.m.)
  -pressure (u.m., v.)
  -priced (u.m.)
  #proof
  -reaching (u.m.)
  -rigger (n.)
  rise (building)
  road
  #seas
  -speed (u.m.)
  stepper
  -tension (u.m.)
  #tide
  -up (u.m.)
  #water
higher-up (n.)
hill
  culture (farming)
  side
  top
hind
  brain
  cast
  gut (n.)
  head
  leg

most
quarter
saddle
sight
wing
hip
  bone
  mold
  shot
hippo (c.f.)
  all one word
histo (c.f.)
  all one word
hit
  -and-miss (u.m.)
  -and-run (u.m.)
  -or-miss (u.m.)
hitchhiker
hoarfrost
hoary-haired (u.m.)
hob
  goblin
  nail
  nob
hobbyhorse
hockshop
hocus-pocus
hod#carrier
hodgepodge
hog
  back
  -backed (u.m.)
  -faced (u.m.)
  fat
  frame
  hide
  nose (machine)
  -nosed (u.m.)
  pen
  sty
  -tie (v.)
  wash
  -wild (u.m.)

hog's-back (geol.)
hogshead
hoistaway (n.)
hold
  all (n., u.m.)
  back (n., u.m.)
  -clear (n., u.m.)
  down (n., u.m.)
  fast (n., u.m.)
  off (n., u.m.)
  out (n., u.m.)
  up (n., u.m.)
holder
  -forth
  -on
  -up
hole
  #in#one
  -high (u.m.)
  -in-the-wall (n.)
  through
hollow
  back
    (bookbinding)
  -backed (u.m.)
  -eyed (u.m.)
  faced
  -ground (u.m.)
holo (c.f.)
  all one word
holy
  #day
  stone
home
  -baked (u.m.)
  body
  born
  bred
  brew
  builder
  #buyer
  comer
  coming

-fed (u.m.)
felt
folk
freeze (u.m., v.)
front
furnishings (n.)
going
grown
lander
life
made
maker
owner
#ownership
plate
#rule
seeker
sick
spun
stead
stretch
town
woven
homeo (c.f.)
  all one word
home#page
homo
  #legalis
  #sapiens
homo (c.f.)
  -ousia, etc.
  rest one word
honey
  -colored (u.m.)
  comb
  -cured (u.m.)
  dew
  drop
  eater
  -laden (u.m.)
  lipped
  moon
  mouthed

pot
sucker
sweet
honor
  bound
  #guard
  #man
hood
  cap
  mold
  wink
hoof
  beat
  mark
  print
  -printed (u.m.)
hook
  ladder
  nose
  -nosed (u.m.)
  pin
  up (n., u.m.)
hooker
  -off
  -on
  -out
  -over
  -up
hoopstick
hop
  about (n., u.m.)
  off (n., u.m.)
  scotch
  toad
hope#chest
hopper
  burn
  dozer
horehound
hormono (c.f.)
  all one word
horn
  bill

blende
blower
-eyed (u.m.)
pipe
stay
tip
hornyhanded
horse
  back
  breaker
  car
  cloth
  dealer
  fair
  fight
  flesh
  hair
  head
  herd
  hide
  hoof
  -hour
  jockey
  laugh
  meat
  mint
  play
  pond
  power-hour
  power-year
  pox
  race
  #sense (n.)
  shoe
  thief
  #trade
  whip
hot
  bed
  blood
  -blooded (u.m.)
  brain
  cake

-cold
dog
foot
head (n.)
-mix (u.m.)
pack
patch
plate
-press (v.)
rod (nonliteral)
-roll (v.)
-rolled (u.m.)
spot
-work (v).
hotelkeeper
houndshark
hourglass
house
  breaking
  broken
  builder
  #call
  cleaner
  -cleaning (u.m.)
  coat
  dress
  father
  furnishing(s) (n.)
  guest
  hold
  husband
  mother
  owner
  parent
  pest
  plant
  -raising (u.m.)
  ridden
  top
  trailer
  wares
  warming
  wife

how
  -do-you-do (n.)
  ever
  soever
hub
  cap
  -deep (u.m.)
  humankind
humble
  bee
  -looking (u.m.)
  mouthed
  -spirited (u.m.)
  humdrum
hump
  back
  -shouldered
    (u.m.)
  humpty-dumpty
  hunchback
hundred
  fold
  -legged (u.m.)
  -percenter
  -pounder
  weight
  hung-up (u.m.)
hunger
  -mad (u.m.)
  -worn (u.m.)
  hurly-burly
hush
  -hush
  #money
  up (n., u.m.)
hydro (c.f.)
  all one word
  hydro#station
hygro (c.f.)
  all one word
hyper (pref.)
  -Dorian, etc.
  linked

text
  rest one word
hypo (c.f.)
  all one word
hystero (c.f.)
  -oophorectomy
  -salpingo-oopho-
    rectomy
  rest one word

I

I
  -bar
  -beam
  -iron
  -rail
ice
  berg
  blind
  #blindness
  blink
  block
  bone
  breaker
  cap
  -clad (u.m.)
  -cold (u.m.)
  -cooled (u.m.)
  -covered (u.m.)
  #cream
  fall
  #fishing
  floe (island)
  flow (current)
  -free (u.m.)
  maker
  melt
  pack
  plant
  plow
  quake
  #storm
  #water

ideo (c.f.)
  -unit
  rest one word
idle
  headed
  -looking (u.m.)
  -minded (u.m.)
ileo (c.f.)
  all one word
ilio (c.f.)
  all one word
ill
  -advised (u.m.)
  -being (n.)
  -born (u.m.)
  -bred (u.m.)
  #breeding (n.)
  -doing (n., u.m.)
  -fated (u.m.)
  -humored (u.m.)
  -looking (u.m.)
  -treat (v.)
  -use (v.)
  #will
  -wisher
  -wishing (u.m.)
in
  -and-in (u.m.)
  -and-out (u.m.)
  -and-outer
  -being (u.m.)
  -flight (u.m.)
  -house
  -law (n.)
  asmuch, sofar
  #re, #rem, #situ,
    etc.
in (pref.)
  active (u.m.)
  breeding
  depth (u.m.)
  hospital (u.m.)
  migration (u.m.)

service
(u.m.), etc.
inch
-deep (u.m.)
-long (u.m.)
meal
-pound
-ton
worm
index-digest
indigo
-blue (u.m.)
-carmine (u.m.)
Indo (c.f.)
chinese
-European, etc.
infra (pref.)
-anal
-auricular
-axillary
-esophageal
-umbilical
rest one word
ink
-black (u.m.)
mixer
pot
slinger
spot
-spotted (u.m)
stain
stand
well
inner
-city (u.m.)
#man
spring
ino (c.f.)
all one word
insect-borne (u.m.)
inter (pref.)
-American, etc.
rest one word

intra (pref.)
-atomic, etc.
rest one word
intro (pref.)
all one word
Irish
-American (u.m.)
-born (u.m.)
iron
#age
back
-braced (u.m.)
clad
fisted
-free (u.m.)
handed
hard
-lined (u.m.)
mold
-red (u.m.)
shod
shot (mineral)
(u.m.)
#shot (golf)
side
-willed (u.m.)
works
ironer-up
island
-born (u.m.)
-dotted (u.m.)
iso (c.f.)
-octane
-oleic
-osmosis
rest one word
ivory
-tinted (u.m.)
type (photog.)
-white (u.m.)
ivy
-clad (u.m.)
-covered (u.m.)

J
J-bolt
jack
ass
hammer
head
-in-the-box
knife
-of-all-trades
-o'-lantern
-plane (v.)
pot
rabbit
screw
jail
bird
house
jam
nut
packed
Java
#applets
Beans
Script
jaw
bone
breaker
-locked (u.m.)
twister
jay
hawk
walk
jelly
bean
roll
jerry
-build (v.)
builder
-built (u.m.)
jet
#airliner
#airplane
-black (u.m.)

lag
liner
port
-powered (u.m.)
prop
-propelled (u.m.)
#propulsion
stream
wash
jewel
-bright (u.m.)
-studded (u.m.)
jib
head
-o-jib
stay
jig
-a-jig
back
-drill (v.)
saw
job
#lot
seeker
#shop
site
joggle#piece
joint#owner
joulemeter
joy
hop
ride
stick
jump
master
off (n., u.m.)
rock
jungle
-clad (u.m.)
-covered (u.m.)
#gym
side
junkpile

jury
  #box
  -fixing (u.m.)
  -rigged (u.m.)
just#in#time
juxta (c.f.)
  -ampullar
  -articular
  rest one word

K

K
  #car
  -ration
  -term
keel
  block
  fat
  haul
  -laying (u.m.)
  #line
keepsake
kerato (c.f.)
  all one word
kettle
  drum
  stitch
key
  board
  bolt
  hole
  lock
  note
  punch
  ring
  seat
  stone
  stop
  word
  worker
kick
  about (n., u.m.)
  back (n., u.m.)

  -in (n., u.m.)
  off (n., u.m.)
  out (n., u.m.)
  up (n., u.m.)
killjoy
kiln
  -dry (u.m., v.)
  eye
  hole
  rib
  stick
  tree
kilo (pref.)
  gram-meter
  voltampere
  watthour
  rest one word
kindheart
king
  bolt
  #crab
  head
  hood
  hunter
  maker
  piece
  pin
kins
  folk
  people
kiss-off (n., u.m.)
kite
  flier
  flying
knapsack
knee
  -braced (u.m.)
  brush
  cap
  -deep (u.m.)
  -high (u.m.)
  hole
  -jerk (u.m.)

  pad
  pan
  strap
knick
  knack
  point
knight
  -errant
  head
  hood
knitback
knock
  about (n., u.m.)
  away (n., u.m.)
  down (n., u.m.)
  -knee (n.)
  -kneed (u.m.)
  off (n., u.m.)
  -on (n., u.m.)
  out (n., u.m.)
  up (n., u.m.)
knocker
  -off
  -up
knot
  hole
  horn
know
  -all (n., u.m.)
  -how (n., u.m.)
  -it-all (n., u.m.)
  -little (n., u.m.)
  -nothing (n., u.m.)
knuckle
  bone
  buster
  -deep (u.m.)
  -kneed (u.m.)

L

L
  -bar

  -beam
  -block
  -shaped
  -square
labio (c.f.)
  all one word
laborsaving
lace
  -edged (u.m.)
  #edging
  wing (insect)
  -winged (u.m.)
  worked
lackluster
ladder-backed (u.m.)
lady
  beetle
  finger
  killer
  ship
lake
  bed
  front
  lander
  shore
  side
lameduck (nonliteral) (n., u.m.)
lamp
  black
  -blown (u.m.)
  -foot
  hole
  -hour
  house
  lighter
  lit
  post
  shade
  stand
  wick

land
#base
-based (u.m.)
#bird
borne
fall
fast
fill
flood
form
grabber
-grant (u.m.)
holding
lady
locked
look
lord
lubber
mark
mass
mine
#office
owner
-poor (u.m.)
right
scape
sick
side
slide
slip
spout
storm
wash
wire
wrack
lantern-jawed
   (u.m.)
lap
belt
-lap
robe
streak
top

weld (v.)
-welded (u.m.)
-welding (u.m.)
large
-eyed
-handed (u.m.)
-minded (u.m.)
mouthed
-scale (u.m.)
lark
-colored (u.m.)
spur
laryngo (c.f.)
   all one word
last
-born (u.m.)
-cited (u.m.)
-ditcher
-named (u.m.)
latch
bolt
key
string
late
-born (u.m.)
comer
-lamented (u.m.)
-maturing (u.m.)
latero (c.f.)
   all one word
lath-backed (u.m.)
lathe-bore (v.)
latter
-day (u.m.)
most
lattice
#stitch
work
laughing
#gas
stock
launch
#pad

site
laundry#room
law
-abiding (u.m.)
book
breaker
-fettered (u.m.)
giver
#office
suit
lawnmower
lay
away (n., u.m.)
back (n., u.m.)
-by (n.)
down (n., u.m.)
-minded (u.m.)
off (n., u.m.)
on (n., u.m.)
out (n., u.m.)
up (n., u.m.)
layer
-on
-out
-over
-up
lazy
bones
boots
#guy
legs
lead
-alpha
-burn (v.)
-filled (u.m.)
-gray (u.m.)
-in (n., u.m.)
line
#line (medical,
   naut. only)
off (n., u.m.)
out (n., u.m.)
#pencil

time
leaden
-eyed (u.m.)
pated
-souled (u.m.)
leader#line
leaf
bud
-clad (u.m.)
-eating (u.m.)
-shaped (u.m.)
stalk
lean
-faced (u.m.)
-looking (u.m.)
-to (n., u.m.)
leap
frog
#year
lease
back (n., u.m.)
hold
leased-line
leather
back
-backed (u.m.)
-bound (u.m.)
-brown (u.m.)
-covered (u.m.)
head
neck
side
ware
leavetaking
lee-bow (v.)
leech
eater
#rope
left
-bank (v.)
#field (sports)
-hand (u.m.)
-handed (u.m.)

-hander
  most
  -sided (u.m.)
  wing (political)
leg
  band
  puller
  rope (v.)
  work
  lend-lease (n., u.m.)
length
  ways
  wise
lepto (c.f.)
  all one word
let
  down (n., u.m.)
  off (n., u.m.)
  up (n., u.m.)
letter
  bomb
  #carrier
  drop
  gram
  head
  -perfect (u.m.)
  press
  space
  writer
leuc(o) (c.f.)
  all one word
liberal-minded
  (u.m.)
lieutenant
  #colonel
  -colonelcy
  #governor
  -governorship
life
  belt
  blood
  boat
  #buoy

#cycle
-cycle (u.m.)
  drop
  float
  giver
  giving
  guard
  hold
  jacket
  long
#net
  raft
  ring
  saver
  -size (u.m.)
  -sized (u.m.)
  span
  spring
  stream
  style
  tide
  time
  vest
  weary (u.m.)
lift-off (n., u.m.)
light
  -armed (u.m.)
  -clad (u.m.)
  -colored (u.m.)
  -drab (u.m.)
  -draft (u.m.)
  face (printing)
  -footed (u.m.)
  handed
  house#keeping
    (nautical)
  #housekeeping
    (domestic)
  mouthed
  -producing (u.m.)
  ship
  -struck (u.m.)
  weight (n., u.m.)

-year
lighter-than-air
  (u.m.)
like
  -looking (u.m.)
  -minded (u.m.)
lily
  handed
  -shaped (u.m.)
  -white (u.m.)
lime
  #juice
  kiln
  lighter
  pit
  quat
  stone
  wash
  water
linch
  bolt
  pin
line
  -bred (u.m.)
  -breed (v.)
  casting
  crew
  cut (printing)
  finder
  -item (u.m.)
  up (n., u.m.)
  walker
link
  up (n., u.m.)
  #up (v.)
lion
  -bold (u.m.)
  -headed (u.m.)
  hearted
  -maned (u.m.)
lip
  read
  service

  stick
listener-in
litho (c.f.)
  -offset
  rest one word
little
  -known (u.m.)
  neck (clam)
  -used (u.m.)
live
  #load
  long
  stock
  #wire
  wire (nonliteral)
liver
  -brown (u.m.)
  -colored (u.m.)
  wurst
living#room
loadmeter
loanword
lob
  fig
  lolly
lobster-tailed (u.m.)
lock
  box
  fast
  hole
  jaw
  nut
  out (n., u.m.)
  pin
  ring
  step
  stitch
  up (n., u.m.)
  washer
locker#room
lode
  star
  stone

log
- book
- in
- jam
- on
- off
- roll
- sheet
- loggerhead

logo (c.f.)
- *all one word*

long
- -awaited (u.m.)
- beard (n.)
- -bearded (u.m.)
- -billed (u.m.)
- bow
- cloth
- -distance (u.m.)
- -drawn (u.m.)
- felt
- hair (n.)
- -haired (u.m.)
- hand (nonliteral)
- -handed (u.m.)
- -handled (u.m.)
- head (n.)
- horn (cattle)
- -horned (u.m.)
- johns
- #jump
- leaf
- -leaved (u.m.)
- -legged (u.m.)
- legs (n.)
- -lived (u.m.)
- mouthed
- -necked (u.m.)
- nose (n.)
- -nosed (u.m.)
- -past (u.m.)
- play (records)
- playing (u.m.)

run (u.m.)
- shoreman
- spun
- standing (u.m.)
- stitch
- #term (n.)
- -term (u.m.)
- wave (radio)
- ways
- wool (sheep)

look
- down (n., u.m.)
- -in (n., u.m.)
- out (n., u.m.)
- over (n., u.m.)
- #over (v.)
- through (n., u.m.)
- looker-on

loop
- hole
- #knot
- stitch

loose
- leaf (u.m.)
- mouthed
- -tongued (u.m.)

lop
- -eared (u.m.)
- sided

loud
- mouthed
- #speaker (orator)
- speaker (radio)
- -voiced (u.m.)

love
- bird
- born
- -inspired (u.m.)
- #knot
- lorn
- seat
- sick

low
- born
- boy
- bred
- brow (nonliteral)
- browed (nonliteral)
- -built (u.m.)
- down (n., u.m.)
- -downer
- -lander
- -lived (u.m.)
- -lying (u.m.)
- -power (u.m.)
- -pressure (u.m.)
- rise
- #water

lower
- case (printing)
- #deck
- most

lug
- bolt
- mark
- sail
- lukewarm

lumber
- jack
- #room

lumbo (c.f.)
- -ovarian
- *rest one word*
- lumen-hour

lunch
- box
- #hour
- room
- time
- lying-in (n., u.m.)

M

M-day
macebearer

machine
- -finished (u.m.)
- gun
- -hour
- -made (u.m.)
- #shop
- #work

macro (c.f.)
- *all one word*

mad
- brain
- cap
- man (n.)
- #money

made
- -over (u.m.)
- -up (u.m.)

magnetite
- -basalt
- -olivinite
- -spinellite

magneto (c.f.)
- -optics
- *rest one word*
- mahjong

maid
- #of#honor
- servant

maiden
- hair
- head
- hood
- #name

mail
- bag
- clad
- clerk
- guard
- -order (u.m.)
- pouch
- room
- slot
- truck

main
frame
mast
pin
sail
sheet
spring
stay
stream
(nonliteral)
top
topmast
#yard
major
-domo
#league
-leaguer
-minor
make
-believe (n., u.m.)
fast (n.)
over
ready (printing)
shift
up (n., u.m.)
weight
maker
-off
-up
making#up
mal (c.f.)
all one word
man
back
-child
-created (u.m.)
-day
eater
-fashion (u.m.)
-grown (u.m.)
handle
hater
-high (u.m.)

hole
-hour
killer
kind
made (u.m.)
-minute
-of-war (ship)
power
servant
-size (u.m.)
slaughter
slayer
stealer
stopper
trap
-woman
-year
manic-depressive
manifold
mantel
piece
shelf
tree
many
-colored (u.m.)
-folded (u.m.)
-layered (u.m.)
plies
-sided (u.m.)
mapreader
marble
head
-looking (u.m.)
-topped (u.m.)
-white (u.m.)
mare's
-nest
-tail
mark
down (n., u.m.)
off (n., u.m.)
shot
up (n., u.m.)

marker
-down
-off
-up
marketplace
marrowbone
marsh
buck
mallow
(confection)
#mallow (plant)
mass
-minded (u.m.)
-produce (v.)
mast
-brown (u.m.)
head
master
#at#arms
mind
#of#ceremonies
piece
ship
#stroke
#workman
mat-covered (u.m.)
match
book
head
-lined (u.m.)
mark
safe
stick
maxi (n.)
maxi (pref.)
all one word
May
#Day
-day (u.m.)
pole
tide
may
be (adv.)

beetle
day (distress call)
hap
mealymouth
mean
-acting (u.m.)
-spirited (u.m.)
time
(meanwhile)
#time
(astronomical)
tone (u.m.)
while
meat
ball
cutter
-eater
-fed (u.m.)
hook
-hungry (u.m.)
packer
works
wrapper
mechanico (c.f.)
all one word
medico (c.f.)
all one word
medio (c.f.)
all one word
medium
-brown (u.m.)
-size(d) (u.m.)
weight (n., u.m.)
meek
-eyed (u.m.)
hearted
-spirited (u.m.)
meetingplace
megalo (c.f.)
all one word
melon
grower
-laden (u.m.)

-shaped (u.m.)
melt
  down (n., u.m.)
  water
men
  folk
  kind
meningo (c.f.)
  all one word
menu-driven
merry
  -go-round
  meeting
  -minded (u.m.)
meshbag
meso (c.f.)
  all one word
mess
  hall
  kit
  room
  tin
  -up (n., u.m.)
meta (pref.)
  all one word
metal
  ammonium
  -clad (u.m.)
  -coated (u.m.)
  -lined (u.m.)
  works
meter
  -amperes
  gram
  -kilogram
  -kilogram-second
  -millimeter
metro (c.f.)
  all one word
mezzo
  graph
  relievo
  soprano

tint
micro (c.f.)
  -organism
  rest one word
mid (c.f.)
  -American, etc.
  -April
  day
  -decade
  -dish
  -ice
  -level
  -1958
  -Pacific, etc.
  -Victorian, etc.
  rest one word
middle
  -aged (u.m.)
  breaker
  brow (nonliteral)
  -burst (v.)
  buster
  #ear
  #ground
  man (nonliteral)
  most
  -of-the-roader
  -sized (u.m.)
  splitter
  weight
midi (n.)
midi (pref.)
  all one word
mighty-handed
  (u.m.)
mil-foot
mild
  -cured (u.m.)
  -mannered (u.m.)
  -spoken (u.m.)
mile
  -long (u.m.)
  -ohm

post
  -pound
  -ton
  -wide (u.m.)
milk
  -fed (u.m.)
  head
  #run
  shake
  shed
  sick
  sop
  -white (u.m.)
mill
  cake
  course
  dam
  feed
  hand
  -headed (u.m.)
  pond
  post
  race
  ring
  stock
  stream
  wright
milli (c.f.)
  gram-hour
  rest one word
mincemeat
mind
  #healer
  -healing (u.m.)
  reader
  set (n.)
  sight
mine
  field
  layer
  ship
  sweeper
  thrower

works
mini (n.)
mini (pref.)
  all one word
minor
  #league
  -leaguer
minute#book
mirror
  -faced (u.m.)
  scope
mis (pref.)
  all one word
mischiefmaking
mist
  bow
  -clad (u.m.)
  -covered (u.m.)
  fall
miter
  #box
  -lock (v.)
mix
  blood
  up (n.)
mixing#room
mizzenmast
mock
  -heroic (u.m.)
  #turtle
  up (n., u.m.)
mocker-up
mocking
  stock
  -up (u.m.)
mold
  made (u.m.)
  #shop
mole
  catcher
  -eyed (u.m.)
  head
  hill

money
  bag
  changer
  getter
  grubber
  lender
  -mad (u.m.)
  maker
  saver
monkey
  -faced (u.m.)
  nut
  pod
  pot
  shine
  #wrench
mono (c.f.)
  -ideistic
  -iodo
  -iodohydrin
  -ion
  -ousian
  rest one word
month
  end
  long (u.m.)
moon
  beam
  blind
  #blindness
  blink
  born
  -bright (u.m.)
  eye
  face
  gazing
  glow
  head
  lighter
  lit
  -mad (u.m.)
  path
  rise

sail
set
shade
shine
shot
sick
struck
tide
walker
-white (u.m.)
moosecall
mop
  head
  stick
  up (n., u.m.)
mopper-up
mopping-up (u.m.)
morning
  #sickness
  #star
  tide
mosquito
  -free (u.m.)
  #net
moss
  back
  -clad (u.m.)
  -green (u.m.)
  -grown (u.m.)
  head
  -lined (u.m.)
most-favored-nation
  (u.m.)
moth
  ball
  -eaten (u.m.)
  hole
  proof
mother
  board
  hood
  -in-law
  -of-pearl

moto (c.f.)
  all one word
motor
  bike
  bus
  cab
  cade
  car
  coach
  cycle
  -driven (u.m.)
  jet
  -minded (u.m.)
  #scooter
  ship
  truck
  van
moundbuilder
mountain
  -high (u.m.)
  side
  top
  -walled (u.m.)
mouse
  -brown (u.m.)
  -eared (u.m.)
  -eaten (u.m.)
  hole
  trap
mouth
  -filling (u.m.)
  -made (u.m.)
  piece
  wash
muck
  rake (v.)
  raker
  sweat
muco (c.f.)
  all one word
mud
  bank
  bath

-colored (u.m.)
  flat
  flow
  guard
  head
  hole
  lark
  sill
  slinger
  -splashed (u.m.)
  stain
  sucker
  track
  #turtle
muddlehead
mule
  back
  #deer
  skinner
multi (c.f.)
  all one word
multiple-purpose
  (u.m.)
muscle
  bound
  power
music
  lover
  -mad (u.m.)
  maker
  room
musico (c.f.)
  all one word
musk
  #deer
  melon
  #ox
  rat
mutton
  #chop (meat)
  chop (shape)
  fist
  head

myria (c.f.)
  all one word
mytho (c.f.)
  all one word
myxo (c.f.)
  all one word

N
nail
  bin
  brush
  head
  -headed (u.m.)
  #hole
  print
  puller
  rod
  -shaped (u.m.)
  -studded (u.m.)
name
  -calling (u.m.)
  -dropping (u.m.)
  plate
  sake
nano (c.f.)
  all one word
naptime
narco (c.f.)
  all one word
narrow
  -mouthed (u.m.)
  minded
naso (c.f.)
  -occipital
  -orbital
  rest one word
nationwide
native-born (u.m.)
navy-blue (u.m.)
naysayer
near
  by
  -miss

sighted
neat's-foot (u.m.)
neck
  band
  bone
  -breaking (u.m.)
  cloth
  -deep (u.m.)
  fast
  guard
  -high (u.m.)
  hole
  lace
  line
  mold
  tie
necro (c.f.)
  all one word
needle
  bill
  case
  -made (u.m.)
  nose (pliers)
  point
  -shaped (u.m.)
  -sharp (u.m.)
  worked
ne'er-do-well
neo (c.f.)
  -Greek, etc.
  rest one word
nephro (c.f.)
  all one word
nerve
  ache
  -celled (u.m.)
  -racked (u.m.)
net
  ball
  braider
  -veined (u.m.)
  work
  #worth

nettle
  fire
  foot
  some
neuro (c.f.)
  all one word
never
  -ending (u.m.)
  more
  theless
new
  born
  -car (u.m.)
  comer
  -created (u.m.)
  fangled
  -fashioned (u.m.)
  -front (v.)
  -made (u.m.)
  -mown (u.m.)
  -rich (u.m.)
newlywed
news
  boy
  case
  cast
  clip
  dealer
  #editor
  letter
  paper
  paper#work
  photo
  print
  reader
  reel
  sheet
  stand
  story
  teller
nick
  -eared (u.m.)
  name

nickel
  plate (v.)
  -plated (u.m.)
  -plating (u.m.)
  type
night
  -black (u.m.)
  #blindness
  cap
  -clad (u.m.)
  clothes
  club
  dress
  fall
  -fly (aviation) (v.)
  -flying (u.m.)
  gown
  -grown (u.m.)
  hawk
  long (u.m.)
  mare
  #school
  shade
  #shift
  shirt
  side
  tide
  walker
nimble
  -fingered (u.m.)
  footed
nimbostratus
  (clouds)
nine
  fold
  #holes
  -lived (u.m.)
  pin
  score
nitpicker
nitro (c.f.)
  -hydro-carbon
  rest one word

no
  -account (n., u.m.)
  -fault
  -fee
  -good (n., u.m.)
  -hitter (n.)
  how
  #man's land
  #one
  -par (u.m.)
  -par-value (u.m.)
  -show (n., u.m.)
  -thoroughfare (n.)
  whit
  -year (funds)
noble
  -born (u.m.)
  -featured (u.m.)
  heartedness
  -looking (u.m.)
  -minded (u.m.)
nol-pros (v.)
non
  -civil-service
       (u.m.)
  -European, etc.
  -interactive
  -pros (v.)
  #sequitur, etc.
  -tumor-bearing
       (u.m.)
  as prefix, one
       word
none
  such
  theless
noon
  day
  tide
  time
north
  -central (u.m.)

east
going
most
-northeast
-sider
nose
  bag
  bleed
  bone
  dive
  down (n., u.m.)
  gay
  guard
  -high (u.m.)
  hole
  -led (u.m.)
  over (n., u.m.)
  pipe
  ring
  -thumbing (u.m.)
  up (n., u.m.)
  wheel
note
  book
  #paper
  worthy
notwithstanding
novel
  -reading (u.m.)
  #writer
  -writing (u.m.)
nucleo (c.f.)
  all one word
nut
  breaker
  -brown (u.m.)
  cake
  cracker
  hatch
  hook
  pecker
  pick
  -shaped (u.m.)

shell
sweet

O

oak
  -beamed (u.m.)
  -clad (u.m.)
  -green (u.m.)
  #leaf
  -leaved (u.m.)
oar
  -footed (u.m.)
  lock
oarsman
oat
  bin
  cake
  -fed (u.m.)
  meal
  seed
oathbreaker
object-oriented
oblong
  -elliptic (u.m.)
  -leaved (u.m.)
  -linear (u.m.)
  -ovate (u.m.)
  -shaped (u.m.)
  -triangular (u.m.)
occipito (c.f.)
  -otic
  rest one word
ocean
  -born (u.m.)
  borne
  -girdled (u.m.)
  going
  side
  -spanning (u.m.)
octo (c.f.)
  all one word
odd
  -jobber

-job man
-looking (u.m.)
man (arbiter)
-numbered (u.m.)
off
-and-on (u.m.)
beat
cast
center (u.m.)
color (u.m.)
-colored (u.m.)
cut (printing)
day
-fall (v.)
-flavor (n., u.m.)
-flow
-go (n.)
going
grade
hand
-hours
line
loading
look
-lying (u.m.)
peak
print
put
-reckoning (n.)
saddle
scape
scour
scum
-season
set
shoot
shore
side
site
-sorts (n.)
spring
stage
street

take
-the-record (u.m.)
type
-wheel (n.)
-wheeler (n.)
-white (u.m.)
#year
office
#boy
holder
seeker
-seeking (u.m.)
oftentimes
ofttimes
ohm
-ammeter
meter
-mile
oil
#burner
cake
can
cloth
coat
cup
-driven (u.m.)
-fed (u.m.)
field
-forming (u.m.)
-harden (v.)
hole
meal
paper
proofing
seed
#shale
skinned
-soaked (u.m.)
spill (n.)
stove
-temper (v.)
tightness
#well

old
-fashioned (u.m.)
-fogy (u.m.)
-growing (u.m.)
-looking (u.m.)
#maid
-maidish (u.m.)
#man
-new
  style (printing)
  timer
#woman
-young
oleo
#butter
#gear
#oil
#strut
*as combining
  form, one word*
olive
-brown (u.m.)
-clad (u.m.)
-drab (u.m.)
-growing (u.m.)
#oil
-skinned (u.m.)
wood
#wood (color)
omni (c.f.)
-ignorant
rest one word
on
-and-off (n., u.m.)
board (u.m.)
-go (n.)
going
line#service
site
*noun, adjective,
  one word*
once
-over (n.)

-run (u.m.)
one
-armed (u.m.)
-decker
-eyed (u.m.)
fold
-half
-handed (u.m.)
ness
-piece (u.m.)
self
-sided (u.m.)
-sidedness
signed (u.m.)
-step (dance)
-striper
time (formerly)
  (u.m.)
-time (one action)
  (u.m.)
-two-three
-way (u.m.)
onion
peel
skin
op-ed
(newspaper)
open
-air (u.m.)
-armed (u.m.)
-back (u.m.)
-backed (u.m.)
band (yarn)
cast
cut (mining)
-end (u.m.)
-ended
-faced (u.m.)
handed
#house
minded
mouthed
#shop

side (u.m.)
-sided (u.m.)
worked
opera
goer
going
#house
operating#system
ophthalmo (c.f.)
all one word
orange
ade
colored (u.m.)
peel
-red (u.m.)
stick
orchard#house
orderly#room
organo (c.f.)
all one word
ornitho (c.f.)
all one word
orrisroot
ortho (c.f.)
all one word
osteo (c.f.)
all one word
other
wise
#world
worldly
oto (c.f.)
all one word
out
-and-out (u.m.)
-and-outer (n.)
-loud (u.m.)
-Machiavelli, etc.
migration
-of-date (u.m.)
-of-door(s) (u.m.)
-of-State (u.m.)
-of-the-way (u.m.)

placement
-to-out (u.m.)
as prefix, one
word
outer
-city (u.m.)
#man
most
wear
outward
-bound (u.m.)
-bounder
ovate
-acuminate (u.m.)
-oblong (u.m.)
ovato (c.f.)
-oblong
-orbicular
rest one word
oven
baked
dried
peel
ware
over
age (surplus)
age (older) (n.,
u.m.)
all (n., u.m.)
-the-counter
(u.m.)
as combining
form, one word
owl-eyed (u.m.)
ox
biter
blood (color)
bow
brake
cart
cheek
eye
-eyed (u.m.)

gall
harrow
hide
horn
shoe
tail
#team
oxy (c.f.)
all one word
oyster
bed
#crab
house
root
seed
shell
-white (u.m.)

P
pace
maker
#setter
-setting (u.m.)
pachy (c.f.)
all one word
pack
builder
cloth
horse
-laden (u.m.)
sack
saddle
staff
thread
up (n., u.m.)
packing#box
padlock
paddlefoot
page
-for-page (u.m.)
#proof (printing)
painkiller
painstaking

paint
box
brush
mixer
pot
spray
stained (u.m.)
pale
belly
-blue (u.m.)
buck
-cheeked (u.m.)
face (n.)
-faced (u.m.)
-looking (u.m.)
-reddish (u.m.)
paleo (c.f.)
-Christian, etc.
rest one word
pallbearer
palm
-green (u.m.)
#leaf
#oil
-shaded (u.m.)
palmi (c.f.)
all one word
pan
-American, etc.
-broil (v.)
#ice
rest one word
Pan
#American Union
hellenic
panel-lined (u.m.)
panic-stricken
(u.m.)
panto (c.f.)
all one word
panty hose
paper
back (n.)

#box
#carrier
cutter
hanger
shell (n., u.m.)
-shelled (u.m.)
-thin (u.m.)
weight
-white (u.m.)
papier#mache
para (c.f. or pref.)
-analgesia
-anesthesia
legal
medic
rest one word
parcel
#carrier
-plate (v.)
#post
parchment
-covered (u.m.)
#maker
-making (u.m.)
parieto (c.f.)
-occipital
rest one word
parimutuel
park
#forest
land
way
part
-finished (u.m.)
#owner
-time (u.m.)
-timer (n.)
#way
parti (c.f.)
all one word
party#line
parvi (c.f.)
all one word

pass
  back (n.)
  book
  key
  out (n., u.m.)
  port
  through (n.,
    u.m.)
  way
  word
passenger-mile
passer(s)-by
passion
  -driven (u.m.)
  -feeding (u.m.)
  -filled (u.m.)
  #play
paste
  down (n., u.m.)
  pot
  up (n., u.m.)
pastureland
patent-in-fee
path
  breaker
  finder
  way
patho (c.f.)
  all one word
patri (c.f.)
  all one word
patrol
  man
  #wagon
pattycake
pawn
  broker
  shop
pay
  back (n., u.m.)
  check
  #cut
  day

dirt
load
off (n., u.m.)
out (n., u.m.)
#raise
roll
sheet
-TV
pea
  #coal
  coat
  cod
  -green (u.m.)
  hen
  jacket
  nut
  pod
  shooter
  -sized (u.m.)
  stick
peace
  -blessed (u.m.)
  breaker
  -loving (u.m.)
  maker
  #pipe
  time
peach
  bloom
  blow (color)
  -colored (u.m.)
  pear-shaped (u.m.)
pearl
  -eyed (u.m.)
  fishing
  -pure (u.m.)
  -set (u.m.)
  -studded (u.m.)
  -white (u.m.)
peat
  -roofed (u.m.)
  moss
  stack

pebble
  -paved (u.m.)
  -strewn (u.m.)
peeloff (n., u.m.)
peep
  eye
  hole
  show
  sight
peer-to-peer
pegleg
pellmell
pen
  -cancel (v.)
  head
  knife
  manship
  #name
  point
  pusher
  rack
  script
  -shaped (u.m.)
  stock
  trough
pencil
  #box
  holder
  -mark (v.)
penny
  -a-liner
  pincher
  weight
  winkle
  worth
pent-up (u.m.)
penta (c.f.)
  -acetate
  rest one word
pepper
  corn
  #jelly
  mint

pot
  -red (u.m.)
peptalk
per
  #annum
  cent
  #centum
  compound
    (chemical)
  current
    (botanical)
  #diem
  salt (chemical)
  #se
  sulfide
peri (pref.)
  -insular
  rest one word
permafrost
pest
  hole
  -ridden (u.m.)
petcock
petit
  grain
  #jury
  #larceny
  #point
petro (c.f.)
  -occipital
  rest one word
pharmaco (c.f.)
  -oryctology
  rest one word
pharyngo (c.f.)
  -esophageal
  -oral
  rest one word
phase
  -in (n., u.m.)
  meter
  out (n., u.m.)
  -wound (u.m.)

pheno (c.f.)
all one word
philo (c.f.)
-French, etc.
rest one word
phlebo (c.f.)
all one word
phonebook
phono (c.f.)
all one word
phospho (c.f.)
all one word
photo (c.f.)
-offset
-oxidation
-oxidative
rest one word
phrasemark (music)
phreno (c.f.)
all one word
phyllo (c.f.)
all one word
phylo (c.f.)
all one word
physico (c.f.)
all one word
physio (c.f.)
all one word
phyto (c.f.)
all one word
piano
forte
graph
#player
pick
aback
ax
lock
-me-up (n., u.m.)
off (n., u.m.)
over (n., u.m.)
#over (v.)
pocket

pole
shaft
up (n., u.m.)
picker-up
picket#line
pickle-cured (u.m.)
picture
#book
#writing
pie
bald
crust
-eater
-eyed
marker
pan
plant
#plate
-stuffed (u.m.)
#tin
piece
-dye (v.)
#goods
meal
mold
piezo (c.f.)
-oscillator
rest one word
pig
-back (v.)
-backed (u.m.)
-bellied (u.m.)
belly
-eyed (u.m.)
face
-faced (u.m.)
foot
-footed (u.m.)
headed
herd
#iron
out
pen

root
stick
sty
tailed
wash
pigeon
gram
hole
-toed (u.m.)
wing
piggyback
pike
-eyed (u.m.)
staff
pile
driver
-driving (u.m.)
hammer
up (n., u.m.)
#weave
woven
pill
pusher
rolling
taker
pillow
case
made
slip
top
pilot
#boat
house
#light
pin
ball
block
bone
case
cushion
-eyed (u.m.)
fall
feather

fire
fold
head
hold
hole
hook
lock
paper
point
prick
rail
setter
spot
stripe
-tailed (u.m.)
up (n., u.m.)
wheel
pinch
back
bar
beck
cock
fist
-hit (v.)
-hitter
penny
pine
apple
-bearing (u.m.)
-clad (u.m.)
#cone
-fringed (u.m.)
#needle
#oil
-shaded (u.m.)
#tar
pink
-blossomed (u.m.)
eye (n.)
-eyed (u.m.)
pipe
-drawn (u.m.)
dream

fitter
layer
line
-shaped (u.m.)
stem
walker
welder
pisci (c.f.)
all one word
pistol-whipped (v.)
piston
head
#pin
#rod
#valve
pit
#boss
#bull
-eyed (u.m.)
fall
head
-headed (u.m.)
hole
mark
-marked (u.m.)
-rotted (u.m.)
saw
side
pitch
-black (u.m.)
blende
#box
-colored (u.m.)
-dark (u.m.)
#darkness
fork
hole
-lined (u.m.)
man
-marked (u.m.)
out (n., u.m.)
#pipe
up (n., u.m.)

place
card
kick
plague-infested
(u.m.)
plain
back (fabric)
-bodied (u.m.)
clothes (u.m.)
clothesman
-headed (u.m.)
-looking (u.m.)
-spoken (u.m.)
woven (u.m.)
plane
#curve
load
-mile
-parallel (u.m.)
table (surveying)
plani (c.f.)
all one word
plano (c.f.)
all one word
plant
#food
life
site
plasterboard
plate
cutter
#glass
-incased (u.m.)
layer
mark
#proof (printing)
-roll (v.)
-rolled (u.m.)
platy (c.f.)
all one word
play
-act (v.)
back (n., u.m.)

bill
book
boy
broker
day
down (n., u.m.)
fellow
goer
going
ground
mate
off (n., u.m.)
pen
reader
room
script
suit
thing
time
wright
#yard
pleasure
-bent (u.m.)
#boat
-seeking (u.m.)
-tired (u.m.)
-weary (u.m.)
pleo (c.f.)
all one word
pleuro (c.f.)
all one word
plow
back (n., u.m.)
-bred (u.m.)
hand
horse
pan
point
-shaped (u.m.)
share
shoe
sole
staff

#tail
wright
plug
-and-play
hole
-in (n., u.m.)
tray
-ugly (n., u.m.)
plumbline
plume-crowned
(u.m.)
pluri (c.f.)
all one word
pluto (c.f.)
all one word
pneumato (c.f.)
-hydato-genetic
(u.m.)
rest one word
pneumo (c.f.)
all one word
pock
mark
-marked (u.m.)
-pit (v.)
pocket
book (purse)
#book (book)
-eyed (u.m.)
knife
-sized (u.m.)
-veto (v.)
poet
-artist
#laureate
-painter
pointblank
Point-to-Point
poison-dipped
(u.m.)
pole
arm
-armed (u.m.)

ax
burn
cat
-dried (u.m.)
horse
-pile (v.)
setter
-shaped (u.m.)
sitter
-stack (v.)
star
timber
trap
-vault (v.)
#vaulter
politico (c.f.)
-orthodox
rest one word
poll
book
#parrot
#tax
poly (c.f.)
all one word
poor
-blooded (u.m.)
farm
-spirited (u.m.)
pop
corn
eye
gun
up (n., u.m.)
poppy
-bordered (u.m.)
cock
-red (u.m.)
seed
pork
barrel (n., u.m.)
#chop
fish
#pie

port
cullis
fire
folio
hole
hook
manteau
-mouthed (u.m.)
side
#wine
post
#bellum
#boat
card
-Christian, etc.
-cold-war (u.m.)
#diem
-free (u.m.)
haste
#hospital
(military)
#meridiem
#mortem (literal)
mortem
(nonliteral)
#partum
#school (military)
audit, graduate,
etc.
as prefix, one
word
postal#card
pot
ash
bellied
boil
eye
hanger
head
herb
hole
hook
hunter

latch
lid
luck
pie
pourri
rack
#roast
shot
potato#field
poultry
#keeper
-keeping (u.m.)
#raiser
-raising (u.m.)
#yard
pound
cake
-foolish (u.m.)
-foot
worth
powder
-blue (u.m.)
box
#house
#keg
#mill
#room
-scorched (u.m.)
power
boat
#mower
-operated (u.m.)
pack
plant
praise
-deserving (u.m.)
-spoiled (u.m.)
worthiness
pre (pref.)
-Incan, etc.
audit, existing,
etc.
rest one word

president
-elect
#pro#tempore
press
#agent
-agentry
board
feeder
-forge (v.)
-made (u.m.)
mark
pack (v.)
plate
#proof (printing)
preter (pref.)
all one word
price
#cutter
-cutting (u.m.)
#fixer
-fixing (u.m.)
#index
list
-support (u.m.)
tag
prick
-eared (u.m.)
mark
seam
priesthood
prime
#minister
-ministerial
(u.m.)
-ministership
-ministry
prince
hood
-priest
print
cloth
out
script

printing
-in (n., u.m.)
#ink
#office
-out (n., u.m.)
prison
bound
-free (u.m.)
-made (u.m.)
prisoner-of-war
(u.m.)
prize
fighter
#ring
taker
winner
-winning (u.m.)
pro
-Ally, etc.
-choice
#football, etc.
#forma
-life
#rata
#tem
#tempore
*as prefix, one
word*
problem-solver
procto (c.f.)
all one word
profit
-and-loss (u.m.)
-sharing (u.m.)
prong
buck
-hoe (v.)
horn
-horned (u.m.)
proof
#press
read
reader

sheet
prop
jet
wash
proso (c.f.)
all one word
proto (c.f.)
-Egyptian, etc.
rest one word
proud
hearted
-looking (u.m.)
-minded (u.m.)
psalmbook
pseudo (c.f.)
-Messiah, etc.
-occidental
-official
-orientalism
-orthorhombic
-osteomalacia
-owner
rest one word
psycho (c.f.)
-organic
rest one word
ptero (c.f.)
all one word
public
hearted
-minded (u.m.)
-spirited (u.m.)
#works
pug
nose
-pile (v.)
pull
back (n., u.m.)
#box
down (n., u.m.)
-in (n., u.m.)
off (n., u.m.)
-on (n., u.m.)

out (n., u.m.)
-push (u.m.)
through (n.,
u.m.)
up (n., u.m.)
puller
-in
-out
pulp
board
wood
punch
board
bowl
card
-drunk (u.m.)
mark
-marked (u.m.)
out (n.)
punctureproof
pup#tent
pure
blood
bred
#line (biological)
purple
-blue (u.m.)
-clad (u.m.)
-colored (u.m.)
heart (wood)
purse
making
-proud (u.m.)
#strings
push
button
card
cart
off (n., u.m.)
-pull (u.m.)
up (n., u.m.)

pussy
cat
foot
#willow
put
back (n., u.m.)
off (n., u.m.)
-on (n., u.m.)
out (n., u.m.)
-put (n.)
-up (n., u.m.)
putter
-forth
-in
-off
-on
-out
-through
-up
pyo (c.f.)
all one word
pyro (c.f.)
all one word
Q
Q
-boat
-fever
quadri (c.f.)
-invariant
rest one word
quarrystone
quarter
-angled (u.m.)
back
-bloom (u.m.)
#boards
-bound (u.m.)
-breed (u.m.)
-cast (u.m.)
-cut (u.m.)
deck
-miler

#note
pace
-phase (u.m.)
saw (v.)
staff
stretch
-yearly (u.m.)
quartermaster
#general
-generalship
quasi
all hyphened
queen#bee
quick
-change (u.m., v.)
-drawn (u.m., v.)
freeze (u.m., v.)
lime
sand
set
silver
step
#time
-witted (u.m.)
quin (c.f.)
all one word
quit
claim
rent

R
rabbit
-backed (u.m.)
-eared (u.m.)
#fever
#foot
mouth
-mouthed (u.m.)
skin
race
about (n., u.m.)
course
goer

horse
track
way
radarscope
radio
generally two
words except
the following
forms
frequency
isotope
telegraph
telephone
rag
bolt
#doll
-made (u.m.)
sorter
tag
time
rail
bird
car
guard
head
-ridden (u.m.)
road
setter
splitter
#train
way#maker
wayman
rain
band
-beaten (u.m.)
bow
check
coat
drop
fall
#forest
-soft (u.m.)
spout

storm
wash
water
rakeoff (n., u.m.)
ram
jet
rod
shackle
ranch
#hand
house
Random-access
range
finder
#light
rider
rapid
#fire
#transit
rash
-brained (u.m.)
-headed (u.m.)
-hearted (u.m.)
-minded (u.m.)
rat
bite
catcher
hole
-infested (u.m.)
#race
-tailed (u.m.)
-tight (u.m.)
trap
rate
#cutter
-cutting (u.m.)
-fixing (u.m.)
payer
-raising (u.m.)
setting
rattle
brain
snake

trap
raw
boned
-edged (u.m.)
hide
-looking (u.m.)
razor
back
-billed (u.m.)
#blade
edge
-keen (u.m.)
-sharp (u.m.)
strop
razzle-dazzle
re (pref.)
-cover (cover
again)
-create (create
again), etc.
-cross-
examination
-ice
-ink
-redirect
evaluate, process,
etc.
rest one word
reading#room
read
out (n.)
through (n., u.m.)
README
ready
-built (u.m.)
-handed (u.m.)
made (u.m.)
-mix (u.m.)
#reference
room
-witted (u.m.)
rear
#end
guard

most
view (u.m.)
ward
reception#room
recordbreaker
recti (c.f.)
  all one word
recto (c.f.)
  all one word
red
  bait (v.)
  -billed (u.m.)
  -blooded (u.m.)
  bone
  buck
  cap (porter)
  coat (n.)
  eye (n.)
  -eyed (u.m.)
  -faced (u.m.)
  -haired (u.m.)
  handed
  head (n.)
  -hot (u.m.)
  -legged (u.m.)
  #line (literal)
  #man
  out (n., u.m.)
  -skinned (u.m.)
  tape (nonliteral)
  #tape (literal)
  -throated (u.m.)
  -yellow (u.m.)
reformat
regionwide
religio (c.f.)
  all one word
remote-access
repair#shop
representative
  #at#large
  -elect
research#worker

resino (c.f.)
  all one word
retro (c.f.)
  -ocular
  -omental
  -operative
  -oral
  rest one word
rheo (c.f.)
  all one word
rhino (c.f.)
  all one word
rhizo (c.f.)
  all one word
rhod(o) (c.f.)
  all one word
rhomb(o) (c.f.)
  all one word
rice
  growing
  #water
rich
  -bound (u.m.)
  -clad (u.m.)
  -looking (u.m.)
rickrack
ridge
  band
  pole
  top
riffraff
rifleshot
rig
  out (n., u.m.)
  -up (n., u.m.)
right
  about
  about-face
  -angle (u.m., v.)
  -angled (u.m.)
  #away
  #field (sports)
  -handed (u.m.)

-hander
-headed (u.m.)
  most
  -of-way
  wing (political)
rim
  -deep (u.m.)
  fire
  lock
  rock
ring
  -adorned (u.m.)
  -banded (u.m.)
  -billed (u.m.)
  bolt
  giver
  head
  -in (n., u.m.)
  lead (v.)
  leader
  -necked (u.m.)
  -off (n., u.m.)
  pin
  -porous (u.m.)
  -shaped (u.m.)
  side
  sight
  stand
  stick
  -tailed (u.m.)
  -up (n., u.m.)
  worm
rip
  cord
  -off (n., u.m.)
  rap
  roaring
  sack
  saw
  snorter
  tide
  -up (n., u.m.)

river
  bank
  bed
  #bottom
  flow
  -formed (u.m.)
  front
  head
  scape
  side
  wash
  -worn (u.m.)
road
  bank
  bed
  block
  builder
  head
  hog
  kill
  map
  #runner (bird)
  #show
  side
  -test (v.)
  way
  -weary (u.m.)
rock
  abye
  bottom
    (nonliteral)
  #climber
  -climbing (u.m.)
  fall (n.)
  -fallen (u.m.)
  fill
  firm
  pile
  -ribbed (u.m.)
  #salt
  shaft
  slide
rod-shaped (u.m.)

roe
  buck
  #deer
roentgeno (c.f.)
  all one word
roll
  about (n., u.m.)
  back (n., u.m.)
  call
  -fed (v.)
  film
  off (n., u.m.)
  -on (n., u.m.)
  out (n., u.m.)
  over (n., u.m.)
  top
  up (n., u.m.)
roller
  #blade
  #coaster
  -made (u.m.)
  -milled (u.m.)
  #skate
Romano (c.f.)
  -canonical, etc.
  -Gallic, etc.
roof
  garden
  line
  top
  tree
room
  #clerk
  keeper
  mate
roominghouse
root
  bound
  cap
  -cutting (u.m.)
  fast
  hold
  #mean#square

#rot
  stalk
  stock
rope
  dance
  layer
  stitch
  walk
rose
  -bright (u.m.)
  bud
  bush
  head
  -headed (u.m.)
  -scented (u.m.)
  -sweet (u.m.)
  tan
  #water
rotor
  craft
  ship
rotten
  -dry (u.m.)
  -minded (u.m.)
rough
  -and-ready (u.m.)
  -and-tumble (n., u.m.)
  cast (u.m., v.)
  -coat (v.)
  -cut (u.m.)
  draw (v.)
  dress (v.)
  dry (u.m., v.)
  -face (v.)
  -faced (u.m.)
  hew
  house
  -legged (u.m.)
  -looking (u.m.)
  neck
  rider
  setter

shod
  -sketch (v.)
  stuff
  tailed
  #work (n.)
  work (v.)
  wrought
rougher
  -down
  -out
  -up
roughing-in (u.m.)
round
  about (n., u.m.)
  about-face
  -faced (u.m.)
  head
  -made (u.m.)
  mouthed
  nose (tool)
  out (n., u.m.)
  robin (petition)
  seam
  table (panel)
  -tailed (u.m.)
  -topped (u.m.)
  #trip
  -tripper
  up (n., u.m.)
rub
  -a-dub
  down (n., u.m.)
rubber
  band
  -down
  -lined (u.m.)
  neck
  -off
  -set (u.m.)
  stamp
    (nonliteral) (n.,
    u.m., v.)
  #stamp (n.)

-stamped (u.m.)
ruby
  -hued (u.m.)
  -red (u.m.)
  -set (u.m.)
  -throated (u.m.)
rudder
  head
  hole
  post
  stock
rule#of#thumb
rum
  -crazed (u.m.)
  runner
  seller
rumpus#room
run
  about (n., u.m.)
  around (n., u.m.)
  away (n., u.m.)
  back (n., u.m.)
  by (n.)
  down (n., u.m.)
  -in (n., u.m.)
  off (n., u.m.)
  -on (n., u.m.)
  out (n., u.m.)
  over (n., u.m.)
  through (n., u.m.)
  up (n., u.m.)
runner-up
Russo (c.f.)
  -Chinese, etc.
  rest one word
rust
  -brown (u.m.)
  -eaten (u.m.)
  proofing
  -resistant (u.m.)
  -stained (u.m.)
rye#field

S

S
- -bend
- -brake
- -iron
- -ray
- -shaped
- -trap
- -wrench

saber
- -legged (u.m.)
- tooth
- -toothed (u.m.)

sable-cloaked (u.m.)

Sabrejet

saccharo (c.f.)
- *all one word*

sack
- bearer
- cloth
- #coat
- -coated (u.m.)
- -making (u.m.)
- -shaped (u.m.)

sacro (c.f.)
- *all one word*

sad
- -eyed (u.m.)
- iron
- #sack
- -voiced (u.m.)

saddle
- back
- -backed (u.m.)
- bag
- bow
- cloth
- -graft (v.)
- #horse
- -making (u.m.)
- nose
- -nosed (u.m.)
- sore

- -stitched (u.m.)
- tree
- -wire (u.m.)

safe
- blower
- cracker
- -deposit (u.m.)
- guard
- hold
- #house
- #site

sage
- brush
- leaf
- -leaved (u.m.)

sail
- cloth
- -dotted (u.m.)
- flying
- saintlike

sales
- book
- clerk
- manship
- people
- person

salmon
- -colored (u.m.)
- -red (u.m.)

salpingo (c.f.)
- -oophorectomy
- -oophoritis
- -ovariotomy
- -ovaritis
- *rest one word*

salt
- box
- cellar
- -cured (u.m.)
- #lick
- mouth
- pack
- pan

- peter
- pit
- pond
- shaker
- spoon
- sprinkler
- water
- works

salver
- form
- -shaped (u.m.)

sample
- #book
- #box
- maker
- -making (u.m.)

sand
- bag
- bank
- bar
- bath
- bin
- blast
- blown
- box
- -built (u.m.)
- -buried (u.m.)
- -cast (u.m., v.)
- culture
- #dune
- fill
- flea
- glass
- heat
- hill
- -hiller
- hog
- hole
- lapper
- lot
- paper
- pile
- pipe

- pit
- -pump (u.m., v.)
- shoe
- spit
- storm
- table
- weld (v.)
- -welded (u.m.)
- -welding (u.m.)

sandy-bottomed
  (u.m.)

sangfroid

sans
- #serif
- #souci

sapphire
- -blue (u.m.)
- -colored (u.m.)

sarco (c.f.)
- *all one word*

sashcord

satin
- #cloth
- -lined (u.m.)
- -smooth (u.m.)

sauce
- dish
- pan

sauer
- braten
- kraut

save-all (n., u.m.)

saw
- back
- belly
- bill (bird)
- -billed (u.m.)
- bones (n.)
- buck
- dust
- -edged (u.m.)
- horse
- setter

timber
  tooth
  -toothed (u.m.)
sax
  cornet
  horn
  tuba
say
  -nothing (n., u.m.)
  -so (n.)
scale
  bark
  down (n., u.m.)
  pan
  -reading (u.m.)
scapegoat
scapulo (c.f.)
  all one word
scar
  -clad (u.m.)
  face
  -faced (u.m.)
  #tissue
scare
  crow
  head
scarfpin
scarlet
  -breasted (u.m.)
  #fever
  -red (u.m.)
scatter
  brain
  good
  #rug
scene
  shifter
  wright
schisto (c.f.)
  all one word
schizo (c.f.)
  all one word

school
  bag
  #board
  book
  bus
  children
  day
  -made (u.m.)
  mate
  ship
  teacher
  -trained (u.m.)
  #year
scientifico (c.f.)
  all one word
scissor
  bill
  -tailed (u.m.)
  -winged (u.m.)
scissors
  hold
  -shaped (u.m.)
  #smith
sclero (c.f.)
  -oophoritis
  -optic
  rest one word
score
  board
  book
  card
  sheet
scot-free
Scoto (c.f.)
  -Britannic, etc.
Scotsman
scout
  #badge
  #car
  hood
  master
scrap
  basket

book
  #paper
  works
scratch
  brush
  -brusher
  -coated (u.m.)
  #pad
  #test
screen
  out (n., u.m.)
  play
screw
  ball
  bolt
  cap
  down (u.m.)
  drive (v.)
  -driven (u.m.)
  driver
  head
  hook
  jack
  -lifted (u.m.)
  nut
  ship
  #thread
  -threaded (u.m.)
  -turned (u.m.)
scroll
  -back
  head
  work
scuttlebutt
scythe-shaped
  (u.m.)
sea
  #base
  -based (u.m.)
  -bathed (u.m.)
  beach
  -beaten (u.m.)
  bed

#bird
-blue (u.m.)
  board
#boat
-born (u.m.)
  borne
  bound
-bred (u.m.)
  coast
-deep (u.m.)
  dog
-driven (u.m.)
  drome
-encircled (u.m.)
  fare (food)
  fighter
#floor
  folk
  food
  front
  girt
  goer
  going
  hound
  lane
#level
  lift
#lion
  mark
  port
  quake
#room
  scape
#scout
  scouting
  shell
  shine
  shore
  sick
  side
  stroke
#time (clock)
  wall

weed
wing
worn
worthiness
-wrecked (u.m.)
seam
blasting
rend (v.)
stitch
weld (v.)
-welded (u.m.)
search
#engine
light
plane
seat
belt
#cover
-mile
second
-class (u.m.)
-degree (u.m.)
-foot
-guess (v.)
hand (adv., u.m.)
#hand (n.)
#in#command
-rate (u.m.)
#sight
-sighted (u.m.)
Secret Service
secretary
#general
-generalcy
-generalship
section#man
seed
bed
cake
case
coat
kin
stalk

seer
band
hand
sucker
seesaw
seismo (c.f.)
all one word
self
dom
-extracting
hood
less
ness
same
reflexive prefix,
use hyphen
sell
off (n., u.m.)
out (n., u.m.)
semi (pref.)
-armor-piercing
(u.m.)
-Christian, etc.
-idleness
-indirect, etc.
annual, arid, etc.
rest one word
send
off (n., u.m.)
out (n., u.m.)
senso (c.f.)
all one word
septi (c.f.)
all one word
septo (c.f.)
all one word
sergeant#at#arms
serio (c.f.)
all one word
sero (c.f.)
all one word
serrate
-ciliate (u.m.)

-dentate (u.m.)
server-based
service
-connected (u.m.)
man
#man#and
#woman
member
person
wide
woman
servo
accelerometer
amplifier
control
mechanism
motor
system
sesqui (c.f.)
all one word
set
-aside (n., u.m.)
back (n., u.m.)
bolt
down (n., u.m.)
-fair (n.)
head
-in (n., u.m.)
off (n., u.m.)
-on (n., u.m.)
out (n., u.m.)
over (n., u.m.)
pin
screw
-stitched (u.m.)
-to (n., u.m.)
up (n., u.m.)
setter
-forth
-in
-on
-out
-to

-up
seven
-branched (u.m.)
fold
penny (nail)
score
-shooter
-up (n.)
severalfold
shade
-giving (u.m.)
-grown (u.m.)
shadow
boxing
gram
graph
#line
shag
bark
-haired (u.m.)
#rug
shake
down (n., u.m.)
out (n., u.m.)
up (n., u.m.)
shallow
-draft (u.m.)
-headed (u.m.)
shame
-crushed (u.m.)
faced
shank
bone
#mill
shapeup (n., u.m.)
share
bone
broker
cropper
holder
out (n., u.m.)
ware

sharp
  -angled (u.m.)
  -cut (u.m.)
  -edged (u.m.)
  -freeze (u.m., v.)
  -freezer
  -looking (u.m.)
  naysayer
  -set (u.m.)
  shod
  shooter
  -tailed (u.m.)
  -witted (u.m.)
shavetail
shear
  pin
  waters
shedhand
sheep
  biter
  crook
  dip
  #dog
  faced
  #farm
  fold
  gate
  herder
  hook
  kill
  -kneed (u.m.)
  nose (apple)
  pen
  shank
  shear (v.)
  shearer (n.)
  shed
  stealer
  walk
  -white (u.m.)
sheer
  off (n., u.m.)
  up (n., u.m.)

sheet
  block
  flood
  #glass
  rock
  ways
shell
  back
  burst
  fire
  fishery
  #game
  hole
  -like
  shocked
shelterbelt
shield-shaped
  (u.m.)
shilly-shally
shin
  bone
  guard
  plaster
shiner-up
ship
  breaker
  broken
  broker
  builder
  lap
  mast
  owning
  -rigged (u.m.)
  shape
  side
  wreck
shipping
  #master
  #room
shirt
  band
  #sleeve
  tail

  waist
shock
  #therapy
  #troops
  #wave
shoe
  black
  brush
  horn
  lace
  pack
  scraper
  shine
  store
  string
  tree
shootoff (n., u.m.)
shop
  folk
  lifter
  -made (u.m.)
  mark
  owner
  -soiled (u.m.)
  talk
  walker
  window
shore
  #bird
  #boat
  fast
  going
  #leave
  side
short
  -armed (u.m.)
  bread
  cake
  change (v.)
  changer
  #circuit
  -circuited (u.m.)
  coming

  cut (n., u.m., v.)
  fall (n.)
  -fed (u.m.)
  hand (writing)
  -handed (u.m.)
  head (whale)
  horn (n., u.m.)
  -horned (u.m.)
  -lasting (u.m.)
  leaf (u.m.)
  -lived (u.m.)
  rib
  run (u.m.)
  sighted
  staff
  stop
  #term
  -term (u.m.)
  wave (radio)
shot
  gun
  hole
  put
  star
shoulder
  #belt
  #blade
  -high (u.m.)
  #strap
show
  boat
  card
  case
  down (n., u.m.)
  off (n., u.m.)
  piece
  place
  room
  through
    (printing) (n.,
    u.m.)
  up (n., u.m.)
shredout (n., u.m.)

shroud
-laid (u.m.)
plate
shut
away (n., u.m.)
down (n., u.m.)
eye (n., u.m.)
-in (n., u.m.)
-mouthed (u.m.)
off (n., u.m.)
out (n., u.m.)
up (u.m.)
shuttlecock
sick
bay
bed
#call
#leave
list
room
sickle-cell (u.m.)
side
arms
band
board
bone
burns
car
check
-cut (u.m.)
dress (v.)
flash
head (printing)
hill
hook
kick
lap
#light (literal)
light (nonliteral)
#line (literal)
line (nonliteral)
long
note

plate
play
saddle
show
slip
splitting
step
stitch
-stitched (u.m.)
sway
swipe
track
walk
wall
-wheeler
winder
sight
hole
read
saver
seeing
setter
sign
off (n., u.m.)
-on (n., u.m.)
post
up (n., u.m.)
silico (c.f.)
all one word
silk
#screen
-stockinged (u.m.)
works
siltpan
silver
-backed (u.m.)
beater
-bright (u.m.)
fish
-gray (u.m.)
-haired (u.m.)
-lead (u.m.)
-leaved (u.m.)

plate (v.)
-plated (u.m.)
point (drawing)
print
tip
-tongued (u.m.)
top
simon-pure (u.m.)
simple
-headed (u.m.)
-minded (u.m.)
-rooted (u.m.)
-witted (u.m.)
simulcast
sin
-born (u.m.)
-bred (u.m.)
sine#die
single
bar
-breasted (u.m.)
-decker
-edged (u.m.)
handed
hood
-loader
-minded (u.m.)
-phase (u.m.)
-seater
stick
#stitch
tree
singsong
sink
head
hole
Sino (c.f.)
-Japanese, etc.
sister
-german
hood
-in-law

sit
down (n., u.m.)
-downer
fast (n., u.m.)
-in
up (n., u.m.)
sitter
-by
-in
-out
sitting#room
sitz
#bath
mark
six
-cylinder (u.m.)
fold
penny (nail)
-ply (u.m.)
-shooter
-wheeler
sizeup (n., u.m.)
ski
#jump
#lift
plane
#suit
skid
lift (truck)
road
#row
skin
-clad (u.m.)
deep
diver
flint
-graft (v.)
skipjack
skirtmarker
skullcap
skunk
head
top

sky
  -blue (u.m.)
  gazer
  -high (u.m.)
  jacker
  lift
  look (v.)
  rocket
  sail
  scape
  scraper
  shine
  writer
slab-sided (u.m.)
slack
  -bake (v.)
  -filled (u.m.)
  #water
slambang
slant-eyed (u.m.)
slap
  bang
  dab
  dash
  down (n., u.m.)
  happy
  jack
  stick
  -up (n., u.m.)
slate
  -blue (u.m.)
  -colored (u.m.)
  works
slaughter
  house
  pen
slave
  -born (u.m.)
  -deserted (u.m.)
  holding
  #market
  owner
  pen

Slavo (c.f.)
  -Hungarian, etc.
sledge
  #hammer
  -hammered (u.m.)
  meter
sleep
  -filled (u.m.)
  talker
  walker
sleepy
  -eyed (u.m.)
  head
  -looking (u.m.)
sleetstorm
sleeveband
sleuthhound
slide
  film
  knot
  #rule
sling
  ball
  shot
slip
  along (u.m.)
  band
  case
  cover
  knot
  #law
  -on (n., u.m.)
  #proof (printing)
  proof
  ring
  sheet
  shod
  sole
  step
  stitch
  stream
  -up (n., u.m.)
  washer

slit
  -eyed (u.m.)
  shell
  #skirt
slop
  -molded (u.m.)
  seller
slopeways
slow
  belly
  down (n., u.m.)
  -footed (u.m.)
  going
  -motion (u.m.)
  mouthed
  poke
  #time
  up (n., u.m.)
  -witted (u.m.)
sluice
  box
  #gate
slum
  dweller
  gullion
  gum
  lord
slumber-bound
  (u.m.)
small
  #arms
  #businessman
  pox
  -scale (u.m.)
  sword
  talk
  -time (u.m.)
  town (u.m.)
smart
  #aleck
  -alecky (u.m.)
  -looking (u.m.)
  #set

  -tongued (u.m.)
smashup (n., u.m.)
smearcase
smoke
  -blinded (u.m.)
  bomb
  chaser
  -dried (u.m.)
  -dry (v.)
  -dyed (u.m.)
  -filled (u.m.)
  house
  jack
  jumper
  -laden (u.m.)
  pot
  screen
  stack
smoking#room
smooth
  bore
  -browed (u.m.)
  -cast (u.m.)
  -mouthed (u.m.)
  -tongued (u.m.)
  -working (u.m.)
snackbar
snail
  -paced (u.m.)
  -slow (u.m.)
snail's#pace
snake
  bite
  -bitten (u.m.)
  -eater
  -eyed (u.m.)
  head
  hole
  pit
snap
  dragon
  head
  hook

-on (n., u.m.)
out (n.)
ring
roll
shooter
shot
-up (u.m.)
snapper
-back
-up
snipe
bill
#eel
-nosed (u.m.)
sniperscope
snooperscope
snow
ball
bank
berg
blind
#blindness
blink
block
-blocked (u.m.)
blower
break
capped
-choked (u.m.)
clad (u.m.)
#cover
-covered (u.m.)
drift
fall
field
flake
line
melt
-melting (u.m.)
mobile
pack
pit
plow

scape
shade
shed
shine
shoe
sled
slide
slip
storm
suit
-topped (u.m.)
#water
-white (u.m.)
snuffbox
so
-and-so
beit (n., conj.)
-called (u.m.)
-seeming (u.m.)
-so
soap
box
bubble
dish
flakes
#opera
rock
stock
suds
sob
#sister
#story
sober
-minded (u.m.)
sides
social
#work
#worker
socio (c.f.)
-official
economic, etc.
sod
buster

culture
#house
soda
jerk
#pop
#water
sofa
#bed
#maker
-making (u.m.)
-ridden (u.m.)
soft
ball
-boiled (u.m.)
#coal
#copy
#drink
#goods
head
-pedal (v.)
-shelled (u.m.)
-soap (nonliteral) (v.)
-soaper (nonliteral) (n.)
-spoken (u.m.)
tack
ware
wood
sole
cutter
plate
somato (c.f.)
all one word
some
day
how
one (anyone)
#one (distributive)
place (adv.)
time (adv., u.m.)
#time (some time ago)

what
son-in-law
song
bird
fest
writer
sonobuoy
sooth
fast
sayer
sore
-eyed (u.m.)
foot (n.)
footed (u.m.)
head (n., u.m.)
sorry-looking (u.m.)
soul
-deep (u.m.)
mate
-searching (u.m.)
sick
sound
-absorbing (u.m.)
#field
film
-minded (u.m.)
off (n., u.m.)
track
#wave
soup
bone
#bowl
#kitchen
#plate
spoon
sour
belly
bread
dough (n.)
faced
-natured (u.m.)
-sweet

source
  book
  #file
south
  -born (u.m.)
  bound
  -central (u.m.)
  east
  going
  lander
  paw
  #side
  -sider
  -southeast
  west
soybean
sow
  back
  belly
space
  bar
  craft
  -cramped (u.m.)
  #key
  mark
  ship
  #time
spade
  -dug (u.m.)
  foot
  -footed (u.m.)
  -shaped (u.m.)
Spanish
  -American
  -born (u.m.)
  -speaking (u.m.)
spare
  -bodied (u.m.)
  rib
  #room
spark
  #plug (literal)
  plug (nonliteral)

speakeasy (n.)
spear
  cast
  head
  -high (u.m.)
  -shaped (u.m.)
spectro (c.f.)
  all one word
speech
  -bereft (u.m.)
  -read (v.)
speed
  boating
  letter
  trap
  up (n., u.m.)
spell
  binding
  check
  down (n., u.m.)
  -free (u.m.)
spend
  -all (n.)
  thrift
spermato (c.f.)
  all one word
spermo (c.f.)
  all one word
spheno (c.f.)
  -occipital
  rest one word
sphygmo (c.f.)
  all one word
spice
  -burnt (u.m.)
  cake
  -laden (u.m.)
spider
  #crab
  -legged
  -spun (u.m.)
  #web (n.)
  web (u.m., v.)

spike
  horn
  -kill (v.)
  -pitch (v.)
spill
  over (n., u.m.)
  way
spin
  back
  #doctor (slang)
  off
spindle
  -formed (u.m.)
  head
  -legged (u.m.)
  legs
  shanks
spine
  bone
  -broken (u.m.)
  -pointed (u.m.)
spino (c.f.)
  -olivary
  rest one word
spirit
  -born (u.m.)
  -broken (u.m.)
  #writing
spit
  ball
  fire
  stick
splanchno (c.f.)
  all one word
splay
  footed
  mouthed
spleen
  -born (u.m.)
  sick
  -swollen (u.m.)
spleno (c.f.)
  all one word

split
  finger
  (crustacean)
  fruit
  mouth
  saw
  #second
  -tongued (u.m.)
  up (n., u.m.)
spoilsport
spondylo (c.f.)
  all one word
sponge
  #bath
  cake
  diver
  -diving (u.m.)
  -shaped (u.m.)
spongio (c.f.)
  all one word
spoolwinder
spoon
  -beaked (u.m.)
  -billed (u.m.)
  bread
  -fed (u.m.)
  -shaped (u.m.)
  ways
sporeformer
sporo (c.f.)
  all one word
sports
  #editor
  person
  wear
  writer
spot
  #check
  -checked (u.m.)
  -face (v.)
  light
  weld (v.)
  welded (u.m.)

-welding (u.m.)
spray-washed (u.m.)
spread
  -eagle (u.m., v.)
  head
  out (n., u.m.)
  over (n., u.m.)
  -set (v.)
spring
  back
    (bookbinding)
  bok
  -born (u.m.)
  buck
  -clean (v.)
  #fever
  finger
  -grown (u.m.)
  halt
  head
  -plow (v.)
  -plowed (u.m.)
  tide (season)
  time
  trap
spritsail
spur
  -clad (u.m.)
  -driven (u.m.)
  gall
  -galled (u.m.)
  -heeled (u.m.)
spy
  glass
  hole
  tower
square
  -bottomed (u.m.)
  -built (u.m.)
  -faced (u.m.)
  flipper
  head
  -headed

#mile
-rigged (u.m.)
#root
-set (u.m.)
shooter
squeeze
  -in (n., u.m.)
  out (n., u.m.)
  up (n., u.m.)
squirrel-headed
  (u.m.)
stackup (n., u.m.)
staff
  -herd (v.)
  -hour
  time
stag
  -handled (u.m.)
  head
  -headed (u.m.)
  horn
  -horned (u.m.)
  hound
  hunter
stage
  coach
  hand
  #set
  -struck (u.m.)
stair
  case
  head
  step
  #well
stake
  head
  out (n.)
stale-worn (u.m.)
stall
  -fed (u.m.)
  -feed (v.)
stand
  by (n., u.m.)

down (n., u.m.)
fast (n., u.m.)
-in (n., u.m.)
off (n., u.m.)
offish
out (n., u.m.)
pat
pipe
point
post
still (n., u.m.)
up (n., u.m.)
standard
  #bearer
  bred
  #gauge
  #time
staphylo (c.f.)
  all one word
star
  blind
  bright
  dust
  gazer
  -led (u.m.)
  light
  lit
  lite (gem)
  nose (mole)
  shake
  shine
  shoot
  -spangled (u.m.)
  stroke
  -studded (u.m.)
  #time
starchworks
stark
  -blind (u.m.)
  -mad (u.m.)
  -naked (u.m.)
  -raving (u.m.)
starter-off

start-stop
startup (n., u.m.)
stat (pref.)
  all one word
State
  -aided (u.m.)
  #line
  -owned (u.m.)
state
  hood
  -of-the-art (u.m.)
  quake
  room
  side
  station#house
stato (c.f.)
  all one word
statute
  -barred (u.m.)
  #book
stay
  -at-home (n., u.m.)
  bar
  bolt
  boom
  lace
  log
  pin
  plow
  sail
  wire
steam
  boating
  car
  -cooked (u.m.)
  -driven (u.m.)
  fitter
  pipe
  plant
  -pocket (v.)
  power (n.)
  #powerplant
  -propelled (u.m.)

roll (v.)
roller (u.m., v.)
ship
table
tightness
steamer#line
steel
  -blue (u.m.)
  -bright (u.m.)
  -cased (u.m.)
  clad
  -framed (u.m.)
  -hard (u.m.)
  head
  plate
  works
steep
  -rising (u.m.)
  -to (u.m.)
  -up (u.m.)
  -walled (u.m.)
steeple
  chase
  -high (u.m.)
  jack
  top
stem
  head
  post
  sickness
  winder
stencil-cutting (u.m.)
steno (c.f.)
  all one word
step
  aunt
  child, etc.
  dance
  down (n., u.m.)
  -in (n., u.m.)
  ladder
  off (n., u.m.)
  -on (n., u.m.)

over (n., u.m.)
-up (n., u.m.)
stepping
  -off (u.m.)
  -out (u.m.)
  stone
stereo (c.f.)
  all one word
stern
  castle
  -faced (u.m.)
  -heavy (u.m.)
  -looking (u.m.)
  most
  post
  #wheel
  -wheeler
sterno (c.f.)
  all one word
stetho (c.f.)
  all one word
stew
  pan
  pot
stick
  -at-it (n., u.m.)
  fast (n.)
  -in-the-mud (n., u.m.)
  out (n., u.m.)
  pin
  -to-it-iveness (n.)
  up (n., u.m.)
sticker
  -in
  -on
  -up
stiff
  -backed (u.m.)
  neck
  -necked (u.m.)
still
  -admired (u.m.)

birth
born
-burn (v.)
-fish (v.)
-hunt (v.)
#life
-recurring (u.m.)
stand
stink
  ball
  bomb
  bug
  damp
  pot
stir
  about (n., u.m.)
  fry
  -up (n., u.m.)
stitch
  down (n., u.m.)
  up (n., u.m.)
stock
  breeder
  broker
  #car
  feeder
  holding
  jobber
  judging
  list
  pile
  pot
  rack
  raiser
  -still (u.m.)
  taker
  truck
  wright
stoke
  hold
  hole
stomach
  #ache

-filling (u.m.)
#pump
-shaped (u.m.)
-sick (u.m.)
-weary (u.m.)
stomato (c.f.)
  all one word
stone
  biter
  blind
  brash
  breaker
  broke
  brood
  cast
  -cold (u.m.)
  #crab
  crusher
  cutter
  -dead (u.m.)
  -deaf (u.m.)
  -eyed (u.m.)
  head
  layer
  lifter
  mason
  shot
  #wall (n.)
  wall (u.m., v.)
  #writing
stony
  -eyed (u.m.)
  #land
stop
  back (n.)
  block
  clock
  cock
  gap
  hound
  list
  log
  -loss (u.m.)

off (n., u.m.)
watch
storage#room
store
  front
  house
storm
  -beaten (u.m.)
  cock
  flow
  -laden (u.m.)
  -swept (u.m.)
  -tossed (u.m.)
  #trooper
  wind
  #window
storyteller
stout
  -armed (u.m.)
  heartedness
  -minded (u.m.)
stove
  brush
  -heated (u.m.)
  pipe
stow
  away (n., u.m.)
  down (n., u.m.)
straddle
  back
  -face (v.)
  -legged (u.m.)
straight
  away
  -backed (u.m.)
  -cut (u.m.)
  edge
  -edged (u.m.)
  #face
  -faced (u.m.)
  forward
  head
  -legged (u.m.)

#line
-lined (u.m.)
-out (n., u.m.)
-spoken (u.m.)
#time
-up (u.m.)
-up-and-down
  (u.m.)
strainslip
strait
  -chested (u.m.)
  jacket
  laced
  stranglehold
strap
  -bolt (v.)
  hanger
  head
  -shaped (u.m.)
  watch
strato (c.f.)
  all one word
straw
  berry#field
  boss
  -built (u.m.)
  hat
  -roofed (u.m.)
  splitting
  stack
  -stuffed (u.m.)
  #vote
  walker
  -yellow (u.m.)
stray
  away (n., u.m.)
  #line
  mark
stream
  bank
  bed
  flow
  head

lined
side
street
  -bred (u.m.)
  car
  cleaner
  -cleaning (u.m.)
  sweeper
  walker
strepto (c.f.)
  all one word
stretchout (n., u.m.)
strike
  breaker
  -in (n., u.m.)
  out (n., u.m.)
  -over (n., u.m.)
striker
  -in
  -out
  -over
string
  course
  halt
  #proof (density)
  ways
strip
  cropping
  #mine
  tease
strong
  -arm (u.m., v.)
  back (nautical)
  -backed (u.m.)
  box
  hold
  #man (literal)
  man (nonliteral)
  -minded (u.m.)
  point (n.)
stub
  runner
  -toed (u.m.)

wing
stubble
  #field
  -mulch (u.m.)
stubbornminded
stucco-fronted
  (u.m.)
stuck
  up (n., u.m.)
  -upper
  -uppish (u.m.)
stud
  bolt
  horse
  mare
stuntman
stupid
  head
  -headed (u.m.)
  -looking (u.m.)
sturdy-limbed (u.m.)
stylebook
stylo (c.f.)
  all one word
sub (pref.)
  -Himalayan, etc.
  machinegun
  #rosa, #specie, etc.
  -subcommittee
  polar, standard,
    etc.
  rest one word
subject
  -object
  -objectivity
subter (pref.)
  all one word
such-and-such
suck
  -egg (n., u.m.)
  hole
  -in (n., u.m.)

sugar
  #beet
  #bowl
  cake
  cane
  -coat (v.)
  -coated (u.m.)
  -cured (u.m.)
  loaf
  plum
  spoon
  sweet
  #water
  works
sulfa (c.f.)
  all one word
sulfo (c.f.)
  all one word
sulfon (c.f.)
  all one word
sullen
  hearted
  -natured (u.m.)
summer
  -clad (u.m.)
  -dried (u.m.)
  -fallow (v.)
  -made (u.m.)
  tide
  time (season)
  #time (daylight
    saving)
sun
  -baked (u.m.)
  bath
  -bathed (u.m.)
  beam
  blind
  #blindness
  bonnet
  bow
  break
  burn

burst
  -cured (u.m.)
  dial
  dog
  down
  dress
  -dried (u.m.)
  -dry (v.)
  fall
  fast
  glade
  glare
  glow
  #hat
  lamp
  lit
  quake
  ray
  rise
  scald
  set
  shade
  shine
  -shot (u.m.)
  shower
  spot
  stricken
  stroke
  struck
  tan
  #time (measure)
  time (dawn)
  up
sunny
  -looking (u.m.)
  -natured (u.m.)
super (pref.)
  -Christian, etc.
  #high frequency
  -superlative
  highway, market,
    etc.
  rest one word

Super Bowl
supra (pref.)
  -abdominal
  -acromial
  -aerial
  anal
  -angular
  -arytenoid
  -auditory
  -auricular
  -axillary
  -Christian, etc.
  rest one word
sur (pref.)
  all one word
sure
  -fire (u.m.)
  -footed (u.m.)
  -slow
surf
  -battered (u.m.)
  board
  #fish
  -swept (u.m.)
swallow
  pipe
  -tailed (u.m.)
swampside
swan
  -bosomed (u.m.)
  dive
  herd
  mark
  neck
  song
swansdown
swash
  buckler
  plate
sway
  back (n., u.m.)
  -backed (u.m.)
  bar

-brace (v.)
swearer-in
sweat
  band
  #gland
  #shirt
  shop
sweep
  back (aviation)
    (n., u.m.)
  forward
    (aviation) (n.,
    u.m.)
  stake
  through (n., u.m.)
  washer
sweet
  bread
  -breathed (u.m.)
  brier
  faced
  heart
  meat
  mouthed
  -pickle (v.)
  -sour
  -sweet
swell
  -butted (u.m.)
  head
  toad
swelled-headed
    (u.m.)
swept
  back (n., u.m.)
  forward (n.,
    u.m.)
  wing (n., u.m.)
swift
  foot
  -footed (u.m.)
  -handed (u.m.)
  -running (u.m.)

swill
  bowl
  tub
swimsuit
swine
  -backed (u.m.)
  bread
  head
  herd
  pox
  sty
swing
  back (n., u.m.)
  bar
  dingle
  #gate
  #shift
  stock
  -swang
  tree
swingle
  bar
  tree
switch
  back
  blade
  box
  gear
  plate
  plug
  rail
  tender
swivel
  #chair
  eye
  -eyed (u.m.)
  -hooked (u.m.)
sword
  -armed (u.m.)
  bearer
  #belt
  bill
  fishing

  play
  -shaped (u.m.)
  stick
syn (pref.)
  all one word
synchro
  cyclotron
  flash
  mesh
  tron
Syro (c.f.)
  -Arabian, etc.
  phenician

T

T
  -ball
  -bandage
  -beam
  -boat
  -bone
  -cloth
  -iron
  -man
  -rail
  -scale (score)
  -shape
  -shaped
  -shirt
  -square
table
  cloth
  -cut (u.m.)
  cutter
  -cutting (u.m.)
  -formed (u.m.)
  #linen
  -shaped (u.m.)
  spoon
  talk
  top
  ware

tachy (c.f.)
  all one word
tag
  -affixing (u.m.)
  lock
  rag
  sore
tail
  band
  #coat
  -cropped (u.m.)
  #end
  -ender
  first
  foremost
  gate
  head
  -heavy (u.m.)
  hook
  lamp
  pin
  pipe
  race
  spin
  stock
  -tied (u.m.)
  twister
  -up (n., u.m.)
  wheel
  wind
tailor
  -cut (u.m.)
  made (u.m.)
  -suited (u.m.)
take
  -all (n.)
  down (n., u.m.)
  -home (n., u.m.)
  -in (n., u.m.)
  off (n., u.m.)
  out (n., u.m.)
  over (n., u.m.)
  up (n., u.m.)

taker
  -down
  -in
  -off
  -over
  -up
tale
  bearer
  carrier
  teller
talkfest
talking-to (n.)
tall
  boy (n.)
  -built (u.m.)
  -looking (u.m.)
tallow
  -faced (u.m.)
  -pale (u.m.)
tally
  #board
  #clerk
  ho
  #room
  #sheet
tame
  -grown (u.m.)
  -looking (u.m.)
tan
  bark
  works
tangent
  -cut (v.)
  -saw (v.)
tangle
  foot
  -haired (u.m.)
tank
  #car
  farm
  ship
  town

tap
bolt
dance
hole
net
off (n., u.m.)
-riveted (u.m.)
room
root
-tap
water
tape
#deck
#drive
#measure
string
-tied (u.m.)
taper
bearer
-fashion (u.m.)
-headed (u.m.)
tapestry
-covered (u.m.)
#maker
-making (u.m.)
#work
tapper-out
tar
-brand (v.)
brush
-coal (u.m.)
-dipped (u.m.)
#paper
-paved (u.m.)
pot
-roofed (u.m.)
works
tariff-protected
(u.m.)
tarpaulin
-covered (u.m.)
#maker
-making (u.m.)

tarso (c.f.)
all one word
task
#force
setter
tattletale
tauro (c.f.)
all one word
tax
-burdened (u.m.)
#collector
eater
-exempt (u.m.)
-free (u.m.)
gatherer
-laden (u.m.)
paid
payer
#roll
-supported (u.m.)
taxi
auto
bus
cab
meter
stand
tea
ball
cake
cart
-colored (u.m.)
cup
dish
kettle
#party
pot
room
-scented (u.m.)
spoon
taster
teamplay
tear
bomb

-dimmed (u.m.)
down (n., u.m.)
drop
#gas
-off (n., u.m.)
-out (n., u.m.)
pit
sheet
stain
-stained (u.m.)
teen
age (u.m.)
ager
teeter-totter
tele (c.f.)
all one word
teleo (c.f.)
all one word
tell
tale
truth
telo (c.f.)
all one word
tempest-rocked
(u.m.)
temporo (c.f.)
-occipital
rest one word
ten
fold
penny (nail)
pins
tender
#boat
-faced (u.m.)
foot
-footed (u.m.)
footish
-handed (u.m.)
heart
loin
-looking (u.m.)
tenement#house

tent
-dotted (u.m.)
pole
-sheltered (u.m.)
#show
terra
#cotta
#firma
mara
terrace-fashion
(u.m.)
test-fly (v.)
tetra (c.f.)
all one word
thanksgiving
thatch-roofed
(u.m.)
text
-based
#file
#mode
theater
goer
going
thenceforth
theo (c.f.)
all one word
theologico (c.f.)
all one word
there
about(s)
above
across
after
against
among
around
at
away
before
between
by
for

fore
from
in
inafter
inbefore
into
on
over
through
tofore
under
until
unto
upon
with
thermo (c.f.)
all one word
thick
-blooded (u.m.)
head
-looking (u.m.)
pated
set (n., u.m.)
skinned
skull (n.)
skulled
-tongued (u.m.)
wit
-witted (u.m.)
-wooded (u.m.)
-woven (u.m.)
thin
-clad (u.m.)
down (n., u.m.)
set (u.m.)
-voiced (u.m.)
thio (c.f.)
all one word
third
-class (u.m.)
-degree (u.m.)
hand (adv., u.m.)
#house

-rate (u.m.)
-rater
thistledown
thoraco (c.f.)
all one word
thorn
back
bill
-covered (u.m.)
-set (u.m.)
-strewn (u.m.)
tail
thorough
-bind (v.)
bred
-dried (u.m.)
fare
going
-made (u.m.)
paced
pin
thought
-free (u.m.)
-out (u.m.)
-provoking (u.m.)
thousand
fold
-headed (u.m.)
-legged (u.m.)
legs (worm)
thrall
born
dom
-less
thread
bare
-leaved (u.m.)
worn
three
-bagger
-cornered (u.m.)
-dimensional
(u.m.)

fold
-in-hand
-master
penny (nail)
-piece (u.m.)
-ply (u.m.)
score
some
-spot
-square
-striper
throat
band
cutter
latch
strap
thrombo (c.f.)
all one word
through
out
put
#road
way
throw
away (n., u.m.)
back (n., u.m.)
-in (n., u.m.)
#line
off (n., u.m.)
-on (n., u.m.)
out (n., u.m.)
over (n., u.m.)
-weight
thrust-pound
thumb
#hole
-made (u.m.)
mark
-marked (u.m.)
nail
print
screw
stall

string
sucker
tack
worn
thunder
bearer
blast
bolt
clap
cloud
head
peal
shower
storm
struck
thymo (c.f.)
all one word
thyro (c.f.)
all one word
tibio (c.f.)
all one word
tick
#feed
seed
tacktoe
tick
tock
ticket
#seller
-selling (u.m.)
#writer
tidal#wave
tiddlywink
tide
flat
head
mark
-marked (u.m.)
race
table
-tossed (u.m.)
waiter
-worn (u.m.)

tie
  back (n.)
  #bar
  #beam
  down (n., u.m.)
  -in (n., u.m.)
  -on (n., u.m.)
  -out (n., u.m.)
  pin
  -plater
  #rod
  #tack
  up (n., u.m.)
tierlift (truck)
tiger
  eye
  #lily
  #shark
  -striped (u.m.)
tight
  -belted (u.m.)
  fisted
  -fitting (u.m.)
  lipped
  rope
  -set (u.m.)
  -tie (v.)
  wad
  wire
tile
  -clad (u.m.)
  #drain
  -red (u.m.)
  setter
  works
  wright
tilt
  hammer
  rotor
  up (n.)
timber
  -built (u.m.)
  head

  -headed (u.m.)
  jack
  line
  -propped (u.m.)
  #wolf
  wright
time
  bomb
  born
  card
  clerk
  clock
  -consuming (u.m.)
  frame
  -honored (u.m.)
  keeper
  killer
  lag
  lock
  outs (n., u.m.)
  piece
  pleaser
  saver
  server
  sheet
  slip
  slot
  span
  -stamp (v.)
  study
  table
  taker
  waster
  worn
tin
  -bearing (u.m.)
  #can
  -capped (u.m.)
  -clad (u.m.)
  cup
  #fish (torpedo)
  foil
  horn

  kettle
  -lined (u.m.)
  man
  pan
  plate
  -plated (u.m.)
  pot
  -roofed (u.m.)
  type
  -white (u.m.)
tinsel
  -bright (u.m.)
  -clad (u.m.)
  -covered (u.m.)
  #town
tintblock (printing)
tip
  burn
  cart
  -curled (u.m.)
  head
  -in (n., u.m.)
  most
  off (n., u.m.)
  over (n., u.m.)
  staff
  stock
  tank
  -tap
  toe
  top
  -up (u.m.)
tire
  changer
  dresser
  fitter
  #gauge
  #iron
  -mile
  #rack
  shaper
  some

tit
  bit
  #for#tat
  mouse
titano (c.f.)
  all one word
tithe
  book
  -free (u.m.)
  payer
  right
title
  holder
  -holding (u.m.)
  #page
  winner
  -winning (u.m.)
to
  -and-fro
  -do (n.)
  #wit
toad
  back
  -bellied (u.m.)
  blind
  fish
  -green (u.m.)
  stool
tobacco
  #grower
  -growing (u.m.)
  #shop
toe
  cap
  #dance
  hold
  -in (n., u.m.)
  -mark (v.)
  nail
  plate
  print
toil
  -beaten (u.m.)

some
-stained (u.m.)
-weary (u.m.)
worn
toilet#room
toll
bar
#bridge
#call
gate
gatherer
house
#line
payer
road
taker
tom
boy
cat
foolery
-tom
tommy
gun
rot
ton
-hour
-kilometer
-mile
-mileage
-mile-day
tone
-deaf (u.m.)
down (n., u.m.)
-producing (u.m.)
up (n., u.m.)
tongue
-baited (u.m.)
-bound (u.m.)
-free (u.m.)
-lash (v.)
#lashing
play
-shaped (u.m.)

shot
sore
tack
tied
tip
#twister
-twisting (u.m.)
tool
bag
#belt
box
builder
#chest
crib
dresser
fitter
#grinder
-grinding (u.m.)
head
holding
kit
mark
plate
post
rack
setter
shed
slide
stock
tooth
ache
#and#nail
-billed (u.m.)
brush
drawer
mark
-marked (u.m.)
paste
pick
plate
powder
puller
-pulling (u.m.)

-set (u.m.)
-shaped (u.m.)
some
wash
top
#brass
cap (n.)
coat
cutter
#dog
-drain (v.)
#drawer
dress (v.)
flight (u.m.)
full
gallant (n., u.m.)
-graft (v.)
hat
-hatted (u.m.)
heavy
kick
knot
liner
mark
mast
milk
most
notch (nonliteral)
rail
rope
sail
-secret (u.m.)
-shaped (u.m.)
side (naut.)
soil
topo (c.f.)
all one word
topsy-turvy
torch
bearer
#holder
lighted
lit

torpedo
#boat
#room
torquemeter
toss
pot
up (n., u.m.)
touch
#and#go
back (n., u.m.)
down (n., u.m.)
hole
-me-not (n., u.m.)
pan
reader
stone
up (n., u.m.)
tough
-headed (u.m.)
-looking (u.m.)
-skinned (u.m.)
tow
away
boat
head
line
mast
#net
-netter
path
rope
#truck
tower
-high (u.m.)
-shaped (u.m.)
town
-bred (u.m.)
#clerk
#crier
-dotted (u.m.)
folk
gate
going

hall
lot
ship
side
site
talk
-weary (u.m.)
towns
fellow
people
toy
#dog
-sized (u.m.)
town
tracheo (c.f.)
 all one word
trachy (c.f.)
 all one word
track
barrow
hound
layer
mark
-mile
side
walker
tractor-trailer
trade
#board
-in (n., u.m.)
-laden (u.m.)
-made (u.m.)
mark
#name
off
#union
#wind
tradespeople
traffic-mile
tragico (c.f.)
 all one word
trail
blazer
breaker

-marked (u.m.)
side
sight
-weary (u.m.)
train
bearer
bolt
crew
line
-mile
shed
sick
stop
tram
-borne (u.m.)
car
rail
road
way
trans (pref.)
alpine
atlantic
-Canadian, etc.
pacific
uranic
 rest one word
transit#time
trap
door
fall
shoot
trashrack
travel
-bent (u.m.)
time
-tired (u.m.)
-worn (u.m.)
trawlnet
tread
mill
wheel
treasure
-filled (u.m.)

#house
-laden (u.m.)
treaty
breaker
-sealed (u.m.)
tree
#belt
-clad (u.m.)
#line
-lined (u.m.)
nail
-ripe (u.m.)
scape
top
#trunk
trellis-covered
 (u.m.)
trench
back
coat
foot
#knife
mouth
#plow
-plowed (u.m.)
tri (c.f.)
-iodide
-ply (u.m.)
state, etc.
 rest one word
tribespeople
tribo (c.f.)
 all one word
tricho (c.f.)
 all one word
trim
-cut (u.m.)
-dressed (u.m.)
-looking (u.m.)
trinitro (c.f.)
 all one word
trip
-free (u.m.)

hammer
wire
triple
-acting (u.m.)
back (sofa)
branched (u.m.)
-edged (u.m.)
fold
#play
-tailed (u.m.)
tree (n.)
trolley#line
troop
ship
#train
tropho (c.f.)
 all one word
tropo (c.f.)
 all one word
trouble
-free (u.m.)
-haunted (u.m.)
maker
shooter
some
truce
breaker
-seeking (u.m.)
truck
driver
#farm
-mile
stop
true
-aimed (u.m.)
-blue (u.m.)
born
bred
-eyed (u.m.)
-false
love (n., u.m.)
penny (n.)
#time

trunk
back
nose
trust
breaking
buster
-controlled (u.m.)
-ridden (u.m.)
worthy
truth
-filled (u.m.)
lover
seeker
-seeking (u.m.)
teller
try
-on (n., u.m.)
out (n., u.m.)
square
works
tube
-eyed (u.m.)
-fed (u.m.)
head
-nosed (u.m.)
works
tuberculo (c.f.)
all one word
tubo (c.f.)
-ovarian
rest one word
tug
boat
#of#war
tumbledown (n., u.m.)
tune
out (n., u.m.)
up (n., u.m.)
tunnel
-boring (u.m.)
-shaped (u.m.)
vision

turbo (c.f.)
-ramjet (u.m.)
rest one word
turf
-built (u.m.)
-clad (u.m.)
-covered (u.m.)
#war
turkey
back
#buzzard
#gobbler
#trot
Turko (c.f.)
-Greek, etc.
rest one word
turn
about (n., u.m.)
about-face
again (n., u.m.)
around (n., u.m.)
back (n., u.m.)
buckle
cap
coat
cock
down (n., u.m.)
gate
-in (n., u.m.)
key
off (n., u.m.)
out (n., u.m.)
over (n., u.m.)
pike
pin
plate
round (n., u.m.)
screw
sheet
sole
spit
stile
stitch

table
tail
-to (n.)
under (n., u.m.)
up (n., u.m.)
turned
-back (u.m.)
-down (u.m.)
-in (u.m.)
-on (u.m.)
-out (u.m.)
-over (u.m.)
turner-off
turtle
back
dove
-footed (u.m.)
neck (u.m.)
#shell
twelve
fold
penny (nail)
score
twenty
-first
fold
-one
twice
-born (u.m.)
-reviewed (u.m.)
-told (u.m.)
twin
#boat
born
-engined (u.m.)
fold
-jet (u.m.)
-motor (u.m.)
-screw (u.m.)
two
-a-day (u.m.)
-along (n.)
(bookbinding)

-decker
-faced (u.m.)
fold
-handed (u.m.)
penny (nail)
-piece (u.m.)
-ply (u.m.)
score
-seater
some
-spot
-step (dance)
-striper
-suiter
-up (n., u.m.)
-way (u.m.)
-wheeler
tympano (c.f.)
all one word
type
case
cast
cutter
face
foundry
script
set
write (v.)
typho (c.f.)
all one word
typo (c.f.)
all one word
tyro (c.f.)
all one word

U

U
-boat
-cut
-magnet
-rail
-shaped
-tube

ultra (pref.)
-ambitious,
-atomic, etc.
-English, etc.
high#frequency
-high-speed (u.m.)
#valorem, etc.
rest one word
un (pref.)
-American, etc.
called-for (u.m.)
heard-of (u.m.)
-ionized (u.m.)
self-conscious
sent-for (u.m.)
thought-of (u.m.)
rest one word
under
age (deficit)
age (younger)
(n., u.m.)
#cultivation
(tillage)
cultivation
(insufficient)
#secretary
-secretaryship
way
*as prefix, one
word*
uni (c.f.)
-univalent
rest one word
union
-made (u.m.)
#shop
unit-set (u.m.)
up
-anchor (u.m., v.)
-and-coming
(u.m.)
#and#up
beat

coast
country
dip
end (v.)
front (n., u.m.)
grade
gradient
keep
lift
load
-over (u.m.)
rate
river
stairs
state
stream
swing
take
tight (n., u.m.)
#tight (v.)
-to-date (u.m.)
#to#date
town
trend
turn
wind
upper
case (printing)
#class
classman
crust (n., u.m.)
cut
#deck
most
urano (c.f.)
all one word
uretero (c.f.)
all one word
urethro (c.f.)
all one word
uro (c.f.)
all one word
used-car (u.m.)

user
#default
-defined
-friendly
#group
#interface
utero (c.f.)
all one word

V

V
-connection
-curve
-engine
-neck
-shaped
-type
vacant
-eyed (u.m.)
-looking (u.m.)
-minded (u.m.)
vagino (c.f.)
all one word
vainglorious
valve
-grinding (u.m.)
-in-head (u.m.)
van
driver
guard
pool
vapor
-filled (u.m.)
-heating (u.m.)
#lock
vase-shaped (u.m.)
vaso (c.f.)
all one word
vegeto (c.f.)
all one word
vein
-mining (u.m.)
-streaked (u.m.)

vellum
-bound (u.m.)
-covered (u.m.)
velvet
-crimson (u.m.)
-draped (u.m.)
-green (u.m.)
-pile (u.m.)
venthole
ventri (c.f.)
all one word
ventro (c.f.)
all one word
vertebro (c.f.)
all one word
vesico (c.f.)
all one word
vibro (c.f.)
all one word
vice
#admiral
-admiralty
#consul
-consulate
#governor
-governorship
#minister
-ministry
-presidency
#president
-president-elect
-presidential
#rector
-rectorship
regal
-regency
#regent
royal
#squad
#versa
#warden
videotape
Vietcong

view
  finder
  point
  vile-natured (u.m.)
vine
  -clad (u.m.)
  -covered (u.m.)
  dresser
  growing
  stalk
vinegar
  -flavored (u.m.)
  -hearted (u.m.)
  -making (u.m.)
  -tart (u.m.)
violet
  -blue (u.m.)`
  -colored (u.m.)
  -eared (u.m.)
  #ray
  -rayed (u.m.)
  #water
violin-shaped (u.m.)
vis-a-vis
viscero (c.f.)
  all one word
vitreo (c.f.)
  all one word
vitro (c.f.)
  -clarain
  -di-trina
  rest one word
vivi (c.f.)
  all one word
voice
  -capable
  #mail
  over (n.)
volleyball
volt
  ammeter
  -ampere
  -coulomb

meter
ohmmeter
  -second
volta (c.f.)
  all one word
vote
  -casting (u.m.)
  getter
  -getting (u.m.)
vow
  -bound (u.m.)
  breaker
  -pledged (u.m.)
vulvo (c.f.)
  all one word

W

W
  -engine
  -shaped
  -surface
  -type
wage
  #earner
  -earning (u.m.)
  #scale
  worker
waist
  band
  belt
  cloth
  coat
  -deep (u.m.)
  -high (u.m.)
  line
waiting
  #list
  #man
  #room
  #woman
walk
  around (n., u.m.)
  away (n., u.m.)

-on (n., u.m.)
out (n., u.m.)
over (n., u.m.)
up (n., u.m.)
way
walkie-talkie
wall
  board
  eyed
  flower
  -like
  -painting (u.m.)
  paper
  plate
  -sided (u.m.)
walled
  -in (u.m.)
  -up (u.m.)
war
  #dance
  -disabled (u.m.)
  -famed (u.m.)
  fare
  head
  horse (nonliteral)
  like
  monger
  -made (u.m.)
  path
  plane
  ship
  -swept (u.m.)
  #time (clock)
  time (duration)
ward
  heeler
  robe
  ship
warm
  blooded
  -clad (u.m.)
  up (n., u.m.)
warmed-over (u.m.)

warpsetter
wash
  basin
  basket
  board
  bowl
  cloth
  -colored (u.m.)
  day
  down (n., u.m.)
  -in (n., u.m.)
  off (n., u.m.)
  out (n., u.m.)
  pot
  rag
  #sale
  stand
  tray
  trough
  tub
  up (n., u.m.)
washed
  -out (u.m.)
  -up (u.m.)
waste
  basket
  land
  leaf
    (bookbinding)
  paper
  site
  word
watch
  band
  case
  #chain
  cry
  dog
  -free (u.m.)
  glass
  tower
water
  bag

bank	pot	#paper	**web**
bearer	power	#stone	-fingered (u.m.)
-bearing (u.m.)	proofing	-yellow (u.m.)	foot
-beaten (u.m.)	quake	**way**	-footed (u.m.)
-bind (v.)	-rot (v.)	back (n., u.m.)	master
#blister	scape	beam	#press
bloom	shed	bill	Web#site
buck	shoot	down (n., u.m.)	**wedge**
color	side	farer	-billed (u.m.)
-colored (u.m.)	-soak (v.)	fellow	-shaped (u.m.)
-cool (v.)	-soaked (u.m.)	going	**weed**
-cooled (u.m.)	-soluble (u.m.)	laid	-choked (u.m.)
#cooler	spout	lay	-hidden (u.m.)
course	stain	mark	hook
craft	#table	post	killer
dog	tight	side	**week**
-drinking (u.m.)	wall	-sore (u.m.)	day
drop	works	-up (n., u.m.)	end
fall	worn	worn	-ender
-filled (u.m.)	**watt**	**weak**	-ending (u.m.)
finder	-hour	-backed (u.m.)	long (u.m.)
flood	meter	-eyed (u.m.)	-old (u.m.)
flow	-second	handed	**weigh**
fog	**wave**	-kneed (u.m.)	bridge
-free (u.m.)	-cut (u.m.)	minded	-in (n., u.m.)
front	form	mouthed	lock
gate	guide	**weather**	out (n., u.m.)
head	-lashed (u.m.)	beaten	shaft
hole	length	blown	**well**
horse	mark	-borne (u.m.)	-being (n.)
-inch	meter	break	-beloved (u.m.)
-laden (u.m.)	-moist (u.m.)	cock	-born (u.m.)
lane	-on (n., u.m.)	glass	-bound (u.m.)
leaf	off (n., u.m.)	going	-bred (u.m.)
#line	-swept (u.m.)	-hardened (u.m.)	-clad (u.m.)
-lined (u.m.)	-worn (u.m.)	#house	-deserving (u.m.)
locked	**wax**	-marked (u.m.)	-doer
log	bill	most	-doing (n., u.m.)
#main	-billed (u.m.)	proofing	-drained (u.m.)
mark	chandler	-stain (v.)	-drilling (u.m.)
melon	cloth	strip	#field
meter	-coated (u.m.)	-stripped (u.m.)	-grown (u.m.)
plant	-headed (u.m.)	worn	head

-headed (u.m.)
hole
-informed (u.m.)
-known (u.m.)
-looking (u.m.)
-meaner
-nigh (u.m.)
-off (u.m.)
-read (u.m.)
-set-up (u.m.)
-settled (u.m.)
side
-spoken (u.m.)
spring
stead
-thought-of (u.m.)
-thought-out (u.m.)
-to-do (u.m.)
-wisher
-wishing (u.m.)
-worn (u.m.)
welterweight
werewolf
west
bound
-central (u.m.)
#end
-faced (u.m.)
going
most
-northwest
#side
-sider
wet
#bar
-cheeked (u.m.)
-clean (v.)
land
-nurse (v.)
pack
wash

whale
back
-backed (u.m.)
bone
-built (u.m.)
-headed (u.m.)
-mouthed (u.m.)
ship
wharf
#boat
hand
head
side
what
abouts (n.)
ever
-is-it (n.)
not (n.)
soever
-you-may-call-it (n.)
wheat
cake
-colored (u.m.)
ear
-fed (u.m.)
field
grower
-rich (u.m.)
stalk
wheel
band
barrow
base
chair
-cut (u.m.)
going
horse (nonliteral)
#load
-made (u.m.)
plate
race
spin

stitch
-worn (u.m.)
wright
when
ever
-issued (u.m.)
soever
where
abouts
after
as
at
by
for
fore
from
in
insoever
into
of
on
over
soever
through
to
under
upon
with
withal
wherever
which
ever
soever
whiffletree
whip
cord
crack
-graft (v.)
#hand
lash
-marked (u.m.)
post
saw

-shaped (u.m.)
socket
staff
stalk
stall
stick
stitch
stock
-tailed (u.m.)
whipper
-in
snapper
whirl
about (n., u.m.)
blast
pool
-shaped (u.m.)
wind
whirlybird
whisk
broom
#tail
whistle
blower (nonliteral)
#blower (literal)
stop
white
back
beard (n.)
#book (diplomatic)
cap (n.)
coat (n.)
-collar (u.m.)
comb (n.)
corn
-eared (u.m.)
-eyed (u.m.)
face
-faced (u.m.)
foot (n.)
-footed (u.m.)

handed
-hard (u.m.)
head
-headed (u.m.)
-hot (u.m.)
#line
out (u.m., v.)
pot
tail
-tailed (u.m.)
-throated (u.m.)
top (n.)
vein
wash
who
ever
soever
whole
-headed (u.m.)
#hog
-hogger
sale
some
whomsoever
whooping#cough
wicker-woven (u.m.)
wicket
keeper
keeping
wide
-angle (u.m.)
-awake (u.m.)
-handed (u.m.)
mouthed
-open (u.m.)
spread
-spreading (u.m.)
widow
#bird
hood
wife
beater
hood

killer
-ridden (u.m.)
wigwag
wild
cat (n.)
-eyed (u.m.)
fire
#land
life
#man
wind
will
-less
-o'-the-wisp
power
wilt-resistant (u.m.)
wind (v.)
down (n., u.m.)
up (n., u.m.)
bag
ball
blown
brace
breaker
burn
catcher
-chapped (u.m.)
chill
fall
fast
-fertilized (u.m.)
firm
flow
#force
gall
-galled (u.m.)
#gauge
hole
-hungry (u.m.)
jammer
lass
mill
pipe

-pollinated (u.m.)
-rode (u.m.)
row
screen
-shaken (u.m.)
-shear (u.m.)
shield
shock
side
sleeve
sock
speed
stop
storm
stream
swept
#tunnel
worn
window
breaker
-breaking (u.m.)
#cleaner
-cleaning (u.m.)
#dresser
-dressing (u.m.)
pane
peeper
#shade
-shop (v.)
-shopping (u.m.)
sill
#work
wine
bag
-black (u.m.)
-drinking (u.m.)
glass
growing
-hardy (u.m.)
pot
#press
-red (u.m.)
seller

taster
tester
vat
wing
band
bar
beat
bolt
bone
borne
bow
cut
#flap
-footed (u.m.)
handed
-heavy (u.m.)
-loading (u.m.)
-loose (u.m.)
nut
over (n., u.m.)
-shaped (u.m.)
-shot (u.m.)
span
-swift (u.m.)
tip
top
wall
-weary (u.m.)
winter
-beaten (u.m.)
-clad (u.m.)
-fallow (v.)
-fed (u.m.)
feed
#green (color)
green (plant, etc.)
-hardy (u.m.)
kill
-made (u.m.)
-sown (u.m.)
tide
time
-worn (u.m.)

wire
bar
-caged (u.m.)
-cut (u.m.)
cutter
dancer
draw (v.)
-edged (u.m.)
#gauge
hair (dog)
-haired (u.m.)
less
#line
photo
puller
#rope
spun
stitch
-stitched (u.m.)
-tailed (u.m.)
tap
walker
works
-wound (u.m.)
wise
acre
crack
guy
head (n.)
-headed (u.m.)
-spoken (u.m.)
wishbone
witch
craft
#hazel
#hunt
-hunting (u.m.)
with
draw
hold
in
out
stand

within
-bound (u.m.)
-named (u.m.)
woe
begone
worn
wolf
-eyed (u.m.)
#fish
hound
pack
woman
folk
hood
kind
womenfolk
wonder
land
strong
-struck (u.m.)
wood
bark (color)
bin
bined
block
-built (u.m.)
-cased (u.m.)
chipper
chopper
chuck
craft
cut
grub
hole
horse
hung (u.m.)
land
-lined (u.m.)
lot
-paneled (u.m.)
pecker
pile
-planing (u.m.)

print
pulp
ranger
rock
#rot
shed
side
stock
turner
-turning (u.m.)
-walled (u.m.)
wind (music)
working (u.m.)
wooden
head (n.)
-hulled (u.m.)
wool
fell
gatherer
grader
growing
head
-laden (u.m.)
-lined (u.m.)
pack
press
shearer
shed
sorter
stock
washer
wheel
-white (u.m.)
winder
woolly
-coated (u.m.)
-headed (u.m.)
-looking (u.m.)
-white (u.m.)
word
-blind (u.m.)
book
builder

catcher
-clad (u.m.)
-deaf (u.m.)
flow
jobber
list
-perfect (u.m.)
play
seller
smith
work
aday (n., u.m.)
-and-turn (u.m.)
away (n., u.m.)
bag
basket
bench
book
card
day
-driven (u.m.)
fare
flow
folk
force
group
hand
-hardened (u.m.)
horse
-hour (u.m.)
housed
life
load
manship
out (n., u.m.)
pace
pan
paper
people
place
room
saving
sheet

shoe
shop
-shy (n., u.m.)
-shyness
site
slip
space
-stained (u.m.)
stand
station
stream
study
table
time
up (n., u.m.)
ways
-weary (u.m.)
week
worn
working
#capital
#load
#room
world
beater
-conscious (u.m.)
#consciousness
#line
#power
-shaking (u.m.)
-weary (u.m.)
worm
-eaten (u.m.)
-eating (u.m.)
hole
-riddled (u.m.)
-ripe (u.m.)
seed
shaft
wood
worn
#away
down (u.m.)

out (u.m.)
outness
worrywart
worth
less
while (n., u.m.)
whileness (n.)
wrap
around (n., u.m.)
-up (n., u.m.)
wreath-crowned
(u.m.)
wreck-free (u.m.)
wring
bolt
staff
wrist
band
bone
drop
fall
lock
#pin
plate
watch
write
back (n., u.m.)
-in (n., u.m.)
off (n., u.m.)
-protect
up (n., u.m.)
writing#room
wrong
doer
-ended (u.m.)
-minded (u.m.)
-thinking (u.m.)
wrought
#iron
-up (u.m.)
wry
bill
-billed (u.m.)

-faced (u.m.)
-looking (u.m.)
-mouthed (u.m.)
neck
-set (u.m.)

X

X
-body
-chromosome
-disease
#rated
-shaped
-virus
x
-axis
#ray (n.)
-ray (u.m.)
xantho (c.f.)
all one word
xeno (c.f.)
all one word
xero (c.f.)
all one word
xylo (c.f.)
all one word

Y

Y
-chromosome
-joint
-level
-potential
-shaped
-track
-tube
Yankee-Doodle
yard
arm
-deep (u.m.)
-long (u.m.)
stick
-wide (u.m.)

yaw
meter
-sighted (u.m.)
year
book
day
end
-hour (u.m.)
long (u.m.)
-old (u.m.)
-round (u.m.)
yellow
back
-backed (u.m.)
-bellied (u.m.)
belly
-billed (u.m.)
brush
#fever
-headed (u.m.)
-tailed (u.m.)
-throated (u.m.)
top
yes
-man
-no
yester
day
year
yoke
fellow
mating
-toed (u.m.)
young
eyed (u.m.)
-headed (u.m.)
-ladylike
-looking (u.m.)
-manlike
-old
-womanhood
youthtide
yuletide

Z

Z
-bar
zero
  axial
  -dimensional
    (u.m.)
  gravity
  #hour

zigzag
zinc
  -coated (u.m.)
  -white (u.m.)
zip
  #gun
  line
  -lipped (u.m.)
  lock

zoo (c.f.)
  all one word
zoologico (c.f.)
  all one word
zygo (c.f.)
  all one word
zygomatico (c.f.)
  -orbital
  rest one word

zymo (c.f.)
  all one word

8. Punctuation

8.1.   Punctuation is used to clarify the meaning of written or printed language. Well-planned word order requires a minimum of punctuation. The trend toward less punctuation calls for skillful phrasing to avoid ambiguity and to ensure exact interpretation. The GPO STYLE MANUAL can only offer general rules of text treatment. A rigid design or pattern of punctuation cannot be laid down, except in broad terms. The adopted style, however, must be consistent and based on sentence structure.

8.2.   The general principles governing the use of punctuation are: If it does not clarify the text it should be omitted; and, in the choice and placing of punctuation marks, the sole aim should be to bring out more clearly the author's thought. Punctuation should aid reading and prevent misreading.

Apostrophes and possessives

8.3.   The possessive case of a singular or plural noun not ending in *s* is formed by adding an apostrophe and *s*. The possessive case of a singular or plural noun ending in *s* or with an *s* sound is formed by adding an apostrophe only. Some irregular plurals require both an apostrophe and an *s*. (For possessives of italicized nouns, see rule 11.6.)

boss', bosses'	man's, men's
child's, children's	medium's, media's
citizen's, citizens'	people's, peoples'
Congress', Congresses'	Essex's, Essexes'
criterion's, criteria's	Jones', Joneses'
Co.'s, Cos.'	Jesus'
erratum's, errata's	Mars'
hostess', hostesses'	Dumas'
lady's, ladies'	Schmitz'

8.4.   In compound nouns, the *'s* is added to the element nearest the object possessed.

comptroller general's decision	attorney at law's fee
attorneys general's appointments	John White, Jr.'s (no comma) account
Mr. Brown of New York's motion	

193

8.5. Joint possession is indicated by placing an apostrophe on the last element of a series, while individual or alternative possession requires the use of an apostrophe on each element of a series.

soldiers and sailors' home	editor's or proofreader's opinion
Brown & Nelson's store	Clinton's or Bush's administration
men's, women's, and children's	Mrs. Smith's and Mrs. Allen's children
clothing	the Army's and the Navy's work
St. Michael's Men's Club	master's and doctor's degrees

8.6. In the use of an apostrophe in firm names, the names of organizations and institutions, the titles of books, and geographic names, the authentic form is to be followed. (Note use of "St.")

Masters, Mates & Pilots' Association	Johns Hopkins University
Dentists' Supply Co. of New York	Hinds' Precedents
International Ladies' Garment	Harpers Ferry
Workers' Union	Hells Canyon
Court of St. James's	Reader's Digest
St. Peter's Church	Actor's Equity Association
St. Elizabeths Hospital	*but* Martha's Vineyard

8.7. Generally, the apostrophe should not be used after names of countries and other organized bodies ending in *s*, or after words more descriptive than possessive (not indicating personal possession), except when plural does not end in *s*.

United States control	teachers college
United Nations meeting	merchants exchange
Southern States industries	children's hospital
Massachusetts laws	Young Men's Christian Association
Bureau of Ships report	
House of Representatives session	*but*
Teamsters Union	Veterans' Administration
editors handbook	(now Department of Veterans
syrup producers manual	Affairs)
technicians guide	Congress' attitude

8.8. Possessive pronouns do not take an apostrophe.

its	yours
ours	hers
theirs	whose

8.9.   Possessive indefinite or impersonal pronouns require an apostrophe.

each other's books   another's idea
some others' plans   someone's guesstimate
one's home is his castle

8.10.   The singular possessive case is used in such general terms as the following:

arm's length   fuller's earth
attorney's fees   miner's inch
author's alterations   printer's ink
confectioner's sugar   traveler's checks
cow's milk   writer's cramp
distiller's grain

8.11.   While an apostrophe is used to indicate possession and contractions, it is not generally necessary to use an apostrophe simply to show the plural form of most acronyms, initialisms, or abbreviations, except where clarity and sense demand such inclusion.

49ers   e'er (ever)
TVers   class of '08 (2008)
OKs   spirit of '76 (1776)
MCing
RIFing   *not* in her '70s (age)
RIFs   better: in her seventies
RIFed
YWCAs   *not* during the '90s
ABCs   better: during the 1990s or
1920s   during the twenties
IOUs
10s (thread)   *but*
4½s (bonds)   he never crosses his t's
3s (golf)   she fails to dot her i's
2 by 4s   a's, &'s, 7's
IQs   watch your p's and q's
don't (do not)   are they l's or 1's
I've (I have)   the Oakland A's
it's (it is/it has)   a number of s's
ne'er (never)   his resume had too many I's

When the plural form of an acronym appears in parentheses, a lower case *s* is included within the parentheses.

(MPDs)   (IPOs)
(MP3s)   (SUVs)
(JPEGs)

8.12. The apostrophe is omitted in abbreviations, and also in shortened forms of certain other words.

Danl., *not* Dan'l   Halloween, *not* Hallowe'en
phone, *not* 'phone   copter, *not* 'copter
coon, *not* 'coon
possum, *not* 'possum   *but* ma'am

8.13. The plural of spelled-out numbers, of words referred to as words, and of words containing an apostrophe is formed by adding *s* or *es*; but *'s* is added to indicate the plural of words used as words if omission of the apostrophe would cause difficulty in reading.

twos, threes, sevens   yeses and noes
ands, ifs, and buts   yeas and nays
ins and outs
the haves and have-nots   *but*
ups and downs   do's and don'ts
whereases and wherefores   which's and that's
pros and cons

8.14. The possessive case is often used in lieu of an objective phrase even though ownership is not involved.

1 day's labor (labor for 1 day)   for charity's sake
12 days' labor   for pity's sake
2 hours' traveltime   several billion dollars' worth
a stone's throw
2 weeks' pay   *but* $10 billion worth

8.15. The possessive case is not used in such expressions as the following, in which one noun modifies another.

day labor (labor by the day)   State prison
quartermaster stores   State rights

8.16.   For euphony, nouns ending in *s* or *ce* and followed by a word beginning with *s* form the possessive by adding an apostrophe only.

for goodness' sake   for acquaintance' sake
Mr. Hughes' service   for conscience' sake
for old times' sake

8.17.   A possessive noun used in an adjective sense requires the addition of *'s*.

He is a friend of John's.   Stern's is running a sale.

8.18.   A noun preceding a gerund should be in the possessive case.

in the event of Mary's leaving   the ship's hovering nearby

Brackets

Brackets, in pairs, are used—

8.19.   In transcripts, congressional hearings, the Congressional Record, testimony in courtwork, etc., to enclose interpolations that are not specifically a part of the original quotation, corrections, explanations, omissions, editorial comments, or a caution that an error is reproduced literally.

We found this to be true at the Government Printing Office [GPO].
He came on the 3d [2d] of July.
Our conference [lasted] 2 hours.
The general [Washington] ordered him to leave.
The paper was as follows [reads]:
I do not know. [Continues reading:]
[Chorus of "Mr. Chairman."]
They fooled only themselves. [Laughter.]
Our party will always serve the people [applause] in spite of the opposition [loud applause]. (If more than one bracketed interpolation, both are included within the sentence.)
The WITNESS. He did it that way [indicating].
Q. Do you know these men [handing witness a list]?
The bill had *not* been paid. [Italic added.] *or* [Emphasis added.]
The statue [sic] was on the statute books.
The WITNESS. This matter is classified. [Deleted.]
[Deleted.]
Mr. JONES. Hold up your hands. [Show of hands.]
Answer [after examining list]. Yes; I do.
Q. [Continuing.]
A. [Reads:]

    A. [Interrupting.]
    [Discussion off the record.]
    [Pause.]
    The WITNESS [interrupting]. It is known——
    Mr. JONES [continuing]. Now let us take the next item.
    Mr. SMITH [presiding]. Do you mean that literally?
    Mr. JONES [interposing]. Absolutely.
    [The matter referred to is as follows:]
    The CHAIRMAN [to Mr. Smith].
    The CHAIRMAN [reading]:
    Mr. KELLEY [to the chairman]. From 15 to 25 percent.
    [Objected to.]
    [Mr. Smith nods.]
    [Mr. Smith aside.]
    [Mr. Smith makes further statement off the record.]
    Mr. JONES [for Mr. Smith].
    A VOICE FROM AUDIENCE. Speak up.
    SEVERAL VOICES. Quiet!

8.20.   In bills, contracts, laws, etc., to indicate matter that is to be omitted.

8.21.   In mathematics, to denote that enclosed matter is to be treated as a unit.

8.22.   When matter in brackets makes more than one paragraph, start each paragraph with a bracket and place the closing bracket at end of last paragraph.

Colon

The colon is used—

8.23.   Before a final clause that extends or amplifies preceding matter.

> Give up conveniences; do not demand special privileges; do not stop work: these are necessary while we are at war.
> Railroading is not a variety of outdoor sport: it is service.

8.24.   To introduce formally any matter that forms a complete sentence, question, or quotation.

> The following question came up for discussion: What policy should be adopted?
> She said: "I believe the time is now or never." [When a direct quotation follows that has more than a few words.]

There are three factors, as follows: First, military preparation; second, industrial mobilization; and third, manpower.

8.25. After a salutation.

My Dear Sir:
Ladies and Gentlemen:
To Whom It May Concern:

8.26. In expressing clock time.

2:40 p.m.

8.27. After introductory lines in lists, tables, and leaderwork, if subentries follow.

Seward Peninsula:
   Council district:
      Northern Light Mining Co.
      Wild Goose Trading Co.
   Fairhaven district: Alaska Dredging Association (single subitem runs in).
Seward Peninsula: Council district (single subitem runs in):
      Northern Light Mining Co.
      Wild Goose Trading Co.

8.28. In Biblical and other citations.

Luke 4:3.
I Corinthians 13:13.
Journal of Education 3:342–358.

8.29. In bibliographic references, between place of publication and name of publisher.

Congressional Directory. Washington: U.S. Government Printing Office.

8.30. To separate book titles and subtitles.

Financial Aid for College Students: Graduate
Germany Revisited: Education in the Federal Republic

8.31. In imprints before the year (en space each side of colon).

U.S. Government Printing Office
Washington : 2008

8.32. In proportions.

Concrete mixed 5:3:1
but 5–2–1 *or* 5-2-1 (when so in copy)

8.33.   In double colon as ratio sign.

    1:2::3:6

Comma

The comma is used—

8.34.   To separate two words or figures that might otherwise be misunderstood.

    Instead of hundreds, thousands came.
    Instead of 20, 50 came.
    December 7, 1941.
    In 2003, 400 men were dismissed.
    To John, Smith was very kind.
    What the difficulty is, is not known.
    but He suggested that that committee be appointed.

8.35.   Before a direct quotation of only a few words following an introductory phrase.

    He said, "Now or never."

8.36.   To indicate the omission of a word or words.

    Then we had much; now, nothing.

8.37.   After each of a series of coordinate qualifying words.

    short, swift streams; *but* short tributary streams

8.38.   Between an introductory modifying phrase and the subject modified.

    Beset by the enemy, they retreated.

8.39.   Before and after *Jr., Sr., Esq., Ph.D., F.R.S., Inc.,* etc., within a sentence except where possession is indicated.

Henry Smith, Jr., chairman	*but*
Peter Johns, F.R.S., London	John Smith 2d (*or* II); Smith, John, II
Washington, DC, schools	Mr. Smith, Junior, also spoke
Motorola, Inc., factory	(where only last name is used)
Brown, A.H., Jr. (*not* Brown, Jr., A.H.)	Alexandria, VA's waterfront

8.40.   To set off parenthetic words, phrases, or clauses.

> Mr. Jefferson, who was then Secretary of State, favored the location of the
>   National Capital at Washington.
> It must be remembered, however, that the Government had no guarantee.
> It is obvious, therefore, that this office cannot function.
> The atom bomb, which was developed at the Manhattan project, was first
>   used in World War II.
> Their high morale might, he suggested, have caused them to put success of
>   the team above the reputation of the college.
> The restriction is laid down in title IX, chapter 8, section 15, of the code.
> *but* The man who fell [restrictive clause] broke his back.
> The dam that gave way [restrictive clause] was poorly constructed.
> He therefore gave up the search.

8.41.   To set off words or phrases in apposition or in contrast.

> Mr. Green, the lawyer, spoke for the defense.
> Mr. Jones, attorney for the plaintiff, signed the petition.
> Mr. Smith, not Mr. Black, was elected.
> James Roosevelt, Democrat, of California.
> Jean's sister, Joyce, was the eldest. (Jean had one sister.)
> *but* Jonathan's brother Moses Taylor was appointed. (Jonathan had more than
>   one brother.)

8.42.   After each member within a series of three or more words, phrases,
letters, or figures used with *and, or,* or *nor.*

> red, white, and blue
> horses, mules, and cattle; *but* horses and mules and cattle
> by the bolt, by the yard, or in remnants
> a, b, and c
> neither snow, rain, nor heat
> 2 days, 3 hours, and 4 minutes (series); *but* 70 years 11 months 6 days (age)

8.43.   Before the conjunction in a compound sentence containing two or
more independent clauses, each of which could have been written as
a simple sentence.

> Fish, mollusks, and crustaceans were plentiful in the lakes, and turtles fre-
>   quented the shores.
> The boy went home alone, and his sister remained with the crowd.

8.44. After a noun or phrase in direct address.

Senator, will the measure be defeated?
Mr. Chairman, I will reply to the gentleman later.
but Yes, sir; he did see it.
No, ma'am; I do not recall.

8.45. After an interrogative clause, followed by a direct question.

You are sure, are you not?   You will go, will you not?

8.46. Between the title of a person and the name of an organization in the absence of the words *of* or *of the.*

Chief, Division of Finance   colonel, 12th Cavalry Regiment
chairman, Committee on   president, University of Virginia
  Appropriations

8.47. Inside closing quotation mark.

He said "four," not "five."
"Freedom is an inherent right," he insisted.
Items marked "A," "B," and "C," inclusive, were listed.

8.48. To separate thousands, millions, etc., in numbers of four or more digits.

4,230   *but* 1,000,000,000 is more clearly
50,491   illustrated as 1 billion
1,250,000

8.49. After the year in complete dates (month, day, year) within a sentence.

The dates of September 11, 1993, to June 12, 1994, were erroneous.
This was reflected in the June 13, 2007, report.
but Production for June 2008 was normal.
The 10 February 2008 deadline passed.

The comma is omitted—

8.50. Between superior figures or letters in footnote references.

Numerous instances may be cited.[12]
Data are based on October production.[ab]

8.51.   Before ZIP (Zone Improvement Plan) Code postal-delivery number.

> Government Printing Office, Washington, DC 20401–0003
> East Rochester, OH 44625–9701

8.52.   Between month, holiday, or season and year in dates.

June 2008	150 B.C.
22d of May 2008	Labor Day 2006
February and March 2008	Easter Sunday 2006
January, February, and March 2008	5 January 2006 (military usage)
January 24 A.D. 2008; 15th of June	spring 2007
A.D. 2008	autumn 2007

8.53.   Between the name and number of an organization.

> Columbia Typographical Union No. 101–12
> American Legion Post No. 33

8.54.   In fractions, in decimals, and in serial numbers, except patent numbers.

> ½₅₀₀
> 1.0947
> page 2632
> 202–275–2303 (telephone number)
> 1721–1727 St. Clair Avenue
> Executive Order 11242
> motor No. 189463
> 1450 kilocycles; 1100 meters

8.55.   Between two nouns one of which identifies the other.

> The Children's Bureau's booklet "Infant Care" continues to be a bestseller.

8.56.   Before an ampersand (&).

> Brown, Wilson & Co.
> Mine, Mill & Smelter Workers

8.57.   Before abbreviations of compass directions.

> 6430 Princeton Dr. SW.

8.58.   In bibliographies, between name of the publication and volume or similar number.

> American Library Association Bulletin 34:238, April 1940.

8.59.   Wherever possible without danger of ambiguity.

> $2 gold
> Executive Order No. 21
> General Order No. 12; *but* General Orders, No. 12
> Public Law 85–1
> He graduates in the year 2010 (not the year 2,010)
> My age is 30 years 6 months 12 days.
> John Lewis 2d (*or* II)
> Murphy of Illinois; Murphy of New York (where only last name is used)
> Carroll of Carrollton; Henry of Navarre (person closely identified with place);
>   *but* Clyde Leo Downs, of Maryland; President Levin, of Yale University
> James Bros. et al.; but James Bros., Nelson Co., et al. (last element of series)

Dash

A 1-em dash is used—

8.60.   To mark a sudden break or abrupt change in thought.

> He said—and no one contradicted him—"The battle is lost."
> If the bill should pass—which God forbid!—the service will be wrecked.
> The auditor—shall we call him a knave or a fool?—approved an inaccurate statement.

8.61.   To indicate an interruption or an unfinished word or sentence. A 2-em dash is used when the interruption is by a person other than the speaker, and a 1-em dash will show self-interruption. Note that extracts must begin with a true paragraph. Following extracts, colloquy must start as a paragraph.

> "Such an idea can scarcely be——"
> "The word 'donation'——"
> "The word 'dona'——"
> He said: "Give me lib——"
> The bill reads "repeal," not "am——"
> Q. Did you see——A. No, sir.
>
> Mr. BROWN [reading]: "The report goes on to say that"—Observe this closely—"during the fiscal year * * *."

8.62.   Instead of commas or parentheses, if the meaning may thus be clarified.

> These are shore deposits—gravel, sand, and clay—but marine sediments underlie them.

8.63. Before a final clause that summarizes a series of ideas.

> Freedom of speech, freedom of worship, freedom from want, freedom from fear—these are the fundamentals of moral world order.

8.64. After an introductory phrase reading into the following lines and indicating repetition of such phrase.

> I recommend—
>> That we submit them for review and corrections;
>> That we then accept them as corrected; and
>> That we also publish them.

8.65. With a preceding question mark, in lieu of a colon.

> How can you explain this?—"Fee paid, $5."

8.66. To precede a credit line or a run-in credit or signature.

>> Lay the proud usurpers low!
>> Tyrants fall in every foe!
>> Liberty's in every blow!
>>> Let us do or die!
>>> —*Robert Burns.*

> Every man's work shall be made manifest.—I Corinthians 3:13.
> This statement is open to question.—GERALD H. FORSYTHE.

8.67. After a run-in sidehead.

8.68. To separate run-in questions and answers in testimony.

> Q. Did he go?—A. No.

A 1-em dash is not used—

8.69. At the beginning of any line of type, except as shown in rule 8.66.

8.70. Immediately after a comma, colon, or semicolon.

A 3-em dash is used—

8.71. In bibliographies to indicate repetition.

> Powell, James W., Jr., Hunting in Virginia's lowlands. 1972. 200 pp.
> ———— Fishing off Delmarva. 1972. 28 pp.

An en dash is used—

8.72. In a combination of (1) figures, (2) capital letters, or (3) figures and capital letters. An en dash, not a hyphen, is used, even when such terms are adjectival modifiers.

figures:

5–20 (bonds)

85–1—85–20 (Public laws. Note em dash between two elements with en dashes)

1–703–765–6593 (telephone number)

230–20–8030 (Social Security number)

$15–$25 (range)

capital letters:

WTOP–AM–FM–TV (radio and television stations)

CBS–TV

AFL–CIO (union merger)

C–SPAN (satellite television)

figures and capitals:

6–A (exhibit identification)

DC–14 (airplane)

I–95 (interstate roadway)

4–H (Club)

LK–66–A(2)–74 (serial number)

but Rule 13e–4

section 12(a)–(b) (en dash used for the word "to")

ACF-Brill Motors Co. (hyphen with capital letters and a word)

loran-C (hyphen with lowercase word and capital letter)

MiG-25 (hyphen with mixed letters with figure)

ALL-AMERICAN ESSAY CONTEST (hyphen in capitalized heading)

Four Corners Monument, AZ-NM-UT-CO (hyphen with two-letter state abbreviations)

8.73. In the absence of the word *to* when denoting a span of time.

2005–2008   January–June   Monday–Friday

An en dash is not used—

8.74. For *to* when the word *from* precedes the first of two related figures or expressions.

From June 1 to July 30, 2005; *not* from June 1–July 30, 2005

8.75. For *and* when the word *between* precedes the first of two related figures or expressions.

Between 2000 and 2008; *not* between 2000–08

Ellipses

8.76. Three asterisks (preferred form) or three periods, separated by en spaces, are used to denote an ellipsis within a sentence, at the beginning or end of a sentence, or in two or more consecutive sentences. To achieve faithful reproduction of excerpt material, editors using period ellipses should indicate placement of the terminal period in relation to an ellipsis at the end of a sentence. Note, in the following examples, the additional spacing necessary to clearly define commas and the terminal period when period ellipses are employed.

> The Senate having tried Andrew Johnson, President of the United States, upon articles of impeachment exhibited against him by the House of Representatives, and two-thirds of the Senators present not having found him guilty of the charges contained in the second, third, and eleventh articles of impeachment, it is therefore
>
> *Ordered and adjudged.* That the said Andrew Johnson, President of the United States be, and he is, acquitted of the charges in said articles made and set forth.

> The Senate having tried Andrew Johnson * * * upon articles of impeachment * * * and two-thirds of the Senators present not having found him guilty of the charges * * *, it is therefore
>
> *Ordered and adjudged.* That the said Andrew Johnson, President of the United States be * * * acquitted of the charges * * *.

> The Senate having tried Andrew Johnson . . . upon articles of impeachment . . . and two-thirds of the Senators present not having found him guilty of the charges . . . , it is therefore
>
> *Ordered and adjudged.* That the said Andrew Johnson, President of the United States be . . . acquitted of the charges. . . .

8.77. Ellipses are not overrun alone at the end of a paragraph.

8.78. When periods are not specifically requested for ellipses in copy that has both periods and asterisks, asterisks will be used.

8.79. A line of asterisks indicates an omission of one or more entire paragraphs. In 26½-pica or wider measure, a line of "stars" means seven asterisks indented 2 ems at each end of the line, with the remaining space divided evenly between the asterisks. In measures less than 26½ picas, five asterisks are used. Quotation marks are not used on a line of asterisks in quoted matter. Where an ellipsis line ends a complete quotation, no closing quote is used.

*   *   *   *   *   *   *

8.80. Indented matter in 26½-pica or wider measure also requires a seven-asterisk line to indicate the omission of one or more entire paragraphs.

8.81. If an omission occurs in the last part of a paragraph immediately before a line of asterisks, three asterisks are used, in addition to the line of asterisks, to indicate such an omission.

8.82. Equalize spacing above and below an ellipsis line.

Exclamation point

8.83. The exclamation point is used to mark surprise, incredulity, admiration, appeal, or other strong emotion which may be expressed even in a declarative or interrogative sentence.

> Who shouted, "All aboard!" [Note omission of question mark.]
> "Great!" he shouted. [Note omission of comma.]
> He acknowledged the fatal error!
> How breathtakingly beautiful!
> Timber!
> Mayday! Mayday!

8.84. In direct address, either to a person or a personified object, *O* is used without an exclamation point, or other punctuation; but if strong feeling is expressed, an exclamation point is placed at the end of the statement.

> O my friend, let us consider this subject impartially.
> O Lord, save Thy people!

8.85. In exclamations without direct address or appeal, *oh* is used instead of *O*, and the exclamation point is omitted.

> Oh, but the gentleman is mistaken.
> Oh dear; the time is so short.

Hyphen

The hyphen (a punctuation mark, not an element in the spelling of words) is used—

8.86. To connect the elements of certain compound words. (See Chapter 6 "Compounding Rules.")

8.87.   To indicate continuation of a word divided at the end of a line. (See Word Division, supplement to the STYLE MANUAL.)

8.88.   Between the letters of a spelled word.

> The Style Board changed New Jerseyite to New J-e-r-s-e-y-a-n.
> A native of Halifax is a H-a-l-i-g-o-n-i-a-n.
> The Chinese repressive action took place in T-i-a-n-a-n-m-e-n Square.

8.89.   To separate elements of chemical formulas.

The hyphen, as an element, may be used—

8.90.   To represent letters deleted or illegible words in copy.

> Oakland's - - bonic plague   Richard Emory H - - - -

Parentheses

Parentheses are used—

8.91.   To set off matter not intended to be part of the main statement or not a grammatical element of the sentence, yet important enough to be included. In colloquy, brackets must be substituted.

> This case (124 U.S. 329) is not relevant.
> The result (see fig. 2) is most surprising.
> The United States is the principal purchaser (by value) of these exports (23 per cent in 1995 and 19 percent in 1996).

8.92.   To enclose a parenthetic clause where the interruption is too great to be indicated by commas.

> You can find it neither in French dictionaries (at any rate, not in Littré) nor in English dictionaries.

8.93.   To enclose an explanatory word not part of a written or printed statement.

> the Winchester (VA) Star; *but* the Star of Winchester, VA
> Portland (OR) Chamber of Commerce; *but* Athens, GA, schools

8.94.   To enclose letters or numbers designating items in a series, either at the beginning of paragraphs or within a paragraph.

> The order of delivery will be: (a) Food, (b) clothing, and (c) tents and other housing equipment.
> You will observe that the sword is (1) old fashioned, (2) still sharp, and (3) unusually light for its size.
> Paragraph 7(B)(1)(*a*) will be found on page 6. (Note parentheses closed up.)

8.95. To enclose a figure inserted to confirm a written or printed statement given in words if double form is specifically requested.

> This contract shall be completed in sixty (60) days.

8.96. A reference in parentheses at the end of a sentence is placed before the period, unless it is a complete sentence in itself.

> The specimen exhibits both phases (pl. 14, *A*, *B*).
> The individual cavities show great variation. (See pl. 4.)

8.97. If a sentence contains more than one parenthetic reference, the one at the end is placed before the period.

> This sandstone (see pl. 6) is in every county of the State (see pl. 1).

8.98. When a figure is followed by a letter in parentheses, no space is used between the figure and the opening parenthesis; but if the letter is not in parentheses and the figure is repeated with each letter, the letter is closed up with the figure.

> 15(*a*). Classes, grades, and sizes.
> 15*a*. Classes, grades, and sizes.

8.99. If both a figure and a letter in parentheses are used before each paragraph, a period and an en space are used after the closing parenthesis. If the figure is not repeated before each letter in parentheses but is used only before the first letter, the period is placed after the figure. However, if the figure is not repeated before each letter in parentheses and no period is used, space is inserted after the number if at least one other lettered subsection appears.

> 15(*a*). When the figure is used before the letter in each paragraph—
> 15(*b*). The period is placed after the closing parenthesis.
> 15. (*a*) When the figure is used before the letter in the first paragraph but not repeated with subsequent letters—
> (*b*) The period is used after the figure only.
> Sec. 12 (a) When no period is used and a letter in parentheses appears after a numbered item—
> (b) Space must be used after the number if at least one other lettered subsection is shown.

8.100. Note position of the period relative to closing parenthesis:

> The vending stand sells a variety of items (sandwiches, beverages, cakes, etc.).
> The vending stand sells a variety of items (sandwiches, beverages, cakes, etc. (sometimes ice cream)).

The vending stand sells a variety of items. (These include sandwiches, beverages, cakes, etc. (6).)

8.101. To enclose bylines in congressional work.

(By Harvey Hagman, archeological correspondent)

8.102. When matter in parentheses makes more than one paragraph, start each paragraph with a parenthesis and place the closing parenthesis at the end of the last paragraph.

Period

The period is used—

8.103. After a declarative sentence that is not exclamatory or after an imperative sentence.

Stars are suns.
He was employed by Sampson & Co.
Do not be late.
On with the dance.

8.104. After an indirect question or after a question intended as a suggestion and not requiring an answer.

Tell me how he did it.
May we hear from you.
May we ask prompt payment.

8.105. In place of a closing parenthesis after a letter or number denoting a series.

a. Bread well baked   1. Punctuate freely
b. Meat cooked rare   2. Compound sparingly
c. Cubed apples stewed   3. Index thoroughly

8.106. Sometimes to indicate ellipsis.

8.107. After a run-in sidehead.

Conditional subjunctive.—The conditional subjunctive is required for all unreal and doubtful conditions.

2. Peacetime preparation.—*a.* The Chairman of the National Security Resources Board, etc.

2. Peacetime preparation—*Industrial mobilization plans.*—The Chairman of the National Security Resources Board, etc.

2. Peacetime preparation.—*Industrial mobilization.*—The Chairman of the National Security Resources Board, etc.

62. *Determination of types.—a. Statement of characteristics.*—Before types of equipment, etc.

Steps in planning for procurement.—(1) *Determination of needs.*—To plan for the procurement of such arms, etc.

62. *Determination of types.—(a) Statement of characteristics.*—Before, etc.

DETERMINATION OF TYPES.—Statement of characteristics.—Before types of, etc.

NOTE.—The source material was furnished.
but Source: U.S. Department of Commerce, Bureau of the Census.

8.108. Paragraphs and subparagraphs may be arranged according to the following scheme. The sequence is not fixed, and variations, in addition to the use of center and side heads or indented paragraphs, may be adopted, depending on the number of parts.

I. Outlines can begin with a capital Roman numeral.
  A. The number of levels and the width of the column determine alignment and indention.
  1. A set space (en space) following the identifier aids alignment.
    a. Usually, typefaces and sizes are chosen to agree with the hierarchy of the head breakdowns.
    (1) Aligning runover lines with the first word which follows the number or letter aids readability.
      (*a*) It is important to vary (alternate) the use of letters and numbers in any outline.
      (i) The lowercase Roman numerals (i), (ii), etc. may be used as parts of the outline or to identify subparts of any previous parts.
      (*aa*) When absolutely necessary, double (or triple) lowercase letters may be used.
II. Where not needed, the capital Roman numerals may be discarded and the outline can begin with the letter A. As in any composition, consistency in indentions and order is essential.

8.109. To separate integers from decimals in a single expression.

13.75 percent	1.25 meters
$3.50	0.08 mile

8.110. In continental European languages, to indicate thousands.

1.317	72.190.175

8.111. After abbreviations, unless otherwise specified. (See Chapter 9, "Abbreviations and Letter Symbols.")

Apr.   RR.
fig.   *but*
Ph.D.   m (meter)
NE. (Northeast)   kc (kilocycle)
SSE. (South-Southeast)   NY (New York)

8.112. After legends and explanatory matter beneath illustrations. Legends without descriptive language do not receive periods.

FIGURE 1.—Schematic drawing.
FIGURE 1.—Continued.
but FIGURE 1 (without legend, no period)

8.113. After *Article 1, Section 1*, etc., at the beginning of paragraphs.

A center period is sometimes used—

8.114. To indicate multiplication. (Use of a multiplication sign is preferable.)

$$a \cdot b \qquad\qquad a \times b$$

The period is omitted—

8.115. After—

Lines in title pages
Center, side, and running heads; *but* is not omitted after run-in
     sideheads
Continued lines
Boxheads of tables
Scientific, chemical, or other symbols
This rule does not apply to abbreviation periods.

8.116. After a quotation mark that is preceded by a period.

She said: "I believe the time is now or never."

8.117. After letters used as names without specific designation.

Officer B, Subject A, Brand X, etc.
A said to B that all is well.
Mr. A told Mr. B that the case was closed.
Mr. X (for unknown or censored name).

but Mr. A. [for Mr. Andrews]. I do not want to go.
Mr. K. [for Mr. King]. The meeting is adjourned.

8.118. After a middle initial which is merely a letter and not an abbreviation of a name.

Daniel D Tompkins
Ross T McIntire
but Harry S. Truman (President Truman's preference)

8.119. After a short name which is not an abbreviation of the longer form.

Alex   Mac
Ed   Sam

8.120. After Roman numerals used as ordinals.

King George V   Super Bowl XLII
Apollo XII insigne

8.121. After words and incomplete statements listed in columns. Full-measure matter is not to be regarded as a column.

8.122. Explanatory matter should be set in 6 point type under leaders or rules.

....
(Name)   (Address)   (Position)

8.123. Immediately before leaders, even if an abbreviation precedes the leaders.

Question mark

The question mark is used—

8.124. To indicate a direct query, even if not in the form of a question.

Did he do it?
He did what?
Can the money be raised? is the question.
Who asked, "Why?" [Note single question mark.]
"Did you hurt yourself, my son?" she asked.

8.125. To express more than one query in the same sentence.

Can he do it? or you? or anyone?

8.126. To express doubt.

> He said the boy was 8(?) feet tall. (No space before question mark.)
> The statue(?) was on the statute books.
> The scientific identification *Dorothia*? was noted. (Roman "?".)

Quotation marks

Quotation marks are used—

8.127. To enclose direct quotations. (Each part of an interrupted quotation begins and ends with quotation marks.)

> The answer is "No."
> He said, "John said, 'No.' " (Note thin space between single and double closing quotes.)
> "John," asked Henry, "why do you go?"

8.128. To enclose any matter following such terms as *entitled, the word, the term, marked, designated, classified, named, endorsed, cited as, referred to as,* or *signed;* but are not used to enclose expressions following the terms *known as, called, so-called,* etc., unless such expressions are misnomers or slang.

> Congress passed the act entitled "An act * * *."
> After the word "treaty", insert a comma.
> Of what does the item "Miscellaneous debts" consist?
> The column "Imports from foreign countries" was not * * *.
> The document will be marked "Exhibit No. 21"; *but* The document may be made exhibit No. 2.
> The check was endorsed "John Adamson."
> It was signed "John."
> *but* Beryllium is known as glucinium in some European countries.
> It was called profit and loss.
> The so-called investigating body.

8.129. To enclose titles of addresses, articles, awards, books, captions, editorials, essays, headings, subheadings, headlines, hearings, motion pictures and plays (including television and radio programs), operas, papers, short poems, reports, songs, studies, subjects, and themes. All principal words are to be capitalized.

> An address on "Uranium-235 in the Atomic Age"
> The article "Germany Revisited" appeared in the last issue.
> He received the "Man of the Year" award.
> "The Conquest of Mexico," a published work (book)
> Under the caption "Long-Term Treasurys Rise"
> The subject was discussed in "Punctuation." (chapter heading)

It will be found in "Part XI: Early Thought."
The editorial "Haphazard Budgeting"
"Compensation," by Emerson (essay)
"United States To Appoint Representative to U.N." (heading for headline)
In "Search for Paradise" (motion picture); "South Pacific" (play)
A paper on "Constant-Pressure Combustion" was read.
"O Captain! My Captain!" (short poem)
The report "Atomic Energy: What It Means to the Nation"; *but* annual report of the Public Printer
This was followed by the singing of "The Star-Spangled Banner."
Under the subhead "Sixty Days of Turmoil" will be found * * *.
The subject (or theme) of the conference is "Peaceful Uses of Atomic Energy."
also Account 5, "Management fees."
Under the heading "Management and Operation."
Under the appropriation "Building of ships, Navy."

8.130.   At the beginning of each paragraph of a quotation, but at the end of the last paragraph only.

8.131.   To enclose a letter or communication, which bears both date and signature, within a letter.

8.132.   To enclose misnomers, slang expressions, sobriquets, coined words, or ordinary words used in an arbitrary way.

His report was "bunk."
It was a "gentlemen's agreement."
The "invisible government" is responsible.
George Herman "Babe" Ruth.
but He voted for the lameduck amendment.

8.133.   Quotation marks close up to adjacent characters except when they precede a fraction or an apostrophe or precede or follow a superior figure or letter, in which case a thin space is used. A thin space is used to separate double and single quotation marks.

Quotation marks are not used—

8.134.   In poetry. The lines of a poem should align on the left, those that rhyme taking the same indention.

Why seek to scale Mount Everest,
    Queen of the air?
Why strive to crown that cruel crest
    And deathward dare?

> Said Mallory of dauntless quest:
> "Because it's there."

8.135. To enclose titles of works of art: paintings, statuary, etc.

8.136. To enclose names of newspapers or magazines.

8.137. To enclose complete letters having date and signature.

8.138. To enclose extracts that are indented or set in smaller type, or solid extracts in leaded matter; but indented matter in text that is already quoted carries quotation marks.

8.139. In indirect quotations.

> Tell her yes. He could not say no.

8.140. Before a display initial which begins a quoted paragraph.

8.141. The comma and the final period will be placed inside the quotation marks. Other punctuation marks should be placed inside the quotation marks only if they are a part of the matter quoted.

> Ruth said, "I think so."
> "The President," he said, "will veto the bill."
> The trainman shouted, "All aboard!"
> Who asked, "Why?"
> The President suggests that "an early occasion be sought * * *."
> Why call it a "gentlemen's agreement"?

8.142. In congressional and certain other classes of work showing amendments, and in courtwork with quoted language, punctuation marks are printed after the quotation marks when not a part of the quoted matter.

> Insert the words "growth", "production", and "manufacture".
> To be inserted after the words "cadets, U.S. Coast Guard;".
> Change "February 1, 1983", to "June 30, 2008".
> "Insert in lieu thereof 'July 1, 1983,'."

8.143. When occurring together, quotation marks should precede footnote reference numbers.

> The commissioner claimed that the award was "unjustified."[1]
> Kelly's exact words were: "The facts in the case prove otherwise."[2]

8.144.   Quotation marks should be limited, if possible, to three sets (double, single, double).

> "The question in the report is, 'Can a person who obtains his certificate of naturalization by fraud be considered a "bona fide" citizen of the United States?'"

Semicolon

The semicolon is used—

8.145.   To separate clauses containing commas.

> Donald A. Peters, Jr., president of the First National Bank, was also a director of New York Central; Harvey D. Jones was a director of Oregon Steel Co. and New York Central; Thomas W. Harrison, chairman of the board of McBride & Co., was also on the board of Oregon Steel Co.
>
> Reptiles, amphibians, and predatory mammals swallow their prey whole or in large pieces, bones included; waterfowl habitually take shellfish entire; and gallinaceous birds are provided with gizzards that grind up the hardest seeds.
>
> Yes, sir; he did see it.
>
> No, sir; I do not recall.

8.146.   To separate statements that are too closely related in meaning to be written as separate sentences, and also statements of contrast.

> Yes; that is right.
>
> No; we received one-third.
>
> It is true in peace; it is true in war.
>
> War is destructive; peace, constructive.

8.147.   To set off explanatory abbreviations or words which summarize or explain preceding matter.

> The industry is related to groups that produce finished goods; i.e., electrical machinery and transportation equipment.
>
> There were three metal producers involved; namely, Jones & Laughlin, Armco, and Kennecott.

The semicolon is not used—

8.148.   Where a comma will suffice.

> Offices are located in New York, NY, Chicago, IL, and Dallas, TX.

Single punctuation

8.149. Single punctuation should be used wherever possible without ambiguity.

> 124 U.S. 321 (no comma)
> Sir: (no dash)
> Joseph replied, "It is a worthwhile effort." (no outside period)

Type

8.150. All punctuation marks, including parentheses, brackets, and superior reference figures, are set to match the type of the words which they adjoin. A lightface dash is used after a run-in boldface sidehead followed by lightface matter. Lightface brackets, parentheses, or quotation marks shall be used when both boldface and lightface matter are enclosed.

> Charts: C&GS 5101 (N.O. **18320**), page **282** (**see above**); N.O. **93491** (**Plan**); page **271**.

9. Abbreviations and Letter Symbols

9.1. Abbreviations and letter symbols are used to save space and to avoid distracting the reader by use of repetitious words or phrases.

9.2. The nature of the publication governs the extent to which abbreviations are used. In text of technical and legal publications, and in parentheses, brackets, footnotes, sidenotes, tables, leaderwork, and bibliographies, many words are frequently abbreviated. Heads, legends, tables of contents, and indexes follow the style of the text.

9.3. Internal and terminal punctuation in symbols represening units of measure are to be omitted to conform with practice adopted by scientific, technical, and industrial groups. Where omission of terminal punctuation causes confusion; e.g., the symbol *in* (inch) mistaken for the preposition *in*, the symbol should be spelled out.

9.4. Standard and easily understood forms are preferable, and they should be uniform throughout a job. Abbreviations not generally known should be followed in the text by the spelled-out forms in parentheses the first time they occur; in tables and leaderwork such explanatory matter should be supplied in a footnote. As the printer cannot rewrite the copy, the author should supply these explanatory forms.

9.5. In technical matter, symbols for units of measure should be used only with figures; similarly, many other abbreviations and symbols should not appear in isolation. For example, energy is measured in foot-pounds, *not* energy is measured in ft•lbs.

Capitals, hyphens, periods (points), and spacing

9.6. In general, an abbreviation follows the capitalization and hyphenation of the word or words abbreviated. It is followed by a period unless otherwise indicated.

    c.o.d.   St.   *but* ft•lb

9.7. Abbreviations and initials of a personal name with points are set without spaces. Abbreviations composed of contractions and initials or numbers, will retain space.

H.S.T.	B.S., LL.D., Ph.D., B.Sc.
J.F.K.	H.R. 116 (*but* S. 116, S. Con.
L.B.J.	Res. 116)
U.S.	C.A.D.C. (*but* App. D.C.)
U.N.	A.B. Secrest, D.D.S.
U.S.C. (*but* Rev. Stat.)	
A.F. of L.-CIO (AFL–CIO	
preferred)	*but*
A.D., B.C.	AT&T
e.s.t.	Texas A&M
i.e., e.g. (*but* op. cit.)	R&D

9.8. Except as otherwise designated, points and spaces are omitted after initials used as shortened names of governmental agencies and of other organized bodies. "Other organized bodies" shall be interpreted to mean organized bodies that have become popularly identified with a symbol, such as MIT (Massachusetts Institute of Technology), GM (General Motors), GMAC (General Motors Acceptance Corp.), etc. (See "List of Abbreviations.") Symbols, when they appear in copy, may be used for acts of Congress. Example: ARA (Area Redevelopment Act).

VFW	TVA	ARC
NLRB	AFL–CIO	ASTM

Geographic terms

9.9. *United States* must be spelled out when appearing in a sentence containing the name of another country. The abbreviation *U.S.* will be used when preceding the word *Government* or the name of a Government organization, except in formal writing (treaties, Executive orders, proclamations, etc.); congressional bills; legal citations and courtwork; and covers and title pages.

U.S. Government
U.S. Congress
U.S. Department of Health and Human Services
U.S. district court
U.S. Supreme Court (*but* Supreme Court of the United States)
U.S. Army (*but* Army of the United States)

U.S. monitor *Nantucket*
U.S.-NATO assistance
U.S. Government efforts to control inflation must be successful if the
United States is to have a stable economy.
but British, French, and United States Governments; United States-British
talks

9.10. With the exceptions in the preceding rule, the abbreviation *U.S.* is used in the adjective position, but is spelled out when used as a noun.

U.S. foreign policy	United States Steel Corp.
U.S. farm-support program	(legal title)
U.S. attorney	Foreign policy of the
U.S. citizen	United States
United States Code (official title)	*not* Temperatures vary in the U.S.

9.11. The names of foreign countries are not abbreviated, with the exception of the former U.S.S.R., which is abbreviated due to its length.

9.12. In other than formal usage as defined in rule 9.9, all States of the United States, Puerto Rico, and the Virgin Islands are abbreviated immediately following any capitalized geographic term, including armory, arsenal, airbase, airport, barracks, depot, fort, Indian agency, military camp, national cemetery (also forest, historic site, memorial, seashore, monument, park), naval shipyard, proving ground, reservation (forest, Indian, or military), and reserve or station (military or naval).

Prince George's County, MD	Arlington National Cemetery, VA
Mount Rainier National Forest, WA	Aberdeen Proving Ground, MD
Stone Mountain, GA	Baltimore-Washington International Airport, MD
National Naval Medical Center, Bethesda, MD	Redstone Arsenal, AL
Mark Twain National Wildlife Refuge, IL-IA-MO (note use of hyphens here)	*but* Leavenworth freight yards, Kansas
Richmond, VA	Altoona sidetrack, Wisconsin

9.13. The Postal Service style of two-letter State, Province, and Freely Associated State abbreviations is to be used.

United States
[Including freely associated States]

Alabama...AL	Kentucky...KY	Ohio...OH
Alaska...AK	Louisiana...LA	Oklahoma...OK
American Samoa...AS	Maine...ME	Oregon...OR
Arizona...AZ	Marshall Islands...MH	Palau...PW
Arkansas...AR	Maryland...MD	Pennsylvania...PA
California...CA	Massachusetts...MA	Puerto Rico...PR
Colorado...CO	Michigan...MI	Rhode Island...RI
Connecticut...CT	Minnesota...MN	South Carolina...SC
Delaware...DE	Mississippi...MS	South Dakota...SD
District of Columbia...DC	Missouri...MO	Tennessee...TN
Federated States of	Montana...MT	Texas...TX
Micronesia...FM	Nebraska...NE	Utah...UT
Florida...FL	Nevada...NV	Vermont...VT
Georgia...GA	New Hampshire...NH	Virgin Islands...VI
Guam...GU	New Jersey...NJ	Virginia...VA
Hawaii...HI	New Mexico...NM	Washington...WA
Idaho...ID	New York...NY	West Virginia...WV
Illinois...IL	North Carolina...NC	Wisconsin...WI
Indiana...IN	North Dakota...ND	Wyoming...WY
Iowa...IA	Northern Mariana	
Kansas...KS	Islands...MP	

Canada

Alberta...AB	Northwest Territories...NT	Prince Edward Island...PE
British Columbia...BC	Nova Scotia...NS	Quebec...QC
Manitoba...MB	Nunavut...NU	Saskatchewan...SK
New Brunswick...NB	Ontario...ON	Yukon...YT
Newfoundland and Labrador...NL		

9.14. The names of other insular possessions, trust territories, and *Long Island, Staten Island,* etc., are not abbreviated.

9.15. The names of Canadian Provinces and other foreign political subdivisions are not abbreviated except as noted in rule 9.13.

Addresses

9.16. Words such as *Street, Avenue, Place, Road, Square, Boulevard, Terrace, Drive, Court,* and *Building,* following a name or number, are abbreviated in footnotes, sidenotes, tables, leaderwork, and lists.

9.17. In addresses, a single period is used with the abbreviations *NW., SW., NE., SE.* (indicating sectional divisions of cities) following name or number. *North, South, East,* and *West* are spelled out at all times.

9.18.   The word *Street* or *Avenue* as part of a name is not abbreviated even in parentheses, footnotes, sidenotes, tables, lists, and leaderwork.

14th Street Bridge   Ninth Avenue Bldg.

9.19.   The words *County, Fort, Mount, Point,* and *Port* are not abbreviated. *Saint (St.)* and *Sainte (Ste.)* should be abbreviated.

Descriptions of tracts of land

9.20.   If fractions are spelled out in land descriptions, *half* and *quarter* are used (not *one-half* nor *one-quarter*).

south half of T. 47 N., R. 64 E.

9.21.   In the description of tracts of public land the following abbreviations are used (periods are omitted after abbreviated compass directions that immediately precede and close up on figures):

SE¼NW¼ sec. 4, T. 12 S., R. 15 E., of the Boise Meridian
lot 6, NE¼ sec. 4, T. 6 N., R. 1 W.
N½ sec. 20, T. 7 N., R. 2 W., sixth principal meridian
Tps. 9, 10, 11, and 12 S., Rs. 12 and 13 W.
T. 2 S., Rs. 8, 9, and 10 E., sec. 26
T. 3 S., R. 1 E., sec. 34, W½E½, W½, and W½SE¼SE¼
sec. 32 (with or without a township number)

9.22.   In case of an unavoidable break in a land-description symbol group at end of a line, use no hyphen and break after fraction.

Names and titles

9.23.   The following forms are not always abbreviations, and copy should be followed as to periods:

Al	Ben	Fred	Walt
Alex	Ed	Sam	Will

9.24.   In signatures, an effort should be made to retain the exact form used by the signer.

George Wythe   Geo. Taylor

9.25.   In company and other formal names, if it is not necessary to preserve the full legal title, such forms as *Bro., Bros., Co., Corp., Inc., Ltd.,* and *&* are used. *Association* and *Manufacturing* are not abbreviated.

Radio Corp. of America	Electronics Manufacturing Co.
Aluminum Co. of America	Texas College of Arts & Industries
Standard Oil Co. of New Jersey	Robert Wilson & Associates, Inc.
H.J. Baker & Bro.	U.S. News & World Report
Jones Bros. & Co.	Baltimore & Ohio Railroad
American Telephone &	Mine, Mill & Smelter Workers
Telegraph Co.	
Norton Enterprises, Inc.	
Maryland Steamship Co., Ltd.	*but*
Chesapeake & Delaware Canal	Little Theater Company
Fairmount Building & Loan	Senate Banking, Housing and
Association	Urban Affairs Committee

9.26.   *Company* and *Corporation* are not abbreviated in names of Federal Government units.

> Commodity Credit Corporation
> Federal Savings and Loan Insurance Corporation
> Pension Benefit Guaranty Corporation

9.27.   In parentheses, footnotes, sidenotes, tables, and leaderwork, abbreviate the words *railroad* and *railway* (*RR.* and *Ry.*), except in such names as "Washington Railway & Electric Co." and "Florida Railroad & Navigation Corp." *SS* for *steamship, MS* for *motorship,* etc., preceding name are used at all times.

9.28.   In the names of informal companionships the word *and* is spelled out.

> Gilbert and Sullivan   Currier and Ives

9.29.   In other than formal usage, a civil, military, or naval title preceding a name is abbreviated if followed by first or given name or initial; but *Mr., Mrs., Miss, Ms., M., MM., Messrs., Mlle., Mme.,* and *Dr.* are abbreviated with or without first or given name or initial.

United States military titles and abbreviations

Officer rank

Officer ranks in the United States military consist of commissioned officers and warrant officers. The commissioned ranks are the highest in the military. These officers hold presidential commissions and are confirmed at their ranks by the Senate. Army, Air Force, and Marine Corps officers are called company grade officers in the pay grades of O–1 to O–3, field grade officers in pay grades O–4 to O–6, and general officers in pay grades O–7 and higher. The equivalent officer groupings in the Navy are called junior grade, mid-grade, and flag.

Warrant officers hold warrants from their service secretary and are specialists and experts in certain military technologies or capabilities. The lowest ranking warrant officers serve under a warrant, but they receive commissions from the President upon promotion to chief warrant officer 2. These commissioned warrant officers are direct representatives of the President of the United States. They derive their authority from the same source as commissioned officers but remain specialists, in contrast to commissioned officers, who are generalists. There are no warrant officers in the Air Force.

	Army	Navy Coast Guard	Marines	Air Force
	General of the Army (Reserved for wartime only)	Fleet Admiral (Reserved for wartime only)		General of the Air Force (Reserved for wartime only)
O10	General GEN Army Chief of Staff	Admiral ADM Chief of Naval Operations and Commandant of the Coast Guard	General Gen. Commandant of the Marine Corps	General Gen. Air Force Chief of Staff
O9	Lieutenant General LTG	Vice Admiral VADM	Lieutenant General Lt. Gen.	Lieutenant General Lt. Gen.
O8	Major General MG	Rear Admiral Upper Half RADM	Major General Maj. Gen.	Major General Maj. Gen.
O7	Brigadier General BG	Rear Admiral Lower Half RDML	Brigadier General Brig. Gen.	Brigadier General Brig. Gen.
O6	Colonel COL	Captain CAPT	Colonel Col.	Colonel Col.
O5	Lieutenant Colonel LTC	Commander CDR	Lieutenant Colonel Lt. Col.	Lieutenant Colonel Lt. Col.
O4	Major MAJ	Lieutenant Commander LCDR	Major Maj.	Major Maj.
O3	Captain CPT	Lieutenant LT	Captain Capt.	Captain Capt.

	Army	Navy Coast Guard	Marines	Air Force
O2	First Lieutenant 1LT	Lieutenant Junior Grade LTJG	First Lieutenant 1st Lt.	First Lieutenant 1st Lt.
O1	Second Lieutenant 2LT	Ensign ENS	Second Lieutenant 2nd Lt.	Second Lieutenant 2nd Lt.
W5	Chief Warrant Officer CW5	Chief Warrant Officer CWO5	Chief Warrant Officer 5 CWO5	NO WARRANT
W4	Chief Warrant Officer 4 CW4	Chief Warrant Officer 4 CWO4	Chief Warrant Officer 4 CWO4	NO WARRANT
W3	Chief Warrant Officer 3 CW3	Chief Warrant Officer 3 CWO3	Chief Warrant Officer 3 CWO3	NO WARRANT
W2	Chief Warrant Officer 2 CW2	Chief Warrant Officer 2 CWO2	Chief Warrant Officer 2 CWO2	NO WARRANT
W1	Warrant Officer 1 WO1	Warrant Officer 1 WO1	Warrant Officer 1 WO	NO WARRANT

Source: http://www.defenselink.mil/specials/insignias/officers.html.

Enlisted rank

Service members in pay grades E–1 through E–3 are usually either in some kind of training status or on their initial assignment. The training includes the basic training phase where recruits are immersed in military culture and values and are taught the core skills required by their service component.

Basic training is followed by a specialized or advanced training phase that provides recruits with a specific area of expertise or concentration. In the Army and Marines, this area is called a military occupational specialty; in the Navy it is known as a rate; and in the Air Force it is simply called an Air Force specialty.

Leadership responsibility significantly increases in the mid-level enlisted ranks. This responsibility is given formal recognition by use of the terms noncommissioned officer and petty officer. An Army sergeant, an Air Force staff sergeant, and a Marine corporal are considered NCO ranks. The Navy NCO equivalent, petty officer, is achieved at the rank of petty officer third class.

At the E–8 level, the Army, Marines, and Air Force have two positions at the same pay grade. Whether one is, for example, a senior master sergeant or a first sergeant in the Air Force depends on the person's job. The same is true for the positions at the E–9 level. Marine Corps master gunnery sergeants and sergeants major receive the same pay but have different responsibilities. All told, E–8s and E–9s have 15 to 30 years on the job, and are commanders' senior advisers for enlisted matters.

A third E–9 element is the senior enlisted person of each service. The sergeant major of the Army, the sergeant major of the Marine Corps, the master chief petty officer of the Navy, and the chief master sergeant of the Air Force are the spokespersons of the enlisted force at the highest levels of their services.

	Army		Navy Coast Guard		Marines		Air Force		
E9	Sergeant Major of the Army (SMA)		Master Chief Petty Officer of the Navy (MCPON) and Coast Guard (MCPOCG)		Sergeant Major of the Marine Corps (SgtMajMC)		Chief Master Sergeant of the Air Force (CMSAF)		
E9	Sergeant Major (SGM)	Command Sergeant Major (CSM)	Master Chief Petty Officer (MCPO)	Fleet/Command Master Chief Petty Officer	Sergeant Major (SgtMaj)	Master Gunnery Sergeant (MGySgt)	Chief Master Sergeant (CMSgt)	First Sergeant	Command Chief Master Sergeant (CCM)
E8	Master Sergeant (MSG)	First Sergeant (1SG)	Senior Chief Petty Officer (SCPO)		Master Sergeant (MSgt)	First Sergeant	Senior Master Sergeant (SMSgt)	First Sergeant	
E7	Sergeant First Class (SFC)		Chief Petty Officer (CPO)		Gunnery Sergeant (GySgt)		Master Sergeant (MSgt)	First Sergeant	
E6	Staff Sergeant (SSG)		Petty Officer First Class (PO1)		Staff Sergeant (SSgt)		Technical Sergeant (TSgt)		
E5	Sergeant (SGT)		Petty Officer Second Class (PO2)		Sergeant (Sgt)		Staff Sergeant (SSgt)		
E4	Corporal (CPL)	Specialist (SPC)	Petty Officer Third Class (PO3)		Corporal (Cpl)		Senior Airman (SrA)		

	Army	Navy Coast Guard	Marines	Air Force
E3	Private First Class (PFC)	Seaman (SN)	Lance Corporal (LCpl)	Airman First Class (A1C)
E2	Private E-2 (PV2)	Seaman Apprentice (SA)	Private First Class (PFC)	Airman (Amn)
E1	Private	Seaman Recruit (SR)	Private	Airman Basic

Source: http://www.defenselink.mil/specials/insignias/enlisted.html.

9.30.   Spell out *Senator, Representative,* and *commandant.*

9.31.   Unless preceded by *the,* abbreviate *Honorable, Reverend,* and *Monsignor* when followed by the first name, initials, or title.

> Hon. Elihu Root; the Honorable Elihu Root; the Honorable Mr. Root
> the Honorables John Roberts, John Paul Stevens, and Ruth Bader Ginsberg
> Rev. Martin Luther King, Jr.; the Reverend Dr. King; Rev. Dr. King; Reverend King (*not* Rev. King, *nor* the Reverend King)
> Rt. Rev. James E. Freeman; the Right Reverend James E. Freeman; Very Rev. Henry Boyd; the Very Reverend Henry Boyd
> Rt. Rev. Msgr. John Bird; the Right Reverend Monsignor John Bird

9.32.   The following and similar forms are used after a name:

> Esq., Jr., Sr.
> 2d, 3d (*or* II, III) (not preceded by comma)
> Degrees: LL.D., M.A., Ph.D., etc.
> Fellowships, orders, etc.: FSA Scot, F.R.S., K.C.B., C.P.A., etc.

9.33.   The abbreviation *Esq.* and other titles such as *Mr., Mrs.,* and *Dr.,* should not appear with any other title or with abbreviations indicating scholastic degrees.

> John L. Smith, Esq., *not* Mr. John L. Smith, Esq., *nor* John L. Smith, Esq., A.M.; *but* James A. Jones, Jr., Esq.
> Ford Maddox, A.B., Ph.D., *not* Mr. Ford Maddox, A.B., Ph.D.
> George Gray, M.D., *not* Mr. George Gray, M.D., *nor* Dr. George Gray, M.D.
> Dwight A. Bellinger, D.V.M.

9.34.   *Sr.* and *Jr.* should not be used without first or given name or initials, but may be used in combination with any title.

> A.K. Jones, Jr., or Mr. Jones, Junior, *not* Jones, Jr., *nor* Jones, Junior
> President J. B. Nelson, Jr.

9.35. When name is followed by abbreviations designating religious and fraternal orders and scholastic and honorary degrees, their sequence is as follows: Orders, religious first; theological degrees; academic degrees earned in course; and honorary degrees in order of bestowal.

> Henry L. Brown, D.D., A.M., D.Lit.
> T.E. Holt, C.S.C., S.T.Lr., LL.D., Ph.D.
> Samuel J. Deckelbaum, P.M.

9.36. Academic degrees standing alone may be abbreviated.

> John was graduated with a B.A. degree; *but* bachelor of arts degree (lowercase when spelled out).
> She earned her Ph.D. by hard work.

9.37. In addresses, signatures, lists of names, and leaderwork but not in tables nor in centerheads, *Mr., Mrs.,* and other titles preceding a name, and *Esq., Jr., Sr., 2d,* and *3d* following a name, are set in roman caps and lowercase if the name is in caps and small caps. If the name is in caps, they are set in caps and small caps, if small caps are available—otherwise in caps and lowercase.

Parts of publications

9.38. The following abbreviations are used for parts of publications mentioned in parentheses, brackets, footnotes, sidenotes, list of references, tables, and leaderwork, when followed by figures, letters, or Roman numerals.

app., apps. (appendix, appendixes)	pl., pls. (plate, plates)
art., arts. (article, articles)	pt., pts. (part, parts)
bull., bulls. (bulletin, bulletins)	sec., secs. (section, sections)
ch., chs. (chapter, chapters)	subch., subchs. (subchapter, subchapters)
col., cols. (column, columns)	subpar., subpars. (subparagraph, subparagraphs)
ed., eds. (edition, editions)	subpt., subpts. (subpart, subparts)
fig., figs. (figure, figures)	subsec., subsecs. (subsection, subsections)
No., Nos. (number, numbers)	
p., pp. (page, pages)	supp., supps. (supplement, supplements)
par., pars. (paragraph, paragraphs)	vol., vols. (volume, volumes)

9.39. The word *article* and the word *section* are abbreviated when appearing at the beginning of a paragraph and set in caps and small caps followed by a period and an en space, except that the first of a series is spelled out.

> Art. 2; Sec. 2; etc.; *but* Article 1; Section 1
> Art. II; Sec. II; etc.; *but* Article I; Section I

9.40. At the beginning of a legend, the word *figure* preceding the legend number is not abbreviated.

Figure 4.—Landscape.

Terms relating to Congress

9.41. The words *Congress* and *session*, when accompanied by a numerical reference, are abbreviated in parentheses, brackets, and text footnotes. In sidenotes, lists of references, tables, leaderwork, and footnotes to tables and leaderwork, the following abbreviations are used:

106th Cong., 1st sess.	Public Law 84, 102d Cong.
1st sess., 106th Cong.	Private Law 68, 102d Cong.

9.42. In references to bills, resolutions, documents and reports in parentheses, brackets, footnotes, sidenotes, tables, and leaderwork, the following abbreviations are used:

H.R. 416 (House bill)	H. Conf. Rept. 10 (House
S. 116 (Senate bill)	conference report)
The examples above may be	H. Doc. 35 (House document)
abbreviated or spelled	S. Doc. 62 (Senate document)
out in text.	H. Rept. 214 (House report)
H. Res. 5 (House resolution)	S. Rept. 410 (Senate report)
H. Con. Res. 10 (House concurrent	Ex. Doc. B (Executive document)
resolution)	Ex. F (92d Cong., 2d sess.)
H.J. Res. 21 (House joint resolution)	Ex. Rept. 9 (92d Cong., 1st sess.)
S. Res. 50 (Senate resolution)	Misc. Doc. 16 (miscellaneous
S. Con. Res. 17 (Senate concurrent	document)
resolution)	Public Res. 47
S.J. Res. 45 (Senate joint resolution)	

9.43. References to statutes in parentheses, footnotes, sidenotes, tables, leaderwork, and congressional work are abbreviated.

Rev. Stat. (Revised Statutes); 43 Rev. Stat. 801; 18 U.S.C. 38
Supp. Rev. Stat. (Supplement to the Revised Statutes)
Stat. L. (Statutes at Large)
but Public Law 85–1; Private Law 68

Calendar divisions

9.44. Names of months followed by the day, or day and year, are abbreviated in footnotes, tables, leaderwork, sidenotes, and in bibliographies. (See examples, rule 9.45.) *May, June,* and *July* are always spelled out. In narrow columns in tables, however, the names of months may be abbreviated even if standing alone. Preferred forms follow:

Jan.	Apr.	Oct.
Feb.	Aug.	Nov.
Mar.	Sept.	Dec.

9.45. In text only, dates as part of a citation or reference within parentheses or brackets are also abbreviated.

(Op. Atty. Gen., Dec. 4, 2005)
(Congressional Record, Sept. 25, 2007)
[From the New York Times, Mar. 4, 2008]
[From the Mar. 4 issue]
On Jan. 25 (we had commenced on Dec. 26, 2005) the work was finished. (In footnotes, tables, leaderwork, and sidenotes)
On January 25, a decision was reached (Op. Atty. Gen., Dec. 4, 2006). (Text, but with citation in parentheses)
but On January 25 (we had commenced on December 26, 2008) the work was finished. (Not a citation or reference in text)

9.46. Weekdays are not abbreviated, but the following forms are used, if necessary, in lists or in narrow columns in tables:

Sun.	Wed.	Fri.
Mon.	Thurs.	Sat.
Tues.		

Time zones

9.47. The following forms are to be used when abbreviating names of time zones:

AKDT—Alaska daylight time	GMAT—Greenwich mean
AKST—Alaska standard time	astronomical time
AKT—Alaska time (implies	GMT—Greenwich mean time
standard or daylight time)	HDT—Hawaii-Aleutian daylight time
AST—Atlantic standard time	(not observed in HI)
AT—Atlantic time	HST—Hawaii-Aleutian standard time
CDT—central daylight time	LST—local standard time
CST—central standard time	MDT—mountain daylight time
CT—central time	MST—mountain standard time
DST—daylight saving (no "s") time	MT— mountain time
EDT—eastern daylight time	PDT—Pacific daylight time
EST—eastern standard time	PST—Pacific standard time
ET—eastern time	PT—Pacific time
GCT—Greenwich civil time	UTC—coordinated universal time

Acronyms and coined words

9.48. To obtain uniform treatment in the formation of acronyms and coined words, apply the formulas that follow:

Use all capital letters when only the first letter of each word or selected words is used to make up the symbol:

> APPR (Army package power reactor)
> EPCOT (Experimental Prototype Community of Tomorrow)
> MAG (Military Advisory Group)
> MIRV (multiple independently targetable reentry vehicle)
> SALT (strategic arms limitation talks); (*avoid* SALT talks)
> STEP (supplemental training and employment program)

Use all capital letters where first letters of prefixes and/or suffixes are utilized as part of established expressions:

> CPR (*c*ardio*p*ulmonary *r*esuscitation)
> ESP (*e*xtra*s*ensory *p*erception)
> FLIR (*f*orward-*l*ooking *i*nfra*r*ed)

Copy must be followed where an acronym or abbreviated form is copyrighted or established by law:

> ACTION (agency of Government; not an acronym)
> MarAd (*Mar*itime *Ad*ministration)
> NACo (*N*ational *A*ssociation of *Co*unties)
> MEDLARS (*Med*ical *L*iterature *A*nalysis and *R*etrieval *S*ystem)

Use caps and lowercase when proper names are used in shortened form, any word of which uses more than the first letter of each word:

Conrail (Consolidated Rail Corporation)
Pepco (Potomac Electric Power Co.)
Inco (International Nickel Co.)
Aramco (Arabian-American Oil Co.)
Unprofor (United Nations Protection Force)

Use lowercase in common-noun combinations made up of more than the first letter of lowercased words:

loran (*long-range navigation*)
sonar (*sound navigation ranging*)
secant (*separation control of aircraft by nonsynchronous techniques*)

9.49. The words *infra* and *supra* are not abbreviated.

Terms of measure

9.50. Compass directions are abbreviated as follows:

N.	S.	ESE.
NE.	NNW.	10° N. 25° W.
E.	W.	NW. by N. ¼ W.
SW.		

9.51. The words *latitude* and *longitude*, followed by figures, are abbreviated in parentheses, brackets, footnotes, sidenotes, tables, and leaderwork, and the figures are always closed up.

lat. 52°33'05" N.   long. 13°21'10" E.

9.52. Avoid breaking latitude and longitude figures at end of line; space out line instead. In case of an unavoidable break at end of line, use hyphen.

9.53. Temperature and gravity are expressed in figures. When the degree mark is used, it must appear closed up to the capital letter, not against the figures. Note the following related abbreviations and letter symbols and their usages:

abs, absolute	API, American Petroleum
Bé, Baumé	Institute
°C,[1] degree Celsius[2]	Twad, Twaddell
°F, degree Fahrenheit	100 °C
°R, degree Rankine	212 °F[1]
K, kelvin	671.67 °R
273.15 K	18 °API
°API	

---

[1] Without figures preceding it, °C or °F should be used only in boxhead and over figure columns in tables.
[2] Preferred form (superseding Centigrade).

9.54. References to meridian in statements of time are abbreviated as follows:

> 10 a.m. (*not* 10:00 a.m.)   12 p.m. (12 noon)
> 2:30 p.m.   12 a.m. (12 midnight)

9.55. The word *o'clock* is not used with abbreviations of time.

> *not* 10 o'clock p.m.

9.56. Metric unit letter symbols are set lowercase roman unless the unit name has been derived from a proper name, in which case the first letter of the symbol is capitalized (for example Pa for pascal and W for watt). The exception is the letter L for liter. The same form is used for singular and plural. The preferred symbol for *cubic centimeter* is *cm*^{3}; use *cc* only when requested.

A space is used between a figure and a unit symbol except in the case of the symbols for degree, minute, and second of plane angle.

> 3 m   45 mm   25 °C   *but* 33°15'21"

Prefixes for multiples and submultiples						Metric units	
E	exa (10^{18})		d	deci (10^{-1})		m	meter (for length)
P	peta (10^{15})		c	centi (10^{-2})		g	gram (for weight or mass)
T	tera (10^{12})		m	milli (10^{-3})		L	liter (for capacity)
G	giga (10^{9})		μ	micro (10^{-6})			
M	mega (10^{6})		n	nano (10^{-9})			
k	kilo (10^{3})		p	pico (10^{-12})			
h	hecto (10^{2})		f	femto (10^{-15})			
da	deka (10)		a	atto (10^{-18})			

	Length		Area		Volume
km	kilometer	km^2	square kilometer	km^3	cubic kilometer
hm	hectometer	hm^2	square hectometer	hm^3	cubic hectometer
dam	decameter	dam^2	square decameter	dam^3	cubic dekameter
m	meter	m^2	square meter	m^3	cubic meter
dm	decimeter	dm^2	square decimeter	dm^3	cubic decimeter
cm	centimeter	cm^2	square centimeter	cm^3	cubic centimeter
mm	millimeter	mm^2	square millimeter	mm^3	cubic millimeter

Weight		Land area		Capacity of containers	
kg	kilogram	ha	hectare	kL	kiloliter
hg	hectogram	a	acre	hL	hectoliter
dag	dekagram			daL	dekaliter
g	gram			L	liter
dg	decigram			dL	deciliter
cg	centigram			cL	centiliter
mg	milligram			mL	milliliter
µg	microgram				

9.57. A similar form of abbreviation applies to any unit of the metric system.

A	amper	V	volt	mF	millifarad
VA	voltampere	W	watt	mH	millihenry
F	farad	kc	kilocycle	µF	microfarad (one-
H	Henry	kV	kilovolt		millionth of a farad)
Hz	Hertz	kVA	kilovoltampere		
J	joule	kW	kilowatt		

9.58. The following forms are used when units of English weight and measure and units of time are abbreviated, the same form of abbreviation being used for both singular and plural:

Length		Area and volume	
in	inch	in²	square inch
ft	foot	in³	cubic inch
yd	yard	mi²	square mile
mi	mile (statute)	ft³	cubic foot

Time		Weight		Capacity	
yr	year	gr	grain	gill	(not abbreviated)
mo	month	dr	dram	pt	pint
d	day	oz	ounce	qt	quart
h	hour	lb	pound	gal	gallon
min	minute	cwt	hundredweight	pk	peck
s	second	dwt	pennyweight	bu	bushel
		ton(s)	(not abbreviated)	bbl	barrel
		but t	metric ton (tonne)		

9.59. In astrophysical and similar scientific matter, magnitudes and units of time may be expressed as follows, if so written in copy.

$$5^h3^m9^s \qquad\qquad\qquad 4.5^h$$

Money

9.60. The following are some of the abbreviations and symbols used for indicating money:

(For the abbreviations of other terms indicating currency, see the table "Currency" in Chapter 17 "Useful Tables.")

$, dol (dollar)	Mex $2,650
c, ct, ¢ (cent, cents)	₱ (peso)
TRL175 (Turkish)	£ (pound)
USD15,000	d (pence)
€ (euro)	

Use "USD" if omission would result in confusion.

Standard word abbreviations

9.61. If abbreviations are required, use these forms:

2,4D (insecticide)
3d—third
4°—quarto
8°—octavo
A1 (rating)
A.A.—Alcoholics Anonymous
AARP—American Association of
  Retired Persons
abbr.—abbreviation
abs.—abstract
acct.—account
ACDA—Arms Control and
  Disarmament Agency
ACTH—adrenocorticotropic
  hormone
A.D.—(anno Domini) in the year
  of our Lord (A.D. 937)
ADDH—attention deficit disorder
  with hyperactivity
ADHD—attention deficit hyper-
  activity disorder
AEF—American Expeditionary
  Forces
AF—audiofrequency
AFB—Air Force Base

AFL–CIO—American Federation
  of Labor and Congress of
  Industrial Organizations
AID—Agency for International
  Development
AIDS—acquired immuno-
  deficiency syndrome
a.k.a.—also known as
A.L.R.—American Law Reports
AM—amplitude modulation (no
  periods)
A.M.—(anno mundi) in the year of
  the world
A.M. or M.A.—master of arts
a.m.—(ante meridiem) before noon
Am. Repts.—American Reports
Amtrak—National Railroad
  Passenger Corporation
AMVETS—American Veterans of
  World War II; Amvet(s)
  (individual)
antilog—antilogarithm (no period)
AOA—Administration on Aging
API—American Petroleum
  Institute

APO—Army post office (no periods)
App. D.C.—District of Columbia Appeal Cases
App. Div.—Appellate Division
APPR—Army package power reactor
approx.—approximately
ARC—American Red Cross
ARS—Agricultural Research Service
ASCS—Agricultural Stabilization and Conservation Service
ASME—American Society of Mechanical Engineers
A.S.N.—Army service number
ASTM—American Society for Testing and Materials
ATM—automatic teller machine
Atl.—Atlantic Reporter; A.2d, Atlantic Reporter, second series
AUS—Army of the United States
Ave.—avenue
AWACS—airborne warning and control system
AWOL—absent without leave
B.A. or A.B.—bachelor of arts
BBB—Better Business Bureau
B.C.—before Christ (1200 B.C.)
B.C.E.—Before Common Era
BCG—(bacillus Calmette-Guerin) antituberculosis vaccine
bf.—boldface
BGN—Board on (not of) Geographic Names
BIA—Bureau of Indian Affairs
BIS—Bank for International Settlements
Blatch. Pr. Cas.—Blatchford's Prize Cases
Bldg.—building
B. Lit(t). or Lit(t).B.—bachelor of literature

BLM—Bureau of Land Management
BLS—Bureau of Labor Statistics
Blvd.—boulevard
b.o.—buyer's option
B.S. or B.Sc.—bachelor of science
c. and s.c.—caps and small caps
ca.—(circa) about
ca—centiare
CACM—Central American Common Market
CAD—computer-aided design
CAP—Civil Air Patrol
CARE—Cooperative for American Remittances to Everywhere, Inc.
CAT scan—computerized axial tomography
C.C.A.—Circuit Court of Appeals
CCC—Commodity Credit Corporation
CCITT—Consultative Committee for International Telegraphy and Telephony
C.Cls.—Court of Claims
C.Cls.R.—Court of Claims Reports
C.C.P.A.—Court of Customs and Patents Appeals
CCR—Commission on Civil Rights
CDC—Centers for Disease Control
C.E.—Common Era
CEA—Council of Economic Advisers
cf.—(confer) compare or see
CFR—Code of Federal Regulations
CFR Supp.—Code of Federal Regulations Supplement
CHAMPUS—Civilian Health and Medical Program of the Uniformed Services
CIA—Central Intelligence Agency
CIC—Counterintelligence Corps
C.J.—(corpus juris) body of law; Chief Justice

CNN—Cable News Network
CO—commanding officer
Co.—company (commercial)
c.o.d.—cash on delivery
COLA—cost-of-living adjustment
Comp. Dec.—Comptroller's
   Decisions (Treasury)
Comp. Gen.—Comptroller
   General Decisions
con.—continued
conelrad—control of
   electromagnetic radiation
   (civil defense)
Conus—continental United States
Corp.—corporation (commercial)
cos—cosine (no period)
cosh—hyperbolic cosine (no
   period)
cot—cotangent (no period)
coth—hyperbolic cotangent (no
   period)
c.p.—chemically pure
C.P.A.—certified public
   accountant
CPI—Consumer Price Index
CPR—cardiopulmonary
   resuscitation
cr.—credit; creditor
C–SPAN—Cable Satellite Public
   Affairs Network
csc—cosecant (no period)
csch—hyperbolic cosecant (no
   period)
Ct.—court
Dall.—Dallas (U.S. Supreme
   Court Reports)
DAR—Daughters of the American
   Revolution
d.b.a.—doing business as
d.b.h.—diameter at breast height
D.D.—doctor of divinity
D.D.S.—doctor of dental surgery
DDT—dichlorodiphenyl-
   trichloroethane

DHS—Department of Homeland
   Security
Dist. Ct.—District Court
D.Lit(t). or Lit(t).D.—doctor of
   literature
DNC—Domestic Names
   Committee (BGN)
do.—(ditto) the same
DOC—Department of Commerce
DOD—Department of Defense
DOE—Department of Energy
DOJ—Department of Justice
DOL—Department of Labor
DOS—Department of State
DOT—Department of
   Transportation
DP—displaced person (no period)
D.P.H.—doctor of public health
D.P.Hy.—doctor of public hygiene
DPT—diphtheria, pertussis,
   tetanus innoculation
dr.—debit; debtor
Dr.—doctor; drive
d.s.t.—daylight saving (no "s") time
D.V.M.—doctor of veterinary
   medicine
E.—east
EDGAR—Electronic Data
   Gathering, Analysis and
   Retrieval (SEC)
EEOC—Equal Employment
   Opportunity Commission
EFTA—European Free Trade
   Association
EFTS—electronic funds transfer
   system
e.g.—(exempli gratia) for example
EHF—extremely high frequency
emcee—master of ceremony
e.o.m.—end of month
EOP—Executive Office of the
   President
EPA—Environmental Protection
   Agency

et al.—(et alii) and others
et seq.—(et sequentia) and the
    following
etc.—(et cetera) and so forth
EU—European Union
Euratom—European Atomic
    Energy Community
Euro—currency (common)
Eurodollars—U.S. dollars used to
    finance foreign trade
Ex. Doc. (with letter)—executive
    document
Ex-Im Bank—Export-Import
    Bank of the United States
f., ff.—and following page (pages)
FAA—Federal Aviation
    Administration
FACS—Faculty of the American
    College of Surgeons
FAO—Food and Agriculture
    Organization
f.a.s.—free alongside ship
FAS—Foreign Agricultural
    Service
FBI—Federal Bureau of
    Investigation
FCA—Farm Credit
    Administration
FCC—Federal Communications
    Commission
FCIC—Federal Crop Insurance
    Corporation
FCSC—Foreign Claims
    Settlement Commission
FDA—Food and Drug
    Administration
FDIC—Federal Deposit Insurance
    Corporation
FDLP—Federal Depository
    Library Program
Fed.—Federal Reporter; F.3d,
    Federal Reporter, third series
FEOF—Foreign Exchange
    Operations Fund

FHA—Federal Housing
    Administration
FmHA—Farmers Home
    Administration
FHLBB—Federal Home Loan
    Bank Board
FHWA—Federal Highway
    Administration
FICA—Federal Insurance
    Contributions Act
FLSA—Fair Labor Standards Act
FM—frequency modulation
FMC—Federal Maritime
    Commission
FMCS—Federal Mediation and
    Conciliation Service
FNMA—Federal National
    Mortgage Association
    (Fannie Mae)
FNS—Food and Nutrition Service
f°—folio
f.o.b.—free on board
FPC—Federal Power Commission
FPO—fleet post office (no periods)
FR—Federal Register
    (publication)
FRG—Federal Republic of
    Germany
FRS—Federal Reserve System
FS—Forest Service
FSLIC—Federal Savings and Loan
    Insurance Corporation
FSS—Federal Supply Service
F.Supp.—Federal Supplement
FTC—Federal Trade Commission
FWS—Fish and Wildlife Service
GAO—Government
    Accountability Office
GATT—General Agreement on
    Tariffs and Trade
GDR—German Democratic
    Republic
GI—general issue; Government
    issue

GIS—Geographic Information System
G.M.&S.—general, medical, and surgical
GNMA—Government National Mortgage Association (Ginnie Mae)
GNP—gross national product
Gov.—Governor
GPO—Government Printing Office
GPS—Global Positioning System
gr. wt.—gross weight
GSA—General Services Administration
GSE—Government-Sponsored Enterprise
H.C.—House of Commons
H. Con. Res. (with number)— House concurrent resolution
H. Doc. (with number)—House document
hazmat—hazardous material
HDTV—high definition television
HE—high explosive (no periods)
HF—high frequency (no periods)
HHS—Health and Human Services (Department of)
HIV—human immunodeficiency virus
H.J. Res. (with number)—House joint resolution
HMO—health-maintenance organization
HOV—high-occupancy vehicle
How.—Howard (U.S. Supreme Court Reports)
H.R. (with number)—House bill
H. Rept. (with number)—House report
H. Res. (with number)—House resolution
HUD—Housing and Urban Development (Department of)

IADB—Inter-American Defense Board
IAEA—International Atomic Energy Agency
ibid.—(ibidem) in the same place
ICBM—intercontinental ballistic missile
id.—(idem) the same
IDA—International Development Association
IDE—integrated drive electronics
i.e.—(id est) that is
IEEE—Institute of Electrical and Electronic Engineers
IF—intermediate frequency (no periods)
IFC—International Finance Corporation
IMCO—Intergovernmental Maritime Consultative Organization
IMF—International Monetary Fund
Insp. Gen. (also IG)—inspector general
Interpol—International Criminal Police Organization
IOU—I owe you
IQ—intelligence quotient
IRA—individual retirement account
IRBM—intermediate range ballistic missile
IRE—Institute of Radio Engineers
IRO—International Refugee Organization
IRS—Internal Revenue Service
ISO—International Standards Organization
ITO—International Trade Organization
ITU—International Telecommunications Union
JAG—Judge Advocate General

jato—jet-assisted takeoff

J.D.—(jurum or juris doctor) doctor of laws

JOBS—Job Opportunities in the Business Sector

JIT—just in time

Jpn.—Japan or Japanese where necessary to abbreviate

Jr.—junior

Judge Adv. Gen.—Judge Advocate General

LAFTA—Latin American Free Trade Association

lat.—latitude

LC—Library of Congress

LCD—liquid crystal display

lc.—lowercase

L.Ed.—Lawyer's edition (U.S. Supreme Court Reports)

liq.—liquid

lf.—lightface

LF—low frequency

LL.B.—bachelor of laws

LL.D.—doctor of laws

loc. cit.—(loco citato) in the place cited

log (no period)—logarithm

long.—longitude

loran (no periods)—long-range navigation

lox (no periods)—liquid oxygen

LPG—liquefied petroleum gas

Ltd.—limited

Lt. Gov.—lieutenant governor

M—money supply: M1, M2, etc.

M.—monsieur; MM., messieurs

m.—(meridies) noon

M—more

MAC—Military Airlift Command

MAG—Military Advisory Group

MarAd—Maritime Administration

MC—Member of Congress (emcee, master of ceremonies)

M.D.—doctor of medicine

MDAP—Mutual Defense Assistance Program

MediCal—Medicaid California

memo—memorandum

MF—medium frequency; microfiche

MFN—most favored nation

MIA—missing in action (plural MIA's)

MIRV—multiple independently targetable reentry vehicle

Misc. Doc. (with number)— miscellaneous document

Mlle.—mademoiselle

Mme.—madam

Mmes.—mesdames

mo.—month

MOS—military occupational specialty

M.P.—Member of Parliament

MP—military police

Mr.—mister (plural Messrs.)

MRI—magnetic resonance imaging

Mrs.—mistress

Ms.—feminine title (plural Mses.)

M.S.—master of science

MS.—MSS., manuscript, manuscripts

MSC—Military Sealift Command

Msgr.—monsignor

m.s.l.—mean sea level

MSNBC—Microsoft National Broadcasting Co.

MTN—multilateral trade negotiations

N.—north

NA—not available; not applicable

NACo.—National Association of Counties

NAFTA—North American Free Trade Agreement

NAS—National Academy of
Sciences
NASA—National Aeronautics and
Space Administration
NATO—North Atlantic Treaty
Organization
NCUA—National Credit Union
Administration
NE.—northeast
n.e.c.—not elsewhere classified
n.e.s.—not elsewhere specified
net wt.—net weight
N.F.—National Formulary
NFAH—National Foundation on
the Arts and the Humanities
NIH—National Institutes of
Health
NIST—National Institute of
Standards and Technology
n.l.—natural log or logarithm
NLRB—National Labor Relations
Board
NNTP—Network News Transfer
Protocol
No.—Nos., number, numbers
NOAA—National Oceanic and
Atmospheric Administration
n.o.i.b.n.—not otherwise indexed
by name
n.o.p.—not otherwise provided
(for)
n.o.s.—not otherwise specified
NOVS—National Office of Vital
Statistics
NPS—National Park Service
NRC—Nuclear Regulatory
Commission
NS—nuclear ship
NSA—National Shipping
Authority
NSC—National Security Council
NSF—National Science
Foundation
n.s.k.—not specified by kind

n.s.p.f.—not specifically provided
for
NW.—northwest
OAPEC—Organization of Arab
Petroleum Exporting
Countries
OAS—Organization of American
States
OASDHI—Old-Age, Survivors,
Disability, and Health
Insurance Program
OASI—Old-Age and Survivors
Insurance
OCD—Office of Civil Defense
OD—officer of the day
OD—overdose; Odd, overdosed
O.D.—doctor of optometry
OECD—Organization for
Economic Cooperation and
Development
OK—Oked, Oking, Oks
OMB—Office of Management and
Budget
Op. Atty. Gen.—Opinions of the
Attorney General
op. cit.—(opere citato) in the work
cited
OPEC—Organization of
Petroleum Exporting
Countries
OSD—Office of the Secretary of
Defense
OTC—Organization for Trade
Cooperation
PA—public address system
Pac.—Pacific Reporter; P.2d,
Pacific Reporter, second
series
PAC—political action committee
(plural PAC's)
Passed Asst. Surg.—passed
assistant surgeon
PBS—Public Building Service
PCV—Peace Corps Volunteer

Pet.—Peters (U.S. Supreme Court Reports)
Ph—phenyl
Phar.D.—doctor of pharmacy
Ph.B. or B.Ph.—bachelor of philosophy
Ph.D. or D.Ph.—doctor of philosophy
Ph.G.—graduate in pharmacy
PHS—Public Health Service
PIN—personal identification number
Pl.—place
p.m.—(post meridiem) after noon
P.O. Box (with number)—*but* post office box (in general sense)
POP—Point of Presence; Post Office Protocol
POW—prisoner of war (plural POWs)
PTSD—post-traumatic-stress disorder
Private Res. (with number)— private resolution
Prof.—professor
pro tem—(pro tempore) temporarily
P.S.—(post scriptum) postscript; public school (with number)
PTA—parent-teachers' association
Public Res. (with number)—public resolution
PX—post exchange
QT—on the quiet
racon—radar beacon
radar—radio detection and ranging
R&D—research and development
rato—rocket-assisted takeoff
Rd.—road
RDT&E—research, development, testing, and evaluation
REA—Rural Electrification Administration

Rev.—reverend
Rev. Stat.—Revised Statutes
RF—radiofrequency
R.F.D.—rural free delivery
Rh—Rhesus (blood factor)
RIF—reduction(s) in force; RIFed, RIFing, RIFs
R.N.—registered nurse
ROTC—Reserve Officers' Training Corps
RR.—railroad
RRB—Railroad Retirement Board
Rt. Rev.—right reverend
Ry.—railway
S.—south; Senate bill (with number)
SAC—Strategic Air Command
SAE—Society of Automotive Engineers
S&L(s)—savings and loan(s)
SALT—strategic arms limitation talks
SAR—Sons of the American Revolution
SBA—Small Business Administration
sc.—(scilicet) namely (see also ss)
s.c.—small caps
S. Con. Res. (with number)— Senate concurrent resolution
s.d.—(sine die) without date
SDI—Strategic Defense Initiative
S. Doc. (with number)—Senate document
SE.—southeast
SEATO—Southeast Asia Treaty Organization
SEC—Securities and Exchange Commission
sec—secant
sech—hyperbolic secant
2d—second
SHF—superhigh frequency
shoran—short range (radio)

SI—Systeme International d'Unités
sic—thus
sin—sine
sinh—hyperbolic sine
S.J. Res. (with number)—Senate joint resolution
sonar—sound, navigation, and ranging (no period)
SOP—standard operating procedure
SOS—wireless distress signal
SP—shore patrol
SPAR—Coast Guard Women's Reserve (semper paratus—always ready)
sp. gr.—specific gravity
Sq.—square (street)
Sr.—senior
S. Rept. (with number)—Senate report
S. Res. (with number)—Senate resolution
SS—steamship
ss—(scilicet) namely (in law) (see also sc.)
SSA—Social Security Administration
SSS—Selective Service System
St.—Ste., SS., Saint, Sainte, Saints
St.—street
Stat.—Statutes at Large
STP—standard temperature and pressure
Sup. Ct.—Supreme Court Reporter
Supp. Rev. Stat.—Supplement to the Revised Statutes
Supt.—superintendent
Surg.—surgeon
Surg. Gen.—Surgeon General
SW.—southwest
S.W.2d—Southwestern Reporter, second series

SWAT—special weapons and tactics (team)
T.—Tps., township, townships
tan—tangent
tann—hyperbolic tangent
TB—tuberculosis
T.D.—Treasury Decisions
TDY—temporary duty
Ter.—terrace
t.m.—true mean
TNT—trinitrotoluol
TV—television
TVA—Tennessee Valley Authority
uc.—uppercase
UHF—ultrahigh frequency
UMTA—Urban Mass Transportation Administration
U.N.—United Nations
UNESCO—United Nations Educational, Scientific, and Cultural Organization
UNICEF—United Nations Children's Fund
U.S.—U.S. Supreme Court Reports
U.S.A.—United States of America
USA—U.S. Army
USAF—U.S. Air Force
U.S.C.—United States Code
U.S.C.A.—United States Code Annotated
U.S.C. Supp.—United States Code Supplement
USCG—U.S. Coast Guard
USDA—U.S. Department of Agriculture
USES—U.S. Employment Service
U.S. 40—U.S. No. 40, U.S. Highway No. 40
USGS—U.S. Geological Survey
USIA—U.S. Information Agency
USMC—U.S. Marine Corps
USN—U.S. Navy

USNR—U.S. Naval Reserve
U.S.P.—United States
    Pharmacopeia
USPS—U.S. Postal Service
U.S.S.—U.S. Senate
v. or vs.—(versus) against
VA—Department of Veterans
    Affairs
VAT—value added tax
VCR—video cassette recorder
VHF—very high frequency
VIP—very important person
viz—(videlicet) namely
VLF—very low frequency
VTR—video tape recording
W.—west

w.a.e.—when actually employed
Wall.—Wallace (U.S. Supreme
    Court Reports)
wf—wrong font
Wheat.—Wheaton (U.S. Supreme
    Court Reports)
WHO—World Health
    Organization
WIPO—World Intellectual
    Property Organization
WMAL—WRC, etc., radio stations
w.o.p.—without pay
Yale L.J.—Yale Law Journal
ZIP Code—Zone Improvement
    Plan Code (Postal Service)
ZIP+4—9-digit ZIP Code

Standard letter symbols for units of measure

9.62.   The same form is used for singular and plural senses.

A—ampere
Å—angstrom
a—are
a—atto (prefix, one-quintillionth)
aA—attoampere
abs—absolute (temperature and
    gravity)
ac—alternating current
AF—audiofrequency
Ah—ampere-hour
A/m—ampere per meter
AM—amplitude modulation
asb—apostilb
At—ampere-turn
at—atmosphere, technical
atm—atmosphere
at wt—atomic weight
au—astronomical units
avdp—avoirdupois
b—barn
B—bel
b—bit
bbl—barrel
bbl/d—barrel per day

Bd—baud
bd. ft.—board foot (obsolete); use fbm
Bé—Baumé
Bev (obsolete); see GeV
Bhn—Brinell hardness number
bhp—brake horsepower
bm—board measure
bp—boiling point
Btu—British thermal unit
bu—bushel
c—¢, ct; cent(s)
c—centi (prefix, one-hundredth)
C—coulomb
°C—degree Celsius
cal—calorie (also: cal_{IT}, International
    Table; cal_{th}—thermochemical)
cd/in²—candela per square inch
cd/m²—candela per square meter
cg—centigram
cd·h—candela-hour
Ci—curie
cL—centiliter
cm—centimeter
c/m—cycles per minute

cm²—square centimeter
cm³—cubic centimeter
cmil—circular mil
cp—candlepower
cP—centipoise
cSt—centistokes
cwt—hundredweight
D—darcy
d—day
d—deci (prefix, one-tenth)
d—pence
da—deka (prefix, 10)
dag—dekagram
daL—dekaliter
dam—dekameter
dam²—square dekameter
dam³—cubic dekameter
dB—decibel
dBu—decibel unit
dc—direct current
dg—decigram
dL—deciliter
dm—decimeter
dm²—square decimeter
dm³—cubic decimeter
dol—dollar
doz—dozen
dr—dram
dwt—deadweight tons
dwt—pennyweight
dyn—dyne
EHF—extremely high frequency
emf—electromotive force
emu—electromagnetic unit
erg—erg
esu—electrostatic unit
eV—electronvolt
°F—degree Fahrenheit
F—farad
f—femto (prefix, one-quadrillionth)
fbm—board foot; board foot measure
fc—footcandle
fL—footlambert
fm—fentometer

FM—frequency modulation
ft—foot
ft²—square foot
ft³—cubic foot
ftH₂O—conventional foot of water
ft•lb—foot-pound
ft•lbf—foot-pound force
ft/min—foot per minute
ft²/min—square foot per minute
ft³/min—cubic foot per minute
ft-pdl—foot poundal
ft/s—foot per second
ft²/s—square foot per second
ft³/s—cubic foot per second
ft/s²—foot per second squared
ft/s³—foot per second cubed
G—gauss
G—giga (prefix, 1 billion)
g—gram; acceleration of gravity
Gal—gal cm/s²
gal—gallon
gal/min—gallons per minute
gal/s—gallons per second
GB—gigabyte
Gb—gilbert
g/cm³—gram per cubic centimeter
GeV—gigaelectronvolt
GHz—gigahertz (gigacycle per second)
gr—grain; gross
h—hecto (prefix, 100)
H—henry
h—hour
ha—hectare
HF—high frequency
hg—hectogram
hL—hectoliter
hm—hectometer
hm²—square hectometer
hm³—cubic hectometer
hp—horsepower
hph—horsepower-hour
Hz—hertz (cycles per second)
id—inside diameter
ihp—indicated horsepower

in—inch
in²—square inch
in³—cubic inch
in/h—inch per hour
inH₂O—conventional inch of water
inHg—conventional inch of mercury
in-lb—inch-pound
in/s—inch per second
J—joule
J/K—joule per kelvin
K—kayser
K—kelvin (use without degree symbol)
k—kilo (prefix, 1,000)
k—thousand (7k=7,000)
kc—kilocycle; see also kHz (kilohertz),
    kilocycles per second
kcal—kilocalory
keV—kiloelectronvolt
kG—kilogauss
kg—kilogram
kgf—kilogram-force
kHz—kilohertz (kilocycles per second)
kL—kiloliter
klbf—kilopound-force
km—kilometer
km²—square kilometer
km³—cubic kilometer
km/h—kilometer per hour
kn—knot (speed)
kΩ—kilohm
kt—kiloton; carat
kV—kilovolt
kVA—kilovoltampere
kvar—kilovar
kW—kilowatt
kWh—kilowatthour
L—lambert
L—liter
lb—pound
lb ap—apothecary pound
lb—avdp, avoirdupois pound
lbf—pound-force
lbf/ft—pound-force foot
lbf/ft²—pound-force per square foot

lbf/ft³—pound-force per cubic foot
lbf/in²—pound-force per square inch
    (see psi)
lb/ft—pound per foot
lb/ft²—pound per square foot
lb/ft³—pound per cubic foot
lct—long calcined ton
ldt—long dry ton
LF—low frequency
lin ft—linear foot
l/m—lines per minute
lm—lumen
lm/ft²—lumen per square foot
lm/m²—lumen per square meter
lm•s—lumen second
lm/W—lumen per watt
l/s—lines per second
L/s—liter per second
lx—lux
M—mega (prefix, 1 million)
M—million (3 M=3 million)
m—meter
m—milli (prefix, one-thousandth)
M1—monetary aggregate
m²—square meter
m³—cubic meter
μ—micro (prefix, one-millionth)
μm—micrometer
mA—milliampere
μA—microampere
MB—megabyte
mbar—millibar
μbar—microbar
Mc—megacycle; see also MHz
    (megahertz), megacycles per
    second
mc—millicycle; see also mHz
    (millihertz), millicycles per
    second
mD—millidarcy
meq—milliquivalent
MeV—megaelectronvolts
mF—millifarad
μF—microfarad

mG—milligauss
mg—milligram
μg—microgram
Mgal/d—million gallons per day
mH—millihenry
μH—microhenry
MHz—megahertz
mHz—millihertz
mi—mile (statute)
mi²—square mile
mi/gal—mile(s) per gallon
mi/h—mile(s) per hour
mil—mil
min—minute (time)
μin—microinch
mL—milliliter
mm—millimeter
mm²—square millimeter
mm³—cubic millimeter
μm²—square micrometer
μm³—cubic micrometer
μμ—micromicron (use of compound
    prefixes obsolete; use pm,
    picometer)
μμf—micromicrofarad (use of
    compound prefixes obsolete; use
    pF)
mmHg—conventional millimeter of
    mercury
mΩ—megohm
mo—month
mol—mole (unit of substance)
mol wt—molecular weight
mp—melting point
ms—millisecond
μs—microsecond
Mt—megaton
mV—millivolt
μV—microvolt
MW—megawatt
mW—milliwatt
μW—microwatt
MWd/t—megawatt-days per ton
Mx—maxwell

n—nano (prefix, one-billionth)
N—newton
nA—nanoampere
nF—nanofarad
N•m—newton meter
N/m²—newton per square meter
nmi—nautical mile
Np—neper
ns—nanosecond
N•s/m²—newton second per square
    meter
nt—nit
od—outside diameter
Oe—oersted (use of A/m, amperes per
    meter, preferred)
oz—ounce (avoirdupois)
p—pico (prefix, one-trillionth)
P—poise
Pa—pascal
pA—picoampere
pct—percent
pdl—poundal
pF—picofarad (micromicrofarad,
    obsolete)
pF—water-holding energy
pH—hydrogen-ion concentration
ph—phot; phase
pk—peck,
p/m—parts per million
ps—picosecond
psi—pounds per square inch
pt—pint
pW—picowatt
qt—quart
quad—quadrillion (10^{15})
°R—rankine
°R—roentgen
R—degree rankine
R—degree reaumur
rad—radian
rd—rad
rem—roentgen equivalent man
r/min—revolutions per minute
rms—root mean square

r/s—revolutions per second
s—second (time)
s—shilling
S—siemens
sb—stilb
scp—spherical candlepower
s•ft—second-foot
shp—shaft horsepower
slug—slug
sr—steradian
sSf—standard saybolt fural
sSu—standard saybolt universal
stdft³—standard cubic foot (feet)
Sus—saybolt universal second(s)
T—tera (prefix, 1 trillion)
Tft³—trillion cubic feet
T—tesla
t—tonne (metric ton)
tbsp—tablespoonful
thm—therm
ton—ton

tsp—teaspoonful
Twad—twaddell
u—(unified) atomic mass unit
UHF—ultrahigh frequency
V—volt
VA—voltampere
var—var
VHF—very high frequency
V/m—volt per meter
W—watt
Wb—weber
Wh—watthour
W/(m•K)—watt per meter kelvin
W/sr—watt per steradian
W/(sr•m²)—watt per steradian square
   meter
x—unknown quantity (italic)
yd—yard
yd²—square yard
yd³—cubic yard
yr—year

Standard Latin abbreviations

9.63.   When Latin abbreviations are used, follow this list.

a.—annus, year; ante, before
A.A.C.—anno ante Christum in the
   year before Christ
A.A.S.—Academiae Americanae
   Socius, Fellow of the American
   Academy [Academy of Arts and
   Sciences]
A.B.—artium baccalaureus, bachelor
   of arts
ab init.—ab initio, from the beginning
abs. re.—absente reo, the defendant
   being absent
A.C.—ante Christum, before Christ
A.D.—anno Domini, in the year of our
   Lord
a.d.—ante diem, before the day
ad fin.—ad finem, at the end, to one end
ad h.l.—ad hunc locum, to this place,
   on this passage

ad inf.—ad infinitum, to infinity
ad init.—ad initium, at the beginning
ad int.—ad interim, in the meantime
ad lib.—ad libitum, at pleasure
ad loc.—ad locum, at the place
ad val.—ad valorem, according to
A.I.—anno inventionis, in the year of
   the discovery
al.—alia, alii, other things, other
   persons
A.M.—anno mundi, in the year of the
   world; Annus mirabilis, the
   wonderful year [1666]; a.m., ante
   meridiem, before noon
an.—anno, in the year; ante, before
ann.—annales, annals; anni, years
A.R.S.S.—Antiquariorum Regiae
   Societatis Socius, Fellow of the
   Royal Society of Antiquaries

A.U.C.—anno urbis conditae, ab urbe conolita, in [the year from] the building of the City [Rome], 753 B.C.

B.A.—baccalaureus artium, bachelor of arts

B. Sc.—baccalaureus scientiae, bachelor of science

C.—centum, a hundred; condemno, I condemn, find guilty

c.—circa, about

cent.—centum, a hundred

cf.—confer, compare

C.M.—chirurgiae magister, master of surgery

coch.—cochlear, a spoon, spoonful

coch. amp.—cochlear amplum, a tablespoonful

coch. mag.—cochlear magnum, a large spoonful

coch. med.—cochlear medium, a dessert spoonful

coch. parv.—cochlear parvum, a teaspoonful

con.—contra, against; conjunx, wife

C.P.S.—custos privati sigilli, keeper of the privy seal

C.S.—custos sigilli, keeper of the seal

cwt.—c. for centum, wt. for weight, hundredweight

D.—Deus, God; Dominus, Lord; d., decretum, a decree; denarius, a penny; da, give

D.D.—divinitatis doctor, doctor of divinity

D.G.—Dei gratia, by the grace of God; Deo gratias, thanks to God

D.N.—Dominus noster, our Lord

D. Sc.—doctor scientiae, doctor of science

d.s.p.—decessit sine prole, died without issue

D.V.—Deo volente, God willing

dwt.—d. for denarius, wt. for weight, pennyweight

e.g.—exempli gratia, for example

et al.—et alibi, and elsewhere; et alii, or aliae, and others

etc.—et cetera, and others, and so forth

et seq.—et sequentes, and those that follow

et ux.—et uxor, and wife

F.—filius, son

f.—fiat, let it be made; forte, strong

fac.—factum similis, facsimile, an exact copy

fasc.—fasciculus, a bundle

fl.—flores, flowers; floruit, flourished; fluidus, fluid

f.r.—folio recto, right-hand page

F.R.S.—Fraternitatis Regiae Socius, Fellow of the Royal Society

f.v.—folio verso, on the back of the leaf

guttat.—guttatim, by drops

H.—hora, hour

h.a.—hoc anno, in this year; hujus anni, this year's

hab. corp.—habeas corpus, have the body—a writ

h.e.—hic est, this is; hoc est, that is

h.m.—hoc mense, in this month; huius mensis, this month's

h.q.—hoc quaere, look for this

H.R.I.P.—hic requiescat in pace, here rests in peace

H.S.—hic sepultus, here is buried; hic situs, here lies; h.s., hoc sensu, in this sense

H.S.S.—Historiae Societatis Socius, Fellow of the Historical Society

h.t.—hoc tempore, at this time; hoc titulo, in or under this title

I—Idus, the Ides; i., id, that; immortalis, immortal

ib. or ibid.—ibidem, in the same place

id.—idem, the same

i.e.—id est, that is

imp.—imprimatur, sanction, let it be printed

I.N.D.—in nomine Dei, in the name of God

in f.—in fine, at the end

inf.—infra, below

init.—initio, in the beginning

in lim.—in limine, on the threshold, at the outset

in loc.—in loco, in its place

in loc. cit.—in loco citato, in the place cited

in pr.—in principio, in the beginning

in trans.—in transitu, on the way

i.q.—idem quod, the same as

i.q.e.d.—id quod erat demonstrandum, what was to be proved

J.—judex, judge

J.C.D.—juris civilis doctor, doctor of civil law

J.D.—jurum or juris doctor, doctor of laws

J.U.D.—juris utriusque doctor, doctor of both civil and canon law

L.—liber, a book; locus, a place

£—libra, pound; placed before figures thus £10; if l., to be placed after, as 401.

L.A.M.—liberalium artium magister, master of the liberal arts

L.B.—baccalaureus literarum, bachelor of letters

lb.—libra, pound (singular and plural)

L.H.D.—literarum humaniorum doctor, doctor of the more humane letters

Litt. D.—literarum doctor, doctor of letters

LL.B.—legum baccalaureus, bachelor of laws

LL.D.—legum doctor, doctor of laws

LL.M.—legum magister, master of laws

loc. cit.—loco citato, in the place cited

loq.—loquitur, he, or she, speaks

L.S.—locus sigilli, the place of the seal

l.s.c.—loco supra citato, in the place above cited

£ s. d.—librae, solidi, denarii, pounds, shillings, pence

M.—magister, master; manipulus, handful; medicinae, of medicine; m., meridies, noon

M.A.—magister artium, master of arts

M.B.—medicinae baccalaureus, bachelor of medicine

M. Ch.—magister chirurgiae, master of surgery

M.D.—medicinae doctor, doctor of medicine

m.m.—mutatis mutandis, with the necessary changes

m.n.—mutato nomine, the name being changed

MS.—manuscriptum, manuscript; MSS., manuscripta, manuscripts

Mus. B.—musicae baccalaureus, bachelor of music

Mus. D.—musicae doctor, doctor of music

Mus. M.—musicae magister, master of music

N.—Nepos, grandson; nomen, name; nomina, names; noster, our; n., natus, born; nocte, at night

N.B.—nota bene, mark well

ni. pri.—nisi prius, unless before

nob.—nobis, for (or on) our part

nol. pros.—nolle prosequi, will not prosecute

non cul.—non culpabilis, not guilty

n.l.—non licet, it is not permitted; non liquet, it is not clear; non longe, not far

non obs.—non obstante, notwithstanding

non pros.—non prosequitur, he does not prosecute

non seq.—non sequitur, it does not
    follow logically
O.—octarius, a pint
ob.—obiit, he, or she, died; obiter,
    incidentally
ob. s.p.—obiit sine prole, died without
    issue
o.c.—opere citato, in the work cited
op.—opus, work; opera, works
op. cit.—opere citato, in the work cited
P.—papa, pope; pater, father; pontifex,
    bishop; populus, people; p.,
    partim, in part; per, by, for; pius,
    holy; pondere, by weight; post,
    after; primus, first; pro, for
p.a.—or per ann., per annum, yearly;
    pro anno, for the year
p. ae.—partes aequales, equal parts
pass.—passim, everywhere
percent.—per centum, by the hundred
pil.—pilula, pill
Ph. B.—philosophiae baccalaureus,
    bachelor of philosophy
P.M.—post mortem, after death
p.m.—post meridiem, afternoon
pro tem.—pro tempore, for the time
    being
prox.—proximo, in or of the next
    [month]
P.S.—postscriptum, postscript; P.SS.,
    postscripta, postscripts
q.d.—quasi dicat, as if one should say;
    quasi dictum, as if said; quasi
    dixisset, as if he had said
q.e.—quod est, which is
Q.E.D.—quod erat demonstrandum,
    which was to be demonstrated
Q.E.F.—quod erat faciendum, which
    was to be done
Q.E.I.—quod erat inveniendum, which
    was to be found out
q.l.—quantum libet, as much as you
    please

q. pl.—quantum placet, as much as
    seems good
q.s.—quantum sufficit, sufficient
    quantity
q.v.—quantum vis, as much as you
    will; quem, quam, quod vide,
    which see; qq. v., quos, quas, or
    quae vide, which see (plural)
R.—regina, queen; recto, right-hand
    page; respublica, commonwealth
℞—recipe, take
R.I.P.—requiescat, or requiescant, in
    pace, may he, she, or they, rest in
    peace
R.P.D.—rerum politicarum doctor,
    doctor of political science
R.S.S.—Regiae Societatis Sodalis,
    Fellow of the Royal Society
S.—sepultus, buried; situs, lies;
    societas, society; socius or
    sodalis, fellow; s., semi, half;
    solidus, shilling
s.a.—sine anno, without date;
    secundum artem, according to
    art
S.A.S.—Societatis Antiquariorum
    Socius, Fellow of the Society of
    Antiquaries
sc.—scilicet, namely; sculpsit, he, or
    she, carved or engraved it
Sc. B.—scientiae baccalaureus,
    bachelor of science
Sc. D.—scientiae doctor, doctor of
    science
S.D.—salutem dicit, sends greetings
s.d.—sine die, indefinitely
sec.—secundum, according to
sec. leg.—secundum legem, according
    to law
sec. nat.—secundum naturam,
    according to nature, or naturally
sec. reg.—secundum regulam,
    according to rule

seq.—sequens, sequentes, sequentia, the following

S.H.S.—Societatis Historiae Socius, Fellow of the Historical Society

s.h.v.—sub hac voce or sub hoc verbo, under this word

s.l.a.n.—sine loco, anno, vel nomine, without place, date, or name

s.l.p.—sine legitima prole, without lawful issue

s.m.p.—sine mascula prole, without male issue

s.n.—sine nomine, without name

s.p.—sine prole, without issue

S.P.A.S.—Societatis Philosophiae Americanae Socius, Fellow of the American Philosophical Society

s.p.s.—sine prole superstite, without surviving issue

S.R.S.—Societatis Regiae Socius or Sodalis, Fellow of the Royal Society

ss—scilicet, namely (in law)

S.S.C.—Societas Sanctae Crucis, Society of the Holy Cross

stat.—statim, immediately

S.T.B.—sacrae theologiae baccalaureus, bachelor of sacred theology

S.T.D.—sacrae theologiae doctor, doctor of sacred theology

S.T.P.—sacrae theologiae professor, professor of sacred theology

sub.—subaudi, understand, supply

sup.—supra, above

t. or temp.—tempore, in the time of

tal. qual.—talis qualis, just as they come; average quality

U.J.D.—utriusque juris doctor, doctor of both civil and canon law

ult.—ultimo, last month (may be abbreviated in writing but should be spelled out in printing)

ung.—unguentum, ointment

u.s.—ubi supra, in the place above mentioned

ut dict.—ut dictum, as directed

ut sup.—ut supra, as above

ux.—uxor, wife

v.—versus, against; vide, see; voce, voice, word

v. —— a., vixit —— annos—lived [so many] years

verb. sap.—verbum [satis] sapienti, a word to the wise suffices

v.g.—verbi gratia, for example

viz—videlicet, namely

v.s.—vide supra, see above

Information technology acronyms and initialisms

9.64.   If abbreviations are required, use these forms:

AARP—Apple Address Resolution Protocol

ABLS—Automated Bid List System

ABM—asynchronous balanced mode

ACES—access certificates for electronic services

ACP—Access Content Package

ACS—Access Content Storage

ACSIS—Acquisition, Classification, and Shipment Information System

AES—advanced encryption standard

AIFF—audio interchange file format

AIP—Archival Information Package

AIS—Archival Information Storage

ANSI—American National Standards Institute

AP—access processor

ARK—archival resource key

ARP—address resolution protocol

ASCII—American Standard Code for Information Interchange

ASP—application service provider
BAC—billing address code
BBS—bulletin board service
BPEL—business process execution
    language
BPI—business process information
BPS—business process storage
CA—certification authority
CCSDS—Consultative Committee for
    Space Data Systems
CD—compact disk
CDN—content delivery network
CDR—critical design review
CD-ROM—compact disk read only
    memory
CE—content evaluator
CFR—Code of Federal Regulations
CGP—Catalog of U.S. Government
    Publications
CMS—content management system
CMYK—cyan, magenta, yellow, black
CO—content originator
COOP—continuity of operations plan
CP—content processor
CPI—content packet information
CRC—cyclic redundancy checks
CSV—comma separated variable
DBMS—database management system
DES—data encryption standard
DIP—Dissemination Information
    Package
DMI—desktop management interface
DNS—domain name system
DO—digital objects
DOI—Digital Object Identifier
DoS—denial of service
DPI—dots per inch
DSR—deployment system review
DSSL—document style and semantics
    language
DVD—digital versatile disc
EA—enterprise architecture
EAD—encoded archival description

EAC—estimate at completion
EAP—enterprise application platform
EBCDIC—Extended Binary Coded
    Decimal Interchange Code
ePub—Electronic Publishing Section
FAQ—frequently asked question
FBCA—Federal Bridge Certificate
    Authority
FDDI—fiber distributed data interface
FDLP—Federal Depository Library
    Program
FDsys—Federal Digital System
FICC—Federal Identity Credentialing
    Committee
FIFO—first in first out
FIPS—Federal Information Processing
    Standard
FOB—free on board
FOSI—format output specification
    instance
FTP—file transfer protocol
GAP—GPO Access Package
GDI—graphical device interface
GFE—government furnished
    equipment
GFI—government furnished
    information
GGP—gateway-to-gateway protocol
GIF—graphics interchange format
GILS—Government Information
    Locator Service
GUI—graphical user interface
HDTV—high definition television
HMAC—key hashed message
    authentication code
HSM—hardware security module
HTML—hypertext markup language
HTTP—hypertext transfer protocol
Hz—Hertz
ICMP—internet control message
    protocol
ID—Information Dissemination
IDD—interface design description

IEEE—Institute of Electronics and Electrical Engineers

IETF—Internet Engineering Task Force

ILS—Integrated Library System

IP—internet protocol

IPR—internal progress review

IPSEC—internet protocol security

ISO—International Organization for Standardization

ISP—internet service provider

ISSN—International Standard Serial Number

IT—information technology

ITU—International Telecommunications Union

JDF—Job Definition Format

JPEG—Joint Photographic Experts Group

LAN—local area network

LDAP—lightweight directory access protocol

LPI—lines per inch

MAC—message authentication code

MARC—Machine Readable Cataloging

METS—Metadata Encoding and Transmission Standard

MHz—megahertz

MIME—multipurpose internet mail extensions

MIPS—millions of instructions per second

MMAR—Materials Management Procurement Regulation

MODS—Metadata Object Descriptive Schema

MPCF—marginally punched continuous forms

NAT—network address translation

NDIIPP—National Digital Information Infrastructure and Preservation Program

NFC—National Finance Center

NIST—National Institute of Standards and Technology

NNTP—network news transfer protocol

OAI—Open Archives Initiative

OAI-PMH—Open Archives Initiative Protocol for Metadata Harvesting

OAIS—Open Archival Information Systems

OCLC—Online Computer Library Center

OCR—optical character recognition

OLTP—online transaction processing

PRONOM—Practical Online Compendium of File Formats

PTR—program tracking report

PURL—persistent uniform resource locator

RAID—redundant array of inexpensive disks

RAM—random access memory

RFC—request for comments

RGB—red, green, blue

RI—representation information

RMA—reliability, maintainability, availability

RPC—remote procedure call

RSA—Rivest, Shamir, Adleman (public key decryption algorithm)

RTF—rich text format

RVTM—requirements verification traceability matrix

SAML—security assertion markup language

SDLC—software/system development life cycle

SDR—system design review

Section 508—Section 508 of the Rehabilitation Act

SGML—standard generalized markup language

SHA—secure hash algorithm

SIP—Submission Information Package
SLIP—serial line internet protocol
SMP—storage management processor
SMS—storage management system
SMTP—simple mail transfer protocol
SNMP—simple network management
 protocol
SPA—simplified purchase agreement
SSL—secure sockets layer
SSP—system security plan
SSR—software specification review
TDES—Triple Data Encryption
 Standard
TIFF—tagged image file format
TLS—transport layer security
UDP—user datagram protocol
URL—uniform resource locator
URN—uniform resource name/
 number

VLAN—virtual local area network
VPN—virtual private network
VRML—virtual reality modeling
 language
W3C—World Wide Web Consortium
WAIS—wide area information service
WAN—wide area network
WAP—wireless application protocol
WAV—waveform audio format
WIP—work in process
WML—wireless markup language
WMS—workflow management system
WWW—World Wide Web
WYSIWYG—what you see is what
 you get
XML—extensible markup language
XMLDsig—xml signature
XMLENC—xml encryption

10. Signs and Symbols

10.1. The increased use of signs and symbols and their importance in technical and scientific work have emphasized the necessity of standardization on a national basis and of the consistent use of the standard forms.

10.2. Certain symbols are standardized—number symbols (the digits, 0, 1, 2, 3, 4, 5, 6, 7, 8, 9); letter symbols (the letters of the alphabet, a, b, c, d, etc.); and graphic symbols (the mathematical signs $+$, $-$, $\pm$, $\times$, $\div$).

10.3. The signs $+$, $-$, $\pm$, $\times$, and $\div$, etc., are closed against accompanying figures and symbols. When the $\times$ is used to indicate "crossed with" (in plant or animal breeding) or magnification, it will be separated from the accompanying words by a space.

i–vii + 1–288 pages	Early June × Bright (crossed with)
The equation A+B	× 4 (magnification)
The result is 4×4	miles ÷ gallons
20,000±5,000	

Symbols with figures

10.4. In technical publications the degree mark is used in lieu of the word *degree* following a figure denoting measurement.

10.5. Following a figure, the spelled form is preferred. The percent symbol is used in areas where space will not allow the word *percent* to be used.

> In that period the price rose 12, 15, and 19 percent.
> *not* In that period the price rose 12 percent, 15 percent, and 19 percent.

10.6. Any symbol set close up to figures, such as the degree mark, number mark, dollar mark, or cent mark, is used before or after each figure in a group or series.

$5 to $8 price range	*but*
5'–7' long, *not* 5–7' long	§ 12 (thin space)
3¢ to 5¢ (no spaces)	¶ 1951 (thin space)
±2 to ±7; 2°±1°	from 15 to 25 percent
#61 to #64	45 to 65 °F *not* 45° to 65° F

259

Letter symbols

10.7.   Letter symbols are set in italic (see rule 10.8) or in roman (see rule 9.56) without periods and are capitalized only if so shown in copy, since the capitalized form may have an entirely different meaning.

Equations

10.8.   In mathematical equations, use italic for all letter symbols—capitals, lowercase, small capitals, and superiors and inferiors (exponents and subscripts); use roman for figures, including superiors and inferiors.

10.9.   If an equation or a mathematical expression needs to be divided, break before +, −, =, etc. However, the equal sign is to clear on the left of other beginning mathematical signs.

10.10.   A short equation in text should not be broken at the end of a line. Space out the line so that the equation will begin on the next line; or better, center the equation on a line by itself.

10.11.   An equation too long for one line is set flush left, the second half of the equation is set flush right, and the two parts are balanced as nearly as possible.

10.12.   Two or more equations in a series are aligned on the equal signs and centered on the longest equation in the group.

10.13.   Connecting words of explanation, such as *hence, therefore,* and *similarly,* are set flush left either on the same line with the equation or on a separate line.

10.14.   Parentheses, braces, brackets, integral signs, and summation signs should be of the same height as the mathematical expressions they include.

10.15.   Inferiors precede superiors if they appear together; but if either inferior or superior is too long, the two are aligned on the left.

Chemical symbols

10.16. The names and symbols listed below are approved by the International Union of Pure and Applied Chemistry. They are set in roman without periods.

Element	Symbol	Atomic No.	Element	Symbol	Atomic No.
Actinium	Ac	89	Mendelevium	Md	101
Aluminum	Al	13	Mercury	Hg	80
Americium	Am	95	Molybdenum	Mo	42
Antimony	Sb	51	Neodymium	Nd	60
Argon	Ar	18	Neon	Ne	10
Arsenic	As	33	Neptunium	Np	93
Astatine	At	85	Nickel	Ni	28
Barium	Ba	56	Niobium	Nb	41
Berkelium	Bk	97	Nitrogen	N	7
Beryllium	Be	4	Nobelium	No	102
Bismuth	Bi	83	Osmium	Os	76
Bohrium	Bh	107	Oxygen	O	8
Boron	B	5	Palladium	Pd	46
Bromine	Br	35	Phosphorus	P	15
Cadmium	Cd	48	Platinum	Pt	78
Calcium	Ca	20	Plutonium	Pu	94
Californium	Cf	98	Polonium	Po	84
Carbon	C	6	Potassium	K	19
Cerium	Ce	58	Praseodymium	Pr	59
Cesium	Cs	55	Promethium	Pm	61
Chlorine	Cl	17	Protactinium	Pa	91
Chromium	Cr	24	Radium	Ra	88
Cobalt	Co	27	Radon	Rn	86
Copper	Cu	29	Rhenium	Re	75
Curium	Cm	96	Rhodium	Rh	45
Darmstadtium	Ds	110	Roentgenium	Rg	111
Dubnium	Db	105	Rubidium	Rb	37
Dysprosium	Dy	66	Ruthenium	Ru	44
Einsteinium	Es	99	Rutherfordium	Rf	104
Erbium	Er	68	Samarium	Sm	62
Europium	Eu	63	Scandium	Sc	21
Fermium	Fm	100	Seaborgium	Sg	106
Fluorine	F	9	Selenium	Se	34
Francium	Fr	87	Silicon	Si	14
Gadolinium	Gd	64	Silver	Ag	47
Gallium	Ga	31	Sodium	Na	11
Germanium	Ge	32	Strontium	Sr	38
Gold	Au	79	Sulfur	S	16
Hafnium	Hf	72	Tantalum	Ta	73
Hassium	Hs	108	Technetium	Tc	43
Helium	He	2	Tellurium	Te	52
Holmium	Ho	67	Terbium	Tb	65
Hydrogen	H	1	Thallium	Tl	81
Indium	In	49	Thorium	Th	90
Iodine	I	53	Thulium	Tm	69
Iridium	Ir	77	Tin	Sn	50
Iron	Fe	26	Titanium	Ti	22
Krypton	Kr	36	Tungsten	W	74
Lanthanum	La	57	Uranium	U	92
Lawrencium	Lr	103	Vanadium	V	23
Lead	Pb	82	Xenon	Xe	54
Lithium	Li	3	Ytterbium	Yb	70
Lutetium	Lu	71	Yttrium	Y	39
Magnesium	Mg	12	Zinc	Zn	30
Manganese	Mn	25	Zirconium	Zr	40
Meitnerium	Mt	109			

Standardized symbols

10.17.   Symbols duly standardized by any national scientific, professional, or technical group are accepted as preferred forms within the field of the group. The issuing office desiring or requiring the use of such standardized symbols should see that copy is prepared accordingly.

Signs and symbols

10.18.   The following list contains some signs and symbols frequently used in printing. The forms and style of many symbols vary with the method of reproduction employed. It is important that editors and writers clearly identify signs and symbols when they appear within a manuscript.

ACCENTS

- ´ acute
- ˘ breve
- ¸ cedilla
- ∧ circumflex
- ·· dieresis
- ` grave
- ¯ macron
- ~ tilde

ARROWS

- → direction
- ↖ direction
- ↝ direction
- ↜ direction
- ↷ direction
- ⬅ bold arrow
- ⇣ open arrow
- ⇌ reversible reaction

BULLETS

- ● solid circle; bullet
- • bold center dot
- • movable accent

CHEMICAL

- ‰ salinity
- ℳ minim
- ‖ exchange
- ↑ gas

CIRCLED SYMBOLS

- ☽ angle in circle
- ⊕ circle with parallel rule
- ▲ triangle in circle
- ☉ dot in circle
- ▲ dot in triangle in circle
- ⊕ cross in circle
- © copyright
- ① Ceres
- ② Pallas
- ③ Juno
- ④ Vesta

CODE

- · No. 1 6 pt. code dot
- · No. 2 8 pt. code dot
- · No. 3 10 pt. code dot
- • No. 4 8 pt. code dot
- • No. 4 10 pt. code dot
- — No. 1 6 pt. code dash
- — No. 2 8 pt. code dash
- — No. 3 10 pt. code dash
- ▬ No. 4 8 pt. code dash
- ▬ No. 4 10 pt. code dash

COMPASS

- ° degree
- °⋅ degree with period
- ′ minute
- ′⋅ minute with period
- ″ second
- ″⋅ second with period
- ″̲ canceled second

DECORATIVE

- ✚ bold cross
- ✠ cross patte
- ■ cross patte
- ✠ cross patte

- ● (184 N)
- ⚷ key
- ⚲ (206 N)
- ¶ paragraph

ELECTRICAL

- ℛ reluctance
- ↔ reaction goes both right and left
- ↕ reaction goes both up and down
- ↕ reversible
- → direction of flow; yields
- → direct current
- ⇄ electrical current
- ⇄ reversible reaction
- ⇄ alternating current
- ⇄ alternating current
- ⇌ reversible reaction beginning at left
- ⇋ reversible reaction beginning at right
- Ω ohm; omega
- MΩ megohm; omega
- µΩ microhm; mu omega
- ω angular frequency, solid angle; omega
- Φ magnetic flux; phi
- Ψ dielectric flux; electrostatic flux; psi
- γ conductivity; gamma

ELECTRICAL—Con.

ρ   resistivity; rho
Λ   equivalent conductivity
HP horsepower

MATHEMATICAL

— vinculum (above letters)
÷ geometrical proportion
−: difference, excess
‖ parallel
‖s parallels
≠ not parallels
│ │ absolute value
· multiplied by
: is to; ratio
÷ divided by
∴ therefore; hence
∵ because
:: proportion; as
≪ is dominated by
> greater than
⊏ greater than
≥ greater than or equal to
≧ greater than or equal to
≷ greater than or less than
≯ is not greater than
< less than
⊐ less than
≶ less than or greater than
≮ is not less than
⋖ smaller than
≤ less than or equal to
≦ less than or equal to
≥ or ≧ greater than or equal to
≲ equal to or less than
≡ equal to or less than
≱ is not greater than equal to or less than
≳ equal to or greater than
≴ is not less than equal to or greater than
⟂ equilateral
⊥ perpendicular to
⊢ assertion sign
≑ approaches

MATHEMATICAL—Con.

≐ approaches a limit
⋎ equal angles
≠ not equal to
≡ identical with
≢ not identical with
⫟ score
≈ or ≒ nearly equal to
= equal to
~ difference
≃ perspective to
≅ congruent to approximately equal
≏ difference between
⟠ geometrically equivalent to
(included in
) excluded from
⊂ is contained in
∪ logical sum or union
∩ logical product or intersection
√ radical
∜ root
√ square root
∛ cube root
∜ fourth root
∜ fifth root
∜ sixth root
π pi
ε base (2.718) of natural system of logarithms; epsilon
ε is a member of; dielectric constant; mean error; epsilon
+ plus
+ bold plus
− minus
− bold minus
/ shill(ing); slash; virgule
± plus or minus
∓ minus or plus
× multiplied by
= bold equal
number
℔ per
% percent
∫ integral
│ single bond
\ single bond
/ single bond

MATHEMATICAL—Con.

‖ double bond
╲ double bond
∥ double bond
⬡ benzene ring
∂ or δ differential; variation
∂ Italian differential
→ approaches limit of
~ cycle sine
⌡ horizontal integral
∮ contour integral
∝ variation; varies as
Π product
Σ summation of; sum; sigma
! or ⌐ factorial product

MEASURE

℔ pound
ℨ dram
ƒℨ fluid dram
℥ ounce
ƒ℥ fluid ounce
O pint

MISCELLANEOUS

§ section
† dagger
‡ double dagger
℀ account of
℅ care of
⫟ score
¶ paragraph
þ Anglo-Saxon
₡ center line
♂ conjunction
⊥ perpendicular to
″ or " ditto
∝ variation
℞ recipe
⊐ move right
⊏ move left
◯ or ⊙ or ① annual
⊙⊙ or ② biennial
∈ element of
℈ scruple
ƒ function
! exclamation mark
⊞ plus in square
♃ perennial

MISCELLANEOUS—Con.

φ diameter
c̄ mean value of c
U mathmodifier
⊂ mathmodifier
⊡ dot in square
△ dot in triangle
⊠ station mark
@ at

MONEY

¢ cent
¥ yen
£ pound sterling
ɱ mills

MUSIC

♮ natural
♭ flat
♯ sharp

PLANETS

☿ Mercury
♀ Venus
⊕ Earth
♂ Mars
♃ Jupiter
♄ Saturn
♅ Uranus
♆ Neptune
♇ Pluto
☊ dragon's head, ascending node
☋ dragon's tail, descending node
☌ conjunction
☍ opposition
☉ or ☉ Sun
☉ Sun's lower limb
☉ Sun's upper limb
☉ solar corona
⊕ solar halo
☽ Moon
● new Moon
☽ first quarter
☾ first quarter
◑ third quarter
◐ last quarter
☾ last quarter
◐ last quarter
○ full Moon
⊕ full Moon

PLANETS—Con.

☽ eclipse of Moon
☽ lunar halo
☽ lunar corona
⚵ Ceres
⚵ Juno

PUNCTUATION

{ } braces
[ ] brackets
( ) parentheses
⟨ ⟩ square parentheses; angle brackets
¡ Spanish open quote
¿ Spanish open quote

SEX

♂ or ⚦ male
☐ male, in charts
♀ female
○ female, in charts
⚥ hermaphrodite

SHAPES

◆ solid diamond
◇ open diamond
○ circle
▲ solid triangle
△ triangle
☐ square
■ solid square
▱ parallelogram
▭ rectangle
▥ double rectangle
★ solid star
☆ open star
∟ right angle
∠ angle
√ check
✓ check
ß German ss
ß italic German ss
☛ solid index
☚ solid index
☜ index
☞ index

GEOLOGIC SYSTEMS [1]

Q Quaternary
T Tertiary
K Cretaceous

J Jurassic
Ƭ Triassic
P Permian
P Pennsylvanian
M Mississippian
D Devonian
S Silurian
O Ordovician
€ Cambrian
p€ Precambrian
C Carboniferous

VERTICAL

| 5 unit vertical
| 8 point vertical
| 9 unit vertical

WEATHER

T thunder
Ƙ thunderstorm; sheet lightning
< sheet lightning
↓ precipitate
⦿ rain
← floating ice crystals
↔ ice needles
▲ hail
⊗ sleet
∾ glazed frost
⊔ hoarfrost
V frostwork
✳ snow or sextile
⊠ snow on ground
⊹ drifting snow (low)
≡ fog
∞ haze
⌓ Aurora

ZODIAC

♈ Aries; Ram
♉ Taurus; Bull
♊ Gemini; Twins
♋ Cancer; Crab
♌ Leo; Lion
♍ Virgo; Virgin
♎ Libra; Balance
♏ Scorpio; Scorpion
♐ Sagittarius; Archer
♑ Capricornus; Goat
♒ Aquarius; Water bearer
♓ Pisces; Fishes

[1] Standard letter symbols used by the Geological Survey on geologic maps. Capital letter indicates the system and one or more lowercased letters designate the formation and member where used.

11. Italic

(See also Chapter 9 "Abbreviations and Letter Symbols" and Chapter 16 "Datelines, Addresses, and Signatures")

11.1.   Italic is sometimes used to differentiate or to give greater prominence to words, phrases, etc. However, an excessive amount of italic defeats this purpose and should be restricted.

Emphasis, foreign words, and titles of publications

11.2.   Italic is not used for mere emphasis, foreign words, or the titles of publications.

11.3.   In nonlegal work, *ante, post, infra,* and *supra* are italicized only when part of a legal citation. Otherwise these terms, as well as the abbreviations *id., ibid., op. cit., et seq.,* and other foreign words, phrases, and their abbreviations, are printed in roman.

11.4.   When "emphasis in original," "emphasis supplied," "emphasis added," or "emphasis ours" appears in copy, it should not be changed; but "underscore supplied" should be changed to "italic supplied." Therefore, when emphasis in quoted or extracted text is referred to by the foregoing terms, such emphasized text must be reflected and set in italic.

11.5.   When copy is submitted with instructions to set "all roman (no italic)," these instructions will not apply to *Ordered, Resolved, Be it enacted,* etc.; titles following signatures or addresses; or the parts of datelines which are always set in italic.

Names of aircraft, vessels, and spacecraft

11.6.   The names of aircraft, vessels, and manned spacecraft are italicized unless otherwise indicated. In lists set in columns and in stubs and reading columns of tables consisting entirely of such names they will be set in roman. Missiles and rockets will be set in caps and lowercase and will not be italicized.

SS *America*; the liner *America*
the Bermuda *Clipper*
USS *Los Angeles* (submarine)
USS *Wisconsin*
ex-USS *Savannah*
USCGS (U.S. Coast and Geodetic
    Survey) ship *Pathfinder*
C.S.N. *Virginia*
CG cutter *Thetus*
the *U–7*
destroyer *31*
H.M.S. *Hornet*
HS (hydrofoil ship) *Denison*
MS (motorship) *Richard*
GTS (gas turbine ship) *Alexander*
NS (nuclear ship) *Savannah*

MV (motor vessel) *Havtroll*
Apollo 13, Atlantis (U.S. spaceships)
West Virginia class or type
the *Missouri's* (roman "s") turret
the *U–7's* (roman "s") deck

but

Air Force One (President's plane)
B–50 (type of plane)
DD–882
LST–1155
MiG; MiG-35
PT–109
F–22 Raptor
F–117 Nighthawk (Stealth fighter)
A–10 Thunderbolt

11.7.   Names of vessels are quoted in matter printed in other than lowercase roman, even if there is italic type available in the series.

Sinking of the "Lusitania"   SINKING OF THE "LUSITANIA"
Sinking of the "Lusitania"   SINKING OF THE "LUSITANIA"

Names of legal cases

11.8.   The names of legal cases are italicized, except for the *v.*, which is always set in lowercase. When requested, the names of such cases may be set in roman with an italic *v.* In matter set in italic, legal cases are set in roman with the *v.* being set roman.

"The Hornet" and "The Hood,"   SMITH v. BROWN ET AL. (heading)
    124 F.2d 45   SMITH v. BROWN ET AL.
Smith v. *Brown et al.*   (heading)
Smith Bros. case (172 App.   *Durham* rule
    Div. 149)   *Brown* decision
Smith Bros. case, *supra*   *John Doe* v. *Richard Roe*
Smith Bros. case   *but* John Doe against Richard Roe,
As cited in *Smith* Bros.   the *Cement* case.

Scientific names

11.9.   The scientific names of genera, subgenera, species, and subspecies (varieties) are italicized, but are set in roman in italic matter; the names of groups of higher rank than genera (phyla, classes, orders, families, tribes, etc.) are printed in roman.

> *A.s. perpallidus*
> *Dorothia?* sp. (roman "?")
> *Tsuga canadensis*
> *Cypripedium parviflorum* var. *pubescens*
> the genera *Quercus* and *Liriodendron*
> the family Leguminosae; the family Nessiteras rhombopteryx
> *Measurements of specimens of* Cyanoderma erythroptera neocara

11.10.   Quotation marks should be used in place of italic for scientific names appearing in lines set in caps, caps and small caps, or boldface, even if there is italic type available in the series.

Words and letters

11.11.   The words *Resolved, Resolved further, Provided, Provided, however, Provided further, And provided further,* and *ordered,* in bills, acts, resolutions, and formal contracts and agreements are italicized; also the words *To be continued, Continued on p. —, Continued from p. —,* and *See* and *see also* (in indexes and tables of contents only).

> *Resolved,* That (resolution)
> *Resolved by the Senate and House of Representatives of the United States of America in Congress assembled,* That
> [*To be continued*] (centered; no period)
> [*Continued from p. 3*] (centered; no period)
> *see also* Mechanical data (index entry)

11.12.   All letters (caps, small caps, lowercase, superiors, and inferiors) used as symbols are italicized. In italic matter roman letters are used. Chemical symbols (even in italic matter) and certain other standardized symbols are set in roman.

> nth degree; x dollars
> $D \div 0.025 V_m^{2.7} = 0.042/G - 1 V_m^{2.7}$
> $5Cu_2S.2(Cu,Fe,Zn)S.2Sb_2S_3O_4$

11.13.   Letter designations in mathematical and scientific matter, except chemical symbols, are italicized.

11.14.   Letter symbols used in legends to illustrations, drawings, etc., or in text as references to such material, are set in italic without periods and are capitalized if so shown in copy.

11.15.   Letters (*a*), (*b*), (*c*), etc., and *a*, *b*, *c*, etc., used to indicate sections or paragraphs, are italicized in general work but not in laws and other legal documents.

11.16.   Internet Web sites and email addresses should be set in roman.

12. Numerals
(See also Chapter 13 "Tabular Work" and Chapter 14 "Leaderwork")

12.1. Most rules for the use of numerals are based on the general principle that the reader comprehends numerals more readily than numerical word expressions, particularly in technical, scientific, or statistical matter. However, for special reasons, numbers are spelled out in certain instances, except in FIC & punc. and Fol. Lit. matter.

12.2. The following rules cover the most common conditions that require a choice between the use of numerals and words. Some of them, however, are based on typographic appearance rather than on the general principle stated above.

12.3. Arabic numerals are preferable to Roman numerals.

Numbers expressed in figures

12.4. A figure is used for a single number of *10* or more with the exception of the first word of the sentence. (See also rules 12.9 and 12.23.)

50 ballots	24 horses	nearly 13 buckets
10 guns	about 40 men	10 times as large

Numbers and numbers in series

12.5. When 2 or more numbers appear in a sentence and 1 of them is *10* or larger, figures are used for each number. (See supporting rule 12.6.)

Each of 15 major commodities (9 metal and 6 nonmetal) was in supply.
but Each of nine major commodities (five metal and four nonmetal) was in supply.
Petroleum came from 16 fields, of which 8 were discovered in 1956.
but Petroleum came from nine fields, of which eight were discovered in 1956.
That man has 3 suits, 2 pairs of shoes, and 12 pairs of socks.
but That man has three suits, two pairs of shoes, and four hats.
Of the 13 engine producers, 6 were farm equipment manufacturers, 6 were principally engaged in the production of other types of machinery, and 1 was not classified in the machinery industry.
but Only nine of these were among the large manufacturing companies, and only three were among the largest concerns.
There were three 6-room houses, five 4-room houses, and three 2-room cottages, and they were built by 20 carpenters. (See rule 12.21.)

There were three six-room houses, five four-room houses, and three two-room cottages, and they were built by nine carpenters.

but If two columns of sums of money add or subtract one into the other and one carries points and ciphers, the other should also carry points and ciphers.

At the hearing, only one Senator and one Congressman testified.

There are four or five things which can be done.

12.6. A unit of measurement, time, or money (as defined in rule 12.9), which is always expressed in figures, does not affect the use of figures for other numerical expressions within a sentence.

Each of the five girls earned 75 cents an hour.

Each of the 15 girls earned 75 cents an hour.

A team of four men ran the 1-mile relay in 3 minutes 20 seconds.

This usually requires from two to five washes and a total time of 2 to 4 hours.

This usually requires 9 to 12 washes and a total time of 2 to 4 hours.

The contractor, one engineer, and one surveyor inspected the 1-mile road.

but There were two six-room houses, three four-room houses, and four two-room cottages, and they were built by nine workers in thirty 5-day weeks. (See rule 12.21.)

12.7. Figures are used for serial numbers.

Bulletin 725	290 U.S. 325
Document 71	Genesis 39:20
pages 352–357	202–512–0724 (telephone number)
lines 5 and 6	the year 2001
paragraph 1	1721–1727 St. Clair Avenue
chapter 2	*but* Letters Patent No. 2,189,463

12.8. A colon preceding figures does not affect their use.

The result was as follows: 12 voted yea, 4 dissented.

The result was as follows: nine voted yea, seven dissented.

Measurement and time

12.9. Units of measurement and time, actual or implied, are expressed in figures.

a. Age:

6 years old	a 3-year-old
52 years 10 months 6 days	at the age of 3 (years implied)

b. Clock time (see also Time):

4:30 p.m.; half past 4

10 o'clock *or* 10 p.m. (*not* 10 o'clock p.m.; 2 p.m. in the afternoon; 10:00 p.m.)

12 p.m. (12 noon)

12 a.m. (12 midnight)

4^h30^m *or* 4.5^h, in scientific work, if so written in copy

0025, 2359 (astronomical and military time)

08:31:04 (stopwatch reading)

c. Dates:

9/11 (referring to the attack on the United States that occurred on September 11, 2001)

June 1985 (*not* June, 1985); June 29, 1985 (*not* June 29th, 1985)

March 6 to April 15, 1990 (*not* March 6, 1990, to April 15, 1990)

May, June, and July 1965 (*but* June and July 1965)

15 April 1951; 15–17 April 1951 (military)

4th of July (*but* Fourth of July, meaning the holiday)

the 1st [day] of the month (*but* the last of April or the first [part] of May, not referring to specific days)

in the year 2000 (*not* 2,000)

In referring to a fiscal year, consecutive years, or a continuous period of 2 years or more, when contracted, the forms 1900–11, 1906–38, 1931–32, 1801–2, 1875–79 are used (*but* upon change of century, 1895–1914 and to avoid multiple ciphers together, 2000–2001). For two or more separate years not representing a continuous period, a comma is used instead of a dash (1875, 1879); if the word *from* precedes the year or the word *inclusive* follows it, the second year is not shortened and the word *to* is used in lieu of the dash (from 1933 to 1936; 1935 to 1936, inclusive).

In dates, *A.D.* precedes the year (A.D. 937); *B.C.* follows the year (254 B.C.); C.E. and B.C.E. follow the year.

d. Decimals: In text a cipher should be supplied before a decimal point if there is no whole unit, and ciphers should be omitted after a decimal point unless they indicate exact measurement.

0.25 inch; 1.25 inches

silver 0.900 fine

specific gravity 0.9547

gauge height 10.0 feet

but .30 caliber (meaning 0.30 inch, bore of small arms); 30 calibers (length)

e. Use spaces to separate groups of three digits in a decimal fraction. (See rule 12.27.)

> 0.123 456 789; *but* 0.1234

f. Degrees, etc. (spaces omitted):

longitude 77°04'06" E.	*but*
35°30'; 35°30' N.	two degrees of justice; 12
a polariscopic test of 85°	degrees of freedom
an angle of 57°	32d degree Mason
strike N. 16° E.	150 million degrees Fahrenheit
dip 47° W. *or* 47° N. 31° W.	30 Fahrenheit degrees
25.5' (preferred) *also* 25'.5	

g. Game scores:

1 up (golf)	7 to 6 (football), etc.
3 to 2 (baseball)	2 all (tie)

h. Market quotations:

4½ percent bonds	gold is 109
Treasury bonds sell at 95	wheat at 2.30
Metropolitan Railroad, 109	sugar, .03; *not* 0.03
Dow Jones average of 10500.76	

i. Mathematical expressions:

multiplied by 3	a factor of 2
divided by 6	square root of 4

j. Measurements:

7 meters	3 ems
about 10 yards	20/20 (vision)
8 by 12 inches	30/30 (rifle)
8- by 12-inch page	12-gauge shotgun
2 feet by 1 foot 8 inches by 1 foot 3	2,500 horsepower
inches	15 cubic yards
2 by 4 (lumber) (*not* 2 x 4 or 2×4)	6-pounder
1½ miles	80 foot-pounds
6 acres	10s (for yarns and threads)
9 bushels	*f*/2.5 (lens aperture)
1 gallon	

but
tenpenny nail
fourfold
three-ply
five votes

six bales
two dozen
one gross
zero miles
seven-story building

k. Money:

$3.65; $0.75; 75 cents; 0.5 cent
$3 (*not* $3.00) per 200 pounds
75 cents apiece
Rs32,25,644 (Indian rupees)
2.5 francs *or* fr2.5
65 yen
₱265

but
two pennies
three quarters
one half
six bits, etc.

l. Percentage:

12 percent; 25.5 percent; 0.5 percent
  (*or* one-half of 1 percent)
thirty-four one hundredths of
  1 percent
3.65 bonds; 3.65s; 5–20 bonds;
  5–20s; 4½s; 3s

50–50 (colloquial expression)
5 percentage points
a 1,100-percent increase, *or* an
  1100-percent increase

m. Proportion:

1 to 4

1–3–5

1:62,500

n. Time (see also Clock time):

6 hours 8 minutes 20 seconds
10 years 3 months 29 days
7 minutes
8 days
4 weeks
1 month
3 fiscal years; third fiscal year
1 calendar year
millennium

but
four centuries
three decades
three quarters (9 months)
statistics of any one year
in a year or two
four afternoons
one-half hour
the eleventh hour

o. Unit modifiers:

5-day week	a 5-percent increase
8-year-old wine	20th-century progress
8-hour day	
10-foot pole	*but*
½-inch pipe	two-story house
5-foot-wide entrance	five-member board
10-million-peso loan	$20 million airfield

p. Vitamins:

B_{12}, B_T, A_1, etc.

Ordinal numbers

12.10. Except as indicated in rules 12.11 and 12.19, and also for day preceding month, figures are used in text and footnotes to text for serial ordinal numbers beginning with *10th*. In tables, leaderwork, footnotes to tables and leaderwork, and in sidenotes, figures are used at all times. Military units are expressed in figures at all times when not the beginning of a sentence, except *Corps*. (For ordinals in addresses, see rule 12.13.)

29th of May, *but* May 29	eighth parallel; 38th parallel
First Congress; 102d Congress	fifth ward; 12th ward
ninth century; 21st century	ninth birthday; 66th birthday
Second Congressional District; 20th	first grade; 11th grade
Congressional District	1st Army
seventh region; 17th region	1st Cavalry Division
323d Fighter Wing	
12th Regiment	*but*
9th Naval District	XII Corps (Army usage)
7th Fleet	Court of Appeals for the Tenth
7th Air Force	Circuit
7th Task Force	Seventeenth Decennial Census (title)

12.11. When ordinals appear in juxtaposition and one of them is *10th* or more, figures are used for such ordinal numbers.

This legislation was passed in the 1st session of the 102d Congress.
He served in the 9th and 10th Congresses.

From the 1st to the 92d Congress.
Their children were in 1st, 2d, 3d, and 10th grades.
We read the 8th and 12th chapters.
but The district comprised the first and second precincts.
He represented the first, third, and fourth regions.
The report was the sixth in a series of 14.

12.12. Ordinals and numerals appearing in a sentence are treated according to the separate rules dealing with ordinals and numerals standing alone or in a group. (See rules 12.4, 12.5, and 12.24.)

The fourth group contained three items.
The fourth group contained 12 items.
The 8th and 10th groups contained three and four items, respectively.
The eighth and ninth groups contained 9 and 12 items, respectively.

12.13. Beginning with *10th*, figures are used in text matter for numbered streets, avenues, etc. However, figures are used at all times and *street, avenue,* etc. are abbreviated in sidenotes, tables, leaderwork, and footnotes to tables and leaderwork.

First Street NW.; *also* in parentheses: (Fifth Street) (13th Street); 810 West 12th Street; North First Street; 1021 121st Street; 2031 18th Street North; 711 Fifth Avenue; 518 10th Avenue; 51–35 61st Avenue

Punctuation

12.14. The comma is used in a number containing four or more digits, except in serial numbers, common and decimal fractions, astronomical and military time, and kilocycles and meters of not more than four figures pertaining to radio.

Chemical formulas

12.15. In chemical formulas full-sized figures are used before the symbol or group of symbols to which they relate, and inferior figures are used after the symbol.

$$6PbS \cdot (Ag,Cu)_2 S \cdot 2As_2 S_3 O_4$$

Numbers spelled out

12.16. Spell out numbers at the beginning of a sentence or head. Rephrase a sentence or head to avoid beginning with figures. (See rule 12.25 for related numbers.)

> Five years ago * * *; *not* 5 years ago * * *
> Five hundred fifty men hired * * *; *not* 550 men hired * * *
> "Five-Year Plan Announced"; *not* "5-Year Plan Announced" (head)
> The year 2065 seems far off * * *; *not* 2065 seems far off * * *
> Workers numbering 207,843 * * *; *not* 207,843 workers * * *
> Benefits of $69,603,566 * * *; *not* $69,603,566 worth of benefits * * *
>
> 1958 REPORT *change to* THE 1958 REPORT
> $3,000 BUDGETED *change to* THE SUM OF $3,000 BUDGETED
> 4 MILLION JOBLESS *change to* JOBLESS NUMBER 4 MILLION

12.17. In verbatim testimony, hearings, transcripts, and question and answer matter, figures are used immediately following Q. and A. or name of interrogator or witness for years (e.g., 2008), sums of money, decimals, street numbers, and for numerical expressions beginning with *101*.

> Mr. BIRCH, Junior. 2008 was a good year.
> Mr. BELL. $1 per share was the return. Two dollars in 1956 was the alltime high. Two thousand ten may be another story.
> Colonel DAVIS. 92 cents.
> Mr. SMITH. 12.8 people.
> Mr. JONES. 1240 Pennsylvania Avenue NW., Washington, DC 20004.
> Mr. SMITH. Ninety-eight persons.
> Q. 101 years? *But* Q. One hundred years?
> A. 200 years.
> Mr. SMITH. Ten-year average would be how much?

12.18. A spelled-out number should not be repeated in figures, except in legal documents. In such instances use these forms:

> five (5) dollars, *not* five dollars (5)
> ten dollars ($10), *not* ten ($10) dollars

12.19. Numbers appearing as part of proper names, used in a hypothetical or inexact sense, or mentioned in connection with serious and dignified subjects such as Executive orders, legal proclamations, and in formal writing are spelled out.

Three Rivers, PA, Fifteenmile Creek, etc.
the Thirteen Original States
in the year two thousand eight
the One Hundred Tenth Congress
millions for defense but not one cent for tribute

three score years and ten
Ten Commandments
Air Force One (Presidential plane)
back to square one
behind the eight ball
our policy since day one

12.20. If spelled out, whole numbers should be set in the following form:

two thousand twenty
one thousand eight hundred fifty
one hundred fifty-two thousand three hundred five
eighteen hundred fifty (serial number)

When spelled out, any number containing a fraction or piece of a whole should use the word "and" when stating the fraction or piece:

sixty-two dollars and four cents
ninety-nine and three-tenths degrees
thirty-three and seventy-five one-hundredths shares

12.21. Numbers of less than *100* preceding a compound modifier containing a figure are spelled out.

two ¾-inch boards
twelve 6-inch guns
two 5-percent discounts

but
120 8-inch boards
three four-room houses

12.22. Indefinite expressions are spelled out.

the seventies; the early seventies;
but the early 1870s *or* 1970s
in his eighties, *not* his '80's *nor* 80's
between two and three hundred horses (*better* between 200 and 300 horses)
twelvefold; thirteenfold; fortyfold; hundredfold; twentyfold to thirtyfold

midthirties (age, years, money)
a thousand and one reasons
but
1 to 3 million
mid-1971; mid-1970s
40-odd people; nine-odd people
40-plus people
100-odd people
3½-fold; 250-fold; 2.5-fold; 41-fold

Words such as *nearly, about, around, approximately,* etc., do not reflect indefinite expressions.

> The bass weighed about 6 pounds.
> She was nearly 8 years old.

12.23. Except as indicated in rules 12.5 and 12.9, a number less than *10* is spelled out within a sentence.

six horses	*but*
five wells	3½ cans
eight times as large	2½ times or 2.5 times

12.24. For typographic appearance and easy grasp of large numbers beginning with *million*, the word *million* or *billion* is used.

The following are guides to treatment of figures as submitted in copy. If copy reads—

> $12,000,000, *change to* $12 million
> 2,750,000,000 dollars, *change to* $2,750 million
> 2.7 million dollars, *change to* $2.7 million
> 2⅜ million dollars, *change to* $2⅜ million
> two and one-half million dollars, *change to* $2½ million
> a hundred cows, *change to* 100 cows
> a thousand dollars, *change to* $1,000
> a million and a half, *change to* 1½ million
> two thousand million dollars, *change to* $2,000 million
> less than a million dollars, *change to* less than $1 million
> *but* $2,700,000, *do not convert* to $2.7 million
> *also* $10 to $20 million; 10 or 20 million; between 10 and 20 million
> 4 million of assets
> amounting to 4 million
> $1,270,000
> $1,270,200,000
> $2¾ billion; $2.75 billion; $2,750 million
> $500,000 to $1 million

300,000; *not* 300 thousand
$½ billion to $1¼ billion (note full figure with second fraction); $1¼ to $1½ billion
three-quarters of a billion dollars
5 or 10 billion dollars' worth

12.25. Related numbers appearing at the beginning of a sentence, separated by no more than three words, are treated alike.

Fifty or sixty more miles away is snowclad Mount Everest.
Sixty and, quite often, seventy listeners responded.
but Fifty or, in some instances, almost 60 applications were filed.

Fractions

12.26. Mixed fractions are always expressed in figures. Fractions standing alone, however, or if followed by *of a* or *of an*, are generally spelled out. (See also rule 12.28.)

three-fourths of an inch; *not* ¾ inch *nor* ¾ of an inch
one-half inch
one-half of a farm; *not* ½ of a farm
one-fourth inch
seven-tenths of 1 percent
three-quarters of an inch
half an inch
a quarter of an inch
one-tenth portion
one-hundredth
two one-hundredths
one-thousandth
five one-thousandths
thirty-five one-thousandths
but
½ to 1¾ pages
½-inch pipe
½-inch-diameter pipe
3½ cans
2½ times

12.27. Fractions (¼, ½, ¾, ⅜, ⅝, ⅞, $^{1}/_{2954}$) or full-sized figures with the shilling mark (1/4, 1/2954) may be used only when either is specifically requested. A comma should not be used in any part of a built-up fraction of four or more digits or in decimals. (See rule 12.9e.)

12.28. Fractions are used in a unit modifier.

½-inch pipe; *not* one-half-inch pipe
¼-mile run
⅞-point rise

Roman numerals

12.29.   A repeated letter repeats its value; a letter placed after one of greater value adds to it; a letter placed before one of greater value subtracts from it; a dashline over a letter denotes multiplied by 1,000.

Numerals

I	1	XXV	25	LXX	70	D	500
II	2	XXIX	29	LXXV	75	DC	600
III	3	XXX	30	LXXIX	79	DCC	700
IV	4	XXXV	35	LXXX	80	DCCC	800
V	5	XXXIX	39	LXXXV	85	CM	900
VI	6	XL	40	LXXXIX	89	M	1,000
VII	7	XLV	45	XC	90	MD	1,500
VIII	8	XLIX	49	XCV	95	MM	2,000
IX	9	L	50	IC	99	MMM	3,000
X	10	LV	55	C	100	MMMM	
XV	15	LIX	59	CL	150	or M$\overline{V}$	4,000
XIX	19	LX	60	CC	200	$\overline{V}$	5,000
XX	20	LXV	65	CCC	300	$\overline{M}$	1,000,000
		LXIX	69	CD	400		

Dates

MDC	1600	MCMXX	1920	MCMLXX	1970
MDCC	1700	MCMXXX	1930	MCMLXXX	1980
MDCCC	1800	MCMXL	1940	MCMXC	1990
MCM or MDCCCC	1900	MCML	1950	MM	2000
MCMX	1910	MCMLX	1960	MMX	2010

13. Tabular Work

(See also Chapter 9 "Abbreviations and Letter Symbols" and Chapter 14 "Leaderwork")

13.1. The object of a table is to present in a concise and orderly manner information that cannot be presented as clearly in any other way.

13.2. Tabular material should be kept as simple as possible, so that the meaning of the data can be easily grasped by the user.

13.3. Tables shall be set without down (vertical) rules when there is at least an em space between columns, except where: (1) In GPO's judgment down rules are required for clarity; or (2) the agency has indicated on the copy they are to be used. The mere presence of down rules in copy or enclosed sample is not considered a request that down rules be used. The publication dictates the type size used in setting tables. Tabular work in the Congressional Record is set 6 on 7. The balance of congressional tabular work sets 7 on 8.

Abbreviations

13.4. To avoid burdening tabular text, commonly known abbreviations are used in tables. Metric and unit-of-measurement abbreviations are used with figures.

13.5. The names of months (except May, June, and July) when followed by the day are abbreviated.

13.6. The words *street, avenue, place, road, square, boulevard, terrace, drive, court,* and *building,* following name or number, are abbreviated. For numbered streets, avenues, etc., figures are used.

13.7. Abbreviate the words *United States* if preceding the word *Government,* the name of any Government organization, or as an adjective generally.

13.8. Use the abbreviations *RR.* and *Ry.* following a name, and *SS, MS,* etc., preceding a name.

13.9. Use *lat.* and *long.* with figures.

13.10. Abbreviate, when followed by figures, the various parts of publications, as *article, part, section,* etc.

13.11. Use, generally, such abbreviations and contractions as *98th Cong., 1st sess., H. Res. 5, H.J. Res. 21, S. Doc. 62, S. Rept. 410, Rev. Stat.,* etc.

13.12. In columns containing names of persons, copy is followed as to abbreviations of given names.

13.13. Periods are not used after abbreviations followed by leaders.

Bearoff

13.14. An en space is used for all bearoffs.

13.15. In a crowded table, when down rules are necessary, the bearoff may be reduced in figure columns.

13.16. Fractions are set flush right to the bearoff of the allotted column width, and not aligned.

13.17. Mathematical signs, parentheses, fractions, and brackets are set with a normal bearoff.

Boxheads

13.18. Periods are omitted after all boxheads, but a dash is used after any boxhead which reads into the matter following.

13.19. Boxheads run crosswise.

13.20. Boxheads are set solid, even in leaded tables.

13.21. Boxheads are centered horizontally and vertically.

Down-rule style (see Rule 13.3)

Sex and age	Employed boys and girls whose work records were obtained						
	Total	Time of year at beginning work [depth of this box does not influence the depth of box on left]					
		June to August		Steptember to May			
	Number	Distri-bution (percent)	Number	Distri-bution (percent)	Number	Distri-bution (percent)	Not re-ported
Boys (12 to 14)............................	3,869	45.5	1,415	9.6	2,405	15.8	49

No-down-rule style (preferred)

TABLE 9.—*Mine production of gold, silver, copper, lead, and zinc in 2008*

Class of material	Short tons	Gold (fine ounces)	Silver (fine ounces)	Copper (pounds)	Lead (pounds)	Zinc (pounds)
		Concentrate shipped to smelters and recoverable metals				
Copper	220,346	763	70,357	14,242,346	9,950	6,260
Lead	3,931	392	48,326	72,500	5,044,750	290,980
Zinc	25,159	269	41,078	263,400	581,590	26,441,270
Total:						
2008	249,436	1,424	159,756	14,578,246	5,636,290	26,738,510
2007	367,430	1,789	432,122	10,622,155	13,544,875	11,923,060
		Crude material shipped to smelters				
Dry gold, dry gold-silver ore	134	52	2,839	2,200		
Copper:						
Crude ore	107,270	844	39,861	2,442,882	124,100	2,200
Slag	421	10	165	285,421		
Lead	528	12	1,693	5,950	110,870	300
Mill cleanings (lead-zinc)	31		254	1,450	8,100	4,300
Total:						
2008	125,749	919	45,444	30,375,754	249,710	6,890
2007	166,184	1,042	47,176	41,601,845	497,125	26,940

13.22. In referring to quantity of things, the word *Number* in boxheads is spelled if possible.

13.23. Column numbers or letters in parentheses may be set under boxheads, and are separated by one line space below the deepest head. (If alignment of parentheses is required within the table, use brackets in boxhead.) These column references align across the table. Units of quantity are set in parentheses within boxheads.

States	Department of Agriculture				Department of Commerce		
	Commodity Credit Corporation, value of commodities donated	Special school milk program[1]	Value of commodities distributed within States	Disaster loans, etc. (payments to assist States in furnishing hay in droughtstriken areas)	Civil Aeronautics Administration— Federal airport program— regular grants	Bureau of Public Roads: Highway construction	
						Regular grants[2]	Emergency grants[3]
	(1)	(2)	(3)	(4)	(5)	(6)	(7)
Alabama	$4,730,154	$1,520,362	$7,970,875		$79,284	$1,176,401	$247,515
Alaska	393,484	269,274	591,487		297,266	12,366,106	472,749
Arizona	4,545,983	823,136	6,512,639		127,749	9,317,853	

13.24. Leaders may be supplied in a column consisting entirely of symbols or years or dates or any combination of these.

Centerheads, flush entries, and subentries

13.25. Heads follow the style of the tables as to the use of figures and abbreviations.

13.26. Punctuation is omitted after centerheads. Flush entries and subentries over subordinate items are followed by a colon (single subentry to run in, preserving the colon), but a dash is used instead of a colon when the entry reads into the matter below.

25	Miscellaneous: Powerplant equipment	$245,040.37
26	Roads, railroads, and bridges	275,900.34
	Total	520,940.71

TRANSMISSION PLANT

42	Structures and improvements	26,253.53
43	Station equipment	966,164.41
	Total	992,417.94

GENERAL PLANT

General plant:	
Norris	753,248.97
Other	15,335.81
Total	768,584.78
Grand total	2,281,943.43

13.27. In reading columns if the centerhead clears the reading matter below by at least an em, the space is omitted; if it clears by less than an em, a space is used. If an overrun, rule, etc., in another column, or in the same column, creates a blank space above the head, the extra space is not added.

13.28. Units of quantity and years used as heads in reading and figure columns are set in italic with space above and no space below.

No-down-rule style (preferred)

The rules are used here to aid readability.

2007								
Oct. 1	35.6	15	Jan. 16	45.2	15	May 8	46.5	15
Oct. 31	45.0	15	Feb. 4	50.2	15	May 22	45.1	18
Nov. 14	40.9	18	Feb. 17	43.4	15	June 9	47.1	14
Dec. 24	41.7	15	Mar. 4	45.6	15	June 24	48.2	16
			Mar. 19	42.7	15	July 9	46.6	17
2008			Apr. 2	40.9	15	July 24	45.9	16
Jan. 3	43.9	15	Apr. 28	47.7	13	Aug. 6	46.5	16

Down-rule style (see Rule 13.3)

2007								
Oct. 1	35.6	15	Jan. 16	45.2	15	May 8	46.5	15
Oct. 31	45.0	15	Feb. 4	50.2	15	May 22	45.1	18
Nov. 14	40.9	18	Feb. 17	43.4	15	June 9	47.1	14
Dec. 24	41.7	15	Mar. 4	45.6	15	June 24	48.2	16
			Mar. 19	42.7	15	July 9	46.6	17
2008			Apr. 2	40.9	15	July 24	45.9	16
Jan. 3	43.9	15	Apr. 28	47.7	13	Aug. 6	46.5	16

Ciphers

13.29. Where the first number in a column or under a cross rule is wholly a decimal, a cipher is added at the left of its decimal point. A cipher used alone in a money or other decimal column is placed in the unit row and is not followed by a period. In mixed units the cipher repeats before decimals unless the group totals.

January	+26.4	0	0	0	0	0	[1]+$0.7	27.1+	+40.4
February	+66.7	0	0	0	0	0	–.9	65.8+	+98.1
March	+143.1	+2.6	–7.5	0	0	0	+12.4	150.6	+224.1

13.30. In columns containing both dollars and cents, ciphers will be supplied on right of decimal point in the absence of figures.

13.31. Where column consists of single decimal, supply a cipher on the right, unless the decimal is a cipher.

0.6
0
3.0
4.2
5.0

13.32. Where column has mixed decimals of two or more places, do not supply ciphers but follow copy.

0.22453
1.263
4
2.60
3.4567
78
12.6
——————
102.14423

13.33. Copy is followed in the use of the word *None* or a cipher to indicate *None* in figure columns. If neither one appears in the copy, leaders are inserted, unless a clear is specifically requested.

13.34. In columns of figures under the heading £ *s d*, if a whole number of pounds is given, one cipher is supplied under *s* and one under *d*; if only shillings are given, one cipher is supplied under *d*.

13.35. In columns of figures under *Ft In*, if only feet are given, supply cipher under *In*; if only inches are given, clear under *Ft*; if ciphers are used for *None*, place one cipher under both *Ft* and *In*.

13.36. In any column containing sums of money, the period and ciphers are omitted if the column consists entirely of whole dollars.

Continued heads

13.37. In continued lines an em dash is used between the head and the word *Continued*. No period is carried after a continued line.

13.38. Continued heads over tables will be worded exactly like the table heading. Notes above tables are repeated; footnote references are repeated in boxheads and in continued lines.

Dashes or rules

13.39. Rules are not carried in reading columns or columns consisting of serial or tracing numbers, but are carried through all figure columns.

13.40. Parallel rules are used to cut off figures from other figures below that are added or subtracted; also, generally, above a grand total.

Ditto (do.)

13.41. The abbreviation *do.* is used to indicate that the previous line is being repeated instead of repeating the line, verbatim, over and over. It is used in reading columns only, lowercased and preceded by leaders (6 periods) when there is matter in preceding column. If ditto marks are requested, closing quotes will be used.

13.42. Capitalize *Do.* in the first and last columns. These are indented 1 or 2 ems, depending on the length of the word being repeated, or the width of the column; the situation will determine as it is encountered.

13.43. In mixed columns made up of figure and reading-matter items, *do.* is used only under the latter items.

13.44. *Do.* is not used—

(1) In a figure or symbol column (tracing columns are figure columns);

(2) In the first line under a centerhead in the column in which the centerhead occurs;

(3) Under a line of leaders or a rule;

(4) Under an item italicized or set in boldface type for a specific reason (italic or boldface *do.* is never used; item is repeated);

(5) Under an abbreviated unit of quantity or other abbreviations; or

(6) Under words of three letters or less.

13.45. *Do.* is used, however, under a clear space and under the word *None* in a reading column.

13.46. *Do.* does not apply to a reference mark on the preceding item. The reference mark, if needed, is added to *do.*

13.47. Leaders are not used before *Do.* in the first column or before or after *Do.* in the last column.

13.48. In a first and/or last column 6 ems or less in width, a 1-em space is used before *Do.* In all other columns 6 ems or less in width, six periods are used. Bearoff is not included.

13.49. In a first and/or last column more than 6 ems in width, 2 ems of space are used before *Do.* In all other columns more than 6 ems in width, six periods are used. Bearoff space is not included. If the preceding line is indented, the indention of *Do.* is increased accordingly.

13.50. *Do.* under an indented item in an inside reading column, with or without matter in preceding column, is preceded by six periods which are indented to align with item above.

Dollar mark

13.51.   The dollar mark or any other money symbol is placed close to the figure; it is used only at the head of the table and under cross rules when the same unit of value applies to the entire column.

13.52.   In columns containing mixed amounts (as money, tons, gallons, etc.), the dollar mark, pound mark, peso mark, or other symbol, as required, is repeated before each sum of money.

13.53.   If several sums of money are grouped together, they are separated from the nonmoney group by a parallel rule, and the symbol is placed on the first figure of the separated group only.

	1958	1967
Water supply available (gallons)	4,000,000	3,000,000
Wheat production (bushels)	9,000,000	8,000,000
Operations:		
Water-dispatching operations	$442,496	$396,800
Malaria control	571,040	426,600
Plant protection	134,971	58,320
Total	1,148,507	881,720
Number of plants	642	525
Percent of budget	96.8	78.8

NOTE.—Preliminary figures.
Source: U.S. Department of Commerce, Bureau of the Census.

13.54.   In a double money column, dollar marks are used in the first group of figures only; en dashes are aligned.

$7–$9
10–12
314–316
1,014–1,016

13.55.   The dollar mark is omitted from a first item consisting of a cipher.

0	*but* $0.12
$300	13.43
500	15.07
700	23.18

13.56.   The dollar mark should be repeated in stub or reading columns.

0 to $0.99 ....
$1 to $24 ....
$25 to $49 ....
$50 to $74 ....

Figure columns

13.57. Figures align on the right, with an en space bearoff. There is no bearoff on leaders.

13.58. In a crowded table the bearoff may be reduced in figure columns only. It is preferable to retain the bearoff.

13.59. Figures in parentheses align if so required.

13.60. In double rows of figures in a single column, connected by a dash, a plus, or minus sign, and in dates appearing in the form 9–4–08, the dashes or signs can be aligned.

13.61. Plus or minus signs at the left of figures are placed against the figures regardless of alignment; plus and minus signs at the right of figures are cleared.

13.62. Words and Roman numerals in figure columns are aligned on the right with the figures, without periods.

Median value of livestock	$224	$62	
Median value of machinery	$54	Small	
Median value of furniture	$211	$100	
Possessing automobiles (percent)	25	17	
Median age (years)			5.5
Median value			$144
Fraternal membership:			
Men		IV	486
Women			None

13.63. Figures (including decimal and common fractions) expressing mixed units of quantity (feet, dollars, etc.) and figures in parentheses are aligned on the right.

13.64. Decimal points are aligned except in columns containing numbers that refer to mixed units (such as pounds, dollars, and percentage) and have irregular decimals.

13.65. It is preferred that all columns in a table consisting entirely of figure columns be centered.

Footnotes and references

13.66. Footnotes to tables are numbered independently from footnotes to text unless requested by committee or department.

13.67.   Superior figures are used for footnote references, beginning with 1 in each table.

13.68.   If figures might lead to ambiguity (for example, in connection with a chemical formula), asterisks, daggers, or italic superior letters, etc., may be used.

13.69.   When items carry several reference marks, the superior-figure reference precedes an asterisk, dagger, or similar character used for reference. These, in the same sequence, precede mathematical signs. A thin space is used to bear off an asterisk, dagger, or similar character.

13.70.   Footnote references are repeated in boxheads or in continued lines over tables.

13.71.   References to footnotes are numbered consecutively across the page from left to right.

13.72.   Footnote references are placed at the right in reading columns and symbol columns, and at the left in figure columns (also at the left of such words as *None* in figure columns), and are separated by a thin space.

13.73.   Two or more footnote references occurring together are separated by spaces, not commas.

13.74.   In a figure column, a footnote reference standing alone is set in parentheses and flushed right. In a reading column, it is set at the left in parentheses and is followed by leaders, but in the last column it is followed by a period, as if it were a word. In a symbol column it is set at the left and cleared.

13.75.   Numbered footnotes are placed immediately beneath the table. If a sign or letter reference in the heading of a table is to be followed, it is not changed to become the first numbered reference mark. The footnote to it precedes all other footnotes. The remaining footnotes in a table will follow this sequence: footnotes (numbers, letters, or symbols); NOTE.—; then Source:.

13.76.   For better makeup or appearance, footnotes may be placed at the end of a lengthy table. A line reading "Footnotes at end of table." is supplied.

13.77. If the footnotes to both table and text fall together at the bottom of a page, the footnotes to the table are placed above the footnotes to the text, and the two groups are separated by a 50-point rule flush left; but if there are footnotes to the text and none to the table, the 50-point rule is retained.

13.78. Footnotes to cut-in and indented tables and tables in rules are set full measure, except when footnotes are short, they can be set in 1 em under indented table.

13.79. Footnotes are set as paragraphs, but two or more short footnotes should be combined into one line, separated by not less than 2 ems.

13.80. The footnotes and notes to tables are set solid.

13.81. Footnotes and notes to tables and boxheads are set the same size, but not smaller than 6 point, unless specified otherwise.

13.82. Footnotes to tables follow tabular style in the use of abbreviations, figures, etc.

13.83. In footnotes, numbers are expressed in figures, even at the beginning of a note or sentence.

13.84. If a footnote consists entirely or partly of a table or leaderwork, it should always be preceded by introductory matter carrying the reference number; if necessary, the copy preparer should add an introductory line, such as " [1] See the following table:".

13.85. An explanatory paragraph without specific reference but belonging to the table rather than to the text follows the footnotes, if any, and is separated from them or from the table by space.

Fractions

13.86. All fractions are set flush right to the bearoff:

Total length	40¾	41	0.42	43	44	0.455	46	47	48	½ in.
Sleeve length	10⅝	10	10	10	11	11	11	11	11	1 in.
Armhole length	8⅝	8½	9	9½	9½	10	10½	10½	11	1 in.
Sleeve cuff length (if cuff is used).	5½	5½	5½	5⁷⁄₁₂	5½	5⁷⁄₁₂	5½	5½	5½	Maximum.
Neck opening	26½	26	27¹⁷⁄₃₂	28¹⁵⁄₃₂	28	29¹⁷⁄₃₂	30	30	31	2 in.
Waist:										
7, 8, 9, 10 cut	23½	24	25½	27¹⁵⁄₃₂	28	29½	31	32	33½	6 pct.
11, 12, 14 cut	22½	23½	25	26½	27½	29	30½	31½	33	6 pct.

13.87.   Fractions standing alone are expressed in figures, even at the beginning of a line, but not at the beginning of a footnote.

Headnotes

13.88.   Headnotes should be set lowercase, but not smaller than 6 point, bracketed, and period omitted at end, even if the statement is a complete sentence; but periods should not be omitted internally if required by sentence structure.

13.89.   Headnotes are repeated under continued heads but the word *Continued* is not added to the headnote.

Indentions and overruns

Subentries

13.90.   The indention of subentries is determined by the width of the stub or reading column. Subentries in columns more than 15 ems wide are indented in 2-em units; in columns 15 ems or less, with short entry lines and few overruns, 2-em indentions are also used. All overruns are indented 1 em more.

13.91.   Subentries in columns of 15 ems or less are indented in 1-em units. Overruns are indented 1 em more.

Total, mean, and average lines

13.92.   All total (also mean and average) lines are indented 3 ems. In very narrow stub columns, total lines may be reduced to 1- or 2-em indentions, depending on length of line.

13.93.   Where overrun of item above conflicts, the total line is indented 1 em more. Runovers of total lines are also indented 1 em more.

13.94.   It is not necessary to maintain uniform indention of the word *Total* throughout the same table. The word *Total* is supplied when not in copy.

Wide stub column—subentries 2 ems	Total, all banks	National banks	Non-national banks	Building associations
ASSETS				
Loans and discounts:				
Loans to banks........................	$74,518	$1,267,493	$947,289	$135,619
Commercial and industrial loans........	2,753,456	450,916	211,597	18,949
Total (total lines generally indent 3 ems)......	2,827,974	718,409	1,158,886	154,568
Real estate loans:				
Secured by farmland....................	12,532	29,854	186,228	19,044
Secured by residential property other than rural and farm	1,011,856	167,765	1,554,084	3,172,837
Total (indent 1 em more to avoid conflict with line above)......	1,024,388	194,619	1,740,312	3,191,881
Securities:				
U.S. Government obligations:				
Direct obligations:				
U.S. savings bonds..................	1,149,764	3,285,721	2,361,796	23,506
Nonmarketable bonds (including investment series A–1965)......	242,500	490,677	732,689	167,735
Total (indent 1 em more than runover above)......	1,392,264	3,776,398	3,094,485	191,241

Italic

13.95. Names of vessels and aircraft (except in columns consisting entirely of such names), titles of legal cases (except *v.* for *versus*), and certain scientific terms are set in italic. The word "Total" and headings in the column do not affect the application of this rule. In gothic typefaces without italic, quotes are allowed.

13.96. Set "See" and "See also" in roman.

Leaders

13.97. Leaders run across the entire table except that they are omitted from a last reading column.

13.98. The style of leadering is guided by two rules: (1) Tables with a single reading column leader from the bottom line, and (2) tables with any combination of more than one reading or symbol column leader from the top line.

13.99. If leadering from the top line, overruns end with a period.

13.100. A column of dates is regarded as a reading column only if leaders are added; in all other cases it is treated as a figure column.

13.101. In tables with tracing figures on left and right of page, leader from top line.

Numerals in tables

13.102. Figures, ordinals, and fractions are used in all parts of a table, except fractions which will be spelled out at the beginning of a footnote.

Parallel and divide tables are discouraged

13.103. Parallel tables are set in pairs of pages, beginning on a left-hand page and running across to facing right-hand page; leader from the top line.

13.104. Heads and headnotes center across the pair of pages, with 2-em hanging indention for three or more lines when combined measure exceeds 30 picas in width. Two-line heads are set across the pair of pages. A single-line head or headnote is divided evenly, each part set flush right and left, respectively. Words are not divided between pages.

13.105. Boxheads and horizontal rules align across both pages.

13.106. Boxheads are not divided but are repeated, with *Continued* added.

13.107. Tracing figures are carried through from the outside columns of both pages and are set to "leader from the top line."

13.108. In divide tables that are made up parallel, with stub column repeated, the head and headnote repeat on each succeeding page, with *Continued* added to the head only.

13.109. Tables with tracing figures or stub, or both, repeating on the left of odd pages, are divide tables and not parallel tables. Over such tables the heads are repeated, with *Continued* added.

Reading columns

13.110. Figures or combinations of figures and letters used to form a reading column align on left and are followed by leaders. *Do.* is not used under such items.

13.111. The en dash is not to be used for *to* in a reading column; if both occur, change to *to* throughout.

13.112. Cut-in items following a colon are indented 2 ems.

13.113. A single entry under a colon line should be run in; retain the colon.

13.114. Numerical terms, including numbered streets, avenues, etc., are expressed in figures, even at the beginning of an item.

Symbol columns

13.115. A column consisting entirely of letters, letters and figures, symbols, or signs, or any combination of these, is called a symbol column. It should be set flush left and cleared, except when it takes the place of the stub, it should then be leadered. No closing period is used when such column is the last column. Blank lines in a last column are cleared. *Do.* is not used in a symbol column.

Symbol	Typical commercial designation	Army product symbol	Filing order symbol	General description	Specification symbol
GM(2)	Gasoline and diesel engine oil, SAE10 and SAE10W grades.	OR10	A	Fuel, grease, chassis, or soap base.	G.&D.
CG	Ball and roller bearing grease.	4l–X–59	N	Extreme pressure	BR
CW[1]	Wheel-bearing grease	OE20[2]	X	do	WBG[3]
	Grease not typified			Further tests being conducted.	
G090	Universal gear lubricant	S.&T.	B	Water-pump grease	80D

13.116. Columns composed of both symbols and figures are treated as figure columns and are set flush right. In case of blank lines in a last column, leaders will be used as in figure columns.

Symbol or catalog number	Typical commercial designation	Symbol or product number	Symbol or filling order symbol	General description	Symbol or specification number
WBD	Chassis grease, cup grease, under pressure.	961	A	Especially adapted to very cold climates.	1359
14L88	Water-pump bearing grease	SWA	352	Under moderate pressure	
5190	Exposed gear chain lubricant	12L	N	High-speed use	AE10
	E.P. hypoid lubricant	863	X	For experimental use only..	NXL
376	Special grade for marine use		468	Free flowing in any weather	749

Tables without rules

13.117. It is preferable to set all tables alike; that is, without either down rules or cross rules and with roman boxheads. When so indicated on copy, by ordering agency, tabular matter may be set without rules, with italic boxheads.

13.118. Column heads over figure columns in 6- or 8-point leaderwork are set in 6-point italic.

13.119. Horizontal rules (spanner) used between a spread or upper level column heading carried over two or more lower level column headings are set continuous and without break, from left to right, between the two levels of such headings.

TABLE 9.—*Changes in fixed assets and related allowances*

	Fixed assets					
		Investment		*Operations*		
	Balance June 30, 2008 (table 9–a)	*Current additions*	*Adjustments*	*Transfers*	*Retirements*	*Balance June 30, 2008*
Supporting and general facilities:						
Transportation and utilities:						
Panama Railroad......	$12,123,197	$306	....	($539)	($284,358)	$11,838,606
Motor Transportation Division	2,242,999	122,597	....	2,143	(147,561)	2,220,178
Steamship line..........	13,653,989	10,247	....	....	....	13,664,236
Power system............	19,364,373	366,311	....	(342)	(290,174)	19,440,168
Communication system......................	2,739,012	151,819	($113,261)	....	(26,100)	2,751,470
Water system and hydroelectric facilities.................	10,590,820	104,039	....	1,661	(48,920)	10,647,600
Total, transportation and utilities..	60,714,390	755,319	(113,261)	2,923	(797,113)	60,562,258
Employee service and facilities:						
Commissary Division	7,012,701	105,952	(130,891)	21,777	(36,418)	6,973,121
Service centers................	3,684,670	29,086	....	530	(230,276)	3,484,010
Housing Division...............	35,729,465	(10,336)	....	(485,548)	(937,916)	34,295,665
Total employee service and facilities...............	46,426,836	124,702	(130,891)	(463,241)	(1,204,610)	44,752,796
Grand total.......................	107,141,236	880,021	(244,152)	(466,164)	(2,001,723)	105,315,054

13.120. More than one figure column, also illustrating use of dollar mark, rule, bearoff, etc.

For property purchased from—			
Central Pipeline Distributing Co.:			
Capital stock issued recorded amount		$75,000	
Undetermined consideration recorded		341	
Pan American Bonded Pipeline Co.: Recorded money outlay		3,476	
M.J. Mitchell: Recorded money outlay		730	
R. Lacy, Inc., and Lynch Refining Co.:			
Recorded money outlay	$157,000		
Note issued	100,000		
Subtotal	257,000		
Less value of oil in lines and salvaged construction material	26,555	230,445	$309,992
For construction, improvements, and replacements, recorded money outlay			522
For construction work in progress, recorded money outlay			933,605
Total			1,244,119

	Quantity (million cubic feet)	Value at point of consumption
Use:		
Residential	34,842	$21,218,778
Commercial	14,404	5,257,468
Industrial:		
Field (drilling, pumping, etc.)	144,052	10,419,000
All other industrial:		
Fuel for petroleum refineries	96,702	
Other, including electric utility plants	346,704	61,440,000
Total	636,704	98,335,246

	Estimated		
	2004	2008	Change
General account:			
Receipts	$64,800	$69,800	+$5,000
Expenditures	(70,300)	(67,100)	(-3,200)
Net improvement, 2008 over 2004			1,800
Deduct 2004 deficit			1,500
Net surplus, estimated for 2008			300

[In U.S.-dollar equivalent]

Balance with the Treasury Department July 1, 2008	$165,367,704.85
Receipts:	
Collections	$564,944,502.99
Return from agency accounts of currencies advanced for liquidation of obligations incurred prior to July 1, 2007	4,450,577.07
Total receipts	569,395,080.06
Total available	734,762,784.91

Units of quantity

13.121. Units of quantity in stub columns are set in lowercase in plural form and placed in parentheses.

Coke (short tons)	4,468,437	[1] 25,526,646	5,080,403	[2] 29,519,871
Diatomite	([123])	([1])	([1])	([123])
Emery (pounds)	765	6,828	1,046	9,349
Feldspar (crude) (long tons)	([1])	([1])	([1])	([1])
Ferroalloys (short tons)	183,465	[2] 18,388,766	259,303	[2] 30,719,756

13.122. Units of quantity and other words as headings over figure columns are used at the beginning of a table or at the head of a continued page or continued column in a double-up table.

13.123. Over figure columns, units of quantity and other words used as headings, and the abbreviations *a.m.* and *p.m.*, if not included in the boxheads, are set in italic and are placed immediately above the figures, without periods other than abbreviating periods. In congressional work (gothic), or at any time when italic is not available, these units should be placed in the boxheads in parentheses. Any well-known abbreviation will be used to save an overrun, but if one unit of quantity is abbreviated, all in the same table will be abbreviated. If units change in a column, the new units are set in italic with space above and no space below. The space is placed both above and below only when there is no italic available.

Quoted tabular work

13.124. When a table is part of quoted matter, quotation marks will open on each centerhead and each footnote paragraph, and if table is end of quoted matter, quotation marks close at end of footnotes. If there are no footnotes and the table is the end of the quotation, quotation marks close at end of last item.

14. Leaderwork

(See also Chapter 9 "Abbreviations and Letter Symbols" and Chapter 13 "Tabular Work")

14.1. Leaderwork is a simple form of tabular work without boxheads or rules and is separated from text by 4 points of space above and below in solid matter and 6 points of space in leaded matter. It consists of a reading (stub) column and a figure column, leadered from the bottom line. It may also consist of two reading columns, aligning on the top line. In general, leaderwork (except indexes and tables of contents, which are set the same style as text) is governed by the same rules of style as tabular work. Unless otherwise indicated, leaderwork is set in 8 point. The period is omitted immediately before leaders.

Bearoff

14.2. No bearoff is required at the right in a single reading column.

Columns

14.3. A figure column is at least an en quad wider than the largest group of figures, but not less than 3 ems in single columns and 2 ems in double-up columns. Total rules are to be the full width of all figure columns.

	Pounds
Year: 2000	655,939
Fiscal year:	
2009	368,233
2010	100,000
Total	1,124,172

14.4. Where both columns are reading columns, they are separated by an em space.

Particulars	Artist
To the French Government:	
The entire collection of French paintings on loan,	Degas.
with the exception of Mlle. DuBourg (Mme.	
Fantin-Latour).	
Avant la Course	Do.
To Col. Axel H. Oxholm, Washington, DC:	
Martha Washington, George Washington, and	Attributed to
Thomas Jefferson.	Jonathan E. Earl,
	Los Angeles, CA.
Roses	Renoir.
Do	Forain.
Roses in a Chinese Vase and Sculpture by Maillol	Vuillard.
Maternity	Gauguin.

Continued heads

14.5. The use of continued heads in leaderwork is not necessary.

Ditto (do.)

14.6. The abbreviation *do.* is indented and capitalized in the stub. It is capitalized and cleared in last reading column.

Dollar mark and ciphers

14.7. In a column containing mixed amounts (as money, tons, gallons, etc.) the figures are aligned on the right, and the dollar mark or other symbol is repeated before each sum of money. If several sums of money are grouped and added or subtracted to make a total, they are separated from the nonmoney group by a parallel rule, and the symbol is placed on the first figure of the separated group only.

14.8. If two columns of sums of money add or subtract one into the other and one carries points and ciphers, the other should also carry points and ciphers.

Flush items and subheads

14.9. Flush items clear the figure column.

14.10. Subheads are centered in full measure.

Footnotes

14.11.   Footnotes to leaderwork follow the style of footnotes to tables.

14.12.   Footnote references begin with 1 in each leadered grouping, and footnotes are placed at the end, separated from it by 4 points of space. Separate notes from matter following by not less than 6 points of space.

14.13.   If the leaderwork runs over from one page to another, the footnotes will be placed at the bottom of the leadered material.[1]

Units of quantity

14.14.   Units of quantity or other words over a stub or figure column are set italic.

14.15.   The following example shows the style to be observed where there is a short colon line at left. In case of only one subentry, run in with colon line and preserve the colon.

	Tons
Baltimore & Ohio RR.:	
Freight carried:	
May	50,000
June	52,000
Coal carried	90,000
Dixie RR.: Freight carried Jan. 1, 1999, including freight carried by all its subsidiaries	[1]2,000

[1]Livestock not included.

14.16.   If there is no colon line, the style is as follows:

	Tons
Freight carried by the Dixie RR. and the Baltimore & Ohio RR. in May	71,500

14.17.   Explanatory matter is set in 6 point under leaders (note omission of period):

(Name)	(Address)	(Position)

---

[1] If footnotes to leaderwork and text fall at bottom of page, leaderwork footnotes are placed above text footnotes. The two groups are separated by a 50-point rule.

14.18. In blank forms, leaders used in place of complete words to be supplied are preceded and followed by a space.

> On this .... day of .... 20 ....

14.19. In half measure doubled up, units of quantity are aligned across the
page.

	Inches		*Inches*
Seedlings:			
Black locust	27	Osage-orange	20
Honey locust	16	Catalpa	16
Green ash	7	Black walnut	10

14.20. Mixed units of quantity and amounts and words in a figure column
are set as follows:

Capital invested	$8,000
Value of implements and stock	$3,000
Land under cultivation (acres)	128.6
Orchard (acres)	21.4
Forest land (square miles)	50
Livestock:	
Horses:	
Number...	8
Value...	$1,500
Cows:	
Number...	18
Estimated weekly production of butter per milk cow	
(pounds)..	7½
Hogs:	
Number	46
Loss from cholera	None

15. Footnotes, Indexes, Contents, and Outlines

Footnotes and reference marks

15.1. Text footnotes follow the style of the text with the exception of those things noted in Chapter 9 "Abbreviations and Letter Symbols." Footnotes appearing in tabular material follow the guidelines set forth in Chapter 13 "Tabular Work."

15.2. In a publication divided into chapters, sections, or articles, each beginning a new page, text footnotes begin with 1 in each such division. In a publication without such divisional grouping, footnotes are numbered consecutively from 1 to 99, and then begin with 1 again. However, in supplemental sections, such as appendixes and bibliographies, which are not parts of the publication proper, footnotes begin with 1.

15.3. Copy preparers must see that references and footnotes are plainly marked.

15.4. If a reference is repeated on another page, it should carry the original footnote; but to avoid repetition of a long note, the copy preparer may use the words "See footnote 3 (6, 10, etc.) on p.—." instead of repeating the entire footnote.

15.5. Unless the copy is otherwise marked: (1) Footnotes to 12-point text are set in 8 point; (2) footnotes to 11-point text are set in 8 point, except in Supreme Court reports, in which they are set in 9 point; (3) footnotes to 10- and 8-point text are set in 7 point.

15.6. Footnotes are set as paragraphs at the bottom of the page and are separated from the text by a 50-point rule, set flush left, with no less than 2 points of space above and below the rule.

15.7. Footnotes to indented matter (other than excerpt footnotes) are set full measure.

15.8. To achieve faithful reproduction of indented excerpt material (particularly legal work) containing original footnotes, these footnotes are also indented and placed at the bottom of the excerpt, separated by 6 points of space. No side dash is used. Reference numbers are not changed to fit the numbering sequence of text footnotes.

15.9. Footnotes must always begin on the page where they are referenced. If the entire footnote will not fit on the page where it is cited, it will be continued at the bottom of the next page.[1]

15.10. Footnotes to charts, graphs, and other illustrations should be placed immediately beneath such illustrative material.

15.11. A cutoff rule is not required between a chart or graph and its footnotes.

15.12. For reference marks use: (1) Roman superior figures, (2) italic superior letters, and (3) symbols. Superior figures (preferred), letters, and symbols are separated from the words to which they apply by thin spaces, unless immediately preceded by periods or commas.

15.13. Where reference figures might lead to ambiguity (for example, in matter containing exponents), asterisks, daggers, etc., or italic superior letters may be used.

15.14. When symbols or signs are used for footnote reference marks, their sequence should be (*) asterisk, (†) dagger, (‡) double dagger, and (§) section mark. Should more symbols be needed, these may be doubled or tripled, but for simplicity and greater readability, it is preferable to extend the assortment by adding other single-character symbols.

15.15. Symbols with established meanings, such as the percent sign (%) and the number mark (#), are likely to cause confusion and should not be used for reference marks.

15.16. To avoid possible confusion with numerals and letters frequently occurring in charts and graphs, it is preferable in such instances to use symbols as reference marks.

---

[1]When a footnote breaks from an odd (right-hand) page to an even (left-hand) page, the word (*Continued*) is set inside parentheses in italic below the last line of the footnote where the break occurs

A 50-point rule is used above each part of the footnote.

When a footnote break occurs on facing pages, i.e., from an even page to an odd page, the (*Continued*) line is not set, but the 50-point rule is duplicated.

15.17. When items carry several reference marks, the superior-figure reference precedes an asterisk, dagger, or similar character used for reference.

15.18. A superior reference mark follows all punctuation marks except a dash, but falls inside a closing parenthesis or bracket if applying only to matter within the parentheses or brackets.

15.19. Two or more superior footnote references occurring together are separated by thin spaces.

Indexes and tables of contents

15.20. Indexes and tables of contents are set in the same style as the text, except that *See* and *see also* are set in italic.

15.21. Where a word occurs in an index page column, either alone or with a figure, it is set flush on the right. If the word extends back into the leaders, it is preceded by an en space.

15.22. For better appearance, Roman numerals should be set in small caps in the figure columns of tables of contents and indexes.

15.23. In indexes set with leaders, if the page numbers will not fit in the leader line, the first number only is set in that line and the other numbers are overrun. If the entry makes three or more lines and the last line of figures is not full, do not use a period at the end.

(For examples of item indentions in a reading column of indexes set with leaders, see index in this MANUAL.)

15.24. Overrun page numbers are indented 3½ ems in measures not over 20 picas and 7 ems in wider measures, more than one line being used if necessary. These indentions are increased as necessary to not less than 2 ems more than the line immediately above or below.

15.25. When copy specifies that all overs are to be a certain number of ems, the runovers of the figure column shall be held in 2 ems more than the specified indention.

15.26. Examples of block-type indexes:

Example 1	*Example 2*
Medical officer, radiological defense, 3	Brazil—Continued
Medicolegal dosage, 44	Exchange restrictions—Continued
Military Liaison Committee, 4	Williams mission (*see also*
Monitoring, 58	Williams, John H., special
Air, 62	mission), exchange control
Personnel, 59	situation, 586–588
Civilian, 60	Trade agreement with United
Military, 59	States, proposed:
Sea, 61	Draft text, 558–567
Ship, 61	Proposals for:
Monitors, radiological defense, 3	Inclusion of all clauses, 531

15.27. In index entries the following forms are used:

Brown, A.H., Jr. (*not* Brown, Jr., A.H.)
Brown, A.H., & Sons (*not* Brown & Sons, A.H.)
Brown, A.H., Co. (*not* Brown Co., A.H.)
Brown, A.H., & Sons Co. (*not* Brown & Sons Co., A.H.)

15.28. In a table of contents, where *chapter, plate,* or *figure* is followed by a number and period, an en space is used after the period. The periods are aligned on the right.

15.29. Subheads in indexes and tables of contents are centered in the full measure.

15.30. In contents using two sizes of lightface type, or a combination of boldface and lightface type, all leaders and page numbers will be set in lightface roman type. Contents set entirely in boldface will use boldface page numbers. All page numbers will be set in the predominant size.

Outlines

15.31. Outlines vary in appearance because there is no one set style to follow in designing them. The width of the measure, the number of levels required for the indentions, and the labeling concept selected to identify each new level all contribute to its individuality.

The following sample outline demonstrates a very basic and structured arrangement. It uses the enumerators listed in rule 8.108 to identify each new indented level.

The enumerators for the first four levels are followed by a period and a fixed amount of space. The enumerators for the second four levels are set in parentheses and followed by the same amount of fixed space.

Each new level indents 2 ems more than the preceding level and data that runs over to the next line aligns with the first word following the enumerator.

Outline example:
I. Balancing a checkbook
   A. Open your check register
      1. Verify all check numbers
         a. Verify no check numbers were duplicated
         b. Verify no check numbers were skipped
   B. Open your bank statement
      1. Put canceled checks in sequence
      2. Compare amounts on checks to those in register
         a. Correct any mistakes in register
         b. Indicate those check numbers cashed
            (1) Mark off check number on the statement
               (a) Verify amount of check
                  (i) Highlight discrepancies on statement
                     (aa) Enter figures on back
                  (ii) Enter missing check numbers on back with amounts
                     (aa) Identify missing check numbers in register
                     (bb) Verify those check numbers were not cashed previously

16. Datelines, Addresses, and Signatures

16.1. The general principle involved in the typography of datelines, addresses, and signatures is that they should be set to stand out clearly from the body of the letter or paper which they accompany. This is accomplished by using caps and small caps and italic, as set forth below. Other typographic details are designed to ensure uniformity and good appearance. Street addresses and ZIP Code numbers are not to be used. In certain lists which carry ZIP Code numbers, regular spacing will be used preceding the ZIP Code. Certain general instructions apply alike to datelines, addresses, and signatures.

General instructions

16.2. Principal words in datelines, addresses, and titles accompanying signatures are capitalized.

16.3. *Mr., Mrs., Miss, Ms.,* and all other titles preceding a name, and *Esq., Jr., Sr.,* and *2d* following a name in address and signature lines, are set in roman caps and lowercase if the name is in caps and small caps or caps and lowercase; if the name is in caps, they are set in caps and small caps, if small caps are available—otherwise in caps and lowercase.

Spacing

16.4. At least 2 points of space should appear between dateline and text or address, address and text, text and signature, and signature and address.

Datelines

16.5. Datelines at the beginning of a letter or paper are set at the right side of the page, the originating office in caps and small caps, the address and date in italic; if the originating office is not given, the address is set in caps and small caps and the date in italic; if only the date is given, it is set in caps and small caps. Such datelines are indented from the right 1 em for a single line; 3 ems and 1 em, successively, for two lines; and 5 ems, 3 ems, and 1 em, successively, for three lines. In measures 30 picas or wider, these indentions are increased by 1 em.

THE WHITE HOUSE,☐☐☐
Washington, DC, January 1, 2008.☐
THE WHITE HOUSE, *July 30, 2008.*☐

TREASURY DEPARTMENT,☐☐☐☐☐
OFFICE OF THE TREASURER,☐☐☐
Washington, DC, January 1, 2008.☐

TREASURY DEPARTMENT, *July 30, 2008.*☐

DEPARTMENT OF COMMERCE,☐☐☐
July 30, 2008.☐

FAIRFAX COUNTY, VA.☐

OFFICE OF JOHN SMITH & CO.,☐☐☐
New York, NY, June 6, 2008.☐

WASHINGTON, *May 20, 2008—10 a.m.*☐

THURSDAY, MAY 8, 2008—2 P.M.☐

JANUARY 24, 2008.☐

WASHINGTON, *November 28, 2008.*☐☐☐
[Received December 5, 2008].☐

ON BOARD USS "CONNECTICUT,"☐☐☐
January 22, 2008.☐

16.6.   Congressional hearings:

TUESDAY, JULY 29, 2008 [1]

HOUSE OF REPRESENTATIVES,☐☐☐☐☐☐☐
COMMITTEE ON THE JUDICIARY,☐☐☐☐☐
SUBCOMMITTEE ON IMMIGRATION,☐☐☐
CITIZENSHIP, REFUGEES,☐☐☐
BORDER SECURITY, AND INTERNAL LAW,☐☐☐
Washington, DC.☐

U.S. SENATE,☐☐☐☐☐
COMMITTEE ON ARMED SERVICES,☐☐☐
Washington, DC.☐

CONGRESS OF THE UNITED STATES,☐☐☐☐☐
JOINT COMMITTEE ON PRINTING,☐☐☐
Washington, DC.☐

---

[1] Normally, dates in House hearings on appropriation bills are set on the right in 10-point caps and small caps.

16.7. Datelines at the end of a letter or paper, either above or below signatures, are set on left in caps and small caps for the address and italic for the date. When the word *dated* is used, dateline is set in roman caps and lowercase.

> ☐May 7, 2008.
> ☐Roanoke, VA.
> ☐Roanoke, VA, *July 1, 2008.*
> ☐Dated July 1, 2008.
> ☐Dated Albany, March 13, 2008.

16.8. Datelines in newspaper extracts are set at the beginning of the paragraph, the address in caps and small caps and the date in roman caps and lowercase, followed by a period and a 1-em dash.

> ☐Aboard USS *Ronald Reagan* April 3, 2008.—
> ☐New York, NY, August 21, 2008.—A message received here from * * *.

Addresses

16.9. Addresses are set flush left at the beginning of a letter or paper in congressional work (or at end in formal usage).

16.10. At beginning or at end:

> To Smith & Jones and
> ☐Brown & Green, Esqs.,
> *Attorneys for Claimant.*
> (Attention of Mr. Green.)
>
> Hon. Dianne Feinstein,
> *U.S. Senate.*
>
> Hon. Nancy Pelosi,
> *U.S. House of Representatives.* (Collective address.)
>
> The President,
> *The White House.*

16.11. A long title following an address is set in italic caps and lowercase, the first line flush left and right, overruns indented 2 ems to clear a following 1-em paragraph indention.

> Hon. Daniel K. Akaka,
> *Chairman, Subcommittee on Oversight of Government Management,*
> ☐☐*the Federal Workforce and the District of Columbia, U.S. Senate,*
> ☐☐*Washington, DC.*

16.12. The name or title forming the first line of the address is set in caps and small caps, but *Mr., Mrs.,* or other title preceding a name, and *Esq., Jr., Sr.,* or *2d* following a name, are set in roman caps and lowercase; the matter following is set in italic. The words *U.S. Army* or *U.S. Navy* immediately following a name are set in roman caps and lowercase in the same line as the name.

> Lt. Gen. ROBERT L. VAN ANTWERP, Jr., U.S. Army,
> *Chief of Engineers.*

> CHIEF OF ENGINEERS, U.S. ARMY. (Full title, all caps and small caps.)

> Lt. Gen. ROBERT L. VAN ANTWERP, Jr.,
> *Chief of Engineers, U.S. Army,*
> *Washington, DC.*

> Hon. LORRAINE C. MILLER,
> *Clerk of the House of Representatives.*

> Hon. ROBERT C. BYRD,
> *U.S. Senator, Washington, DC.*

> Hon. JIM WEBB,
> *Russell Senate Office Building, Washington, DC.*

> The COMMITTEE ON APPROPRIATIONS,
> *House of Representatives.*

16.13. General (or collective) addresses are set in italic caps and lowercase, flush left, with overruns indented 2 ems and ending with a colon, except when followed by a salutation, in which case a period is used.

16.14. Examples of general addresses when not followed by salutation (note the use of colon at end of italic line):

> *To the Officers and Members of the Daughters of the American*
> ☐☐*Revolution, Washington, DC:*

> *To the American Diplomatic and Consular Officers:*

> *To Whom It May Concern:*

> *Collectors of Customs:*

> *To the Congress of the United States:*

16.15. Example of general address when followed by salutation (note the use of period at end of italic line):

> *Senate and House of Representatives.*
> ☐GENTLEMEN: You are hereby * * *.

16.16. Examples illustrating other types of addresses:

To the EDITOR:

To JOHN L. NELSON, *Greeting:*

To JOHN L. NELSON, *Birmingham, AL, Greeting:*

To the CLERK OF THE HOUSE OF REPRESENTATIVES:

CHIEF OF ENGINEERS
(Through the Division Engineer).
☐MY DEAR SIR: I have the honor * * *.
☐MR. REED: I have the honor * * *.
☐DEAR MR. REED: I have the honor * * *.

Lt. (jg.) JOHN SMITH,
Navy Department:
☐The care shown by you * * *.

STATE OF NEW YORK,
County of New York, ss:
☐Before me this day appeared * * *.

DISTRICT OF COLUMBIA, *ss:*
☐Before me this day appeared * * *.

Envelope addresses

U.S. House of Representatives
Committee on Education and Labor
2181 Rayburn House Office Building
Washington, DC 20515

Signatures

16.17. Signatures, preceded by an em dash, are sometimes run in with last line of text.

16.18. Signatures are set at the right side of the page. They are indented 1 em for a single line; 3 ems and 1 em, successively, for two lines; and 5 ems, 3 ems, and 1 em, successively, for three lines. In measures 30 picas or wider, these indentions are increased by 1 em.

16.19. The name or names are set in caps and small caps; *Mr., Mrs.,* and all other titles preceding a name, and *Esq., Jr., Sr.,* and *2d* following a name, are set in roman caps and lowercase; the title following name is set in italic. Signatures as they appear in copy must be followed in regard to abbreviations.

16.20. If name and title make more than half a line, they are set as two lines.

16.21. Two to eight independent signatures, with or without titles, are aligned on the left, at approximately the center of the measure.

> ROBERT E. SCHWENK.
> QUEEN E. HUGHES.
> ERICA N. PROPHET.
> ANDRE RODGERS,
> Commander, U.S. Navy (Retired).☐
> WILLIAM H. COUGHLIN, Chairman.

16.22. More than eight signatures, with or without titles, are set full measure, roman caps and lowercase, run in, indented 5 and 7 ems in measures of 26½ picas or wider; in measures less than 26½ picas, indent 2 and 3 ems.

> ☐☐☐☐☐Brown, Shipley & Co.; Denniston, Cross & Co.; Fruhling & ☐☐☐☐☐☐☐Groschen, Attorneys; C.J. Hambro & Sons; Hardy, ☐☐☐☐☐☐☐Nathan & Co.; Heilbut, Symons & Co.; Harrison Bros. & ☐☐☐☐☐☐☐Co., by George Harrison; Hoare, Miller & Co.; Thomas ☐☐☐☐☐☐☐Eaton Co.

16.23. The punctuation of closing phrases is governed by the sense. A detached complimentary close is made a new paragraph.

16.24. Examples of various kinds of signatures:

> UNITED STATES IMPROVEMENT CO.,
> (By) JOHN SMITH, Secretary.
>
> TEXARKANA TEXTILE MERCHANTS &
> MANUFACTURERS' ASSOCIATION,
> JOHN L. JONES, Secretary.
>
> TEXARKANA TEXTILE MERCHANTS &
> MANUFACTURERS' ASSOCIATION,
> JOANNE WILDER,
> Board Member and Secretary.☐
>
> JOHN W. SMITH☐☐☐
> (And 25 others).☐
>
> JOHN SMITH,☐☐☐☐☐
> Lieutenant Governor☐☐☐
> (For the Governor of Maine).☐

NORTH AMERICAN ICE CO.,
SYLVIA ROONEY, *Secretary.*
JOHN [his thumbmark] SMITH.☐

NITA M. LOWEY,
FRANK WOLF,
Managers on the Part of the House.☐

JOSEPH R. BIDEN, Jr.,
RICHARD LUGAR,
Managers on the Part of the Senate.☐

☐I am, very respectfully, yours,
(Signed)☐FRED C. KLEINSCHMIDT,☐☐☐
Assistant Clerk, Court of Claims.☐

☐On behalf of the Philadelphia Chamber of Commerce:
GEO. W. PHILIPS.
SAML. CAMPBELL.

☐I have the honor to be,
☐☐☐Very respectfully, your obedient servant,
(Signed)☐John R. King
(Typed)☐JOHN R. KING,
Secretary.☐

or

(S)☐John R. King
JOHN R. KING,
Secretary.☐

☐Attest:
RICHARD ROE, *Notary Public.*☐

☐By the Governor:
NATHANIEL COX, *Secretary of State.*☐

☐Approved.
JOHN SMITH, *Governor.*☐

☐By the President:
CONDOLEEZZA RICE, *Secretary of State.*☐

☐Respectfully submitted.
MARY FARRELL, *U.S. Indian Agent.*☐

☐☐☐Yours truly,
Capt. JAMES STALEY, Jr.,☐☐☐
Superintendent.☐

☐☐☐Respectfully yours,
Mrs. FRANK E. (BETTY) SHEFFIELD.☐

☐☐☐Very respectfully,
RON GOLDEN, *U.S. Indian Agent.*☐

16.25.   In quoted matter:

☐☐☐"Very respectfully,

"Todd S. Gilbert.
"Paul Hartman.
"Dolores Hicks.
"Albert H. Jones.
"Joan C. Nugent.
"Brandon Proctor."

16.26.   Examples of various kinds of datelines, addresses, and signatures:

Re weather reports submitted by the International Advisory Committee of ☐☐the Weather Council.

Mr. John D. Dingell,
Chairman, House Committee on Energy and Commerce,
Washington, DC.

☐Dear Mr. Dingell: We have been in contact with your office, etc.

John L. "Jack" Hayes,☐☐☐☐☐
Executive Director,☐☐☐
National Weather Service.☐

———

Lincoln Park, MI, *February 15, 2008.*☐

Re Romeo O. Umanos, Susanna M. Umanos, case No. S–254, U.S. ☐☐Citizenship and Immigration Services, application pending.

Hon. Russell D. Feingold,
Chairman, Subcommittee on the Constitution,
Committee on the Judiciary, Washington, DC.

☐Dear Mr. Feingold: You have for some time * * *.
☐☐☐Sincerely yours,

Edward Pultorak,☐☐☐
Architectural Designer.☐

Hon. ZOE LOFGREN,
Chairman, Subcommittee on Immigration, Citizenship, Refugees,
☐☐*Border Security and International Law of the Committee on*
☐☐*the Judiciary, House of Representatives, Washington, DC.*
☐DEAR MS. LOFGREN: You have for some time * * *.

U.S. DEPARTMENT OF ☐☐☐☐☐
COMMERCE,☐☐☐☐☐
NATIONAL WEATHER SERVICE,☐☐☐
Washington, March 3, 2008.☐

Hon. GENE GREEN,
House of Representatives,
Washington, DC.
☐DEAR MR. GREEN: We will be glad to
give you any further information.
☐☐☐Sincerely yours,
F.W. REICHELDERFER,☐☐☐
Chief of Service.☐

NEW YORK, NY, *February 8, 2008.*☐

To: All supervisory employees of production plants, northern and
☐☐eastern divisions, New York State.
From: Production manager.
Subject: Regulations concerning vacations, health and welfare plans,
☐☐and wage contract negotiations.
☐It has come to our attention that the time * * *.

WASHINGTON, DC, *May 16, 2008.*☐

The Honorable the SECRETARY OF THE NAVY.
☐DEAR MR. SECRETARY: This is in response to your letter * * *.
☐☐☐Very sincerely yours,
[SEAL]☐GEORGE W. BUSH.☐

EAST LANSING, MI, *June 10, 2008.*☐

To Whom It May Concern:

☐I have known Kyu Yawp Lee for 7 years and am glad to testify as to his fine character. He has been employed * * *.

☐Wishing you success in your difficult and highly important job, we are,

☐☐☐Sincerely yours,

AGOSTINO J. GONINO.

LOUISE M. GONINO.

U.S. DEPARTMENT OF VETERANS AFFAIRS,☐☐☐☐☐☐☐

OFFICE OF THE SECRETARY OF☐☐☐☐☐

VETERANS AFFAIRS,☐☐☐

Washington, DC.☐

Hon. PATRICK J. LEAHY,

Chairman, Committee on the Judiciary,

U.S. Senate, Washington, DC.

☐DEAR SENATOR LEAHY: Further reference is made to your reply * * *.

☐☐☐Sincerely yours,

GORDON M. MANSFIELD,☐☐☐☐☐☐☐

Deputy Secretary☐☐☐☐☐

(For and in the absence of☐☐☐

James B. Peake, Secretary).☐

WASHINGTON, DC, *September 16, 2008.*☐

Mr. WILLIAM E. JONES, Jr.,

Special Assistant to the Attorney General, Attorney for Howard ☐☐*Sutherland, Director, Office of Alien Property.*

☐DEAR MR. JONES: In reply to your letter * * *.

☐☐☐Yours truly,

(Signed)☐THOMAS E. RHODES,☐☐☐

Special Assistant to the Attorney General.☐

☐P.S.—A special word of thanks to you from J.R. Brown for your fine ☐☐help.

T.E.R.☐

TOKYO, JAPAN, *November 13, 2008.*☐
U.S. DEPARTMENT OF HOMELAND SECURITY,
U.S. CITIZENSHIP AND NATURALIZATION SERVICES,
Detroit, MI.
☐GENTLEMEN: This letter will testify to the personal character * * *.
☐☐☐Very truly yours,

Mrs. GRACE C. LOHR,☐☐☐☐☐
Inspector General Section, HQ, AFFE,☐☐☐
APO 343, San Francisco, CA.☐

16.27.   The word *seal* appearing with the signature of a notary or of an organized body, such as a company, is spaced 1 em from the signature. The word *seal* is to be set in small caps and bracketed.

[SEAL]☐RICHARD ROE,☐☐☐
Notary Public.☐

[SEAL]☐J.M. WILBER.☐

[SEAL]☐BARTLETT, ROBINS & CO.☐

16.28.   Presidential proclamations after May 23, 1967, do not utilize the seal except when they pertain to treaties, conventions, protocols, or other international agreements. Copy will be followed literally with respect to the inclusion of and between elements of numerical expressions.

NOW, THEREFORE, I, GEORGE W. BUSH, President of the United States of America, by virtue of the authority vested in me by the Constitution and laws of the United States, do hereby proclaim September 27, 2008, as National Hunting and Fishing Day. I call upon the people of the United States to join me in recognizing the contributions of America's hunters and anglers, and all those who work to conserve our Nation's fish and wildlife resources.

  *   *   *   *   *   *   *

IN WITNESS WHEREOF, I have hereunto set my hand this twenty-sixth day of September, in the year of our Lord two thousand eight, and of the Independence of the United States of America the two hundred and thirty-third.

GEORGE W. BUSH.☐

17. Useful Tables

This chapter contains useful tables presented in GPO style. The tables display various design features most frequently used in Government publications and can be considered examples of GPO style.

U.S. Presidents and Vice Presidents

President	Years	Vice President	Years
George Washington	(1789–1797)	John Adams	(1789–1797)
John Adams	(1797–1801)	Thomas Jefferson	(1797–1801)
Thomas Jefferson	(1801–1809)	Aaron Burr	(1801–1805)
		George Clinton	(1805–1809)
James Madison	(1809–1817)	George Clinton	(1809–1812)
		Vacant	(1812–1813)
		Elbridge Gerry	(1813–1814)
		Vacant	(1814–1817)
James Monroe	(1817–1825)	Daniel D. Tompkins	(1817–1825)
John Quincy Adams	(1825–1829)	John C. Calhoun	(1825–1829)
Andrew Jackson	(1829–1837)	John C. Calhoun	(1829–1832)
		Vacant	(1832–1833)
		Martin Van Buren	(1833–1837)
Martin Van Buren	(1837–1841)	Richard M. Johnson	(1837–1841)
William Henry Harrison	(1841)	John Tyler	(1841)
John Tyler	(1841–1845)	Vacant	(1841–1845)
James K. Polk	(1845–1849)	George M. Dallas	(1845–1849)
Zachary Taylor	(1849–1850)	Millard Fillmore	(1849–1850)
Millard Fillmore	(1850–1853)	Vacant	(1850–1853)
Franklin Pierce	(1853–1857)	William R. King	(1853)
		Vacant	(1853–1857)
James Buchanan	(1857–1861)	John C. Breckinridge	(1857–1861)
Abraham Lincoln	(1861–1865)	Hannibal Hamlin	(1861–1865)
		Andrew Johnson	(1865)
Andrew Johnson	(1865–1869)	Vacant	(1865–1869)
Ulysses S. Grant	(1869–1877)	Schuyler Colfax	(1869–1873)
		Henry Wilson	(1873–1875)
		Vacant	(1875–1877)
Rutherford B. Hayes	(1877–1881)	William A. Wheeler	(1877–1881)
James A. Garfield	(1881)	Chester A. Arthur	(1881)
Chester A. Arthur	(1881–1885)	Vacant	(1881–1885)
Grover Cleveland	(1885–1889)	Thomas A. Hendricks	(1885)
		Vacant	(1885–1889)
Benjamin Harrison	(1889–1893)	Levi P. Morton	(1889–1893)
Grover Cleveland	(1893–1897)	Adlai E. Stevenson	(1893–1897)
William McKinley	(1897–1901)	Garret A. Hobart	(1897–1901)
		Theodore Roosevelt	(1901)
Theodore Roosevelt	(1901–1909)	Vacant	(1901–1905)
		Charles W. Fairbanks	(1905–1909)
William H. Taft	(1909–1913)	James S. Sherman	(1909–1912)
		Vacant	(1912–1913)
Woodrow Wilson	(1913–1921)	Thomas R. Marshall	(1913–1921)
Warren G. Harding	(1921–1923)	Calvin Coolidge	(1921–1923)
Calvin Coolidge	(1923–1929)	Vacant	(1923–1925)
		Charles G. Dawes	(1925–1929)
Herbert Hoover	(1929–1933)	Charles Curtis	(1929–1933)
Franklin D. Roosevelt	(1933–1945)	John Nance Garner	(1933–1941)
		Henry A. Wallace	(1941–1945)
		Harry S. Truman	(1945)
Harry S. Truman	(1945–1953)	Vacant	(1945–1949)
		Alben W. Barkley	(1949–1953)
Dwight D. Eisenhower	(1953–1961)	Richard M. Nixon	(1953–1961)

U.S. Presidents and Vice Presidents—Continued

President	Years	Vice President	Years
John F. Kennedy	(1961–1963)	Lyndon B. Johnson	(1961–1963)
Lyndon B. Johnson	(1963–1969)	Vacant	(1963–1965)
		Hubert H. Humphrey	(1965–1969)
Richard M. Nixon	(1969–1974)	Spiro T. Agnew	(1969–1973)
		Gerald R. Ford	(1973–1974)
Gerald R. Ford	(1974–1977)	Nelson Rockefeller	(1974–1977)
Jimmy Carter	(1977–1981)	Walter F. Mondale	(1977–1981)
Ronald Reagan	(1981–1989)	George H.W. Bush	(1981–1989)
George H.W. Bush	(1989–1993)	J. Danforth Quayle	(1989–1993)
William J. Clinton	(1993–2001)	Albert Gore, Jr.	(1993–2001)
George W. Bush	(2001–)	Richard B. Cheney	(2001–)

Most Populous U.S. Cities by State [1]
[2006 Census estimates]

Alabama:
Birmingham ... 229,424
Montgomery* ... 201,998
Mobile ... 192,830
Huntsville ... 168,132
Tuscaloosa ... 83,052
Alaska:
Anchorage ... 278,700
Fairbanks ... 31,142
Juneau* ... 30,737
Wasilla ... 9,236
Sitka City and Borough ... 8,920
Arizona:
Phoenix* ... 1,512,986
Tucson ... 518,956
Mesa ... 447,541
Glendale ... 246,531
Chandler ... 240,595
Arkansas:
Little Rock* ... 184,422
Fort Smith ... 83,461
Fayetteville ... 68,726
Springdale ... 63,082
Jonesboro ... 60,489
California:
Los Angeles ... 3,849,378
San Diego ... 1,256,951
San Jose ... 929,936
San Francisco ... 744,041
Sacramento* ... 453,781
Colorado:
Denver* ... 566,974
Colorado Springs ... 372,437
Aurora ... 303,582
Lakewood ... 140,024
Fort Collins ... 129,467
Connecticut:
Bridgeport ... 137,912
Hartford* ... 124,512
New Haven ... 124,001
Stamford ... 119,261
Waterbury ... 107,251

Delaware:
Wilmington ... 72,826
Dover* ... 34,735
Newark ... 30,014
Middletown ... 10,272
Milford ... 7,852
District of Columbia:
Washington ... 581,530
Florida:
Jacksonville ... 794,555
Miami ... 404,048
Tampa ... 332,888
St. Petersburg ... 248,098
Tallahassee* ... 159,012
Georgia:
Atlanta* ... 486,411
Augusta ... 189,366
Columbus ... 188,660
Savannah ... 127,889
Athens ... 111,580
Hawaii:
Honolulu* ... 377,357
Hilo ... 40,759
Kailua ... 36,513
Kaneohe ... 34,970
Waipahu ... 33,108
Idaho:
Boise* ... 198,638
Nampa ... 76,587
Meridian ... 59,832
Pocatello ... 53,932
Idaho Falls ... 52,786
Illinois:
Chicago ... 2,833,321
Aurora ... 170,617
Rockford ... 155,138
Naperville ... 142,901
Springfield* ... 116,482
Indiana:
Indianapolis* ... 785,597
Fort Wayne ... 248,637
Evansville ... 115,738

Most Populous U.S. Cities by State [1]—Continued

[2006 Census estimates]

Indiana—Continued		**Mississippi—Continued**	
South Bend	104,905	Biloxi	44,342
Gary	97,715	Southaven	41,295
Iowa:		**Missouri:**	
Des Moines*	193,886	Kansas City	447,306
Cedar Rapids	124,417	St. Louis	347,181
Davenport	99,514	Springfield	150,797
Sioux City	83,262	Independence	109,400
Waterloo	65,998	Jefferson City*	39,274
Kansas:		**Montana:**	
Wichita	357,698	Billings	100,148
Overland Park	166,722	Missoula	64,081
Kansas City	143,801	Great Falls	56,215
Topeka*	122,113	Bozeman	35,061
Olathe	114,662	Helena*	27,885
Kentucky:		**Nebraska:**	
Louisville	554,496	Omaha	419,545
Lexington	270,789	Lincoln*	241,167
Owensboro	55,525	Bellevue	47,594
Bowling Green	53,176	Grand Island	44,632
Frankfort*	27,077	Kearney	29,385
Louisiana:		**Nevada:**	
Baton Rouge*	229,553	Las Vegas	552,539
New Orleans	223,388	Henderson	240,614
Shreveport	200,199	Reno	210,255
Lafayette	114,214	North Las Vegas	197,567
Lake Charles	70,224	Carson City*	55,289
Maine:		**New Hampshire:**	
Portland	63,011	Manchester	109,497
Lewiston	35,734	Nashua	87,157
Bangor	31,008	Concord*	42,378
South Portland	23,784	Rochester	30,117
Augusta*	18,560	Dover	28,422
Maryland:		**New Jersey:**	
Baltimore	631,366	Newark	281,402
Rockville	59,114	Jersey City	241,789
Frederick	58,882	Paterson	148,708
Gaithersburg	57,934	Elizabeth	126,179
Annapolis*	36,408	Trenton*	83,923
Massachusetts:		**New Mexico:**	
Boston*	590,763	Albuquerque	504,949
Worcester	175,454	Las Cruces	86,268
Springfield	151,176	Santa Fe*	72,056
Lowell	103,229	Rio Rancho	71,607
Cambridge	101,365	Roswell	45,582
Michigan:		**New York:**	
Detroit	871,121	New York	8,214,426
Grand Rapids	193,083	Buffalo	276,059
Warren	134,589	Rochester	208,123
Sterling Heights	127,991	Yonkers	197,852
Lansing*	114,276	Albany*	93,963
Minnesota:		**North Carolina:**	
Minneapolis	372,833	Charlotte	630,478
St. Paul*	273,535	Raleigh*	356,321
Rochester	96,975	Greensboro	236,865
Duluth	84,167	Durham	209,009
Bloomington	80,869	Winston-Salem	196,990
Mississippi:		**North Dakota:**	
Jackson*	176,614	Fargo	90,056
Gulfport	64,316	Bismarck*	58,333
Hattiesburg	48,012	Grand Forks	50,372

Most Populous U.S. Cities by State [1]—Continued

[2006 Census estimates]

North Dakota—Continued		Tennessee—Continued	
Minot	34,745	Clarksville	113,175
West Fargo	21,508	Texas:	
Ohio:		Houston	2,144,491
Columbus*	733,203	San Antonio	1,296,682
Cleveland	444,313	Dallas	1,232,940
Cincinnati	332,252	Austin*	709,893
Toledo	298,446	Fort Worth	653,320
Akron	209,704	Utah:	
Oklahoma:		Salt Lake City*	178,858
Oklahoma City*	537,734	West Valley	119,841
Tulsa	382,872	Provo	113,984
Norman	102,827	West Jordan	94,309
Broken Arrow	88,314	Sandy	94,203
Lawton	87,540	Vermont:	
Oregon:		Burlington	38,358
Portland	537,081	South Burlington	17,014
Salem*	152,239	Rutland	16,964
Eugene	146,356	Barre	9,078
Gresham	97,105	Montpelier*	7,954
Beaverton	89,643	Virginia:	
Pennsylvania:		Virginia Beach	435,619
Philadelphia	1,448,394	Norfolk	229,112
Pittsburgh	312,819	Chesapeake	220,560
Allentown	107,294	Richmond*	192,913
Erie	102,036	Newport News	178,281
Harrisburg*	47,164	Washington:	
Rhode Island:		Seattle	582,454
Providence*	175,255	Spokane	198,081
Warwick	85,925	Tacoma	196,532
Cranston	81,479	Vancouver	158,855
Pawtucket	72,998	Olympia*	44,645
East Providence	49,123	West Virginia:	
South Carolina:		Charleston*	50,846
Columbia*	119,961	Huntington	49,007
Charleston	107,845	Parkersburg	31,755
North Charleston	87,482	Wheeling	29,330
Rock Hill	61,620	Morgantown	28,654
Mount Pleasant	59,113	Wisconsin:	
South Dakota:		Milwaukee	573,358
Sioux Falls	142,396	Madison*	223,389
Rapid City	62,715	Green Bay	100,353
Aberdeen	24,071	Kenosha	96,240
Watertown	20,526	Racine	79,592
Pierre*	14,095	Wyoming:	
Tennessee:		Cheyenne*	55,314
Memphis	670,902	Casper	52,089
Nashville*	552,120	Laramie	25,688
Knoxville	182,337	Gillette	23,899
Chattanooga	155,190	Rock Springs	19,324

[1] The five most populous cities of each state are listed except where the capital city did not fall into the top five, in which case the fifth most populous city was replaced by the capital city.

* State capital.

Source: Information courtesy of the U.S. Census Bureau.

Principal Foreign Countries as of June 2008

Country	UN member	Capital	Chief of state	Legislative body	Government type
Afghanistan	Yes	Kabul	President	National Assembly of House of People, House of Elders.	Islamic Republic.
Albania	...do...	Tirana (Tirane)	...do...	Assembly (unicameral)	Emerging Democracy.
Algeria	...do...	Algiers	...do...	National People's Assembly, Council of Nations.	Republic.
Andorra	...do...	Andorra la Vella	Executive Council President	General Council of the Valleys (unicameral).	Parliamentary Democracy.
Angola	...do...	Luanda	President	National Assembly (unicameral).	Republic: multiparty presidential regime.
Antigua and Barbuda	...do...	Saint John's	Queen (represented by Governor General).	Parliament (bicameral).	Constitutional Monarchy with a parliamentary system of government.
Argentina	...do...	Buenos Aires	President	National Congress (bicameral).	Republic.
Armenia	...do...	Yerevan	...do...	National Assembly (Parliament)	Do.
Australia	...do...	Canberra	Queen (represented by Governor General).	Federal Parliament (bicameral).	Federal Parliamentary Democracy.
Austria	...do...	Vienna	President	Federal Assembly (bicameral).	Federal Republic.
Azerbaijan	...do...	Baku (Baki, Baky).	...do...	National Assembly (unicameral).	Republic.
Bahamas, The	...do...	Nassau.	Queen (represented by Governor General).	Parliament (bicameral).	Constitutional Parliamentary Democracy.
Bahrain	...do...	Manama.	King	Legislature (bicameral).	Constitutional Monarchy.
Bangladesh	...do...	Dhaka.	President	National Parliament (unicameral).	Parliamentary Democracy.
Barbados	...do...	Bridgetown	Queen (represented by Governor General).	Parliament (bicameral).	Do.
Belarus	...do...	Minsk.	President	National Assembly (bicameral).	Republic in name, although in fact a dictatorship.
Belgium	...do...	Brussels.	King	Parliament (bicameral).	Federal Parliamentary Democracy under a Constitutional Monarchy.
Belize	...do...	Belmopan.	Queen (represented by Governor General).	National Assembly (bicameral).	Parliamentary Democracy.
Benin	...do...	Porto-Novo.	President	National Assembly (unicameral).	Republic.
Bhutan	...do...	Thimphu.	King	Parliament (bicameral).	In transition to Constitutional Monarchy; special treaty relationship with India.
Bolivia	...do...	La Paz.	President	National Congress (bicameral).	Republic.
Bosnia and Herzegovina.	...do...	Sarajevo.	Chairman of the Presidency	Parliamentary Assembly (bicameral).	Emerging Federal Democratic Republic.
Botswana	...do...	Gaborone.	President	Parliament (bicameral).	Parliamentary Republic.
Brazil	...do...	Brasilia.	...do...	National Congress (bicameral).	Federal Republic.
Brunei	...do...	Bandar Seri.	Sultan and Prime Minister.	Legislative Council	Constitutional Sultanate.

Principal Foreign Countries as of June 2008—Continued

Country	UN member	Capital	Chief of state	Legislative body	Government type
Bulgaria	Yes	Sofia	President	National Assembly (unicameral)	Parliamentary Democracy.
Burkina Faso	..do	Ouagadougou	..do	..do	Parliamentary Republic.
Burma (Myanmar)[1]	..do	Rangoon (Yangon)	Chairman of the State Peace and Development Council (SPDC).	People's Assembly (unicameral)	Military Junta.
Burundi	..do	Bujumbura	President	Parliament (bicameral)	Republic.
Cambodia	..do	Phnom Penh	King	National Assembly (bicameral)	Multiparty Democracy under a Constitutional Monarchy.
Cameroon	..do	Yaounde	President	National Assembly (unicameral)	Republic; Multiparty Presidential Regime.
Canada	..do	Ottawa	Queen (represented by Governor General).	Parliament (bicameral)	Constitutional Monarchy that is also a Parliamentary Democracy and a Federation.
Cape Verde	..do	Praia	President	National Assembly (unicameral)	Republic.
Central African Republic.	..do	Bangui	..do	..do	Do.
Chad	..do	N'Djamena	..do	..do	Do.
Chile	..do	Santiago	..do	National Congress (bicameral)	Do.
China	..do	Beijing	..do	National People's Congress (unicameral).	Communist State.
Colombia	..do	Bogota	..do	Congress (bicameral)	Republic, Executive Branch dominates government structure.
Comoros	..do	Moroni	..do	Assembly of the Union (unicameral)	Republic.
Congo, Democratic Republic of the.	..do	Kinshasa	..do	Legislature (bicameral)	Do.
Congo, Republic of the.	..do	Brazzaville	..do	Parliament (bicameral)	Do.
Costa Rica	..do	San Jose	..do	Legislative Assembly (unicameral)	Democratic Republic.
Cote d'Ivoire (Ivory Coast).	..do	Yamoussoukro	..do	National Assembly (unicameral)	Republic; Multiparty Presidential Regime (est. 1960).[2]
Croatia	..do	Zagreb	..do	Assembly (unicameral)	Presidential/Parliamentary Democracy.
Cuba	..do	Havana	..do	National Assembly of People's Power (unicameral).	Communist State.
Cyprus	..do	Nicosia (Lefkosia)	..do	House of Representatives (unicameral)	Republic.
Czech Republic	..do	Prague	..do	Parliament (bicameral)	Parliamentary Democracy.
Denmark	..do	Copenhagen	Queen	People's Assembly (unicameral)	Constitutional Monarchy.
Djibouti	..do	Djibouti	President	Chamber of Deputies (unicameral)	Republic.
Dominica	..do	Roseau	..do	House of Assembly (unicameral)	Parliamentary Democracy.
Dominican Republic	..do	Santo Domingo	..do	National Congress (bicameral)	Democratic Republic.

Country		Capital		Legislature	Type of government
Ecuador	Yes	Quito	President	National Congress (unicameral)	Republic.
Egypt	do	Cairo	do	People's Assembly (bicameral)	Do.
El Salvador	do	San Salvador	do	Legislative Assembly (unicameral)	Do.
Equatorial Guinea	do	Malabo	do	House of People's Representatives (unicameral).	Do.
Eritrea	do	Asmara (Asmera)	do	National Assembly (unicameral)	Transitional Government.
Estonia	do	Tallinn	do	Parliament (unicameral)	Parliamentary Republic.
Ethiopia	do	Addis Ababa	do	Parliament (bicameral)	Federal Republic.
Fiji	do	Suva (on Viti Levu)	do	....do....	Republic.
Finland	do	Helsinki	do	Parliament (unicameral)	Do.
France	do	Paris	do	Parliament (bicameral)	Do.
Gabon	do	Libreville	do	Legislature (bicameral)	Republic; Multiparty Presidential Regime.
Gambia, The	do	Banjul	do	National Assembly (unicameral)	Republic.
Georgia	do	T'bilisi	do	Parliament (unicameral, also known as Supreme Council).	Do.
Germany	do	Berlin	do	Parliament (bicameral)	Federal Republic.
Ghana	do	Accra	do	Parliament (unicameral)	Constitutional Democracy.
Greece	do	Athens	do	....do....	Parliamentary Republic.
Grenada	do	Saint George's	Queen (represented by Governor General).	Parliament (bicameral)	Parliamentary Democracy.
Guatemala	do	Guatemala	President	Congress of the Republic (unicameral).	Constitutional Democratic Republic.
Guinea	do	Conakry	do	People's National Assembly (unicameral).	Republic.
Guinea-Bissau	do	Bissau	do	National People's Asssembly (unicameral).	Do.
Guyana	do	Georgetown	do	National Assembly (unicameral)	Do.
Haiti	do	Port-au-Prince	do	National Assembly (bicameral)	Do.
Holy See (Vatican City)	No	Vatican City	Pope	Pontifical Commission for the State of Vatican City (unicameral).	Ecclesiastical.
Honduras	Yes	Tegucigalpa	President	National Congress (unicameral)	Democratic Constitutional Republic.
Hungary	do	Budapest	do	National Assembly (unicameral)	Parliamentary Democracy.
Iceland	do	Reykjavik	do	Parliament (unicameral)	Constitutional Republic.
India	do	New Delhi	do	Parliament (bicameral)	Federal Republic.
Indonesia	do	Jakarta	do	House of Representatives	Republic.
Iran	do	Tehran	Supreme Leader	Islamic Consultative Assembly (unicameral).	Theocratic Republic.
Iraq	do	Baghdad	President	Council of Representatives	Parliamentary Democracy.
Ireland	do	Dublin	do	Parliament (bicameral)	Republic, Parliamentary Democracy.
Israel	do	Jerusalem[3]	do	Knesset (unicameral)	Parliamentary Democracy.
Italy	do	Rome	do	Parliament (bicameral)	Republic.

Principal Foreign Countries as of June 2008—Continued

Country	UN member	Capital	Chief of state	Legislative body	Government type
Jamaica	Yes	Kingston	Queen (represented by Governor General).	Parliament (bicameral)	Constitutional Parliamentary Democracy.
Japan	do	Tokyo	Emperor	Diet (bicameral)	Constitutional Monarchy with a Parliamentary Government.
Jordan	do	Amman	King	National Assembly (bicameral)	Constitutional Monarchy.
Kazakhstan	do	Astana	President	Parliament (bicameral)	Republic, Authoritarian Presidential rule, with little power outside the Executive Branch.
Kenya	do	Nairobi	do	National Assembly (unicameral)	Republic.
Kiribati	do	Tarawa	do	House of Parliament (unicameral)	Do.
Korea, North	do	Pyongyang	Premier	Supreme People's Assembly (unicameral).	Communist State one-man dictatorship.
Korea, South	do	Seoul	President	National Assembly (unicameral)	Republic.
Kosovo	No	Pristina (Prishtine)	do	Kosovo Assembly of the Provisional Government (unicameral).	Do.
Kuwait	Yes	Kuwait	Amir	National Assembly (unicameral)	Constitutional Emirate.
Kyrgyzstan	do	Bishkek	President	Supreme Council (unicameral)	Republic.
Laos	do	Vientiane	do	National Assembly (unicameral)	Communist State.
Latvia	do	Riga	do	Parliament (unicameral)	Parliamentary Democracy.
Lebanon	do	Beirut	do	National Assembly (unicameral)	Republic.
Lesotho	do	Maseru	King	Parliament (bicameral)	Parliamentary Constitutional Monarchy.
Liberia	do	Monrovia	President	National Assembly (bicameral)	Republic.
Libya	do	Tripoli	Revolutionary Leader[4]	General People's Congress (unicameral).	Jamahiriya.[5]
Liechtenstein	do	Vaduz	Prince	Parliament or Landtag (unicameral)	Constitutional Monarchy.
Lithuania	do	Vilnius	President	Parliament or Seimas (unicameral)	Parliamentary Democracy.
Luxembourg	do	Luxembourg	Grand Duke	Chamber of Deputies (unicameral)	Constitutional Monarchy.
Macedonia, former Yugoslav Republic.	do	Skopje	President	Assembly or Sobranie (unicameral)	Parliamentary Democracy.
Madagascar	do	Antananarivo	do	Legislature (bicameral)	Republic.
Malawi	do	Lilongwe	do	National Assembly (unicameral)	Multiparty Democracy.
Malaysia	do	Kuala Lumpur	Paramount Ruler	Parliament (bicameral)	Constitutional Monarchy.
Maldives	do	Male	President	People's Council (unicameral)	Republic.
Mali	do	Bamako	do	National Assembly (unicameral)	Do.
Malta	do	Valletta	do	House of Representatives (unicameral).	Do.
Marshall Islands	do	Majuro	do	Legislature (unicameral)	Constitutional Government in free association with the U.S.

Country		Capital	Chief of state	Legislature	Form of government
Mauritania	Yes	Nouakchott	President	Legislature (bicameral)	Democratic Republic.
Mauritius	do	Port Louis	do	National Assembly (unicameral)	Parliamentary Democracy.
Mexico	do	Mexico	do	National Congress (bicameral)	Federal Republic.
Micronesia, Federated States of.	do	Palikir	do	Congress (unicameral)	Constitutional Government in free association with the U.S.
Moldova	do	Chisinau	do	Parliament (unicameral)	Republic.
Monaco	do	Monaco	Prince	National Council (unicameral)	Constitutional Monarchy.
Mongolia	do	Ulaanbaatar	President	State Great Hural (unicameral)	Mixed Parliamentary/Presidential.
Montenegro	do	Podgorica	do	Assembly (unicameral)	Republic.
Morocco	do	Rabat	King	Parliament (bicameral)	Constitutional Monarchy.
Mozambique	do	Maputo	President	Assembly of the Republic (unicameral)	Republic.
Namibia	do	Windhoek	do	Legislature (bicameral)	Do.
Nauru	do	No official capital; government offices in Yaren District.	do	Parliament (unicameral)	Do.
Nepal	do	Kathmandu	Prime Minister	330 seat Interim Parliament	Constitutional Monarchy.
Netherlands	do	Amsterdam	Queen	States General (bicameral)	Do.
New Zealand	do	Wellington	do	House of Representatives (unicameral)	Parliamentary Democracy.
Nicaragua	do	Managua	President	National Assembly (unicameral)	Republic.
Niger	do	Niamey	do	do	Do.
Nigeria	do	Abuja	do	National Assembly (bicameral)	Federal Republic.
Norway	do	Oslo	King	Parliament (Storting), (modified unicameral)[6].	Constitutional Monarchy.
Oman	do	Muscat	Sultan and Prime Minister	Majlis Oman (bicameral)	Monarchy.
Pakistan	do	Islamabad	President	Parliament (bicameral)	Federal Republic.
Palau	do	Melekeok	do	National Congress (bicameral)	Constitutional Government in free association with the U.S.
Panama	do	Panama	do	National Assembly (unicameral)	Constitutional Democracy.
Papua New Guinea	do	Port Moresby	Queen	National Parliament (unicameral)	Constitutional Parliamentary Democracy.
Paraguay	do	Asuncion	President	Congress (bicameral)	Constitutional Republic.
Peru	do	Lima	do	Congress of the Republic of Peru (unicameral).	Do.
Philippines	do	Manila	do	Congress (bicameral)	Republic.
Poland	do	Warsaw	do	National Assembly (bicameral)	Do.
Portugal	do	Lisbon	do	Assembly of the Republic (unicameral)	Parliamentary Democracy.
Qatar	do	Doha	Amir	Advisory Council (unicameral)	Emirate.
Romania	do	Bucharest	President	Parliament (bicameral)	Republic.
Russia	do	Moscow	do	Federal Assembly (bicameral)	Federation.
Rwanda	do	Kigali	do	Parliament (bicameral)	Republic; presidential, multiparty system.
Saint Kitts and Nevis	do	Basseterre	Queen	National Assembly (unicameral)	Parliamentary Democracy.

Principal Foreign Countries as of June 2008—Continued

Country	UN member	Capital	Chief of state	Legislative body	Government type
Saint Lucia	Yes	Castries	Queen	Parliament (bicameral)	Parliamentary Democracy.
Saint Vincent and the Grenadines	do	Kingstown	do	House of Assembly (unicameral)	Do.
Samoa	do	Apia	Chief of State	Legislative Assembly (unicameral)	Do.
San Marino	do	San Marino	Co-Chiefs of State (Captains Regent)	Grand and General Council (unicameral)	Republic.
Sao Tome and Principe	do	Sao Tome	President	National Assembly (unicameral)	Do.
Saudi Arabia	do	Riyadh	King and Prime Minister	Consultative Council	Monarchy.
Senegal	do	Dakar	President	Parliament (bicameral)	Republic.
Serbia	do	Belgrade	do	National Assembly (unicameral)	Do.
Seychelles	do	Victoria	do	...do	Do.
Sierra Leone	do	Freetown	do	Parliament (unicameral)	Constitutional Democracy.
Singapore	do	Singapore	do	...do	Parliamentary Republic.
Slovakia	do	Bratislava	do	National Council (unicameral)	Parliamentary Democracy.
Slovenia	do	Ljubljana	do	Parliament (bicameral)	Parliamentary Republic.
Solomon Islands	do	Honiara	Queen	National Parliament (unicameral)	Parliamentary Democracy.
Somalia	do	Mogadishu	Transitional Federal President	National Assembly (unicameral)	No permanent National Government; transitional Parliamentary Federal Government.
South Africa	do	Pretoria	President	Parliament (bicameral)	Republic.
Spain[7]	do	Madrid	King	General Courts or National Assembly (bicameral)	Parliamentary Monarchy.
Sri Lanka	do	Colombo	President	Parliament (unicameral)	Republic.
Sudan	do	Khartoum	do	National Legislature (bicameral)	Government of National Unity (GNU).
Suriname	do	Paramaribo	do	National Assembly (unicameral)	Constitutional Democracy.
Swaziland	do	Mbabane	King	Parliament (bicameral)	Monarchy.
Sweden	do	Stockholm	King	Parliament (unicameral)	Constitutional Monarchy.
Switzerland	do	Bern	President	Federal Assembly (bicameral)	Formally a Confederation but similar in structure to a Federal Republic.
Syria	do	Damascus	do	People's Council (unicameral)	Republic under an authoritarian military-dominated regime.
Tajikistan	do	Dushanbe	do	Supreme Assembly (bicameral)	Republic.
Taiwan	No	Taipei	do	Legislative Yuan (unicameral)	Multiparty Democracy.
Tanzania	Yes	Dar es Salaam	do	National Assembly (unicameral)	Republic.
Thailand	do	Bangkok	King	National Assembly (bicameral)	Constitutional Monarchy.
Timor-Leste	do	Dili	President	National Parliament (unicameral)	Republic.

Country		Capital	Chief of State	Legislative Branch	Type of Government
Togo	Yes	Lome	President	National Assembly (unicameral)	Republic under transition to multiparty democratic rule.
Tonga	do	Nuku'alofa	King	Legislative Assembly (unicameral)	Constitutional Monarchy.
Trinidad and Tobago	do	Port-of-Spain	President	Parliament (bicameral)	Parliamentary Democracy.
Tunisia	do	Tunis	do	Chamber of Deputies and the Chamber of Advisors (bicameral).	Republic.
Turkey	do	Ankara	do	Grand National Assembly of Turkey (unicameral).	Republican Parliamentary Democracy
Turkmenistan	do	Ashgabat (Ashkhabad).	do	Two Parliamentary Bodies: People's Council and a National Assembly.	Republic; Authoritarian Presidential rule, with little power outside the executive branch.
Tuvalu	do	Funafuti	Queen	Parliament (also called House of Assembly; unicameral).	Constitutional Monarchy with a Parliamentary Democracy.
Uganda	do	Kampala	President	National Assembly (unicameral).	Republic.
Ukraine	do	Kyiv (Kiev)	do	Supreme Council (unicameral).	Do.
United Arab Emirates.	do	Abu Dhabi	do	Federal National Council (FNC) (unicameral).	Federation with specified powers delegated to the UAE federal government and other powers reserved to member emirates.
United Kingdom	do	London	Queen	Parliament (bicameral).	Constitutional Monarchy.
Uruguay	do	Montevideo	President	General Assembly (bicameral)	Constitutional Republic.
Uzbekistan	do	Tashkent	do	Supreme Assembly (bicameral)	Republic; authoritarian presidential rule, with little power outside the executive branch.
Vanuatu	do	Port-Vila (on Efate).	do	Parliament (unicameral)	Parliamentary Republic.
Venezuela	do	Caracas	do	National Assembly (unicameral)	Federal Republic.
Vietnam	do	Hanoi	do	do	Communist State.
Yemen	do	Sanaa	do	Legislature (bicameral).	Republic.
Zambia	do	Lusaka	do	National Assembly (unicameral).	Do.
Zimbabwe	do	Harare	Executive President	Parliament (bicameral).	Parliamentary Democracy.

[1] Since 1989, the military authorities in Burma have promoted the name Myanmar as a conventional name for their state; this decision was not approved by any sitting legislature in Burma, and the U.S. Government did not adopt the name, which is a derivative of the Burmese short-form name Myanma Naingngandaw.

[2] Government currently under power sharing agreement mandated by international mediators.

[3] In 1950, the Israel Parliament proclaimed Jerusalem as the capital. The United States does not recognize Jerusalem as the capital and the U.S. Embassy continues to be located in Tel Aviv.

[4] Holds no official title, but is de facto Chief of State.

[5] In theory, governed by the populace through local councils; in practice, an authoritarian state.

[6] No accurate English equivalents.

[7] The Law of Succession, July 27, 1947, declared that Spain was constituted a Kingdom.

Source: World Factbook 2008, Central Intelligence Agency, http://www.cia.gov/library/publications/the-world-factbook/index.html.

Demonyms: Names of Nationalities

[Demonym is a name given to a people or inhabitants of a place.]

Country	Demonym*	Country	Demonym*
Afghanistan	Afghan.	Costa Rica	Costa Rican.
Albania	Albanian.	Cote d'Ivoire	Ivorian.
Algeria	Algerian.	Croatia	Croat or Croatian.
American Samoa	American Samoan.	Cuba	Cuban.
Andorra	Andorran.	Cyprus	Cypriot.
Angola	Angolan.	Czech Republic	Czech.
Anguilla	Anguillan.	Denmark	Dane.
Antigua and Barbuda	Antiguan Barbudan.	Djibouti	Djiboutian.
Argentina	Argentine.	Dominica	Dominican.
Armenia	Armenian.	Dominican Republic	Dominican.
Aruba	Aruban.	Ecuador	Ecuadorian.
Australia	Australian.	Egypt	Egyptian.
Austria	Austrian.	El Salvador	Salvadoran.
Azerbaijan	Azerbaijani.	Equatorial Guinea	Equatorial Guinean or Equatoguinean.
The Bahamas	Bahamian.	Eritrea	Eritrean.
Bahrain	Bahraini.	Estonia	Estonian.
Bangladesh	Bangladeshi.	Ethiopia	Ethiopian.
Barbados	Barbadian or Bajan.	Falkland Islands	Falkland Islander.
Belarus	Belarusian.	Faroe Islands	Faroese (singular and plural).
Belgium	Belgian.		
Belize	Belizean.		
Benin	Beninese (singular and plural).	Fiji	Fijian.
		Finland	Finn.
Bermuda	Bermudian.	France	Frenchman (men) or Frenchwoman (women).
Bhutan	Bhutanese (singular and plural).		
Bolivia	Bolivian.	French Polynesia	French Polynesian.
Bosnia and Herzegovina	Bosnian, Herzegovinian.	Gabon	Gabonese (singular and plural).
Botswana	Motswana (singular), Batswana (plural).		
		The Gambia	Gambian.
Brazil	Brazilian.	Georgia	Georgian.
British Virgin Islands	British Virgin Islander.	Germany	German.
Brunei	Bruneian.	Ghana	Ghanaian.
Bulgaria	Bulgarian.	Gibraltar	Gibraltarian.
Burkina Faso	Burkinabe (singular and plural).	Greece	Greek.
		Greenland	Greenlander.
Burma (Myanmar[1])	Burmese (singular and plural).	Grenada	Grenadian.
		Guam	Guamanian.
Burundi	Burundian.	Guatemala	Guatemalan.
Cambodia	Cambodian.	Guernsey	Channel Islander.
Cameroon	Cameroonian.	Guinea	Guinean.
Canada	Canadian.	Guinea-Bissau	Guinean.
Cape Verde	Cape Verdean.	Guyana	Guyanese (singular and plural).
Cayman Islands	Caymanian.		
Central African Republic	Central African.	Haiti	Haitian.
Chad	Chadian.	Honduras	Honduran.
Chile	Chilean.	Hong Kong	Chinese/Hong Konger.
China	Chinese (singular and plural).	Hungary	Hungarian.
		Iceland	Icelander.
Christmas Island	Christmas Islander.	India	Indian.
Cocos (Keeling) Islands	Cocos Islander.	Indonesia	Indonesian.
Colombia	Colombian.	Iran	Iranian.
Comoros	Comoran.	Iraq	Iraqi.
Congo, Democratic Republic of the.	Congolese (singular and plural).	Ireland	Irishman (men), Irishwoman (women), Irish (collective plural).
Congo, Republic of the	Congolese (singular and plural).		
Cook Islands	Cook Islander.	Israel	Israeli.

Demonyms: Names of Nationalities—Continued

[Demonym is a name given to a people or inhabitants of a place.]

Country	Demonym*	Country	Demonym*
Italy	Italian.	Netherlands	Dutchman (men), Dutchwoman (women), Dutch (collective).
Jamaica	Jamaican.		
Japan	Japanese (singular and plural).		
Jersey	Channel Islander.	Netherlands Antilles	Dutch Antillean.
Jordan	Jordanian.	New Caledonia	New Caledonian.
Kazakhstan	Kazakhstani.	New Zealand	New Zealander.
Kenya	Kenyan.	Nicaragua	Nicaraguan.
Kiribati	I-Kiribati (singular and plural).	Niger	Nigerien.
		Nigeria	Nigerian.
Korea, North	Korean.	Niue	Niuean.
Korea, South	Korean.	Norfolk Island	Norfolk Islander.
Kosovo	Kosovar (Albanian), Kosovac (Serbian).	Norway	Norwegian.
		Oman	Omani.
Kuwait	Kuwaiti.	Pakistan	Pakistani.
Kyrgyzstan	Kyrgyzstani.	Palau	Palauan.
Laos	Lao or Laotian.	Panama	Panamanian.
Latvia	Latvian.	Papua New Guinea	Papua New Guinean.
Lebanon	Lebanese (singular and plural).	Paraguay	Paraguayan.
		Peru	Peruvian.
Lesotho	Mosotho (singular), Basotho (plural).	Philippines	Filipino.
		Pitcairn Islands	Pitcairn Islander.
Liberia	Liberian.	Poland	Pole.
Libya	Libyan.	Portugal	Portuguese (singular and plural).
Liechtenstein	Liechtensteiner.		
Lithuania	Lithuanian.	Qatar	Qatari.
Luxembourg	Luxembourger.	Romania	Romanian.
Macau	Chinese (singular and plural).	Russia	Russian.
		Rwanda	Rwandan.
Macedonia	Macedonian.	Saint Helena	Saint Helenian.
Madagascar	Malagasy (singular and plural).	Saint Kitts and Nevis	Kittian and Nevisian.
		Saint Lucia	Saint Lucian.
Malawi	Malawian.	Saint Pierre and Miquelon	Frenchman (men), Frenchwoman (women).
Malaysia	Malaysian.		
Maldives	Maldivian.		
Mali	Malian.	Saint Vincent and the Grenadines.	Saint Vincentian or Vincentian.
Malta	Maltese (singular and plural).		
		Samoa	Samoan.
Marshall Islands	Marshallese (singular and plural).	San Marino	Sammarinese (singular and plural).
Mauritania	Mauritanian.	Sao Tome and Principe	Sao Tomean.
Mauritius	Mauritian.	Saudi Arabia	Saudi.
Mayotte	Mahorais (singular and plural).	Senegal	Senegalese (singular and plural).
Mexico	Mexican.	Serbia	Serb.
Micronesia, Federated States of.	Micronesian.	Seychelles	Seychellois (singular and plural).
Moldova	Moldovan.	Sierra Leone	Sierra Leonean.
Monaco	Monegasque or Monacan.	Singapore	Singaporean.
		Slovakia	Slovak.
Mongolia	Mongolian.	Slovenia	Slovene.
Montenegro	Montenegrin.	Solomon Islands	Solomon Islander.
Montserrat	Montserratian.	Somalia	Somali.
Morocco	Moroccan.	South Africa	South African.
Mozambique	Mozambican.	Spain	Spaniard.
Namibia	Namibian.	Sri Lanka	Sri Lankan.
Nauru	Nauruan.	Sudan	Sudanese (singular and plural).
Nepal	Nepalese (singular and plural).	Suriname	Surinamer.

Demonyms: Names of Nationalities—Continued

[Demonym is a name given to a people or inhabitants of a place.]

Country	Demonym*	Country	Demonym*
Swaziland	Swazi.	Turkmenistan	Turkmen.
Sweden	Swede.	Tuvalu	Tuvaluan.
Switzerland	Swiss (singular and plural).	Uganda	Ugandan.
		Ukraine	Ukrainian.
Syria	Syrian.	United Arab Emirates	Emirati.
Taiwan	Taiwan (singular and plural).	United Kingdom	Briton or British (collective plural).
Tajikistan	Tajikistani.	United States	American.
Tanzania	Tanzanian.	Uruguay	Uruguayan.
Thailand	Thai (singular and plural).	Uzbekistan	Uzbekistani.
		Vanuatu	Ni-Vanuatu (singular and plural).
Timor-Leste	Timorese (singular and plural).	Venezuela	Venezuelan.
Togo	Togolese (singular and plural).	Vietnam	Vietnamese (singular and plural).
Tokelau	Tokelauan.	Virgin Islands	Virgin Islander.
Tonga	Tongan.	Wallis and Futuna	Wallisian, Futunan.
Trinidad and Tobago	Trinidadian, (singular Tobagonian.	Western Sahara	Sahrawi, Sahraoui.
		Yemen	Yemeni.
Tunisia	Tunisian.	Zambia	Zambian.
Turkey	Turk.	Zimbabwe	Zimbabwean.

[1] Since 1989 the military authorities in Burma have promoted the name Myanmar as a conventional name for their state; this decision was not approved by any sitting legislature in Burma, and the U.S. Government did not adopt the name, which is a derivative of the Burmese short-form name Myanma Naingngandaw.

*NOTE.—Plural references add s unless otherwise indicated.

Source: Information courtesy of World Factbook as of July 24, 2008; for more information see www.cia.gov/library/publications/the-world-factbook/fields/21110.html.

Currency

[As of July 2008]

Country	Currency	ISO 4217 code*
Afghanistan	Afghani	AFA
Akrotiri	Euro	EUR
Albania	Lek	ALL
Algeria	Algerian dinar	DZD
American Samoa	U.S. dollar	USD
Andorra	Euro	EUR
Angola	Kwanza	AOA
Anguilla	East Caribbean dollar	XCD
Antigua and Barbuda	East Caribbean dollar	XCD
Argentina	Argentine peso	ARS
Armenia	Dram	AMD
Aruba	Aruban guilder/florin	AWG
Australia	Australian dollar	AUD
Austria	Euro	EUR
Azerbaijan	Azerbaijani manat	AZN
Bahamas	Bahamian dollar	BSD
Bahrain	Bahraini dinar	BHD
Bangladesh	Taka	BDT
Barbados	Barbadian dollar	BBD
Belarus	Belarusian ruble	BYR
Belgium	Euro	EUR
Belize	Belizean dollar	BZD
Benin	Communaute Financiere Africaine franc	XOF[1]
Bermuda	Bermudian dollar	BMD

Currency—Continued
[As of July 2008]

Country	Currency	ISO 4217 code*
Bhutan	Ngultrum and Indian rupee	BTN/INR
Bolivia	Boliviano	BOB
Bosnia and Herzegovina	Convertible mark	BAM
Botswana	Pula	BWP
Brazil	Real	BRL
British Indian Ocean Territory	British Pound and U.S. Dollar	GBP/USD
British Virgin Islands	U.S. dollar	USD
Brunei	Bruneian dollar	BND
Bulgaria	Lev	BGL
Burkina Faso	Communaute Financiere Africaine franc	XOF[1]
Burma (Myanmar[3])	Kyat	MMK
Burundi	Burundi franc	BIF
Cambodia	Riel	KHR
Cameroon	Communaute Financiere Africaine franc	XAF[2]
Canada	Canadian dollar	CAD
Cape Verde	Cape Verdean escudo	CVE
Cayman Islands	Caymanian dollar	KYD
Central African Republic	Communaute Financiere Africaine franc	XAF[2]
Chad	Communaute Financiere Africaine franc	XAF[2]
Chile	Chilean peso	CLP
China	Renminbi, also called yuan	RMB/CNY
Christmas Island	Australian dollar	AUD
Cocos (Keeling) Islands	Australian dollar	AUD
Colombia	Colombian peso	COP
Comoros	Comoran franc	KMF
Congo, Democratic Republic of the	Congolese franc	CDF
Congo, Republic of the	Communaute Financiere Africaine franc	XAF[2]
Cook Islands	NZ dollar	NZD
Costa Rica	Costa Rican colon	CRC
Cote d'Ivoire (Ivory Coast)	Communaute Financiere Africaine franc	XOF[1]
Croatia	Kuna	HRK
Cuba	Cuban peso and convertible peso	CUP/CUC
Cyprus	Euro	EUR
Czech Republic	Czech koruna	CZK
Denmark	Danish krone	DKK
Dhekelia	Euro	EUR
Djibouti	Djiboutian franc	DJF
Dominica	East Caribbean dollar	XCD
Dominican Republic	Dominican peso	DOP
Ecuador	U.S. dollar	USD
Egypt	Egyptian pound	EGP
El Salvador	U.S. dollar	USD
Equatorial Guinea	Communaute Financiere Africaine franc	XAF[2]
Eritrea	Nakfa	ERN
Estonia	Estonian kroon	EEK
Ethiopia	Birr	ETB
Falkland Islands (Islas Malvinas)	Falkland pound	FKP
Faroe Islands	Danish krone	DKK
Fiji	Fijian dollar	FJD
Finland	Euro	EUR
France	Euro	EUR
French Polynesia	Comptoirs Francais du Pacifique franc	XPF
Gabon	Communaute Financiere Africaine franc	XAF[2]
Gambia, The	Dalasi	GMD
Gaza Strip	New Israeli shekel	ILS
Georgia	Lari	GEL
Germany	Euro	EUR
Ghana	Ghana cedi	GHC
Gibraltar	Gibraltar pound	GIP

Currency—Continued

[As of July 2008]

Country	Currency	ISO 4217 code*
Greece	Euro	EUR
Greenland	Danish krone	DKK
Grenada	East Caribbean dollar	XCD
Guam	U.S. dollar	USD
Guatemala	Quetzal and U.S. dollar	GTQ/USD
Guernsey	Guernsey pound and British pound	**/GBP
Guinea	Guinean franc	GNF
Guinea-Bissau	Communaute Financiere Africaine franc	XOF[1]
Guyana	Guyanese dollar	GYD
Haiti	Gourde	HTG
Holy See (Vatican City)	Euro	EUR
Honduras	Lempira	HNL
Hong Kong	Hong Kong dollar	HKD
Hungary	Forint	HUF
Iceland	Icelandic krona	ISK
India	Indian rupee	INR
Indonesia	Indonesian rupiah	IDR
Iran	Iranian rial	IRR
Iraq	New Iraqi dinar	NID
Ireland	Euro	EUR
Isle of Man	Isle of Man pound also called manx	IMP
Israel	New Israeli shekel	ILS
Italy	Euro	EUR
Jamaica	Jamaican dollar	JMD
Japan	Yen	JPY
Jersey	Jersey pound and British pound	**/GBP
Jordan	Jordanian dinar	JOD
Kazakhstan	Tenge	KZT
Kenya	Kenyan shilling	KES
Kiribati	Australian dollar	AUD
Korea, North	North Korean won	KPW
Korea, South	South Korean won	KRW
Kosovo	Euro and Serbian Dinar	EUR/RSD
Kuwait	Kuwaiti dinar	KWD
Kyrgyzstan	Som	KGS
Laos	Kip	LAK
Latvia	Latvian lat	LVL
Lebanon	Lebanese pound	LBP
Lesotho	Loti and South African rand	LSL/ZAR
Liberia	Liberian dollar	LRD
Libya	Libyan dinar	LYD
Liechtenstein	Swiss franc	CHF
Lithuania	Litas	LTL
Luxembourg	Euro	EUR
Macau	Pataca	MOP
Macedonia	Macedonian denar	NKD
Madagascar	Ariary	MGA
Malawi	Malawian kwacha	MWK
Malaysia	Ringgit	MYR
Maldives	Rufiyaa	MVR
Mali	Communaute Financiere Africaine franc	XOF[1]
Malta	Euro	EUR
Marshall Islands	U.S. dollar	USD
Mauritania	Ouguiya	MRO
Mauritius	Mauritian rupee	MUR
Mayotte	Euro	EUR
Mexico	Mexican peso	MXN
Micronesia, Federated States of	U.S. dollar	USD
Moldova	Moldovan leu	MDL

Currency—Continued
[As of July 2008]

Country	Currency	ISO 4217 code*
Monaco	Euro	EUR
Mongolia	Togrog/tugrik	MNT
Montenegro	Euro	EUR
Montserrat	East Caribbean dollar	XCD
Morocco	Moroccan dirham	MAD
Mozambique	Metical	MZM
Namibia	Namibian dollar and South African rand	NAD/ZAR
Nauru	Australian dollar	AUD
Nepal	Nepalese rupee	NPR
Netherlands	Euro	EUR
Netherlands Antilles	Netherlands Antillean guilder	ANG
New Caledonia	Comptoirs Francais du Pacifique franc	XPF
New Zealand	New Zealand dollar	NZD
Nicaragua	Gold cordoba	NIO
Niger	Communaute Financiere Africaine franc	XOF[1]
Nigeria	Naira	NGN
Niue	New Zealand dollar	NZD
Norfolk Island	Australian dollar	AUD
Northern Mariana Islands	U.S. dollar	USD
Norway	Norwegian krone	NOK
Oman	Omani rial	OMR
Pakistan	Pakistani rupee	PKR
Palau	U.S. dollar	USD
Panama	Balboa and U.S. dollar	PAB/USD
Papua New Guinea	Kina	PGK
Paraguay	Guarani	PYG
Peru	Nuevo sol	PEN
Philippines	Philippine peso	PHP
Pitcairn Islands	New Zealand dollar	NZD
Poland	Zloty	PLN
Portugal	Euro	EUR
Puerto Rico	U.S. dollar	USD
Qatar	Qatari rial	QAR
Romania	Romanian leu	RON
Russia	Russian ruble	RUB
Rwanda	Rwandan franc	RWF
Saint Barthelemy	Euro	EUR
Saint Helena	Saint Helenian pound	SHP
Saint Kitts and Nevis	East Caribbean dollar	XCD
Saint Lucia	East Caribbean dollar	XCD
Saint Martin	Euro	EUR
Saint Pierre and Miquelon	Euro	EUR
Saint Vincent and the Grenadines	East Caribbean dollar	XCD
Samoa	Tala	SAT
San Marino	Euro	EUR
Sao Tome and Principe	Dobra	STD
Saudi Arabia	Saudi riyal	SAR
Senegal	Communaute Financiere Africaine franc	XOF[1]
Serbia	Serbian dinar	RSD
Seychelles	Seychelles rupee	SCR
Sierra Leone	Leone	SLL
Singapore	Singapore dollar	SGD
Slovakia	Slovak koruna	SKK
Slovenia	Euro	EUR
Solomon Islands	Solomon Islands dollar	SBD
Somalia	Somali shilling	SOS
South Africa	Rand	ZAR
Spain	Euro	EUR
Sri Lanka	Sri Lankan rupee	LKR

Currency—Continued
[As of July 2008]

Country	Currency	ISO 4217 code*
Sudan	Sudanese pound	SDG
Suriname	Surinam dollar	SRD
Svalbard	Norwegian krone	NOK
Swaziland	Lilangeni	SZL
Sweden	Swedish krona	SEK
Switzerland	Swiss franc	CHF
Syria	Syrian pound	SYP
Taiwan	New Taiwan dollar	TWD
Tajikistan	Somoni	TJS
Tanzania	Tanzanian shilling	TZS
Thailand	Baht	THB
Timor-Leste	U.S. dollar	USD
Togo	Communaute Financiere Africaine franc	XOF[1]
Tokelau	New Zealand dollar	NZD
Tonga	Pa'anga	TOP
Trinidad and Tobago	Trinidad and Tobago dollar	TTD
Tunisia	Tunisian dinar	TND
Turkey	Turkish lira	TRY
Turkmenistan	Turkmen manat	TMM
Turks and Caicos Islands	U.S. dollar	USD
Tuvalu	Australian dollar	AUD
Uganda	Ugandan shilling	UGX
Ukraine	Hryvnia	UAH
United Arab Emirates	Emirati dirham	AED
United Kingdom	British pound	GBP
United States	U.S. dollar	USD
Uruguay	Uruguayan peso	UYU
Uzbekistan	Soum	UZS
Vanuatu	Vatu	VUV
Venezuela	Bolivar	VEB
Vietnam	Dong	VND
Virgin Islands	U.S. dollar	USD
Wallis and Futuna	Comptoirs Francais du Pacifique franc	XPF
West Bank	New Israeli shekel and Jordanian dinar	ILS/JOD
Western Sahara	Moroccan dirham	MAD
Yemen	Yemeni rial	YER
Zambia	Zambian kwacha	ZMK
Zimbabwe	Zimbabwean dollar	ZWD

[1] Responsible authority is the Central Bank of the West African States.

[2] Responsible authority is the Bank of the Central African States.

[3] Since 1989 the military authorities in Burma have promoted the name Myanmar as a conventional name for their state; this decision was not approved by any sitting legislature in Burma, and the U.S. Government did not adopt the name, which is a derivative of the Burmese short-form name Myanma Naingngandaw.

* ISO 4217 is the international standard of 3-letter codes used to define names of currencies; it is used in place of currency symbols or names. For more information see www.iso.org/iso/support/faqs/faqs_widely_used_standards/widely_used_standards_other/currency_codes/currency_codes_list-1.htm.

** There is no currency code for Island monies. Guernsey and Jersey are both British crown dependencies, but not part of the UK. However, the UK Government is constitutionally responsible for their international representation.

Source: World Factbook: www.cia.gov/library/publications/the-world-factbook/fields/2065.html.

Metric and U.S. Measures [1]

Length

Metric unit	U.S. unit
10 millimeters...............................1 centimeter.	12 inches..1 foot (ft).
10 centimeters.............................1 decimeter.	3 feet...1 yard.
10 decimeters..................................1 meter.	22 yards..1 chain.
10 meters....................................1 dekameter.	10 chains..................................1 furlong (660 ft).
10 dekameters.............................1 hectometer.	8 furlongs..................................1 mile (5,280 ft).
10 hectometers............................1 kilometer.	1 nautical mile ....1.1508 mile.
1 kilometer ....1,000 meters.	1 league.............................3 nautical miles.

Mass Weight

Metric unit	U.S. unit
10 milligrams (mg)........................1 centigram.	16 ounces...1 pound.
10 centigrams ....1 decigram (100 mg).	100 pounds (lbs)...................1 hundredweight.
10 decigrams................1 gram (1,000 mg).	20 hundredweight..................1 ton (2,000 lbs).
10 grams (g) ....1 dekagram.	
10 dekagrams.................1 hectogram (100 g).	
10 hectograms ....1 kilogram (1,000 g).	
1,000 kilograms...............................1 metric ton.	

Volume

Metric unit	U.S. liquid capacity
10 milliliters...................................1 centiliter.	3 teaspoons.......................................1 tablespoon.
10 centiliters..................................1 deciliter.	2 tablespoons..........................1 fluid ounce (fl oz).
10 deciliters......................................1 liter.	1 cup...8 fl oz.
1,000 liters ....1 cubic meter.	2 cups...1 pint.
	2 pints ....1 quart.
	4 quarts...1 gallon.
	42 gallons.............................1 petroleum barrel.
	U.S. dry measure [2]
	2 pints ....1 quart.
	4 quarts...1 gallon.
	2 gallons ....1 peck.
	4 pecks...1 bushel.
	8 bushels...1 quarter.

Temperature Conversion [3]

Celsius	Fahrenheit	Kelvin	Celsius	Fahrenheit	Kelvin
100..................................	212	373.1	0....................................	32	273.1
50....................................	122	323.1	−10	14	263.1
40....................................	104	313.1	−20................................	−4	253.1
30....................................	86	303.1	−30................................	−22	243.1
20....................................	68	293.1	−40................................	−40	233.1
10....................................	50	283.1	−50................................	−58	223.1
			−273.1..........................	−459.7	0

[1] At this time, only three countries—Burma, Liberia, and the United States—have not adopted the International System of Units (SI, or metric system) as their official system of weights and measures.

[2] Dry measurements are mainly used for measuring grain or fresh produce. Do not confuse dry measure for liquid measure as they are not the same.

[3] The equation for converting temperatures is as follows: °C to °F: multiply by 9, then divide by 5, then add 32; °F to °C: subtract 32, then multiply by 5, then divide by 9.

Common Measures and Their Metric Equivalents

U.S. to metric	Metric to U.S.
Inch .... 2.54 centimeters.	Centimeter .... 0.3937 inch.
Foot .... 0.3048 meter.	Meter .... 3.2808 feet.
Yard .... 0.9144 meter.	Do .... 1.0936 yards.
Mile .... 1.6093 kilometers.	Kilometer .... 0.6214 mile.
Nautical mile .... 1.852 kilometers.	Do .... 0.5399 nautical mile.
League .... 5.556 kilometers.	Do .... 0.1799 league.
Square inch .... 6.452 square centimeters.	Square centimeter .... 0.155 square inch.
Square foot .... 0.0929 square meter.	Square meter .... 10.7639 square feet.
Square yard .... 0.836 square meter.	Do .... 1.196 square yards.
Acre .... 0.4047 hectare.	Hectare .... 2.471 acres.
Square mile .... 259 hectares.	Do .... 0.0039 square mile.
Cubic inch .... 16.39 cubic centimeters.	Cubic centimeter .... 0.06 cubic inch.
Cubic foot .... 0.0283 cubic meter.	Cubic meter .... 35.3146 cubic feet.
Cubic yard .... 0.7646 cubic meter.	Do .... 1.3079 cubic yards.
Cord .... 128 cubic feet.	
Ounce (liquid) .... 29.574 milliliters.	Milliliter .... 0.0338 ounce (liquid).
Pint (liquid) .... 473.176 milliliters.	
Quart (liquid) .... 946.35 milliliters.	Liter .... 1.06 quarts (liquid).
Gallon (liquid) .... 3.79 liters.	Do .... 0.26 gallon (liquid).
Pint (dry) .... 550.61 milliliters.	
Quart (dry) .... 1101 milliliters.	Do .... 0.91 quart (dry).
Quart, imperial .... 1137 milliliters.	
Gallon (dry) .... 4.40 liters.	Do .... 0.23 gallon (dry).
Gallon, imperial .... 4.55 liters.	
Peck .... 8.810 liters.	Do .... 0.1135 peck.
Peck, imperial .... 9.092 liters.	
Bushel .... 35.24 liters.	Do .... 0.028 bushel.
Bushel, imperial .... 36.37 liters.	
Grain [1] .... 64.799 milligrams.	
Ounce [2] .... 28.35 grams.	Gram .... 0.04 ounce.
Ounce, troy [3] .... 31.103 grams.	Do .... 0.032 troy ounce.
Pound [2] .... 0.4536 kilogram.	Kilogram .... 2.20 pounds.
Pound, troy .... 12 troy ounces.	
Ton, short .... 907.185 kilograms.	
Do .... 2,000 pounds.	
Ton, metric .... 1,000 kilograms.	
Do .... 2,204.6 pounds.	
Ton, long .... 1,016.047 kilograms.	
Do .... 2,240 pounds.	

[1] The grain is used to measure in ballistics and archery; grains were originally used in medicine but have been replaced by milligrams.

[2] Avoirdupois; avoirdupois is the measure of mass of everyday items.

[3] The troy ounce is used in pricing silver, gold, platinum, and other precious metals and gemstones.

Measurement Conversion

Fraction	Decimal inches	Milli-meters	Picas	Points	Fraction	Decimal inches	Milli-meters	Picas	Points
1/16	.0625	1.587	0p4.5	4.5	7/8	.875	22.225	5p3	63
1/8	.125	3.175	0p9	9	15/16	.9375	23.812	5p7.5	67.5
3/16	.1875	4.762	1p1.5	13.5	1	1	25.4	6	72
1/4	.25	6.35	1p6	18	1¼	1.25	31.75	7p6	90
5/16	.3125	7.937	1p10.5	22.5	1½	1.5	38.1	9	108
3/8	.375	9.525	2p3	27	1¾	1.75	44.5	10p6	126
7/16	.4375	11.112	2p7.5	31.5	2	2	50.8	12	144
1/2	.5	12.7	3	36	2½	2.5	63.5	15	180
9/16	.5625	14.287	3p4.5	40.5	3	3	76.2	18	216
5/8	.625	15.875	3p9	45	3½	3.5	88.9	21	252
11/16	.6875	17.462	4p1.5	49.5	4	4	100.6	24	288
3/4	.75	19.05	4p6	54	5	5	127	30	360
13/16	.8125	20.637	4p10.5	58.5	6	6	152.4	36	432

18. Geologic Terms and Geographic Divisions

Geologic terms

For capitalization, compounding, and use of quotations in geologic terms, copy is to be followed. Geologic terms quoted verbatim from published material should be left as the original author used them; however, it should be made clear that the usage is that of the original author.

Formal geologic terms are capitalized: Proterozoic Eon, Cambrian Period. Structural terms such as arch, anticline, or uplift are capitalized when preceded by a name: Cincinnati Arch, Cedar Creek Anticline, Ozark Uplift. See Chapter 4 geographic terms for more information.

Divisions of Geologic Time
[Most recent to oldest]

Eon	Era	Period
Phanerozoic	Cenozoic	Quarternary.
		Tertiary (Neogene, Paleogene).
	Mesozoic	Cretaceous.
		Jurassic.
		Triassic.
	Paleozoic	Permian.
		Carboniferous (Pennsylvanian, Mississippian).
		Devonian.
		Silurian.
		Ordovician.
		Cambrian.
Proterozoic	Neoproterozoic	Ediacaran.
		Cryogenian.
		Tonian.
	Mesoproterozoic	Stenian.
		Ectasian.
		Calymmian.
	Paleoproterozoic	Statherian.
		Orosirian.
		Rhyacian.
		Siderian.
Archean	Neoarchean.	
	Mesoarchean.	
	Paleoarchean.	
	Eoarchean.	
Hadean.		

Source: Information courtesy of the U.S. Geological Survey; for graphic see http://pubs.usgs.gov/fs/2007/3015/fs2007-3015.pdf.

Physiographic regions

Physiographic regions are based on terrain texture, rock type, and geologic structure and history. The classification system has three tiers: divisions, which are broken into provinces, and some provinces break further into sections. All names are capitalized, not the class; for graphic see http://tapestry. usgs.gov/physiogr/physio.html.

Physiographic Regions of the Lower 48 United States

Division	Province	Section
Laurentian Upland	Superior Upland.	
Atlantic Plain	Continental Shelf.	
	Coastal Plain	Embayed.
		Sea Island.
		Floridian.
		East Gulf Coastal Plain.
		Mississippi Alluvial Plain.
		West Gulf Coastal Plain.
Appalachian Highlands	Piedmont	Piedmont Upland.
		Piedmont Lowlands.
	Blue Ridge	Northern.
		Southern.
	Valley and Ridge	Tennessee.
		Middle.
		Hudson Valley.
	St. Lawrence Valley	Champlain.
		Northern.
	Appalachian Plateaus	Mohawk.
		Catskill.
		Southern New York.
		Allegheny Mountain.
		Kanawha.
		Cumberland Plateau.
		Cumberland Mountain.
	New England	Seaboard Lowland.
		New England Upland.
		White Mountain.
		Green Mountain.
		Taconic.
	Adirondack.	
Interior Plains	Interior Low Plateaus	Highland Rim.
		Lexington Plain.
		Nashville Basin.
	Central Lowland	Eastern Lake.
		Western Lake.
		Wisconsin Driftless.
		Till Plains.
		Dissected Till Plains.
		Osage Plains.

Division	Province	Section
	Great Plains.............................	Missouri Plateau, glaciated.
		Missouri Plateau, unglaciated.
		Black Hills.
		High Plains.
		Plains Border.
		Colorado Piedmont.
		Raton.
		Pecos Valley.
		Edwards Plateau.
		Central Texas.
Interior Highlands......................	Ozark Plateaus.............................	Springfield-Salem Plateaus.
		Boston "Mountains."
	Ouachita......................................	Arkansas Valley.
		Ouachita Mountains.
Rocky Mountain System............	Southern Rocky Mountains.	
	Wyoming Basin.	
	Middle Rocky Mountains.	
	Northern Rocky Mountains.	
Intermontane Plateaus	Columbia Plateau	Walla Walla Plateau.
		Blue Mountain.
		Payette.
		Snake River Plain.
		Harney.
	Colorado Plateaus	High Plateaus of Utah.
		Uinta Basin.
		Canyon Lands.
		Navajo.
		Grand Canyon.
		Datil.
	Basin and Range	Great Basin.
		Sonoran Desert.
		Salton Trough.
		Mexican Highland.
		Sacramento.
Pacific Mountain System............	Cascade-Sierra Mountains.........	Northern Cascade Mountains.
		Middle Cascade Mountains.
		Southern Cascade Mountains.
		Sierra Nevada.
	Pacific Border	Puget Trough.
		Olympic Mountains.
		Oregon Coast Range.
		Klamath Mountains.
		California Trough.
		California Coast Ranges.
		Los Angeles Ranges.
	Lower California.	

Source: Information courtesy of the U.S. Geological Survey.

Geographic divisions

The Public Land Survey System (PLSS) has a hierarchy of lines. Principal meridians and base lines and their related townships, sections, and subdivisions of sections are incorporated in the description of land conveyed by the Federal Government and others.

The Principal Meridians and Base Lines of the United States [1]

Black Hills Meridian and Base Line. (South Dakota)	New Mexico Principal Meridian and Base Line. (New Mexico-Colorado)
Boise Meridian and Base Line. (Idaho)	Point of Beginning and Geographer's Line. (Ohio)
Chickasaw Meridian and Base Line. (Mississippi-Tennessee)	Principal Meridian and Base Line. (Montana)
Choctaw Meridian and Base Line. (Mississippi)	
Cimarron Meridian and Base Line. (Oklahoma)	Salt Lake Meridian and Base Line. (Utah)
Copper River Meridian and Base Line. (Alaska)	San Bernardino Meridian and Base Line. (California-Nevada)
Fairbanks Meridian and Base Line. (Alaska)	Second Principal Meridian and Base Line. (Illinois-Indiana)
Fifth Principal Meridian and Base Line. (Arkansas-Iowa-Minnesota-Missouri-North Dakota-South Dakota)	Seward Principal Meridian and Base Line. (Alaska)
First Principal Meridian and Base Line. (Ohio-Indiana)	Sixth Principal Meridian and Base Line. (Colorado-Kansas-Nebraska-South Dakota-Wyoming)
Fourth Principal Meridian and Base Line. (Illinois)	St. Helena Meridian and Base Line. (Louisiana)
Fourth Principal Meridian and Base Line Wisconsin. (Minnesota-Wisconsin)	St. Stephens Meridian and Base Line. (Alabama-Mississippi)
Gila and Salt River Meridian and Base Line. (Arizona)	Tallahassee Meridian and Base Line. (Florida)
Humboldt Meridian and Base Line. (California)	Third Principal Meridian and Base Line. (Illinois)
Huntsville Meridian and Base Line. (Alabama-Mississippi)	Uintah Special Meridian and Base Line. (Utah)
Indian Meridian and Base Line. (Oklahoma)	Umiat Principal Meridian and Base Line. (Alaska)
Kateel River Principal Meridian and Base Line. (Alaska)	Ute Principal Meridian and Base Line. (Colorado)
Louisiana Meridian and Base Line. (Louisiana-Texas)	Washington Meridian and Base Line. (Mississippi)
Michigan Meridian and Base Line. (Michigan-Ohio)	Willamette Meridian and Base Line. (Oregon-Washington)
Mount Diablo Meridian and Base Line. (California-Nevada)	Wind River Meridian and Base Line. (Wyoming)
Navajo Meridian and Base Line. (Arizona-New Mexico)	

[1] Information courtesy of the U.S. Department of the Interior, Bureau of Land Management.

Public Land Surveys Having No Initial Point as an Origin for Both Township and Range Numbers[1]

Between the Miamis, north of Symmes Purchase. (Ohio)	Scioto River Base. (Ohio)
	Twelve-Mile-Square Reserve. (Ohio)
Muskingum River Survey. (Ohio)	United States Military Survey. (Ohio)
Ohio River Base. (Indiana)	West of the Great Miami. (Ohio)
Ohio River Survey. (Ohio)	

[1] Information courtesy of the U.S. Department of the Interior, Bureau of Land Management.
Sources: Manual of Instructions for the Survey of the Public Lands of the United States, Bureau of Land Management, GPO; Initial Points of the Rectangular Survey System, C. Albert White, 1996. See http://www.blm.gov/wo/st/en/prog/more/cadastralsurvey.html for more information on prinicipal meridians and base lines.

Major Rivers of the World

River	Length (in miles)	River	Length (in miles)
Nile (Africa)	4,160	MacKenzie (Canada)	2,635
Amazon (S. America)	4,000	Mekong (Vietnam)	2,600
Yangtze (China)	3,964	Niger (Africa)	2,590
Yellow (China)	3,395	Yenisey (Russia)	2,543
Ob-Irtysh (Russia)	3,362	Missouri (U.S.)	2,540
Amur (Asia)	2,744	Parana (S. America)	2,485
Lena (Russia)	2,734	Mississippi (U.S.)	2,340
Congo (Africa)	2,718	Murray-Darling (Australia)	2,310

NOTE.—Information compiled from numerous public domain Web sites; references cite different lengths for the same river depending on origin.

Major Rivers of the United States

River	Length (in miles)	River	Length (in miles)
Missouri	2,540	Ohio	1,310
Mississippi	2,340	Red	1,290
Yukon	1,980	Brazos	1,280
Rio Grande	1,900	Columbia	1,240
St. Lawrence	1,900	Snake	1,040
Arkansas	1,460	Platte	990
Colorado	1,450	Pecos	926
Atchafalaya	1,420	Canadian	906

Source: Information courtesy of the U.S. Geological Survey; see http://ga.water.usgs.gov/edu/riversofworld.html.

States, capitals, and counties

The following includes parishes, boroughs, census divisions, districts, islands, municipalities, and municipios of the 50 States, U.S. possessions, and territories. County totals include city counties as defined by the National Association of Counties. See www.naco.org for more information.

ALABAMA (AL) (67 counties)
Capital: Montgomery

Autauga	Cleburne	Fayette	Lowndes	Russell
Baldwin	Coffee	Franklin	Macon	St. Clair
Barbour	Colbert	Geneva	Madison	Shelby
Bibb	Conecuh	Greene	Marengo	Sumter
Blount	Coosa	Hale	Marion	Talladega
Bullock	Covington	Henry	Marshall	Tallapoosa
Butler	Crenshaw	Houston	Mobile	Tuscaloosa
Calhoun	Cullman	Jackson	Monroe	Walker
Chambers	Dale	Jefferson	Montgomery	Washington
Cherokee	Dallas	Lamar	Morgan	Wilcox
Chilton	De Kalb	Lauderdale	Perry	Winston
Choctaw	Elmore	Lawrence	Pickens	
Clarke	Escambia	Lee	Pike	
Clay	Etowah	Limestone	Randolph	

ALASKA (AK) (27 entities: 16 boroughs,* 11 census areas)
Capital: Juneau

Aleutians East*	Juneau*	North Slope*	Wade Hampton
Aleutians West	Kenai Peninsula*	Northwest Arctic*	Wrangell-
Anchorage*	Ketchikan	Prince of Wales-	Petersburg
Bethel	Gateway*	Outer Ketchikan	Yakutat*
Bristol Bay*	Kodiak Island*	Sitka*	Yukon-Koyukuk
Denali*	Lake and	Skagway-Hoonah-	
Dillingham	Peninsula*	Angoon	
Fairbanks	Matanuska-	Southeast	
North Star*	Susitna*	Fairbanks	
Haines*	Nome	Valdez-Cordova	

AMERICAN SAMOA (AS) (5 entities: 2 islands,* 3 districts)
Capital: Pago Pago

Eastern	Manu'a	Rose*	Swains*	Western

ARIZONA (AZ) (15 counties)
Capital: Phoenix

Apache	Gila	La Paz	Navajo	Santa Cruz
Cochise	Graham	Maricopa	Pima	Yavapai
Coconino	Greenlee	Mohave	Pinal	Yuma

ARKANSAS (AR) (75 counties)
Capital: Little Rock

Arkansas	Craighead	Howard	Miller	Randolph
Ashley	Crawford	Independence	Mississippi	St. Francis
Baxter	Crittenden	Izard	Monroe	Saline
Benton	Cross	Jackson	Montgomery	Scott
Boone	Dallas	Jefferson	Nevada	Searcy
Bradley	Desha	Johnson	Newton	Sebastian
Calhoun	Drew	Lafayette	Ouachita	Sevier
Carroll	Faulkner	Lawrence	Perry	Sharp
Chicot	Franklin	Lee	Phillips	Stone
Clark	Fulton	Lincoln	Pike	Union
Clay	Garland	Little River	Poinsett	Van Buren
Cleburne	Grant	Logan	Polk	Washington
Cleveland	Greene	Lonoke	Pope	White
Columbia	Hempstead	Madison	Prairie	Woodruff
Conway	Hot Spring	Marion	Pulaski	Yell

CALIFORNIA (CA) (58 counties)
Capital: Sacramento

Alameda	Imperial	Modoc	San Diego	Solano
Alpine	Inyo	Mono	San Francisco	Sonoma
Amador	Kern	Monterey	San Joaquin	Stanislaus
Butte	Kings	Napa	San Luis	Sutter
Calaveras	Lake	Nevada	Obispo	Tehama
Colusa	Lassen	Orange	San Mateo	Trinity
Contra Costa	Los Angeles	Placer	Santa Barbara	Tulare
Del Norte	Madera	Plumas	Santa Clara	Tuolumne
El Dorado	Marin	Riverside	Santa Cruz	Ventura
Fresno	Mariposa	Sacramento	Shasta	Yolo
Glenn	Mendocino	San Benito	Sierra	Yuba
Humboldt	Merced	San Bernardino	Siskiyou	

COLORADO (CO) (64 counties)
Capital: Denver

Adams	Crowley	Gunnison	Mesa	Rio Blanco
Alamosa	Custer	Hinsdale	Mineral	Rio Grande
Arapahoe	Delta	Huerfano	Moffat	Routt
Archuleta	Denver	Jackson	Montezuma	Saguache
Baca	Dolores	Jefferson	Montrose	San Juan
Bent	Douglas	Kiowa	Morgan	San Miguel
Boulder	Eagle	Kit Carson	Otero	Sedgwick
Broomfield	El Paso	La Plata	Ouray	Summit
Chaffee	Elbert	Lake	Park	Teller
Cheyenne	Fremont	Larimer	Phillips	Washington
Clear Creek	Garfield	Las Animas	Pitkin	Weld
Conejos	Gilpin	Lincoln	Prowers	Yuma
Costilla	Grand	Logan	Pueblo	

CONNECTICUT (CT) (8 counties)
Capital: Hartford

Fairfield	Litchfield	New Haven	Tolland
Hartford	Middlesex	New London	Windham

DELAWARE (DE) (3 counties)
Capital: Dover

Kent	New Castle	Sussex

DISTRICT OF COLUMBIA (DC) (single entity)

FEDERATED STATES OF MICRONESIA (FM) (4 States)
Capital: Palikir

Chuuk	Kosrae	Pohnpei	Yap

FLORIDA (FL) (67 counties)
Capital: Tallahassee

Alachua	Calhoun	De Sota	Gadsden	Hendry
Baker	Charlotte	Dixie	Gilchrist	Hernando
Bay	Citrus	Duval	Glades	Highlands
Bradford	Clay	Escambia	Gulf	Hillsborough
Brevard	Collier	Flagler	Hamilton	Holmes
Broward	Columbia	Franklin	Hardee	Indian River

Jackson	Madison	Okeechobee	Putnam	Suwannee
Jefferson	Manatee	Orange	St. Johns	Taylor
Lafayette	Marion	Osceola	St. Lucie	Union
Lake	Martin	Palm Beach	Santa Rosa	Volusia
Lee	Miami-Dade	Pasco	Sarasota	Wakulla
Leon	Monroe	Pinellas	Seminole	Walton
Levy	Nassau	Polk	Sumter	Washington
Liberty	Okaloosa			

GEORGIA (GA) (159 counties)
Capital: Atlanta

Appling	Cobb	Grady	McDuffie	Sumter
Atkinson	Coffee	Greene	McIntosh	Talbot
Bacon	Colquitt	Gwinnett	Meriwether	Taliaferro
Baker	Columbia	Habersham	Miller	Tattnall
Baldwin	Cook	Hall	Mitchell	Taylor
Banks	Coweta	Hancock	Monroe	Telfair
Barrow	Crawford	Haralson	Montgomery	Terrell
Bartow	Crisp	Harris	Morgan	Thomas
Ben Hill	Dade	Hart	Murray	Tift
Berrien	Dawson	Heard	Muscogee	Toombs
Bibb	Decatur	Henry	Newton	Towns
Bleckley	De Kalb	Houston	Oconee	Treutlen
Brantley	Dodge	Irwin	Oglethorpe	Troup
Brooks	Dooly	Jackson	Paulding	Turner
Bryan	Dougherty	Jasper	Peach	Twiggs
Bulloch	Douglas	Jeff Davis	Pickens	Union
Burke	Early	Jefferson	Pierce	Upson
Butts	Echols	Jenkins	Pike	Walker
Calhoun	Effingham	Johnson	Polk	Walton
Camden	Elbert	Jones	Pulaski	Ware
Candler	Emanuel	Lamar	Putnam	Warren
Carroll	Evans	Lanier	Quitman	Washington
Catoosa	Fannin	Laurens	Rabun	Wayne
Charlton	Fayette	Lee	Randolph	Webster
Chatham	Floyd	Liberty	Richmond	Wheeler
Chattahoochee	Forsyth	Lincoln	Rockdale	White
Chattooga	Franklin	Long	Schley	Whitfield
Cherokee	Fulton	Lowndes	Screven	Wilcox
Clarke	Gilmer	Lumpkin	Seminole	Wilkes
Clay	Glascock	Macon	Spalding	Wilkinson
Clayton	Glynn	Madison	Stephens	Worth
Clinch	Gordon	Marion	Stewart	

GUAM (GU) (single entity)
Capital: Agana

HAWAII (HI) (4 counties)
Capital: Honolulu

Hawaii	Honolulu	Kauai	Maui

IDAHO (ID) (44 counties)
Capital: Boise

Ada	Bonneville	Custer	Kootenai	Owyhee
Adams	Boundary	Elmore	Latah	Payette
Bannock	Butte	Franklin	Lemhi	Power
Bear Lake	Camas	Fremont	Lewis	Shoshone
Benewah	Canyon	Gem	Lincoln	Teton
Bingham	Caribou	Gooding	Madison	Twin Falls
Blaine	Cassia	Idaho	Minidoka	Valley
Boise	Clark	Jefferson	Nez Perce	Washington
Bonner	Clearwater	Jerome	Oneida	

ILLINOIS (IL) (102 counties)
Capital: Springfield

Adams	DuPage	Jo Daviess	McHenry	Saline
Alexander	Edgar	Johnson	McLean	Sangamon
Bond	Edwards	Kane	Menard	Schuyler
Boone	Effingham	Kankakee	Mercer	Scott
Brown	Fayette	Kendall	Monroe	Shelby
Bureau	Ford	Knox	Montgomery	Stark
Calhoun	Franklin	La Salle	Morgan	Stephenson
Carroll	Fulton	Lake	Moultrie	Tazewell
Cass	Gallatin	Lawrence	Ogle	Union
Champaign	Greene	Lee	Peoria	Vermilion
Christian	Grundy	Livingston	Perry	Wabash
Clark	Hamilton	Logan	Piatt	Warren
Clay	Hancock	Macon	Pike	Washington
Clinton	Hardin	Macoupin	Pope	Wayne
Coles	Henderson	Madison	Pulaski	White
Cook	Henry	Marion	Putnam	Whiteside
Crawford	Iroquois	Marshall	Randolph	Will
Cumberland	Jackson	Mason	Richland	Williamson
De Kalb	Jasper	Massac	Rock Island	Winnebago
De Witt	Jefferson	McDonough	St. Clair	Woodford
Douglas	Jersey			

INDIANA (IN) (92 counties)
Capital: Indianapolis

Adams	Elkhart	Jefferson	Noble	Starke
Allen	Fayette	Jennings	Ohio	Steuben
Bartholomew	Floyd	Johnson	Orange	Sullivan
Benton	Fountain	Knox	Owen	Switzerland
Blackford	Franklin	Kosciusko	Parke	Tippecanoe
Boone	Fulton	La Porte	Perry	Tipton
Brown	Gibson	LaGrange	Pike	Union
Carroll	Grant	Lake	Porter	Vanderburgh
Cass	Greene	Lawrence	Posey	Vermillion
Clark	Hamilton	Madison	Pulaski	Vigo
Clay	Hancock	Marion	Putnam	Wabash
Clinton	Harrison	Marshall	Randolph	Warren
Crawford	Hendricks	Martin	Ripley	Warrick
Daviess	Henry	Miami	Rush	Washington
De Kalb	Howard	Monroe	St. Joseph	Wayne
Dearborn	Huntington	Montgomery	Scott	Wells
Decatur	Jackson	Morgan	Shelby	White
Delaware	Jasper	Newton	Spencer	Whitley
Dubois	Jay			

IOWA (IA) (99 counties)
Capital: Des Moines

Adair	Cherokee	Franklin	Johnson	Montgomery
Adams	Chickasaw	Fremont	Jones	Muscatine
Allamakee	Clarke	Greene	Keokuk	O'Brien
Appanoose	Clay	Grundy	Kossuth	Osceola
Audubon	Clayton	Guthrie	Lee	Page
Benton	Clinton	Hamilton	Linn	Palo Alto
Black Hawk	Crawford	Hancock	Louisa	Plymouth
Boone	Dallas	Hardin	Lucas	Pocahontas
Bremer	Davis	Harrison	Lyon	Polk
Buchanan	Decatur	Henry	Madison	Pottawattamie
Buena Vista	Delaware	Howard	Mahaska	Poweshiek
Butler	Des Moines	Humboldt	Marion	Ringgold
Calhoun	Dickinson	Ida	Marshall	Sac
Carroll	Dubuque	Iowa	Mills	Scott
Cass	Emmet	Jackson	Mitchell	Shelby
Cedar	Fayette	Jasper	Monona	Sioux
Cerro Gordo	Floyd	Jefferson	Monroe	Story

Tama	Van Buren	Washington	Winnebago	Worth
Taylor	Wapello	Wayne	Winneshiek	Wright
Union	Warren	Webster	Woodbury	

KANSAS (KS) (105 counties)
Capital: Topeka

Allen	Doniphan	Jackson	Morris	Saline
Anderson	Douglas	Jefferson	Morton	Scott
Atchison	Edwards	Jewell	Nemaha	Sedgwick
Barber	Elk	Johnson	Neosho	Seward
Barton	Ellis	Kearny	Ness	Shawnee
Bourbon	Ellsworth	Kingman	Norton	Sheridan
Brown	Finney	Kiowa	Osage	Sherman
Butler	Ford	Labette	Osborne	Smith
Chase	Franklin	Lane	Ottawa	Stafford
Chautauqua	Geary	Leavenworth	Pawnee	Stanton
Cherokee	Gove	Lincoln	Phillips	Stevens
Cheyenne	Graham	Linn	Pottawatomie	Sumner
Clark	Grant	Logan	Pratt	Thomas
Clay	Gray	Lyon	Rawlins	Trego
Cloud	Greeley	Marion	Reno	Wabaunsee
Coffey	Greenwood	Marshall	Republic	Wallace
Comanche	Hamilton	McPherson	Rice	Washington
Cowley	Harper	Meade	Riley	Wichita
Crawford	Harvey	Miami	Rooks	Wilson
Decatur	Haskell	Mitchell	Rush	Woodson
Dickinson	Hodgeman	Montgomery	Russell	Wyandotte

KENTUCKY (KY) (120 counties)
Capital: Frankfort

Adair	Boyd	Campbell	Crittenden	Franklin
Allen	Boyle	Carlisle	Cumberland	Fulton
Anderson	Bracken	Carroll	Daviess	Gallatin
Ballard	Breathitt	Carter	Edmonson	Garrard
Barren	Breckinridge	Casey	Elliott	Grant
Bath	Bullitt	Christian	Estill	Graves
Bell	Butler	Clark	Fayette	Grayson
Boone	Caldwell	Clay	Fleming	Green
Bourbon	Calloway	Clinton	Floyd	Greenup

Hancock	Knox	Marshall	Nicholas	Shelby
Hardin	Larue	Martin	Ohio	Simpson
Harlan	Laurel	Mason	Oldham	Spencer
Harrison	Lawrence	McCracken	Owen	Taylor
Hart	Lee	McCreary	Owsley	Todd
Henderson	Leslie	McLean	Pendleton	Trigg
Henry	Letcher	Meade	Perry	Trimble
Hickman	Lewis	Menifee	Pike	Union
Hopkins	Lincoln	Mercer	Powell	Warren
Jackson	Livingston	Metcalfe	Pulaski	Washington
Jefferson	Logan	Monroe	Robertson	Wayne
Jessamine	Lyon	Montgomery	Rockcastle	Webster
Johnson	Madison	Morgan	Rowan	Whitley
Kenton	Magoffin	Muhlenberg	Russell	Wolfe
Knott	Marion	Nelson	Scott	Woodford

LOUISIANA (LA) (64 parishes)
Capital: Baton Rouge

Acadia	Concordia	La Salle	Red River	Tangipahoa
Allen	De Soto	Lafayette	Richland	Tensas
Ascension	East Baton	Lafourche	Sabine	Terrebonne
Assumption	Rouge	Lincoln	St. Bernard	Union
Avoyelles	East Carroll	Livingston	St. Charles	Vermilion
Beauregard	East Feliciana	Madison	St. Helena	Vernon
Bienville	Evangeline	Morehouse	St. James	Washington
Bossier	Franklin	Natchitoches	St. John the	Webster
Caddo	Grant	Orleans	Baptist	West Baton
Calcasieu	Iberia	Ouachita	St. Landry	Rouge
Caldwell	Iberville	Plaquemines	St. Martin	West Carroll
Cameron	Jackson	Pointe Coupee	St. Mary	West Feliciana
Catahoula	Jefferson	Rapides	St. Tammany	Winn
Claiborne	Jefferson Davis			

MAINE (ME) (16 counties)
Capital: Augusta

Androscoggin	Hancock	Lincoln	Piscataquis	Waldo
Aroostook	Kennebec	Oxford	Sagadahoc	Washington
Cumberland	Knox	Penobscot	Somerset	York
Franklin				

MARSHALL ISLANDS (MH) (33 municipalities)
Capital: Majuro

Ailinginae	Bokak	Kili	Mejit	Toke
Ailinglaplap	Ebon	Kwajalein	Mili	Ujae
Ailuk	Enewetak	Lae	Namorik	Ujelang
Arno	Erikub	Lib	Namu	Utirik
Aur	Jabat	Likiep	Rongelap	Wotho
Bikar	Jaluit	Majuro	Rongrik	Wotje
Bikini	Jemo	Maloelap		

MARYLAND (MD) (24 counties)
Capital: Annapolis

Allegany	Caroline	Frederick	Montgomery	Talbot
Anne Arundel	Carroll	Garrett	Prince George's	Washington
Baltimore	Cecil	Harford	Queen Anne's	Wicomico
Baltimore City	Charles	Howard	St. Mary's	Worcester
Calvert	Dorchester	Kent	Somerset	

MASSACHUSETTS (MA) (14 counties)
Capital: Boston

Barnstable	Dukes	Hampden	Nantucket	Suffolk
Berkshire	Essex	Hampshire	Norfolk	Worcester
Bristol	Franklin	Middlesex	Plymouth	

MICHIGAN (MI) (83 counties)
Capital: Lansing

Alcona	Cass	Gogebic	Kalamazoo	Marquette
Alger	Charlevoix	Grand	Kalkaska	Mason
Allegan	Cheboygan	Traverse	Kent	Mecosta
Alpena	Chippewa	Gratiot	Keweenaw	Menominee
Antrim	Clare	Hillsdale	Lake	Midland
Arenac	Clinton	Houghton	Lapeer	Missaukee
Baraga	Crawford	Huron	Leelanau	Monroe
Barry	Delta	Ingham	Lenawee	Montcalm
Bay	Dickinson	Ionia	Livingston	Montmorency
Benzie	Eaton	Iosco	Luce	Muskegon
Berrien	Emmet	Iron	Mackinac	Newaygo
Branch	Genesee	Isabella	Macomb	Oakland
Calhoun	Gladwin	Jackson	Manistee	Oceana

Ogemaw	Otsego	Saginaw	Schoolcraft	Washtenaw
Ontonagon	Ottawa	St. Clair	Shiawassee	Wayne
Osceola	Presque Isle	St. Joseph	Tuscola	Wexford
Oscoda	Roscommon	Sanilac	Van Buren	

MINNESOTA (MN) (87 counties)
Capital: St. Paul

Aitkin	Dakota	Lac qui Parle	Norman	Sibley
Anoka	Dodge	Lake	Olmsted	Stearns
Becker	Douglas	Lake of the	Otter Tail	Steele
Beltrami	Faribault	Woods	Pennington	Stevens
Benton	Fillmore	Le Sueur	Pine	Swift
Big Stone	Freeborn	Lincoln	Pipestone	Todd
Blue Earth	Goodhue	Lyon	Polk	Traverse
Brown	Grant	Mahnomen	Pope	Wabasha
Carlton	Hennepin	Marshall	Ramsey	Wadena
Carver	Houston	Martin	Red Lake	Waseca
Cass	Hubbard	McLeod	Redwood	Washington
Chippewa	Isanti	Meeker	Renville	Watonwan
Chisago	Itasca	Mille Lacs	Rice	Wilkin
Clay	Jackson	Morrison	Rock	Winona
Clearwater	Kanabec	Mower	Roseau	Wright
Cook	Kandiyohi	Murray	St. Louis	Yellow
Cottonwood	Kittson	Nicollet	Scott	Medicine
Crow Wing	Koochiching	Nobles	Sherburne	

MISSISSIPPI (MS) (82 counties)
Capital: Jackson

Adams	Clay	Hinds	Lamar	Montgomery
Alcorn	Coahoma	Holmes	Lauderdale	Neshoba
Amite	Copiah	Humphreys	Lawrence	Newton
Attala	Covington	Issaquena	Leake	Noxubee
Benton	DeSoto	Itawamba	Lee	Oktibbeha
Bolivar	Forrest	Jackson	Leflore	Panola
Calhoun	Franklin	Jasper	Lincoln	Pearl River
Carroll	George	Jefferson	Lowndes	Perry
Chickasaw	Greene	Jefferson Davis	Madison	Pike
Choctaw	Grenada	Jones	Marion	Pontotoc
Claiborne	Hancock	Kemper	Marshall	Prentiss
Clarke	Harrison	Lafayette	Monroe	Quitman

Rankin	Stone	Tishomingo	Warren	Wilkinson
Scott	Sunflower	Tunica	Washington	Winston
Sharkey	Tallahatchie	Union	Wayne	Yalobusha
Simpson	Tate	Walthall	Webster	Yazoo
Smith	Tippah			

MISSOURI (MO) (115 counties)
Capital: Jefferson City

Adair	Clay	Iron	Montgomery	St. Clair
Andrew	Clinton	Jackson	Morgan	St. Francois
Atchison	Cole	Jasper	New Madrid	St. Louis
Audrain	Cooper	Jefferson	Newton	St. Louis City
Barry	Crawford	Johnson	Nodaway	Ste. Genevieve
Barton	Dade	Knox	Oregon	Saline
Bates	Dallas	Laclede	Osage	Schuyler
Benton	Daviess	Lafayette	Ozark	Scotland
Bollinger	DeKalb	Lawrence	Pemiscot	Scott
Boone	Dent	Lewis	Perry	Shannon
Buchanan	Douglas	Lincoln	Pettis	Shelby
Butler	Dunklin	Linn	Phelps	Stoddard
Caldwell	Franklin	Livingston	Pike	Stone
Callaway	Gasconade	Macon	Platte	Sullivan
Camden	Gentry	Madison	Polk	Taney
Cape Girardeau	Greene	Maries	Pulaski	Texas
Carroll	Grundy	Marion	Putnam	Vernon
Carter	Harrison	McDonald	Ralls	Warren
Cass	Henry	Mercer	Randolph	Washington
Cedar	Hickory	Miller	Ray	Wayne
Chariton	Holt	Mississippi	Reynolds	Webster
Christian	Howard	Moniteau	Ripley	Worth
Clark	Howell	Monroe	St. Charles	Wright

MONTANA (MT) (56 counties)
Capital: Helena

Beaverhead	Broadwater	Cascade	Daniels	Fallon
Big Horn	Carbon	Chouteau	Dawson	Fergus
Blaine	Carter	Custer	Deer Lodge	Flathead

Gallatin	Lewis and Clark	Musselshell	Ravalli	Sweet Grass
Garfield	Liberty	Park	Richland	Teton
Glacier	Lincoln	Petroleum	Roosevelt	Toole
Golden Valley	Madison	Phillips	Rosebud	Treasure
Granite	McCone	Pondera	Sanders	Valley
Hill	Meagher	Powder River	Sheridan	Wheatland
Jefferson	Mineral	Powell	Silver Bow	Wibaux
Judith Basin	Missoula	Prairie	Stillwater	Yellowstone
Lake				

NEBRASKA (NE) (93 counties)
Capital: Lincoln

Adams	Cuming	Greeley	Loup	Sarpy
Antelope	Custer	Hall	Madison	Saunders
Arthur	Dakota	Hamilton	McPherson	Scotts Bluff
Banner	Dawes	Harlan	Merrick	Seward
Blaine	Dawson	Hayes	Morrill	Sheridan
Boone	Deuel	Hitchcock	Nance	Sherman
Box Butte	Dixon	Holt	Nemaha	Sioux
Boyd	Dodge	Hooker	Nuckolls	Stanton
Brown	Douglas	Howard	Otoe	Thayer
Buffalo	Dundy	Jefferson	Pawnee	Thomas
Burt	Fillmore	Johnson	Perkins	Thurston
Butler	Franklin	Kearney	Phelps	Valley
Cass	Frontier	Keith	Pierce	Washington
Cedar	Furnas	Keya Paha	Platte	Wayne
Chase	Gage	Kimball	Polk	Webster
Cherry	Garden	Knox	Red Willow	Wheeler
Cheyenne	Garfield	Lancaster	Richardson	York
Clay	Gosper	Lincoln	Rock	
Colfax	Grant	Logan	Saline	

NEVADA (NV) (17 counties)
Capital: Carson City

Carson City	Elko	Lander	Mineral	Storey
Churchill	Esmeralda	Lincoln	Nye	Washoe
Clark	Eureka	Lyon	Pershing	White Pine
Douglas	Humboldt			

NEW HAMPSHIRE (NH) (10 counties)
Capital: Concord

Belknap	Cheshire	Grafton	Merrimack	Strafford
Carroll	Coos	Hillsborough	Rockingham	Sullivan

NEW JERSEY (NJ) (21 counties)
Capital: Trenton

Atlantic	Cumberland	Hunterdon	Morris	Somerset
Bergen	Essex	Mercer	Ocean	Sussex
Burlington	Gloucester	Middlesex	Passaic	Union
Camden	Hudson	Monmouth	Salem	Warren
Cape May				

NEW MEXICO (NM) (33 counties)
Capital: Santa Fe

Bernalillo	Dona Ana	Lincoln	Rio Arriba	Sierra
Catron	Eddy	Los Alamos	Roosevelt	Socorro
Chaves	Grant	Luna	San Juan	Taos
Cibola	Guadalupe	McKinley	San Miguel	Torrance
Colfax	Harding	Mora	Sandoval	Union
Curry	Hidalgo	Otero	Santa Fe	Valencia
De Baca	Lea	Quay		

NEW YORK (NY) (62 counties)
Capital: Albany

Albany	Dutchess	Madison	Otsego	Steuben
Allegany	Erie	Monroe	Putnam	Suffolk
Bronx	Essex	Montgomery	Queens	Sullivan
Broome	Franklin	Nassau	Rensselaer	Tioga
Cattaraugus	Fulton	New York	Richmond	Tompkins
Cayuga	Genesee	Niagara	Rockland	Ulster
Chautauqua	Greene	Oneida	St. Lawrence	Warren
Chemung	Hamilton	Onondaga	Saratoga	Washington
Chenango	Herkimer	Ontario	Schenectady	Wayne
Clinton	Jefferson	Orange	Schoharie	Westchester
Columbia	Kings	Orleans	Schuyler	Wyoming
Cortland	Lewis	Oswego	Seneca	Yates
Delaware	Livingston			

NORTH CAROLINA (NC) (100 counties)
Capital: Raleigh

Alamance	Chowan	Guilford	Mitchell	Rutherford
Alexander	Clay	Halifax	Montgomery	Sampson
Alleghany	Cleveland	Harnett	Moore	Scotland
Anson	Columbus	Haywood	Nash	Stanly
Ashe	Craven	Henderson	New Hanover	Stokes
Avery	Cumberland	Hertford	Northampton	Surry
Beaufort	Currituck	Hoke	Onslow	Swain
Bertie	Dare	Hyde	Orange	Transylvania
Bladen	Davidson	Iredell	Pamlico	Tyrrell
Brunswick	Davie	Jackson	Pasquotank	Union
Buncombe	Duplin	Johnston	Pender	Vance
Burke	Durham	Jones	Perquimans	Wake
Cabarrus	Edgecombe	Lee	Person	Warren
Caldwell	Forsyth	Lenoir	Pitt	Washington
Camden	Franklin	Lincoln	Polk	Watauga
Carteret	Gaston	Macon	Randolph	Wayne
Caswell	Gates	Madison	Richmond	Wilkes
Catawba	Graham	Martin	Robeson	Wilson
Chatham	Granville	McDowell	Rockingham	Yadkin
Cherokee	Greene	Mecklenburg	Rowan	Yancey

NORTH DAKOTA (ND) (53 counties)
Capital: Bismarck

Adams	Divide	LaMoure	Pembina	Stark
Barnes	Dunn	Logan	Pierce	Steele
Benson	Eddy	McHenry	Ramsey	Stutsman
Billings	Emmons	McIntosh	Ransom	Towner
Bottineau	Foster	McKenzie	Renville	Traill
Bowman	Golden Valley	McLean	Richland	Walsh
Burke	Grand Forks	Mercer	Rolette	Ward
Burleigh	Grant	Morton	Sargent	Wells
Cass	Griggs	Mountrail	Sheridan	Williams
Cavalier	Hettinger	Nelson	Sioux	
Dickey	Kidder	Oliver	Slope	

NORTHERN MARIANA ISLANDS (MP) (4 municipalities)
Capital: Saipan

Northern Islands	Rota	Saipan	Tinian

OHIO (OH) (88 counties)
Capital: Columbus

Adams	Darke	Hocking	Miami	Sandusky
Allen	Defiance	Holmes	Monroe	Scioto
Ashland	Delaware	Huron	Montgomery	Seneca
Ashtabula	Erie	Jackson	Morgan	Shelby
Athens	Fairfield	Jefferson	Morrow	Stark
Auglaize	Fayette	Knox	Muskingum	Summit
Belmont	Franklin	Lake	Noble	Trumbull
Brown	Fulton	Lawrence	Ottawa	Tuscarawas
Butler	Gallia	Licking	Paulding	Union
Carroll	Geauga	Logan	Perry	Van Wert
Champaign	Greene	Lorain	Pickaway	Vinton
Clark	Guernsey	Lucas	Pike	Warren
Clermont	Hamilton	Madison	Portage	Washington
Clinton	Hancock	Mahoning	Preble	Wayne
Columbiana	Hardin	Marion	Putnam	Williams
Coshocton	Harrison	Medina	Richland	Wood
Crawford	Henry	Meigs	Ross	Wyandot
Cuyahoga	Highland	Mercer		

OKLAHOMA (OK) (77 counties)
Capital: Oklahoma City

Adair	Coal	Harmon	Love	Osage
Alfalfa	Comanche	Harper	Major	Ottawa
Atoka	Cotton	Haskell	Marshall	Pawnee
Beaver	Craig	Hughes	Mayes	Payne
Beckham	Creek	Jackson	McClain	Pittsburg
Blaine	Custer	Jefferson	McCurtain	Pontotoc
Bryan	Delaware	Johnston	McIntosh	Pottawatomie
Caddo	Dewey	Kay	Murray	Pushmataha
Canadian	Ellis	Kingfisher	Muskogee	Roger Mills
Carter	Garfield	Kiowa	Noble	Rogers
Cherokee	Garvin	Latimer	Nowata	Seminole
Choctaw	Grady	Le Flore	Okfuskee	Sequoyah
Cimarron	Grant	Lincoln	Oklahoma	Stephens
Cleveland	Greer	Logan	Okmulgee	Texas

Tillman	Wagoner	Washita	Woods	Woodward
Tulsa	Washington			

OREGON (OR) (36 counties)
Capital: Salem

Baker	Deschutes	Jefferson	Malheur	Umatilla
Benton	Douglas	Josephine	Marion	Union
Clackamas	Gilliam	Klamath	Morrow	Wallowa
Clatsop	Grant	Lake	Multnomah	Wasco
Columbia	Harney	Lane	Polk	Washington
Coos	Hood River	Lincoln	Sherman	Wheeler
Crook	Jackson	Linn	Tillamook	Yamhill
Curry				

PALAU (PW) (16 States)
Capital: Melekeok

Aimeliik	Kayangel	Ngaraard	Ngatpang	Ngiwal
Airai	Koror	Ngarchelong	Ngchesar	Peleliu
Angaur	Melekeok	Ngardmau	Ngeremlengui	Sonsorol
Hatohobei				

PENNSYLVANIA (PA) (67 counties)
Capital: Harrisburg

Adams	Chester	Fulton	McKean	Snyder
Allegheny	Clarion	Greene	Mercer	Somerset
Armstrong	Clearfield	Huntingdon	Mifflin	Sullivan
Beaver	Clinton	Indiana	Monroe	Susquehanna
Bedford	Columbia	Jefferson	Montgomery	Tioga
Berks	Crawford	Juniata	Montour	Union
Blair	Cumberland	Lackawanna	Northampton	Venango
Bradford	Dauphin	Lancaster	Northumberland	Warren
Bucks	Delaware	Lawrence	Perry	Washington
Butler	Elk	Lebanon	Philadelphia	Wayne
Cambria	Erie	Lehigh	Pike	Westmoreland
Cameron	Fayette	Luzerne	Potter	Wyoming
Carbon	Forest	Lycoming	Schuylkill	York
Centre	Franklin			

PUERTO RICO (PR) (78 municipios)
Capital: San Juan

Adjuntas	Cataño	Gurabo	Maunabo	San Germán
Aguada	Cayey	Hatillo	Mayagüez	San Juan
Aguadilla	Ceiba	Hormigueros	Moca	San Lorenzo
Aguas Buenas	Ciales	Humacao	Morovis	San Sebastián
Aibonito	Cidra	Isabela	Naguabo	Santa Isabel
Añasco	Coamo	Jayuya	Naranjito	Toa Alta
Arecibo	Comerío	Juana Díaz	Orocovis	Toa Baja
Arroyo	Corozal	Juncos	Patillas	Trujillo Alto
Barceloneta	Culebra	Lajas	Peñuelas	Utuado
Barranquitas	Dorado	Lares	Ponce	Vega Alta
Bayamón	Fajardo	Las Marías	Quebradillas	Vega Baja
Cabo Rojo	Florida	Las Piedras	Rincón	Vieques
Caguas	Guánica	Loíza	Río Grande	Villalba
Camuy	Guayama	Luquillo	Sabana Grande	Yabucoa
Canóvanas	Guayanilla	Manatí	Salinas	Yauco
Carolina	Guaynabo	Maricao		

RHODE ISLAND (RI) (5 counties)
Capital: Providence

Bristol	Kent	Newport	Providence	Washington

SOUTH CAROLINA (SC) (46 counties)
Capital: Columbia

Abbeville	Cherokee	Fairfield	Lancaster	Orangeburg
Aiken	Chester	Florence	Laurens	Pickens
Allendale	Chesterfield	Georgetown	Lee	Richland
Anderson	Clarendon	Greenville	Lexington	Saluda
Bamberg	Colleton	Greenwood	Marion	Spartanburg
Barnwell	Darlington	Hampton	Marlboro	Sumter
Beaufort	Dillon	Horry	McCormick	Union
Berkeley	Dorchester	Jasper	Newberry	Williamsburg
Calhoun	Edgefield	Kershaw	Oconee	York
Charleston				

SOUTH DAKOTA (SD) (66 counties)
Capital: Pierre

Aurora	Bennett	Brookings	Brule	Butte
Beadle	Bon Homme	Brown	Buffalo	Campbell

Charles Mix	Fall River	Hyde	McPherson	Shannon
Clark	Faulk	Jackson	Meade	Spink
Clay	Grant	Jerauld	Mellette	Stanley
Codington	Gregory	Jones	Miner	Sully
Corson	Haakon	Kingsbury	Minnehaha	Todd
Custer	Hamlin	Lake	Moody	Tripp
Davison	Hand	Lawrence	Pennington	Turner
Day	Hanson	Lincoln	Perkins	Union
Deuel	Harding	Lyman	Potter	Walworth
Dewey	Hughes	Marshall	Roberts	Yankton
Douglas	Hutchinson	McCook	Sanborn	Ziebach
Edmunds				

TENNESSEE (TN) (95 counties)
Capital: Nashville

Anderson	Decatur	Henderson	Maury	Sequatchie
Bedford	DeKalb	Henry	McMinn	Sevier
Benton	Dickson	Hickman	McNairy	Shelby
Bledsoe	Dyer	Houston	Meigs	Smith
Blount	Fayette	Humphreys	Monroe	Stewart
Bradley	Fentress	Jackson	Montgomery	Sullivan
Campbell	Franklin	Jefferson	Moore	Sumner
Cannon	Gibson	Johnson	Morgan	Tipton
Carroll	Giles	Knox	Obion	Trousdale
Carter	Grainger	Lake	Overton	Unicoi
Cheatham	Greene	Lauderdale	Perry	Union
Chester	Grundy	Lawrence	Pickett	Van Buren
Claiborne	Hamblen	Lewis	Polk	Warren
Clay	Hamilton	Lincoln	Putnam	Washington
Cocke	Hancock	Loudon	Rhea	Wayne
Coffee	Hardeman	Macon	Roane	Weakley
Crockett	Hardin	Madison	Robertson	White
Cumberland	Hawkins	Marion	Rutherford	Williamson
Davidson	Haywood	Marshall	Scott	Wilson

TEXAS (TX) (254 counties)
Capital: Austin

Anderson	Archer	Bailey	Bee	Borden
Andrews	Armstrong	Bandera	Bell	Bosque
Angelina	Atascosa	Bastrop	Bexar	Bowie
Aransas	Austin	Baylor	Blanco	Brazoria

Brazos	Dimmit	Henderson	Llano	Real
Brewster	Donley	Hidalgo	Loving	Red River
Briscoe	Duval	Hill	Lubbock	Reeves
Brooks	Eastland	Hockley	Lynn	Refugio
Brown	Ector	Hood	Madison	Roberts
Burleson	Edwards	Hopkins	Marion	Robertson
Burnet	El Paso	Houston	Martin	Rockwall
Caldwell	Ellis	Howard	Mason	Runnels
Calhoun	Erath	Hudspeth	Matagorda	Rusk
Callahan	Falls	Hunt	Maverick	Sabine
Cameron	Fannin	Hutchinson	McCulloch	San Augustine
Camp	Fayette	Irion	McLennan	San Jacinto
Carson	Fisher	Jack	McMullen	San Patricio
Cass	Floyd	Jackson	Medina	San Saba
Castro	Foard	Jasper	Menard	Schleicher
Chambers	Fort Bend	Jeff Davis	Midland	Scurry
Cherokee	Franklin	Jefferson	Milam	Shackelford
Childress	Freestone	Jim Hogg	Mills	Shelby
Clay	Frio	Jim Wells	Mitchell	Sherman
Cochran	Gaines	Johnson	Montague	Smith
Coke	Galveston	Jones	Montgomery	Somervell
Coleman	Garza	Karnes	Moore	Starr
Collin	Gillespie	Kaufman	Morris	Stephens
Collingsworth	Glasscock	Kendall	Motley	Sterling
Colorado	Goliad	Kenedy	Nacogdoches	Stonewall
Comal	Gonzales	Kent	Navarro	Sutton
Comanche	Gray	Kerr	Newton	Swisher
Concho	Grayson	Kimble	Nolan	Tarrant
Cooke	Gregg	King	Nueces	Taylor
Coryell	Grimes	Kinney	Ochiltree	Terrell
Cottle	Guadalupe	Kleberg	Oldham	Terry
Crane	Hale	Knox	Orange	Throckmorton
Crockett	Hall	La Salle	Palo Pinto	Titus
Crosby	Hamilton	Lamar	Panola	Tom Green
Culberson	Hansford	Lamb	Parker	Travis
Dallam	Hardeman	Lampasas	Parmer	Trinity
Dallas	Hardin	Lavaca	Pecos	Tyler
Dawson	Harris	Lee	Polk	Upshur
Deaf Smith	Harrison	Leon	Potter	Upton
Delta	Hartley	Liberty	Presidio	Uvalde
Denton	Haskell	Limestone	Rains	Val Verde
DeWitt	Hays	Lipscomb	Randall	Van Zandt
Dickens	Hemphill	Live Oak	Reagan	Victoria

Walker	Webb	Wilbarger	Winkler	Young
Waller	Wharton	Willacy	Wise	Zapata
Ward	Wheeler	Williamson	Wood	Zavala
Washington	Wichita	Wilson	Yoakum	

UTAH (UT) (29 counties)
Capital: Salt Lake City

Beaver	Duchesne	Kane	San Juan	Utah
Box Elder	Emery	Millard	Sanpete	Wasatch
Cache	Garfield	Morgan	Sevier	Washington
Carbon	Grand	Piute	Summit	Wayne
Daggett	Iron	Rich	Tooele	Weber
Davis	Juab	Salt Lake	Uintah	

VERMONT (VT) (14 counties)
Capital: Montpelier

Addison	Chittenden	Grand Isle	Orleans	Windham
Bennington	Essex	Lamoille	Rutland	Windsor
Caledonia	Franklin	Orange	Washington	

VIRGIN ISLANDS (VI) (3 islands)
Capital: Charlotte Amalie

St. Croix	St. John	St. Thomas

VIRGINIA (VA) (95 counties)
Capital: Richmond

Accomack	Buckingham	Fairfax	Henrico	Mathews
Albemarle	Campbell	Fauquier	Henry	Mecklenburg
Alleghany	Caroline	Floyd	Highland	Middlesex
Amelia	Carroll	Fluvanna	Isle of Wight	Montgomery
Amherst	Charles City	Franklin	James City	Nelson
Appomattox	Charlotte	Frederick	King and Queen	New Kent
Arlington	Chesterfield	Giles	King George	Northampton
Augusta	Clarke	Gloucester	King William	Northumberland
Bath	Craig	Goochland	Lancaster	Nottoway
Bedford	Culpeper	Grayson	Lee	Orange
Bland	Cumberland	Greene	Loudoun	Page
Botetourt	Dickenson	Greensville	Louisa	Patrick
Brunswick	Dinwiddie	Halifax	Lunenburg	Pittsylvania
Buchanan	Essex	Hanover	Madison	Powhatan

Prince Edward	Richmond	Scott	Stafford	Washington
Prince George	Roanoke	Shenandoah	Surry	Westmoreland
Prince William	Rockbridge	Smyth	Sussex	Wise
Pulaski	Rockingham	Southampton	Tazewell	Wythe
Rappahannock	Russell	Spotsylvania	Warren	York

WASHINGTON (WA) (39 counties)
Capital: Olympia

Adams	Douglas	King	Pacific	Stevens
Asotin	Ferry	Kitsap	Pend Oreille	Thurston
Benton	Franklin	Kittitas	Pierce	Wahkiakum
Chelan	Garfield	Klickitat	San Juan	Walla Walla
Clallam	Grant	Lewis	Skagit	Whatcom
Clark	Grays Harbor	Lincoln	Skamania	Whitman
Columbia	Island	Mason	Snohomish	Yakima
Cowlitz	Jefferson	Okanogan	Spokane	

WEST VIRGINIA (WV) (55 counties)
Capital: Charleston

Barbour	Grant	Logan	Nicholas	Summers
Berkeley	Greenbrier	Marion	Ohio	Taylor
Boone	Hampshire	Marshall	Pendleton	Tucker
Braxton	Hancock	Mason	Pleasants	Tyler
Brooke	Hardy	McDowell	Pocahontas	Upshur
Cabell	Harrison	Mercer	Preston	Wayne
Calhoun	Jackson	Mineral	Putnam	Webster
Clay	Jefferson	Mingo	Raleigh	Wetzel
Doddridge	Kanawha	Monongalia	Randolph	Wirt
Fayette	Lewis	Monroe	Ritchie	Wood
Gilmer	Lincoln	Morgan	Roane	Wyoming

WISCONSIN (WI) (72 counties)
Capital: Madison

Adams	Chippewa	Dunn	Iowa	Lafayette
Ashland	Clark	Eau Claire	Iron	Langlade
Barron	Columbia	Florence	Jackson	Lincoln
Bayfield	Crawford	Fond du Lac	Jefferson	Manitowoc
Brown	Dane	Forest	Juneau	Marathon
Buffalo	Dodge	Grant	Kenosha	Marinette
Burnett	Door	Green	Kewaunee	Marquette
Calumet	Douglas	Green Lake	La Crosse	Menominee

Milwaukee	Pierce	Rusk	Taylor	Washington
Monroe	Polk	St. Croix	Trempealeau	Waukesha
Oconto	Portage	Sauk	Vernon	Waupaca
Oneida	Price	Sawyer	Vilas	Waushara
Outagamie	Racine	Shawano	Walworth	Winnebago
Ozaukee	Richland	Sheboygan	Washburn	Wood
Pepin	Rock			

WYOMING (WY) (23 counties)
Capital: Cheyenne

Albany	Crook	Laramie	Platte	Teton
Big Horn	Fremont	Lincoln	Sheridan	Uinta
Campbell	Goshen	Natrona	Sublette	Washakie
Carbon	Hot Springs	Niobrara	Sweetwater	Weston
Converse	Johnson	Park		

Common misspellings

Geographers and cartographers omit the possessive apostrophe in place-names; however, apostrophes appearing in legally constituted names of counties should not be changed.

The names of the following counties are often misspelled and/or confused:

Allegany in Maryland and New York
Alleghany in North Carolina and Virginia
Allegheny in Pennsylvania
Andrew in Missouri
Andrews in Texas
Aransas in Texas
Arkansas in Arkansas
Barber in Kansas
Barbour in Alabama and West Virginia
Brevard in Florida
Broward in Florida
Brooke in West Virginia
Brooks in Georgia and Texas
Bulloch in Georgia
Bullock in Alabama
Burnet in Texas

Burnett in Wisconsin
Cheboygan in Michigan
Sheboygan in Wisconsin
Clarke in Alabama, Georgia, Iowa, Mississippi, and Virginia
Clark in all other States
Coffee in Alabama, Georgia, and Tennessee
Coffey in Kansas
Coal in Oklahoma
Cole in Missouri
Coles in Illinois
Cook in Illinois and Minnesota
Cooke in Texas
Davidson in North Carolina and Tennessee

Davie in North Carolina
Daviess in Indiana, Kentucky,
    and Missouri
Davis in Iowa and Utah
Davison in South Dakota
De Kalb in Alabama, Georgia,
    Illinois, and Indiana
DeKalb in Tennessee and Missouri
Dickenson in Virginia
Dickinson in Iowa, Kansas, and
    Michigan
Dickson in Tennessee
Forrest in Mississippi
Forest in all other States
Glascock in Georgia
Glasscock in Texas
Green in Kentucky and Wisconsin
Greene in all other States
Harford in Maryland
Hartford in Connecticut
Huntingdon in Pennsylvania
Huntington in Indiana
Johnston in North Carolina and
    Oklahoma
Johnson in all other States
Kanabec in Minnesota
Kennebec in Maine
Kearney in Nebraska
Kearny in Kansas
Kenedy in Texas
Linn in Iowa, Kansas, Missouri,
    and Oregon
Lynn in Texas
Loudon in Tennessee
Loudoun in Virginia
Manatee in Florida
Manistee in Michigan
Merced in California
Mercer in all other States

Morton in Kansas
Norton in Kansas
Muscogee in Georgia
Muskogee in Oklahoma
Park in Colorado and Montana
Parke in Indiana
Pottawatomie in Kansas and
    Oklahoma
Pottawattamie in Iowa
Prince George in Virginia
Prince George's in Maryland
Sanders in Montana
Saunders in Nebraska
Smyth in Virginia
Smith in all other States
Stafford in Virginia
Strafford in New Hampshire
Stanley in South Dakota
Stanly in North Carolina
Stark in Illinois, North Dakota,
    and Ohio
Starke in Indiana
Stephens in Georgia, Oklahoma,
    and Texas
Stevens in Kansas, Minnesota,
    and Washington
Storey in Nevada
Story in Iowa
Terrell in Georgia and Texas
Tyrrell in North Carolina
Tooele in Utah
Toole in Montana
Vermillion in Indiana
Vermilion in all other States
Woods in Oklahoma
Wood in all other States
Wyandot in Ohio
Wyandotte in Kansas

19. Congressional Record

Code of laws of the United States and rules for publication of the Congressional Record

TITLE 44, SECTION 901. CONGRESSIONAL RECORD: ARRANGEMENT, STYLE, CONTENTS, AND INDEXES.—The Joint Committee on Printing shall control the arrangement and style of the Congressional Record, and while providing that it shall be substantially a verbatim report of proceedings, shall take all needed action for the reduction of unnecessary bulk. It shall provide for the publication of an index of the Congressional Record semimonthly during and at the close of sessions of Congress.

TITLE 44, SECTION 904. CONGRESSIONAL RECORD: MAPS, DIAGRAMS, ILLUSTRATIONS.—Maps, diagrams, or illustrations may not be inserted in the Record without the approval of the Joint Committee on Printing.

General rules

The rules governing document work (FIC & punc.) apply to the Congressional Record, except as may be noted herein. The same general style should be followed in the permanent (bound) Record as is used in the daily Record. It is important to be familiar with the exceptions and the forms peculiar to the Record.

Much of the data printed in the Congressional Record is forwarded to the GPO via fiber optic transmission using the captured keystrokes of the floor reporters. Element identifier codes are programmatically inserted, and galley output is accomplished without manual intervention. It is not cost effective to prepare the accompanying manuscript as per the GPO STYLE MANUAL and it is too time-consuming to update and change the data once it is already in type form. Therefore, the Record is to be FIC & punc. It is not necessary to stamp the manuscript FIC & punc. because of its volume. However, Record style, as stated in the following rules, will be followed.

Daily and permanent Record texts are set in 8-point type on a 9-point body. Extracts are set in 7-point type on an 8-point body.

An F-dash will be used preceding 8-point cap lines in the proceedings of the Senate and House.

All 7-point extracts and poetry will carry 2 points of space above and below unless heads appear, which generate their own space.

All extracts are set 7 point unless otherwise ordered by the Joint Committee on Printing.

Except as noted below, all communications from the President must be set in 8 point, but if such communications contain extracts, etc., the extracts are set in 7 point.

An address of the President delivered outside of Congress or referred to as an extract is set in 7 point.

A letter from the President to the Senate is set in 7 point when any form of treaty is enclosed that is to be printed in the Record in connection therewith. The letter is set in 7 point whether the treaty follows or precedes it or is separated from it by intervening matter.

In all quoted amendments and excerpts of bills and in reprinting bills, the style and manuscript as printed in the bill will be followed.

Except where otherwise directed, profanity, obscene wording, or extreme vulgarisms are to be deleted and a 3-em dash substituted.

All manuscript submitted in a foreign language will not be printed. It will be returned for translation and resubmitted for printing in the next Record.

Extreme caution must be used in making corrections in manuscript, and no important change will be made without proper authorization.

Observe the lists of names of Senators, Representatives, and Delegates, committees of both Houses, and duplicate names. Changes caused by death, resignation, or otherwise must be noted. There is no excuse for error in the spelling of names of Senators, Representatives, or department officials. In case of doubt, the Congressional Directory will be the authority.

Datelines should be followed on Extensions of Remarks. If any question arises as to the proper date to be used, a supervisor must be consulted.

Indented matter in leaderwork will be 1 em only.

Queries must not be made on proofs.

Capitalization

(See also Chapter 3 "Capitalization Rules")

If the name of the Congressional Record is mentioned, it must be set in caps and small caps and never abbreviated, even when appearing in citations, except in extract matter, then cap/lowercase.

The name of a Senator or a Representative preceding his or her direct remarks is set in caps and is followed by a period with equal spacing to be used.

The name of a Senator or a Representative used in connection with a bill or other paper—that is, in an adjectival sense—is lowercased, as the Hawkins bill, the Fish amendment, etc.; but FISH's amendment, etc.

The names of Members and Members-elect of both Houses of the Congress, including those of the Vice President and Speaker, will be printed in caps and small caps if mention is made of them, except in extract matter.

Deceased Members' names will be set in caps and small caps in eulogies only on the first day the House or Senate is in session following the death of a Member, in a speech carrying date when the Member was eulogized, or on memorial day in the Senate and House. Eulogy day in one House will be treated the same in the other.

Certificates of Senators-elect of a succeeding Congress are usually presented to the current Congress, and in such cases the names of the Senators-elect must be in caps and small caps.

Names of Members of Congress must be set in caps and lowercase in votes, in lists set in columns, in the list of standing and select committees, in contested-election cases, in lists of pairs, and in all parts of tabular matter (head, body, and footnotes).

Observe that the names of all persons not certified Members of Congress are to be set in caps and lowercase; that is, names of secretaries, clerks, messengers, and others.

Names of proposed Federal boards, commissions, services, etc., are capitalized.

Capitalize principal words and quote after each of the following terms: *Address, article, book, caption, chapter heading, editorial, essay, heading, headline, motion picture* or *play* (including TV or radio program), *paper, poem, report, song, subheading, subject, theme,* etc. Also, following the word *entitled,* except with reference to bill titles which are treated as follows: "A bill (or an act) transferring certain functions of the Price Administrator to the Petroleum Administrator for War," etc.

Figures

Follow the manuscript as to the use of numerals. Dollar amounts in Record manuscript are to be followed.

Figures appearing in manuscript as "20 billion 428 million 125 thousand dollars" should be followed.

Tabular matter and leaderwork

Record tables may be set either one or three columns in width, as follows:

One-column table: 14 picas (168 points).

Three-column table: 43½ picas (522 points). Footnote(s) will be set 43½ picas.

All short footnotes should be run in with 2 ems between each.

Italic

Italic, boldface, caps, or small caps shall not be used for emphasis; nor shall unusual indentions be used. This does not apply to literally reproduced quotations from historical, legal, or official documents. If italic other than restricted herein is desired, the words should be underscored and "Fol. ital." written on each folio. Do not construe this to apply to *"Provided," "Provided further," "Ordered," "Resolved," "Be it enacted,"* etc.

Names of vessels must be set in italic, except in headings, where they will be quoted.

The prayer delivered in either House must be set in 8-point roman. If prefaced or followed by a quotation from the Bible, such quotation must be set in 8-point italic. Extracts from the Bible or other literature contained in the body of the prayer will be set in 8-point roman and quoted.

When general or passing mention is made of a case in 8 point, the title is set in roman, as Smith Bros. case. When a specific citation is indicated and reference follows, use italic for title, as *Smith Bros.* case (172 App. Div. 149).

In 8 point manuscript, titles of cases are always set in italic if followed by references. In 7 point, manuscript is followed.

In 8-point matter, when only the title of a case is given, set in roman, as United States versus 12 Diamond Rings.

When *versus* is used in other than legal phrases and for the purposes of showing contrast, it is not abbreviated or set in italic, as "airplanes versus battleships."

Miscellaneous

Do not quote any communication carrying date and signature. However, a letter (or other communication) bearing both date and signature that appears within a letter shall be quoted.

Do not put quotation marks on centerheads in 7-point extracts unless centerheads belong to original matter.

In newspaper extracts, insert place and date at beginning of paragraph. Use caps and small caps for name of place and roman lowercase for spelled-out date. Connect date and extract by a period and an em dash. If date and place are credited in a bracket line above extract, they need not be used again at the beginning of the paragraph.

Each *Whereas* in a preamble must begin a new paragraph. The *Therefore be it* must be preceded by a colon and be run in with the last *Whereas. Be it* will run in with the word *Therefore*, but must not be supplied when not in manuscript. Note the following:

Whereas it has been deemed advisable to, etc.: Therefore be it	*Resolved*, That the committee, etc.

In the titles of legal cases manuscript is followed as to spelling, abbreviations, and use of figures.

Use single punctuation in citations of cases and statutes:

United States v. *12 Diamond Rings* (124 U.S. 329; R.S. p. 310, sec. 1748).

Indent asterisk lines 2 ems on each side. Use five asterisks.

If a title is used as part of the name of an organization, vessel, etc., spell; thus, General Ulysses S. Grant Post No. 76, Grand Army of the Republic.

The order of subdivision of the Constitution of the United States is as follows: article I, section 2, clause 3.

If an exhibit appears at the end of a speech, the head *Exhibit* is set in 7-point caps and small caps.

In extracts containing votes the names must be run in, as Mr. Smith of Texas, AuCoin, and Clay, etc.

In a Senator's or a Representative's remarks, when amendments, sections, etc., are referred to by number, follow the manuscript.

In text references to Senate and House reports and in executive and miscellaneous documents, follow the manuscript.

In headings and text references to resolutions and memorials, follow the manuscript.

In gross or en gros

When a bill comes to final action, in the presentment of amendments collectively for a vote, either the term "*in gross*" or the French equivalent "*en gros*" may be used.

Examples of Congressional Record

USE OF CAPS AND SMALL CAPS

[Note the use of parentheses and brackets in the following examples. Each will be used as submitted, as long as they are consistent throughout.]

Mr. WEBB. (Name all caps when a Member or visitor addresses Senate or House.)

On motion by [or of] Mr. WEBB, it was, etc.

The VICE PRESIDENT resumed the chair.

The PRESIDING OFFICER (Mr. LEVIN). Is there objection?

The SPEAKER called the House to order.

Mr. ETHERIDGE's amendment was adopted.

Mr. HARE. Madam Speaker, I yield to Mr. HOYER.

Mr. HOYER said: If not paired, I would vote "no" on this bill.

A MEMBER. And debate it afterward.

SEVERAL SENATORS. I object.

But: Several Senators addressed the Chair.

Mr. KENNEDY, Mr. WEBB (and others). Let it be read.

The ACTING SECRETARY. In line 11, after the word "*Provided*", it is proposed, etc.

Mrs. CAPPS was recognized, and yielded her time to Mr. CARDOZA.

[When two Members from the same State have the same surname, full name is used.]

On motion of Ms. LINDA T. SÁNCHEZ of California . . .

On motion of Ms. LORETTA SANCHEZ of California . . .

Mr. LINCOLN DIAZ-BALART of Florida and Mr. MARIO DIAZ-BALART of Florida rose to a point of order.

The CHAIRMAN appointed Mr. CAMPBELL of California and Mr. INSLEE as conferees.

[Extracts that consist of colloquies will use caps and small caps for names of persons speaking, as shown below:]

Mr. DEFAZIO. I think this bill is so well understood that no time will be required for its discussion.

Ms. NORTON. Does this bill come from the Committee on Armed Services?

The SPEAKER. It does.

SPECIAL ORDERS GRANTED

By unanimous consent, permission to address the House, following the legislative and any special orders heretofore entered, was granted to:

Mr. HOYER, for 1 hour, on Wednesday, February 2.

Mr. ENGEL (at the request of Mr. HOYER), for 1 hour, on February 2.

(The following Members (at the request of Mr. HALL of New York) and to revise and extend their remarks and include therein extraneous matter:)

Mrs. BACHMANN, for 5 minutes, today.

Mr. HOLDEN, for 5 minutes, today.

Mr. INSLEE, for 60 minutes, today.

[Note the following double action:]

(Mr. HOYER asked and was given permission to extend his remarks at this point in the RECORD and to include extraneous matter.)

(Mr. HOYER addressed the House. His remarks will appear hereafter in the Extensions of Remarks.)

The SPEAKER pro tempore. Under a previous order of the House, the gentleman from Nebraska (Mr. FORTENBERRY) is recognized for 5 minutes.

(Mr. FORTENBERRY addressed the House. His remarks will appear hereafter in the Extensions of Remarks.)

PUNCTUATION

Mr. REID. Mr. President, I call up my amendment which is identified as "unprinted amendment No. 1296," and ask that it be stated.

The bill was reported to the Senate as amended, and the amendment was concurred in.

The bill was reported to the Senate without amendment, ordered to be engrossed for a third reading, read the third time, and passed.

The bill was ordered to be engrossed for a third reading, read the third time, and passed.

[Use this form when title of bill is given:]

The bill was ordered to be engrossed and read the third time, was read the third time, and passed.

The title was amended so as to read: "A bill for the relief of Maude S. Burman."

A motion to reconsider was laid on the table. [House.]

[Use this form when title of bill is not given:]

The bill was ordered to be engrossed and read a third time, was read the third time, and passed, and a motion to reconsider was laid on the table. [House.]

The bill was ordered to be engrossed and read a third time, and passed.

The amendments were ordered to be engrossed and the bill to be read a third time.

The amendment was agreed to, and the bill as amended was ordered to be engrossed and read a third time; and being engrossed, it was accordingly read the third time and passed.

There was no objection, and, by unanimous consent, the Senate proceeded . . .

The question was taken, and the motion was agreed to.

The question being taken, the motion was agreed to.

Ordered to lie on the table and to be printed.

Ms. EDWARDS of Maryland. Mr. Chairman, I move to strike the requisite number of words.

(Ms. EDWARDS of Maryland asked and was given permission to revise and extend her remarks.)

[Note use of interrogation mark in the following:]

Mr. KERRY. Mr. President, what does this mean?—

We have never received a dollar of this amount.

POM-376. A resolution adopted by the House of Representatives of the State of Rhode Island expressing its opposition to federal proposals to authorize increases in the size or weight of commercial motor vehicles; to the Committee on Commerce, Science, and Transportation.

HOUSE RESOLUTION NO. 8296

Whereas, The State of Rhode Island is committed to protecting the safety of motorists on its highways and to protecting taxpayers' investment in our highway infrastructure; and

Whereas, The General Assembly of the State of Rhode Island and Providence Plantations resolved jointly to urge the Congress of the United States to . . .

Resolved, That this House of Representatives of the State of Rhode Island and Providence Plantations hereby reaffirms its opposition to proposals, at all levels of government, that would authorize increases in the size and weight of commercial motor vehicles because of the impact that these increases would have on highway infrastructure, especially on highway infrastructure, especially bridges; and be it further

Resolved, That the Secretary of State be and he hereby is authorized and directed to transmit duly certified copies of this resolution to the President and Vice President of the United States, the Speaker of the United States House of Representatives, the Majority Leader of the United States Senate and the Rhode Island Delegation to the Congress of the United States.

[Note use of italic in title of cases:]

. . . This is the occasion America did not have to consider what other options might guarantee maternal safety while protecting the unborn. This is our national opportunity to reconsider *Roe* v. *Wade*, 410 U.S. 113 (1973).

Roe against Wade and its companion case, *Doe* v. *Bolton*, 410 U.S. 179 (1973), granted abortion the elevated status of a fundamental constitutional right and invalidated almost all effective restrictions on abortion throughout the 9 months of pregnancy . . . .

PARENTHESES AND BRACKETS

[The use of parentheses and brackets will be followed as submitted for acronyms, symbols, or abbreviations.]

This legislation would exempt certain defined Central Intelligence Agency [CIA] operational files from the search and review process of the Freedom of Information Act [FOIA], thus permitting the Agency to respond much more quickly to those FOIA requests which are at all likely to result in the release of information.

Mr. BACA. Madam Speaker, I now yield 5 minutes to the gentleman from Indiana (Mr. HILL).

(Mr. BUTTERFIELD asked and was given permission to revise and extend his remarks in the Record.)

Ms. HARMAN. There is no "may not" about it. Here is the form in which they are printed.

Mr. DOYLE. I am in hopes we shall be able to secure a vote on the bill tonight.

["Vote! Vote!"]

Mr. YOUNG. The Chair rather gets me on that question. [Laughter.] I did not rise. [Cries of "Vote! Vote!"]

Mrs. CAPPS [one of the tellers]. I do not desire to press the point that no quorum has voted.

The CHAIRMAN [after a pause]. If no gentleman claims the floor, the Clerk will proceed with the reading of the bill.

Mr. HALL of Texas. Then he is endeavoring to restrict the liberty of the individual in the disbursement of his own money. [Applause on the Republican side.]

Mr. KENNEDY. Mr. Speaker, I desire to ask unanimous consent that the time of the gentleman—[Cries of "Regular Order!"]

[Laughter.]

The SPEAKER. Is there objection to the consideration of this bill at this time? [After a pause.] There is no objection.

The CHAIRMAN [rapping with his gavel]. Debate is exhausted.

Mr. MORAN of Virginia. Patrick Henry said

Ceasar had his Brutus, Charles I his Cromwell, and George III——

[here he was interrupted by cries of "Treason, Treason"]

and George III may profit by their example. If this be treason, let us make the most of it!

(Mr. MILLER of Florida addressed the Committee [or House]. His remarks will appear hereafter in the Extensions of Remarks.)

[Names of Senators or Representatives appearing in remarks of other Members of Congress should be enclosed in brackets, except in listing of tellers or when some title other than "Mr." is used, as in the following examples:]

Mr. LIEBERMAN. Mr. President, I thank my friend from Rhode Island [Senator WHITEHOUSE] for that magnificent exchange of correspondence between the Hebrew congregation of Newport, RI, and President Washington.

May I say that Senator WHITEHOUSE, in his own bearing and substance, lives out the promise of religious freedom that our first President gave to all Americans.

Perhaps I should say I say that as one of the descendants of the Stock of Abraham who is privileged to be a Member of the Senate today. I thank Senator WHITEHOUSE. I thank Senator COBURN.

I am going to take the liberty, if I may, to speak for a few minutes while we are waiting for either Senator MURKOWSKI, Senators WEBB or MARTINEZ, who are going to read documents before I conclude.

[In Senate manuscript a Senator is referred to as "the Senator from —— [Mr. ——]." Do not supply name and brackets if name does not appear in manuscript.]

[Note that brackets are used only when Mr., etc., appears in manuscript.]

[See also use of Mr., Mrs., Miss, Ms. in explanation of votes under "Pairs."]

VOTING IN THE HOUSE AND IN COMMITTEE OF THE WHOLE

[Note that a dash is used only when a comma is necessary to separate the ayes and noes. If only the ayes or the noes are given, no punctuation is to be used. If the word and is used to connect the ayes and noes, as ayes 52 and noes 65, or 52 ayes and 65 noes, the dash is omitted after the word were or being.]

On the question of ordering the yeas and nays there were 18 ayes and 88 noes.

The House divided; and there were— ayes 52, noes 65.

So (no further count being called for) the amendment of Mr. MORAN of Virginia was not agreed to.

So (two-thirds having voted in favor thereof) the rules were suspended, and the bill was passed.

So (two-thirds not having voted in favor thereof) the motion was rejected.

The CHAIRMAN. The gentleman raises the point of no quorum. The Chair will count. [After counting.]

Two hundred and seventeen present, a quorum. The noes have it, and the amendment is rejected.

The question being taken on the motion of Mr. HOYER to suspend the rules and pass the bill, it was agreed to (two-thirds voting in favor thereof).

So (the affirmative not being one-fifth of the whole vote) the yeas and nays were not ordered.

The question was taken by a viva voice vote, and the Speaker announced that two-thirds appeared to have voted in the affirmative and [after a pause] that the bill was passed.

The yeas and nays were ordered, there being 43 in the affirmative, more than one-fifth of the last vote.

The question being taken on Mr. KENNEDY's motion, there were—ayes 18, noes 35.

The question being taken on concurring in the amendments of the Senate, there were—ayes 101, noes 5.

The question was taken; and on a division [demanded by Mr. HOYER] there were—ayes 17, noes 29.

Mr. HOYER. Mr. Chairman, I demand a recorded vote, and pending that, I make the point of order that a quorum is not present.

The CHAIRMAN. Evidently a quorum is not present.

The Chair announces that pursuant to clause 2, rule XXIII, he will vacate proceedings under the call when a quorum of the Committee appears.

Members will record their presence by electronic device.

The call was taken by electronic device.

☐ 1715

[The above box followed by a four-digit number indicates floor time in the House (5:15 p.m.)]

QUORUM CALL VACATED

The CHAIRMAN. One hundred Members have appeared. A quorum of the Committee of the Whole is present.

Pursuant to rule XXIII, clause 2, further proceedings under the call shall be considered as vacated.

The Committee will resume its business.

The pending business is the demand of the gentleman from Minnesota [Mr. OBERSTAR] for a recorded vote.

A recorded vote was refused.

So the amendment to the amendment offered as a substitute for the amendment was rejected.

The CHAIRMAN. The question is on the amendment offered by the gentleman from Pennsylvania [Mr. ENGLISH] as a substitute for the amendment offered by the gentlewoman from South Dakota [Ms. HERSETH SANDLIN].

The question was taken; and the Chairman announced that the noes appeared to have it.

RECORDED VOTE

Mr. ENGLISH. Mr. Chairman, I demand a recorded vote.

A recorded vote was ordered.

The vote was taken by electronic device, and there were—ayes 228, noes 188, answered "present" 1, not voting 47, as follows

[Roll No. 509]

AYES—228

Abercrombie	Baird	Berman
Ackerman	Baldwin	Berry
Allen	Barrow	Bishop (GA)
Altmire	Bean	Bishop (NY)
Arcuri	Becerra	Blumenauer
Baca	Berkley	Boren

NOES—188

Aderholt	Bartlett (MD)	Blackburn
Akin	Barton (TX)	Blunt
Alexander	Biggert	Boehner
Bachmann	Bilbray	Bonner
Bachus	Bilirakis	Bono Mack
Barrett (SC)	Bishop (UT)	Boozman

ANSWERED "PRESENT"—1

Andrews

NOT VOTING—17

Boswell	Frank (MA)	Inslee
Cooper	Gilchrest	Lucas
Cubin	Herger	Miller, Gary
Doolittle	Hunter	Paul

·

☐ 1311

Mr. RYAN of Wisconsin changed his vote from "aye" to "no."

Ms. WASSERMAN SCHULTZ, Ms. HOOLEY, and Ms. ROS-LEHTINEN changed their vote from "no" to "aye."

[The Speaker's vote is recorded only in the "Ayes" or "Noes." It is never recorded as "not voting."]

[If the Speaker votes, his name is not used, but at the end of the "yeas" or "nays," according to his vote, insert: "The Speaker."

So the amendment offered as a substitute for the amendment was agreed to.

The result of the vote was announced as above recorded.

VOTING BY YEAS AND NAYS

Senate

QUORUM CALL

The clerk will call the roll.

The assistant legislative clerk proceeded to call the roll, and the following Senators entered the Chamber and answered to their names:

[Quorum No. 42]

Akaka	Bennett	Brownback
Alexander	Biden	Bunning
Allard	Bingaman	Burr
Barrasso	Bond	Byrd
Bacus	Boxer	Cantwell
Bayh	Brown	Cardin

The PRESIDING OFFICER [Mr. WEBB]. A quorum is not present.

Mr. REID. Mr. President, I move that the Sergeant at Arms be instructed to require the attendance of absent Senators, and I ask for the yeas and nays on the motion.

THE PRESIDING OFFICER. Is there a sufficient second? There is a sufficient second.

The yeas and nays were ordered.

The PRESIDING OFFICER. The question is on agreeing to the motion of the Senator from Nevada. On this question the yeas and nays have been ordered, and the clerk will call the roll.

The Assistant legislative clerk called the roll.

Mr. DURBIN. I announce that the Senator from Ohio (Mr. BROWN), the Senator from Massachusetts (Mr. KENNEDY), the Senator from Illinois (Mr. OBAMA), the Senator from Arkansas (Mr. PRYOR), and the

Senator from Montana (Mr. TESTER) are necessarily absent.

Mr. KYL. The following Senators are necessarily absent: the Senator from Minnesota (Mr. COLEMAN), the Senator from Nevada (Mr. ENSIGN), the Senator from South Carolina (Mr. GRAHAM), the Senator from New Hampshire (Mr. GREGG), the Senator from Arizona (Mr. McCAIN), the Senator from Alaska (Ms. MURKOWSKI), the Senator from South Dakota (Mr. THUNE), the Senator from Louisiana (Mr. VITTER), and the Senator from Mississippi (Mr. WICKER).

Further, if present and voting, the Senator from Minnesota (Mr. COLEMAN) would have voted "yea."

The result was announced—yeas 76, nays 10, as follows:

[Rollcall Vote No. 163 Leg.]

YEAS—76

Akaka	Conrad	Kohl
Alexander	Corker	Landrieu
Allard	Craig	Lautenberg
Baucus	Dodd	Leahy
Bayh	Dole	Levin
Bennett	Domenici	Lieberman
Biden	Dorgan	Lincoln
Bingaman	Durbin	Lugar
Bond	Feingold	Martinez
Boxer	Feinstein	McCaskill
Brownback	Grassley	McConnell
Byrd	Hagel	Menendez
Cantwell	Harkin	Mikulski
Cardin	Hatch	Murray
Carper	Hutchison	Nelson (FL)
Casey	Inouye	Nelson (NE)
Chambliss	Isakson	Reed
Clinton	Johnson	Reid
Cochran	Kerry	Roberts
Collins	Klobuchar	Rockefeller

Salazar	Snowe	Voinovich
Sanders	Specter	Warner
Schumer	Stabenow	Webb
Sessions	Stevens	Whitehouse
Smith	Sununu	Wyden

NAYS—10

Barrasso	Cornyn	Inhofe
Bunning	Crapo	Kyl
Burr	DeMint	
Coburn	Enzi	

NOT VOTING—14

Brown	Kennedy	Tester
Coleman	McCain	Thune
Ensign	Murkowski	Vitter
Graham	Obama	Wicker
Gregg	Pryor	

So the motion was agreed to.

.

PAIRS

[The word *with* must always be used in pairs in the House, not *and*; and manuscript must be altered to conform thereto, as Mr. Smith with Mr. Jones—*not* Mr. Smith and Mr. Jones. Note use of lowercase for names in list of pairs in House.]

The Clerk announced the following pairs:

On this vote: .

Mr. Abercrombie for, with Mr. Aderholt against.

Until further notice:

Mr. Baca with Mrs. Bachmann.

Mrs. Capps with Mr. Calvert.

Mr. Artur Davis of Alabama with Mr. Lincoln Diaz-Balart of Florida.

Mr. Ackerman with Mr. Young of Alaska.

Mr. HALL of New York, Mrs. DRAKE, Messrs. FOSTER, HILL, and ISRAEL changed their votes from "nay" to "yea."

So the bill was passed.

The result of the vote was announced as above recorded.

A motion to reconsider was laid on the table.   .

Mr. BACA. Mr. Speaker, I voted, but, being paired with the gentlelady from Minnesota, Mrs. BACHMANN, I withdraw my vote.

Mr. ARTUR DAVIS of Alabama. Mr. Speaker, I have a pair with the gentleman from Florida, Mr. LINCOLN DIAZ BALART of Florida, who, if present, would have voted "yea." I voted "nay." I withdraw my vote and vote "present."

[In House pairs do not use brackets when members are referred to by name. In Senate pairs observe the following use of brackets:]

Mr. DOMENICI (when his name was called). I am paired on this question with the senior Senator from Massachusetts [Mr. KENNEDY]. If he were here, I should vote "yea."

CALL OF THE HOUSE   .

Mr. MURTHA. Ms. Speaker, I move a call of the House.

A call of the House was ordered.

The call was taken by electronic device and the following Members responded to their names:

[Roll No. 41]

Abercrombie	Baird	Berman
Ackerman	Baldwin	Berry
Allen	Barrow	Bishop (GA)
Altmire	Bean	Bishop (NY)
Arcuri	Becerra	Blumenauer
Baca	Berkley	Boren

[No reference will be made of the names of those not voting.]

FORMS OF TITLES

[Always in roman lowercase, flush and hang 1 em, if more than two lines.]

H.J. RES. 2

Joint resolution authorizing the Secretary of the Treasury to issue to the public 2 per centum bonds or certificates, etc.

Resolved by the Senate and House of Representatives of the United States of America in Congress assembled, That the . . .

H.R. 4487

A bill to authorize the Rock Island and Southwestern Railway Company to construct a bridge, etc.

Be it enacted by the Senate and House of Representatives of the United States of

America in Congress assembled, That it shall be lawful for the Rock Island and Southwestern Railway Company, a corporation organized under the general incorporation, etc.

ADDRESSES AND SIGNATURES

[No line spacing, street addresses, or ZIP Code numbers are to be used in communications in the Record.]

The Honorable the SECRETARY OF THE ☐☐NAVY.

☐DEAR MR. SECRETARY: This is in response to your letter, etc.

☐☐☐Very sincerely yours,
BILL CLINTON.☐
———
COLUMBIA, MO,☐☐☐
January 17, 2008.☐
Hon. IKE SKELTON,
Cannon House Office Building,
Washington, DC.

☐The President's farm message of today . . . farmers and prevent the spread of this depression to every part of our country.
MISSOURI FARMERS
ASSOCIATION,
F.V. HEINKEL, *President.*
———
JANUARY 20, 2008.☐
Hon. JOHN B. CONNALLY, Jr.,
The Secretary of the Treasury, Department
☐☐*of the Treasury, Washington, DC.*
☐DEAR MR. SECRETARY: Mindful of the tremendous workload, etc.

I would appreciate your comment on the foregoing proposal.

Your proposal seems to be in the best interest of all concerned.

☐☐☐Sincerely yours,
JOHN P. SARBANES,☐☐☐
Member of Congress.☐
———
ALEXANDRIA, MN,☐☐☐
November 10, 2008.☐
Hon. AMY KLOBUCHAR,
Senate Office Building,
Washington, DC.

☐We oppose the nomination of John Smith for Secretary of Agriculture because he resists family farms.

RAYMOND WAGNER.☐
☐BRANDON, MN.
———
JANUARY 17, 1972.☐
Re resignation from committee.
Hon. CARL ALBERT,
The Speaker, U.S. House of Representa-
☐☐*tives, U.S. Capitol, Washington, DC.*

☐DEAR MR. SPEAKER: Having changed my politics from Republican to Democrat, etc.

☐With my best wishes.
☐☐☐Sincerely,
VINCENT J. DELLAY.☐
———
U.S. SENATE,☐☐☐☐☐
PRESIDENT PRO TEMPORE,☐☐☐
Washington, DC, March 17, 2008.☐
To the Senate:

☐Being temporarily absent from the Senate, I appoint Hon. MAX BAUCUS, a Senator from the State of Montana, to perform the duties of the Chair during my absence.

ROBERT C. BYRD,☐☐☐
President pro tempore.☐

DESIGNATION OF SPEAKER PRO TEMPORE

☐The SPEAKER pro tempore laid before the House the following communication from the Speaker:

WASHINGTON, DC,☐☐☐
June 17, 2008.☐
☐I hereby appoint the Honorable RICK LARSEN to act as Speaker pro tempore on this day.

NANCY PELOSI,☐☐☐
Speaker of the House of Representatives.☐
———
☐☐THE INTERNATIONAL UNION OF UNITED☐☐☐
☐☐☐BREWERY, FLOUR, CEREAL, SOFT☐☐☐
☐☐☐DRINKS & DISTILLERY WORKERS OF☐☐☐
☐☐☐AMERICA,
Cincinnati, OH, March 25, 2007.☐
To the Senate of the United States.
To the United States House of Representa-
☐☐*tives.*
☐HONORABLE SIRS: April 7, 2007, being the 60th anniversary of the modification, etc.

[Two to eight independent signatures, with or without titles, are aligned on the left.]

To the Honorable Senate and House of
☐☐*Representatives of the United States of*
☐☐*America Now Assembled at Washington,*
☐☐*DC:*
☐The undersigned, officers of the Navy of the United States, respectfully show unto

your honorable bodies the following information, etc.

JAMES G. GREEN.
W.H. SOUTHERLAND.
THOMAS HARRISON.
F.F. FLETCHER.
ROBERT WHELAN.
C.C. WILSON.

☐Respectfully submitted,
KARL F. FELLER,
   International President.☐
THOMAS RUSCH,
   Director of Organization.☐
ARTHUR GILDEA,
   Secretary-Treasurer.☐
JOSEPH E. BRADY,
   Director of Legislation.☐

[More than eight signatures, with or without titles, are set full measure, caps and lowercase, run in, indented 2 and 3 ems, as follows:]

Gene H. Rosenblum, Cochairman; Paul H. Ray, Cochairman; Cynthia Asplund, James Pedersen, George Doty, Thomas St. Martin; Joan O'Neill; Lloyd Moosebrugger; Sam Kaplan; Ronald Nemer; Dean Potter; Philip Archer; Thomas McDonough; Mrs. Lloyd Moosebrugger; Minnesota Young Democratic Civil Rights Committee.

JOHN SMITH,☐☐☐☐☐
Lieutenant Governor☐☐☐
(For the Governor of Maine).☐

TEXARKANA TEXTILE
MERCHANTS &
MANUFACTURERS'
ASSOCIATION,
JOHN L. JONES,
   Secretary.

CREDITS

[From the Wall Street Journal,
Oct. 31, 2007]

SURVEILLANCE SANITY

(By Benjamin Civiletti, Dick Thornburgh and William Webster)

Following the terrorist attacks of Sept. 11, 2001, President Bush authorized the National Security Agency to target al Qaeda communications into and out of the country. Mr. Bush concluded that this was essential for protecting the country, that using the Foreign Intelligence Surveillance Act would not permit the necessary speed and agility, and that he had the constitutional power to authorize such surveillance without court orders to defend the country.

Since the program became public in 2006, Congress has been asserting appropriate oversight. Few of those who learned the details of the program have criticized its necessity. Instead, critics argued that if the president found FISA inadequate, he should have gone to Congress and gotten the changes necessary to allow the program to proceed under court orders. That process is now underway. The administration has brought the program under FISA, and the Senate Intelligence Committee recently reported out a bill with a strong bipartisan majority of 13–2, that would make the changes to FISA needed for the program to continue. This bill is now being considered by the Senate Judiciary Committee.

POETRY

[If poetry is quoted, each stanza should start with quotation marks, but only the last stanza should end with them. The lines of the poem should align on the left, those that rhyme taking the same indention. Poems are flush left; overs 3 ems; 2 points of space between stanzas, and 2 points of space above and below.]

CASEY AT THE BAT

The outlook wasn't brilliant for the Mudville nine that day:
The score stood four to two, with but one inning more to play.

And then when Cooney died at first, and Barrows did the same,
A pall-like silence fell upon the patrons of the game.

A straggling few got up to go in deep despair.
The rest clung to that hope which springs eternal in the human breast;
They thought, if only Casey could get but a whack at that—
We'd put up even money now, with Casey at the bat.

But Flynn preceded Casey, as did also
Jimmy Blake,
And the former was a hoodoo and the latter
was a cake;
So upon that stricken multitude grim mel-
ancholy sat,
For there seemed but little chance of
Casey's getting to the bat.

But Flynn let drive a single, to the wonder-
ment of all,
And Blake, the much despised, tore the
cover off the ball;
And when the dust had lifted, and the men
saw what had occurred,
There was Jimmy safe at second and Flynn
a-hugging third.

Then from five thousand throats and more
there rose a lusty yell;
It rumbled through the valley, it rattled in
the dell;
It pounded on the mountain and recoiled
upon the flat,
For Casey, mighty Casey, was advancing
to the bat.

There was ease in Casey's manner as he
stepped into his place;
There was pride in Casey's bearing and a
smile lit Casey's face.
And when, responding to the cheers, he
lightly doffed his hat,
No stranger in the crowd could doubt 'twas
Casey at the bat.

Ten thousand eyes were on him as he
rubbed his hands with dirt;
Five thousand tongues applauded when he
wiped them on his shirt.
Then while the writhing pitcher ground
the ball into his hip,
Defiance gleamed in Casey's eye, a sneer
curled Casey's lip.

And now the leather-covered sphere came
hurtling through the air,
And Casey stood a-watching it in haughty
grandeur there.

Close by the sturdy batsman the ball
unheeded sped—
"That ain't my style," said Casey. "Strike
one," the umpire said.

From the benches, black with people, there
went up a muffled roar,
Like the beating of the storm-waves on a
stern and distant shore.
"Kill him! Kill the umpire!" shouted some-
one on the stand;
And it's likely they'd a-killed him had not
Casey raised his hand.

With a smile of Christian charity great
Casey's visage shone;
He stilled the rising tumult; he bade the
game go on;
He signaled to the pitcher, and once more
the dun sphere flew;
But Casey still ignored it, and the umpire
said, "Strike two."

"Fraud!" cried the maddened thousands,
and echo answered fraud;
But one scornful look from Casey and the
audience was awed.
They saw his face grow stern and cold, they
saw his muscles strain,
And they knew that Casey wouldn't let
that ball go by again.

The sneer is gone from Casey's lip, his teeth
are clenched in hate;
He pounds with cruel violence his bat upon
the plate.
And now the pitcher holds the ball, and
now he lets it go,
And now the air is shattered by the force of
Casey's blow.

Oh, somewhere in this favored land the sun
is shining bright;
The band is playing somewhere, and some-
where hearts are light,
And somewhere men are laughing, and
somewhere children shout;
But there is no joy in Mudville—mighty
Casey has struck out.

—Ernest Lawrence Thayer.

EXTRACTS

[Extracts must be set in 7 point unless ordered otherwise by the Joint Committee on
Printing. This does not refer to a casual quotation of a few words or a quotation that would
not make more than 3 lines of 7-point type.
The beginning of the 7-point extract must
start with a true paragraph; 8-point type following is always a paragraph.]

On February 29, Sue Payton, who is
the Air Force's Assistant Secretary
for Acquisition, said at a DOD news
briefing:

We have been extremely open and trans-
parent. We have had a very thorough review
of what we're doing. We've got it nailed.

A week later, she told the House
Appropriations Subcommittee on
Defense:

The Air Force followed a carefully
structured source selection process,—

They what?

designed to provide transparency, maintain
integrity, and ensure a fair competition.

And throughout the last 4 months, Air Force officials have insisted that they selected the cheapest plane that best met their criteria and that they made no mistakes.

[Note, as above, that following an excerpt, the 8 point must begin with a paragraph.]

[An address of the President delivered outside of Congress or referred to as an extract will be set in 7 point.]

SCHEME OF TEXT HEADINGS

[In 8-point, heads are 8-point caps. After the cap head, all sub heads are 7-point small caps, regardless of any perceived hierarchy.

[In 7-point, the progression is as follows (in descending order):

7-point caps and small caps.

7-point small caps.

7-point italic lowercase.

7-point roman caps and lowercase.

7-point roman lowercase.]

USE OF DOUBLE HEADS

This is something which has been entirely overlooked by the . . .

ANALYSIS OF SPECIFIC PROVISIONS OF THE COMMITTEE BILL

AMENDMENTS CHANGING THE INTERSTATE COMMERCE PROVISIONS OF THE ACE

As the law stands today, it applies only to an employee who . . .

EXECUTIVE PROGRAM

ESTATE TAX CONVENTION WITH CANADA

AMENDMENTS SUBMITTED

RECIPROCAL TRADE AGREEMENTS

SPECTER AMENDMENT NO. 1194

HEADS USED IN EXTENSIONS OF REMARKS

DEPARTMENT OF DEFENSE AUTHORIZATION ACT, 2000

SPEECH OF

HON. JOHN CONYERS, JR.

OF MICHIGAN

IN THE HOUSE OF REPRESENTATIVES

Wednesday, February 3, 1999

The House in Committee of the Whole House on the State of the Union had under consideration the bill (H.R. 1401) to authorize appropriations for fiscal year 2000 for the Armed Forces . . .

[The words "Speech of" are to be used only when on manuscript and is an indication that that particular Extension of Remarks is to be inserted in the proceedings of the bound Record of the date used in the heading.]

MISSING CHILDREN

HON. ORRIN G. HATCH

OF UTAH

IN THE SENATE OF THE UNITED STATES

Wednesday, February 3, 1999

Mr. HATCH. Mr. President, I rise before this distinguished assembly to focus additional attention on the tragedy of missing children. The Department of Health and Human Services has estimated that approximately 1.3 million children disappear each year. A significant number do not leave of their own accord. . . .

CONGRESSIONAL PROCEEDINGS

SENATE

TUESDAY, JULY 15, 2008

(Legislative day of Monday, July 14, 2008)[1]

The Senate met at 9:30 a.m., on the expiration of the recess, and was called to order by the Honorable SHELDON WHITEHOUSE, a Senator from the State of Rhode Island.

[Above line to be used only when Senate had been in recess.]

The Senate met at 9:30 a.m., and was called to order by the Honorable BENJAMIN L. CARDIN, a Senator from the State of Maryland.

[Note.—Entire prayer set in 8 point.]

PRAYER

. The Chaplain, Dr. Barry C. Black, offered the following prayer:

Let us pray.

Our Father in heaven, we thank You for the beautiful differences in the human family, for its varied shapes and sizes, its features and colors, its abilities and talents. Deliver us from the forces that would destroy our unity by eliminating our diversity.

Bless the Members of this body. Help them in their debates to distinguish between substance and semantics, between rhetoric and reality. Free them from personal and partisan preoccupations that would defeat their aspirations and deprive Americans of just and equitable solutions. May our lawmakers avoid the works of darkness and put on Your armor of light.

We pray in Your holy Name. Amen.

PLEDGE OF ALLEGIANCE

The Honorable BENJAMIN L. CARDIN led the Pledge of Allegiance, as follows:

[1] To be used only when the Senate had been in recess.

I pledge allegiance to the Flag of the United States of America, and to the Republic for which it stands, one nation under God, indivisible, with liberty and justice for all.

APPOINTMENT OF ACTING PRESIDENT PRO TEMPORE

The PRESIDING OFFICER. The clerk will please read a communication to the Senate from the President pro tempore (Mr. BYRD).

The legislative clerk read the following letter:

U.S. SENATE,
PRESIDENT PRO TEMPORE,
Washington, DC, June 11, 2008.
To the Senate:
Under the provisions of rule I, section 3, of the Standing Rules of the Senate, I hereby appoint the Honorable BENJAMIN L. CARDIN, a Senator from the State of Maryland, to perform the duties of the Chair.
ROBERT C. BYRD,
President pro tempore.

Mr. CARDIN thereupon assumed the chair as Acting President pro tempore.

RECOGNITION OF THE MAJORITY LEADER

The ACTING PRESIDENT pro tempore. The majority leader is recognized.

SCHEDULE

Mr. REID. Mr. President, following my remarks and those of Senator MCCONNELL, there will be a period of morning business for 1 hour, with Senators permitted to speak therein for up to 10 minutes each. The majority will control the first 30 minutes;

the Republicans will control the second 30 minutes.

Following morning business, the Senate will resume consideration of the motion to proceed to S. 3044, the Consumer-First Energy Act. The first 4 hours of debate will be equally divided and controlled in 30-minute alternating blocks of time, with the majority controlling the first 30 minutes and Republicans controlling the next 30 minutes.

Upon conclusion of the controlled time, Senators will be permitted to speak for up to 10 minutes each.

As a reminder, yesterday, I filed cloture on the motion to proceed to S. 3101, the Medicare Improvements for Patients and Providers Act. That cloture vote will occur tomorrow morning.

RESERVATION OF LEADER TIME

The ACTING PRESIDENT pro tempore. Under the previous order, the leadership time is reserved.

MORNING BUSINESS

The ACTING PRESIDENT pro tempore. Under the previous order, the Senate will proceed to a period of morning business for up to 1 hour, with Senators permitted to speak therein for up to 10 minutes each, with the time equally divided and controlled between the two leaders or their designees, with the majority controlling the first half and the Republicans controlling the final half.

Mr. CARDIN. Mr. President, I ask unanimous consent that the order for the quorum call be rescinded.

The PRESIDING OFFICER. Without objection, it is so ordered.

CONCLUSION OF MORNING BUSINESS

The PRESIDING OFFICER. Morning business is now closed.

CONSUMER-FIRST ENERGY ACT OF 2008—MOTION TO PROCEED

The PRESIDING OFFICER. Under the previous order, the Senate will resume consideration of the motion to proceed to S. 3044, which the clerk will report.

The legislative clerk read as follows:

Motion to proceed to S. 3044, a bill to provide energy price relief and hold oil companies and other entities accountable for their actions with regard to high energy prices, and for other purposes.

The PRESIDING OFFICER. The Senator from Maryland is recognized.

Mr. CARDIN. Mr. President, I take this time on behalf of Marylanders who are worried. They are worried because of the high cost of energy. They . . .

CONSUMER-FIRST ENERGY ACT OF 2008—MOTION TO PROCEED— Continued

[Note the use of bullets signifying that which was not spoken on the floor.]

ADDITIONAL STATEMENTS

CONGRATULATING MS. BAILEE CARROLL MAYFIELD

● Mr. BUNNING. Mr. President, today I congratulate Ms. Bailee Carroll Mayfield on receiving the American Veterans, AMVETS, scholarship award. The AMVETS National Scholarship Committee has awarded Ms. Mayfield a $4,000 scholarship after competing successfully against nearly 200 applicants. AMVETS has recognized Ms. Mayfield as an outstanding high school senior exhibiting academic excellence, promise and merit.

The AMVETS organization awards only six scholarships per year. Each scholarship is awarded to a high school senior who is the child or grandchild of a United States veteran, and is seeking a postsecondary education. Ms. Mayfield plans to utilize her scholarship at Eastern Kentucky University to pursue a career in psychology.

Ms. Mayfield has proven herself to be an exemplary student, rightfully receiving the AMVETS Scholarship Award. She is an inspiration to the citizens of Kentucky and to students everywhere. I look forward to seeing all that she will accomplish in the future.●

MESSAGES FROM THE PRESIDENT

Messages from the President of the United States were communicated to the Senate by Mr. Thomas, one of his secretaries.

EXECUTIVE MESSAGES REFERRED

As in executive session the Presiding Officer laid before the Senate messages from the President of the United States submitting sundry nominations which were referred to the appropriate committees.

(The nominations received today are printed at the end of the Senate proceedings.)

REPORT ON THE ISSUANCE OF AN EXECUTIVE ORDER CONTINUING CERTAIN RESTRICTIONS ON NORTH KOREA AND NORTH KOREAN NATIONALS IMPOSED UNDER THE TRADING WITH THE ENEMY ACT—PM 55

The PRESIDING OFFICER laid before the Senate the following message from the President of the United States, together with an accompanying report; which was referred to the Committee on Banking, Housing, and Urban Affairs:

To the Congress of the United States:

Pursuant to the International Emergency Economic Powers Act, as amended (50 U.S.C. 1701 *et seq.*) (IEEPA), I hereby report that I have issued an Executive Order continuing certain restrictions on North Korea and North Korean nationals imposed pursuant to the exercise of authorities under the Trading With the Enemy Act (50 U.S.C. App. 1 *et seq.*) (TWEA). . . .

I am enclosing a copy of the Executive Order and proclamation I have issued.

GEORGE W. BUSH.

THE WHITE HOUSE, *June 26, 2008.*

[The above to be 8 point.]
[When communications from the President contain extracts, etc., such extracts must be in 7 point.]

MESSAGES FROM THE HOUSE

At 12:49 p.m., a message from the House of Representatives, delivered by Mrs. Cole, one of its reading clerks, announced that the House has agreed to the following concurrent resolution, in which it requests the concurrence of the Senate:

H. Con. Res. 377. Concurrent resolution authorizing the use of the rotunda of the Capitol for a ceremony commemorating the 60th Anniversary of the beginning of the integration of the United States Armed Forces.

ENROLLED BILLS SIGNED

At 1:09 p.m., a message from the House of Representatives, delivered by Mrs. Cole, one of its reading clerks, announced that the Speaker has signed the following enrolled bills:

H.R. 6040. An act to amend the Water Resources Development Act of 2007 to clarify the authority of the Secretary of the Army to provide reimbursement for travel expenses incurred by members of the Committee on Levee Safety.

H.R. 6327. An act to amend the Internal Revenue Code of 1986 to extend the funding and expenditure authority of the Airport and Airway Trust Fund, and for other purposes.

The enrolled bills were subsequently signed by the President pro tempore (Mr. BYRD).

At 8:19 p.m., a message from the House of Representatives, delivered by Ms. Niland, one of its reading clerks, announced that the House has passed the following bill, in which it requests the concurrence of the Senate:

H.R. 6377. An act to direct the Commodity Futures Trading Commission to utilize all its authority, including its emergency powers, to curb immediately the role of excessive speculation in any contract market within the jurisdiction and control of the Commodity Futures Trading Commission, on or through which energy futures or swaps are traded, and to eliminate excessive speculation, price distortion, sudden or unreasonable fluctuations or unwarranted changes in prices, or other unlawful activity that is causing major market disturbances that prevent the market from accurately reflecting the forces of supply and demand for energy commodities.

MEASURES REFERRED

The following bills were read the first and the second times by unanimous consent, and referred as indicated:

H.R. 6275. An act to amend the Internal Revenue Code of 1986 to provide individuals temporary relief from the alternative minimum tax, and for other purposes; to the Committee on Finance.

H.R. 6358. An act to require certain standards and enforcement provisions to prevent child abuse and neglect in residential programs, and for other purposes; to the Committee on Health, Education, Labor, and Pensions.

MEASURES PLACED ON THE CALENDAR

The following bill was read the first and second times by unanimous consent, and placed on the calendar:

H.R. 3546. An act to authorize the Edward Byrne Memorial Justice Assistance Grant Program at fiscal year 2006 levels through 2012.

MEASURES READ THE FIRST TIME

The following bills were read the first time:

H.R. 3195. An act to restore the intent and protections of the Americans with Disabilities Act of 1990.

S. 3202. A bill to address record high gas prices at the pump, and for other purposes.

ENROLLED BILL PRESENTED

The Secretary of the Senate reported that on today, June 26, 2008, she had presented to the President of the United States the following enrolled bill:

S. 3180. An act to temporarily extend the programs under the Higher Education Act of 1965.

EXECUTIVE AND OTHER COMMUNICATIONS

The following communications were laid before the Senate, together with accompanying papers, reports, and documents, and were referred as indicated:

EC–6746. A communication from the Under Secretary of Defense (Acquisition, Technology and Logistics), transmitting, pursuant to law, an annual report relative to the conduct of the Defense Acquisition Challenge Program for fiscal year 2007; to the Committee on Armed Services.

REPORT ON CLASSIFIED INFORMATION (S. DOC. NO. 107)

Mr. WARNER. Mr. President, the Committee on Armed Services of the Senate has recently requested the Office of Public Relations of the Department of the Navy to submit to it a report on classified information. The Department of the Navy has complied with the request, and I now present the report and ask that it be published as a Senate document.

The VICE PRESIDENT. Without objection, the report will be printed as a document as requested by the Senator from Virginia.

[Note the insertion of S. Doc. No. — in cases where papers are ordered to be printed as a document. To be inserted only when ordered to be printed or its equivalent is in manuscript.]

Third reading and passage of a bill.

MISSOURI RIVER BRIDGE NEAR ST. CHARLES, MO

The bill (S. 4174) to extend the times for commencing and completing the construction of a bridge across the Missouri River at or near St. Charles, MO, was considered, ordered to be engrossed for a third reading, read the third time, and passed, as follows:

S. 4174

Be it enacted by the Senate and House of Representatives of the United States of America in Congress assembled, That the times for commencing and completing the construction of the bridge across the Missouri River, etc.

GOVERNMENT OF THE TERRITORY OF HAWAII

The Senate proceeded to consider the bill (S. 1881) to amend an act entitled "An act to provide a government for the Territory of Hawaii," approved April 30, 1900, as amended, to establish a Hawaiian Homes Commission, and for other purposes, which had been reported from the Committee on Interior and Insular Affairs with amendments.

The first amendment was, on page 4 line 22, to strike out "Keaaupaha" and insert "Keaaukaha".

The amendment was agreed to.

The next amendment was, on page 6, line 19, after the figure "(1)", to insert "by further authorization of Congress and", so as to make the paragraph read:

(1) by further authorization of Congress and for a period of five years after the first meeting of the Hawaiian Homes Commission only those lands situated on the island of Molokaki, etc.

The Amendment was agreed to.

The bill was ordered to be engrossed for a third reading, read the third time, and passed.

Forms of amendments

The joint resolution (S.J. Res. 4) requesting the President to negotiate a treaty or treaties for the protection of salmon in retrain parts of the Pacific Ocean was announced as next in order.

Mr. INOUYE. Mr. President, I have just had an opportunity to examine this joint resolution. I offer this amendment.

The PRESIDING OFFICER. The Secretary will state the amendment offered by the Senator from Arizona.

The READING CLERK. On page 1, line 11, it is proposed to strike out the words "both within and", so as to make the joint resolution read:

Resolved by the Senate and House of Representatives of the United States of America in Congress assembled, That the President of the United States be, and he is hereby, requested to negotiate on behalf of the United States, as promptly as is practicable, etc.

Mr. REID. Mr. President, I observe in the report of the bill by the chairman of the Foreign Relations Committee that it is reported as a Senate joint resolution. I ask for a modification of it so that it will be a Senate resolution instead of a Senate joint resolution.

The LEGISLATIVE CLERK. It is proposed to strike out "S.J. Res. 4" and insert "S. Res. 85".

The PRESIDING OFFICER. Is there objection to the modification? The Chair hears one and it will be so modified.

Mr. INOUYE. Would it not be necessary to change the resolving clause also? The resolving clause reads:

Resolved by the Senate and House of Representatives of the United States of America in Congress assembled,

The amendment was agreed to.

[Note use of words, figures, and punctuation in the following example. Follow manuscript.]

The next amendment was, on page 34, in line 9, under the heading "Employees' Compensation Commission", before the word "assistants", to strike out "five" and insert "three"; in line 10, after the word "clerks" and before the words "of class 3", to strike out "seven" and insert "five"; in line 11, before the words "of class 2", to strike out "twelve" and insert "nine"; in the same line, before the words "of class 1", to strike out "twenty-seven" and insert "twenty"; in line 12, before the words "at $1.000 each", to strike out "three" and insert "two"; and in line 18, to strike out "$124,940" and insert "$102,590", so as to read:

EMPLOYEE'S COMPENSATION COMMISSION

Salaries: Three Commissioners at $4,000 each; secretary, $2,750; attorney, $4,000; chief statistician, $3,000; chief of accounts, $2,500; accountant, $2,250; claim examiners—chief $2,250, assistant $2,000, assistant $1,800, three assistants at $1,600 each; special agents—two at $1,800 each, two at $1,600 each; clerks—five of class 3, nine of class 2, twenty of class 1, two at $1,000 each; in all $102,590.

Mr. BAYH submitted an amendment intended to be proposed by him to the sundry civil appropriation bill, which was ordered to lie on the table and to be printed, as follows:

Add a new section, as follows: *"That the President of the Senate appoint three Members of the Senate; and the Speaker of the House three Members of the House."*

The Senate resumed the consideration of the bill (H.R. 4075) to limit the immigration of aliens into the United States.

[An executive session usually being open, the following precedes the recess or adjournment heading:]

NATIONAL DRUG CONTROL STRATEGY FOR 2003—PM 15

The PRESIDING OFFICER laid before the Senate the following message from the President of the United

States, together with accompanying report; which was referred to the Committee on the Judiciary.

To the Congress of the United States:

I am pleased to transmit the 2003 National Drug Control Strategy, consistent with the Office of National Drug Control Policy Reauthorization Act of 1998 (12 U.S.C. 1705).

A critical component of our Strategy is to teach young people . . .

GEORGE W. BUSH. ☐
THE WHITE HOUSE, *February 12, 2003.*

To the Senate of the United States:

To the end that I may receive the advice and consent of the Senate to ratification, I transmit herewith a treaty of arbitration and conciliation between the United States and Switzerland, signed at Washington on March 17, 1952.

HARRY S. TRUMAN. ☐
THE WHITE HOUSE, *March 17, 1952.*

[A letter from the President to the Senate is set in 7-point type when any form of treaty is encloses that is to be printed in the Record in connection therewith. The letter is set in 7-point type whether the treaty follows or precedes it or separated from it by intervening matter.]

RECESS UNTIL TOMORROW AT 10:30 A.M.

Mr. REID. Mr. President, I know of no further business to come before the Senate. I move, in accordance with the order previously entered, that the Senate stand in recess until the hour of 10:30 a.m. tomorrow.

The motion was agreed to and, at 7:34 p.m., the Senate recessed until Wednesday, June 18, 2008, at 10:30 a.m.

[After the recess or adjournment the following may appear:]

NOMINATIONS

Executive Nominations received by the Senate.

[Under the heads *Nominations, Confirmations, Withdrawal,* and *Rejection,* the following scheme for subheads is to be followed:

[Heads indicating service, or branch or department of Government and subheads indicating subdivision or type of service—7-point small caps.]

[Subheads indicating new rank of appointee—7-point italic initial cap.

[Text is set in 5 point caps.

[Note: Nominations will be set first name, middle name (or first middle initial), and last name throughout followed by period. Asterisks, if any, precede names as in executive nominations.]

Executive nominations received by the Senate:

DEPARTMENT OF STATE

RICHARD G OLSON, JR., OF NEW MEXICO, A CAREER MEMBER OF THE SENIOR FOREIGN SERVICE, CLASS OF COUNSELOR, TO BE AMBASSADOR EXTRAORDINARY AND PLENIPOTENTIARY OF THE UNITED STATES OF AMERICA TO THE UNITED ARAB REPUBLIC.

DEPARTMENT OF LABOR

BRENT R. OLSON, JR. OF VIRGINIA, TO BE AN ASSISTANT SECRETARY OF LABOR, VICE EMILY STOVER DEROCCO.

IN THE ARMY

THE FOLLOWING NAMED OFFICERS FOR APPOINTMENT TO THE GRADE INDICATED IN THE RESERVE OF THE ARMY UNDER TITLE 10, U.S.C., SECTION 12203:

To be colonel

KENNETH L. BEALE, JR.
THOMAS H. NROUILLARD

CONFIRMATIONS

NATIONAL COMMISSION ON LIBRARIES AND INFORMATION SCIENCE

HAROLD C. CROTTY, OF MICHIGAN, TO BE A MEMBER OF THE NATIONAL COMMISSION.

HOUSE OF REPRESENTATIVES

TUESDAY, SEPTEMBER 9, 2008

[When the Speaker is in the Chair, follow this style.]

The House met at 9:30 a.m.

The Chaplain, the Reverend Daniel P. Coughlin, offered the following prayer:

Water, not only the essential planetary element, O Lord, water itself ushers in new human life. For Your people of covenant, both old and new, the symbol of water is complex, never stable, always fresh and beautiful, sometimes fearful and tragic.

As the Spring of Salvation, we call upon Your Holy Name to calm the waters of anxiety in mid-America. Enable Your people to cross these present waters of disaster and bring them to Your promised land of fruitful plenty.

In the book of Joshua, water upon the fleece is Joshua's own test of Your presence in the midst of trouble; later the way his people take water unto themselves becomes their measurement.

End this waterboarding of America's fields and rural towns even if we can no longer define torture ourselves. By the wellspring of Your Spirit, mix all our human endeavors with our natural resources in such an outstanding victory that believers and unbelievers alike will be touched again as in Joshua's day and acclaim: "Their hearts melted and became as water!"

This is our prayer now and forever. Amen.

[When the Speaker is not in the Chair, follow this style.]

The House met at 12:30 and was called to order by the Speaker pro tempore (Mr. LARSEN of Washington).

---

[1] Head is not used when the Speaker is in the chair. See preceding example.

DESIGNATION OF SPEAKER PRO TEMPORE

The SPEAKER pro tempore laid before the House the following communication from the Speaker:

WASHINGTON, DC,
June 17, 2008.

I hereby appoint the Honorable RICK LARSEN to act as Speaker pro tempore on this day.

NANCY PELOSI,
Speaker of the House of Representatives.

PRAYER[1]

The Chaplain, the Reverend Daniel P. Coughlin, offered the following prayer:

O God, who rules all the world from everlasting to everlasting, during the time given them, help this Congress to set a great agenda for this Nation and its future. Grasping a sense of the urgent needs of Your people, may this week provide a sense of priorities. May the desires of the common good overshadow particular concerns and personal preferences.

Inspire each Member to draw upon his or her best instinct and highest ideal so true goodness overcomes every evil and determined work whittles away at every problem, until this great Nation becomes Your living glory for all the world to see.

Show us the way, fill us with life, and let truth reign, both now and forever. Amen.

THE JOURNAL

The SPEAKER pro tempore. The Chair has examined the Journal of the last day's proceedings and announces to the House his approval thereof.

Pursuant to clause 1, rule I, the Journal stands approved.

PLEDGE OF ALLEGIANCE

The SPEAKER pro tempore. Will the gentleman from Iowa (Mr. BOSWELL) come forward and lead the House in the Pledge of Allegiance.

Mr. BOSWELL led the Pledge of Allegiance as follows:

I pledge allegiance to the Flag of the United States of America, and to the Republic for which it stands, one nation under God, indivisible, with liberty and justice for all.

SWEARING IN OF THE HONORABLE DONNA EDWARDS, OF MARYLAND, AS A MEMBER OF THE HOUSE

Mr. HOYER. Madam Speaker, I ask unanimous consent that the gentlewoman from Maryland, the Honorable DONNA EDWARDS, be permitted to take the oath of office today.

Her certificate of election has not arrived, but there is no contest and no question has been raised with regard to her election.

The SPEAKER. Is there objection to the request of the gentleman from Maryland?

There was no objection.

The SPEAKER. Will Representative-elect EDWARDS and the members of the Maryland delegation present themselves in the well.

Ms. EDWARDS of Maryland appeared at the bar of the house and took the oath of office, as follows:

Do you solemnly swear or affirm that you will support and defend the Constitution of the United States against all enemies, foreign and domestic; that you will bear true faith and allegiance to the same; that you take this obligation freely, without and mental reservation or purpose of evasion; and that you will well and faithfully discharge the duties of the office on which you are about to enter, so help you God.

The SPEAKER. Congratulations. You are now a Member of the 110th Congress.

WELCOMING THE HONORABLE DONNA EDWARDS TO THE HOUSE OF REPRESENTATIVES

[Welcoming speeches follow.]
[Initial speech of new Representative follows.]

ANNOUNCEMENT BY THE SPEAKER

The SPEAKER. Under clause 5(d) of rule XX, the Chair announces to the House that, in light of the administration of the oath of office to the gentlewoman from Maryland (Mrs. EDWARDS), the whole number of the House is 435.

OATH OF OFFICE OF MEMBERS

The oath of office required by the sixth article of the Constitution of the United States, and as provided by section 2 of the act of May 13, 1884 (23 Stat. 22), to be administered to Members, Resident Commissioner, and Delegates or the House of Representatives, the text of which is carried in 5 U.S.C. 3331:

"I, AB, do solemnly swear (or affirm) that I will support and defend the Constitution of the united States against all enemies, foreign and domestic; that you will bear true faith and allegiance to the same; that you take this obligation freely, without and mental reservation or purpose of evasion; and that you will well and faithfully discharge the duties of the office on which you are about to enter, so help you God.

has been subscribed to in person and filed in duplicate with the Clerk of the House of Representatives by the following Member of the 110th Congress, pursuant to Public Law 412 of the 80th Congress entitled "An act to amend section 30 of the Revised Statues of

the United States" (2 U.S.C. 25, approved February 18, 1948:
DONNA F. EDWARDS, 4th District of Maryland

MESSAGE FROM THE SENATE

A message from the Senate by Ms. Curtis, one of its clerks, announced that the Senate concurs in the amendment of the House to the bill (S. 2146) "An Act to authorize the Administrator of the Environmental Protection Agency to accept, as part of a settlement, diesel emission reduction Supplemental Environmental Projects, and for other purposes."

[Above usage occurs when there is only one bill referenced. For more than one bill, use the following style.]

MESSAGE FROM THE SENATE

A message from the Senate by Ms. Curtis, one of its clerks, announced that the Senate has passed without amendment bills and a concurrent resolution of the House of the following titles:

H.R. 430. An act to designate the United States bankruptcy courthouse located at 271 Cadman Plaza East in Brooklyn, New York, as the "Conrad B. Duberstein United States Bankruptcy Courthouse".

H.R. 781. An act to redesignate Lock and Dam No. 5 of the McClellan-Kerr Arkansas River Navigation System near Redfield, Arkansas, authorized by the Rivers and Harbors Act approved July 24, 1946, as the "Colonel Charles D. Maynard Lock and Dam".

H.R. 1019. An act to designate the United States customhouse building located at 31 Gonzalez Clemente Avenue in Mayagüez, Puerto Rico, as the "Rafael Martínez Nadal United States Customhouse Building".

H.R. 2728. An act to designate the station of the United States Border Patrol located at 25762 Madison Avenue in Murrieta, California, as the "Theodore L. Newton, Jr. and George F. Azrak Border Patrol Station".

H.R. 3712. An act to designate the United States courthouse located at 1716 Spielbusch Avenue in Toledo, Ohio, as the "James M. Ashley and Thomas W.L. Ashley United States Courthouse".

H.R. 4140. An act to designate the Port Angeles Federal Building in Port Angeles, Washington, as the "Richard B. Anderson Federal Building".

H. Con. Res. 32. Concurrent resolution honoring the members of the United States Air Force who were killed in the June 25, 1996, terrorist bombing of the Khobar Towers United States military housing compound near Dhahran, Saudi Arabia.

The message also announced that the Senate has passed bills of the following titles in which the concurrence of the House is requested:

S. 2403. An act to designate the new Federal Courthouse, located in the 700 block of East Broad Street, Richmond, Virginia, as the "Spottswood W. Robinson III and Robert R. Merhige, Jr. Federal Courthouse".

S. 2837. An act to designate the United States courthouse located at 225 Cadman Plaza East, Brooklyn, New York, as the "Theodore Roosevelt United States Courthouse".

S. 3009. An act to designate the Federal Bureau of Investigation building under construction in Omaha, Nebraska, as the "J. James Exon Federal Bureau of Investigation Building".

S. 3145. An act to designate a portion of United States Route 20A, located in Orchard Park, New York, as the "Timothy J. Russert Highway".

[Observe that bills from the Senate to the House read *An act*. If the manuscript should read *A bill*, change to *An act* in conformity with this rule, and place number first. Note also the following forms:]

FOOD, CONSERVATION, AND ENERGY ACT OF 2008—VETO MESSAGE FROM THE PRESIDENT OF THE UNITED STATES (H. DOC. NO. 110-125)

The SPEAKER pro tempore laid before the House the following veto message from the President of the United States:

To the House of Representatives:

I am returning herewith without my approval H.R. 6124, the "Food, Conservation, and Energy Act of 2008."

The bill that I vetoed on May 21, 2008, H.R. 2419, which became Public Law

110–234, did not include the title III provisions that are in this bill. . . . For similar reasons, I am vetoing the bill before me today.

GEORGE W. BUSH.
THE WHITE HOUSE, *June 18, 2008.*

The SPEAKER pro tempore. The objections of the President will be spread at large upon the Journal, and the veto message and the bill will be printed as a House document.

The question is, Will the House, on reconsideration, pass the bill, the objections of the President to the contrary notwithstanding?

The gentleman from Minnesota (Mr. PETERSON) is recognized for 1 hour.

[Debate and vote follow.]

MESSAGE FROM THE PRESIDENT

A message in writing from the President of the United States was communicated to the House by Mr. Leomar, one of his secretaries, who also informed the House that on the following dates the President approved and signed bills and a joint resolution of the House of the following titles:

On June 2, 1971:
H.R. 4209. An act to amend the Revised Organic Act of the Virgin Islands.

On June 4, 1971:
H.R. 5765, An act to extend for 6 months the time for filing the comprehensive report of the Commission on the Organization of the Government of the District of Columbia; and

H.J. Res. 583. Joint resolution designating the last full week in July of 1971 as "National Star Route Mail Carriers Week."

[Observe that bills coming from the President take the form of *An act.* This rule must be followed invariably, even if the manuscript reads *A bill.*]

IOWANS UNITED IN TIME OF TROUBLE

(Mr. BOSWELL asked and was given permission to address the House for 1 minute and to revise and extend his remarks.)

Mr. BOSWELL. Mr. Speaker, today I come to share with you that Iowa is in a lot of trouble. We have had extensive floods, etc.

MRS. VIRGINIA THRIFT

Mr. GOSS. Ms. Speaker, by direction of the Committee on House Administration, I offer a privileged resolution (H. Res. 321) and ask for its immediate consideration.

The Clerk read as follows:

H. RES. 321

Resolved, That there shall be paid out of the contingent fund of the House to Mrs. Virginia Thrift, widow of Chester R. Thrift, late an employee of the House, an amount equal to six months' salary compensation at the rate he was receiving at the time of his death, and an additional amount not to exceed $250 to defray funeral expenses of the said Chester R. Thrift.

The Resolution was agreed to.

A motion to reconsider was laid on the table.

BILLS PRESENTED TO THE PRESIDENT

Ms. MATSUI, from the Committee on Rules, reported that that committee did on this day present to the President, for his approval, bills of the House of the following titles:

H.R. 3331. An act for the relief of Harry L. Smith; and

H.R. 3366. An act to amend section 409 of the Interstate Commerce Act, relating to joint rates of freight forwarders and common carriers by motor vehicle.

ENROLLED BILLS SIGNED

Ms. Lorraine C. Miller, Clerk of the House, reported and found truly enrolled bills of the House of the following titles, which were thereupon signed by the Speaker:

H.R. 430. An act to designate the United States bankruptcy courthouse located at 271 Cadman Plaza East in Brooklyn, New

York, as the "Conrad B. Duberstein United States Bankruptcy Courthouse".

H.R. 781. An act to redesignate Lock and Dam No. 5 of the McClellan-Kerr Arkansas River Navigation System near Redfield, Arkansas, authorized by the Rivers and Harbors Act approved July 24, 1946, as the "Colonel Charles D. Maynard Lock and Dam".

H.R. 1019. An act to designate the United States customhouse building located at 31 Gonzalez Clemente Avenue in Mayagüez, Puerto Rico, as the "Rafael Martinez Nadal United States Customhouse Building".

THE COMMON CALENDAR

The SPEAKER. The Clerk will call the first bill on the Private Calendar.

JOHN SIMS

The Clerk called the first bill on the Private Calendar, H.R. 399, for the relief of John Sims.

H.R. 399

Be it enacted by the Senate and House of Representatives of the United States of America in Congress assembled, That the Secretary of the Treasury is authorized and directed to pay to John Sims, Mobile, Alabama, the sum of $5,000.

The SPEAKER. The gentleman from Florida offers an amendment, which the Clerk will report.

The Clerk read as follows:

Amendment by Mr. STEARNS: In line 4, after the word "pay", add a comma and the following words: "out of any money in the Treasury not otherwise appropriated".

The SPEAKER. The question is on agreeing to the amendment.

The amendment was agreed to.

On motion of Mr. STEARNS, a motion to reconsider the vote by which the bill was passed was laid on the [*not upon*] the table.

SENATE BILLS REFERRED

Bills of the Senate of the following titles were taken from the Speaker's table and, under the rule, referred as follows:

S. 2403. An act to designate the new Federal Courthouse, located in the 700 block of East Broad Street, Richmond, Virginia, as the "Spottswood W. Robinson III and Robert R. Merhige, Jr. Federal Courthouse"; to the Committee on Transportation and Infrastructure.

S. 2837. An act to designate the United States courthouse located at 225 Cadman Plaza East, Brooklyn, New York, as the "Theodore Roosevelt United States Courthouse"; to the Committee on Transportation and Infrastructure.

S. 3009. An act to designate the Federal Bureau of Investigation building under construction in Omaha, Nebraska, as the "J. James Exon Federal Bureau of Investigation Building"; to the Committee on Transportation and Infrastructure.

S. 3145. An act to designate a portion of United States Route 20A, located in Orchard Park, New York, as the "Timothy J. Russert Highway"; to the Committee on Transportation and Infrastructure.

[In the reference of Senate acts to House committees the name of the committee will be repeated after the act, though there may be several acts referred to the same committee.]

COMMITTEE OF THE WHOLE HOUSE ON THE STATE OF THE UNION

SAVING ENERGY THROUGH PUBLIC TRANSPORTATION ACT OF 2008

The SPEAKER pro tempore. Pursuant to House Resolution 1304 and rule XVIII, the Chair declares the House in the Committee of the Whole House on the State of the Union for the consideration of the bill, H.R. 6052.

☐ 1408

IN THE COMMITTEE OF THE WHOLE

Accordingly, the House resolved itself into the Committee of the Whole House on the State of the Union for the consideration of the bill (H.R. 6052) to promote increased public transportation use, to promote increased use of alternative fuels in providing public transportation, and for other purposes, with Ms. DeGette in the chair.

The Clerk read the title of the bill.

The CHAIRMAN. Pursuant to the rule, the bill is considered read the first time.

The gentleman from Minnesota (Mr. Oberstar) and the gentleman from Florida (Mr. Mica) each will control 30 minutes.

The Chair recognizes the gentleman from Minnesota.

Mr. OBERSTAR. Madam Chairman, I rise in support of H.R. 6052, the Saving Energy Through Public Transportation Act of 2008. . . .

Mr. MICA. Madam Chairman, I rise today in strong support of H.R. 6052, the "Saving Energy Through Public Transportation Act of 2008". This bill promotes energy savings for all Americans by increasing public transportation use in the United States. . . .

The CHAIRMAN. All time for general debate has expired.

Pursuant to the rule, the bill shall be considered read for amendment under the 5-minute rule.

The text of the bill is as follows:

H.R. 6052

Be it enacted by the Senate and House of Representatives of the United States of America in Congress assembled,

SECTION 1. SHORT TITLE.

This Act may be cited as the "Saving Energy Through Public Transportation Act of 2008".

SEC. 2. FINDINGS.

Congress finds the following:

(1) In 2007, people in the United States took more than 10.3 billion trips using public transportation, the highest level in 50 years. . . .

The CHAIRMAN. No amendment to the bill shall be in order except those printed in House Report 110–734. Each amendment may be offered only in the order printed in the report, by a Member designated in the report, shall be considered read, shall be debatable for the time specified in the report, equally divided and controlled

by the proponent and an opponent, shall not be subject to amendment, and shall not be subject to a demand for division of the question.

AMENDMENT NO. 1 OFFERED BY MR. OBERSTAR

The CHAIRMAN. It is now in order to consider amendment No. 1 printed in House Report 110–734.

Mr. OBERSTAR. Madam Chairman, I have an amendment at the desk.

The CHAIRMAN. The Clerk will designate the amendment.

The text of the amendment is as follows:

Amendment No. 1 offered by Mr. Oberstar:

Page 3, after line 23, insert the following:

(9) Public transportation stakeholders should engage and involve local communities in the education and promotion of the importance of utilizing public transportation. . . .

The CHAIRMAN. Pursuant to House Resolution 1304, the gentleman from Minnesota (Mr. Oberstar) and a Member opposed each will control 5 minutes.

The Chair recognizes the gentleman from Minnesota.

Mr. OBERSTAR. I yield myself such time as I may consume. . . .

I yield back the balance of my time.

Mr. OBERSTAR. I have no further speakers on this amendment, and I yield back the balance of my time.

The CHAIRMAN. The question is on the amendment offered by the gentleman from Minnesota (Mr. Oberstar).

The amendment was agreed to.

The CHAIRMAN. There being no other amendments, under the rule, the Committee rises.

Accordingly, the Committee rose; and the Speaker pro tempore (Mr. Ross) having assumed the chair, Ms. DeGette, Chairman of the Committee of the Whole House on the State of the Union, reported that that Committee, having had under consideration the bill (H.R. 6052) to promote increased public transportation use, to promote increased use of alternative fuels in providing public transportation, and for other purposes, pursuant to House Resolution 1304, she reported the bill back to the House with sundry amendments adopted by the Committee of the Whole.

The SPEAKER pro tempore. Under the rule, the previous question is ordered.

Is a separate vote demanded on any amendment reported from the Committee of the Whole? If not, the Chair will put them en gros.

The amendments were agreed to.

The SPEAKER pro tempore. The question is on the engrossment and third reading of the bill.

The bill was ordered to be engrossed and read a third time, and was read the third time.

The SPEAKER pro tempore. The question is on the passage of the bill.

The question was taken; and the Speaker pro tempore announced that the ayes appeared to have it.

(Voting occurs)

So the bill was passed.

The result of the vote was announced as above recorded.

A motion to reconsider was laid on the table.

CONFERENCE REPORT AND STATEMENT

Conference reports and statements to be set in 7 point.

Use 3-point space before and after conference report and statement.

In the House the names of Members are to be first.

Follow manuscript literally in the report. Observe the form *Amendments numbered 1, 2, 3, etc.*, and when the amendment is to make an independent paragraph, the phrase *And the Senate* [or *House*] *agree to the same* will be a paragraph by itself; otherwise it will be run in after the amendment with a semicolon. Examples of each are given in the report following.

In the statement change *numbered*, when in manuscript, to *No.*, as *amendment No. 1*, but do not supply *No.* or *amendment* if omitted in manuscript; otherwise regular style will prevail.

CONFERENCE REPORT (H. REPT. 97–747)

The committee of conference on the disagreeing votes of the two Houses on the amendments of the Senate to the bill (H.R. 6863) making supplemental appropriations for the fiscal year ending September 30, 1982, and for other purposes, having met, after full and free conference, have agreed to recommend and do recommend to their respective Houses as follows:

That the Senate recede from its amendments numbered 7, 9, 14, 31, 38, 39, 40, 52, 53, 56, 75, 76, 80, 81, 94, 102, 109, 116, 118, 129, 133, 141, 142, 148, 152, 154, 155, 162 163, 164, 171, 173, 179, and 181.

That the House recede from its disagreement to the amendments of the Senate numbered 20, 23, 25, 26, 28, 30, 32, 33, 34, 35, 36, 46, 48, 54, 61, 678, 70, 77, 78, 79, 87, 99, 101, 14, 105, 106, 110, 111, 125, 127, 134, 136, 139, 156, 157, 165, 167, 168, 170, 174, 175, and 176, and agree to the same.

Amendment numbered 16:

That the House recede from its disagreement to the amendment of the Senate numbered 16, and agree to the same with an amendment, as follows:

In lieu of the sum proposed by said amendment insert *$4,400,000*; and the Senate agree to the same.

Amendment numbered 27:

That the House recede from its disagreement to the amendment of the Senate numbered 27, and agree to the same with an amendment, as follows:

In lieu of the sum proposed by said amendment insert $53,700,000; and the Senate agree to the same.

JOHN T. MYERS
(except amendments 54 and 177),
CLARENCE E. MILLER,
LAWRENCE COUGHLIN,
STENY H. HOYER,
GEORGE M. O'BRIEN,
Managers on the Part of the House.
DALE BUMPERS,
DANIEL K. INOUYE,
ERNEST F. HOLLINGS,
TOM HARKIN,
RICHARD H. BRYAN,
J. BENNETT JOHNSON,
RON WYDEN,
PATRICK J. LEAHY,
DIANNE FEINSTEIN,
Managers on the Part of the Senate.

JOINT EXPLANATORY STATEMENT OF THE COMMITTEE OF CONFERENCE

The managers on the part of the House and the Senate at the conference on the disagreeing votes of the two Houses on the amendments of the Senate to the bill (H.R. 6863), making supplemental appropriations for the fiscal year 1982, rescinding certain budget authority, and for other purposes, submit the following joint statement to the House and the Senate in explanation of the effect of the action agreed upon by the managers and recommended in the accompanying conference report:

TITLE I
CHAPTER I—DEPARTMENT OF AGRICULTURE
SOIL CONSERVATION SERVICE
CONSERVATION OPERATIONS

Amendment No. 1: Reported in technical disagreement. The managers on the part of the House will offer a motion to recede and concur in the amendment of the Senate which allows the Soil Conservation Service to exchange a parcel of land in Bellingham, Washington, for other land.

In lieu of the matter inserted by said amendment, insert the following:

FOOD AND NUTRITION SERVICE
CHILD NUTRITION PROGRAMS

If the funds available for Nutrition Education and Training grants authorized under section 19 of the Child Nutrition Act of 1966, as amended, require a ratable reduction in those grants, the minimum grand for each State shall be $50,000.

The managers on the part of the Senate will move to concur in the amendment of the House to the amendment of the Senate.

Committee on Agriculture: Solely for consideration of title I of the House bill and title I of the Senate amendment:

E DE LA GARZA,
THOMAS S. FOLEY,
DAVID R. BOWEN,
FRED RICHMOND,
BILL WAMPLER,
PAUL FINDLEY
(on all matters except as listed below),
TOM HAGEDORN
(on all matters except as listed below),

Amendments

[As figures are used in bills to express sums of money, dates, paragraph numbers, etc., amendments involving such expressions must be set in figures thus: Strike out "$840" and insert "$1,000", etc. for other enumerations, etc., follow the manuscript as the data is picked up from the bill and used for the Record and then picked up from the Record and used for the report.]

EMANUEL F. LENKERSDORF

The Clerk called the bill (H.R. 2520) for the relief of Emanuel F. Lenkersdorf.

There being no objection, the Clerk read the bill as follows:

H.R. 2520

Be it enacted by the Senate and House of Representatives of the United States of America in Congress assembled, That for the purposes of the Immigration and Nationality Act, Emanuel F. Lenkersdorf shall be held and considered to have been lawfully admitted to the United States for permanent residence as of the date of the enactment of this Act, upon payment of the required visa fee. Upon the granting of permanent residence to such alien as provided for in this Act, the Secretary of State shall instruct the proper officer to deduct one number from the total number of immigrant visas and conditional entries which are made available to natives of the country of the alien's birth under paragraphs (1) through (8) of section 203(a) of the Immigration and Nationality Act.

With the following committee amendment:

On page 2, strike lines 4 through 6 and insert in lieu thereof: "which are made available to natives of the country of the alien's birth under section 203(a) of the Immigration and Nationality Act or, if applicable, from the total number of such visas which are made available to such natives under section 202(3) of such Act.".

The committee amendment was agreed to.

The bill was ordered to be engrossed and read a third time, was read the third time, and passed, and a motion to reconsider was laid on the table.

CONTESTED ELECTION, CARTER AGAINST LeCOMPTE—MESSAGE FROM THE CLERK OF THE HOUSE OF REPRESENTATIVES (H. DOC. NO. 235)

The SPEAKER laid before the House the following message from the Clerk of the House of Representatives, which was read and, with the accompanying papers, referred to the Committee on House Administration:

JULY 29, 2008.
The Honorable the SPEAKER,
House of Representatives.

SIR: *I have the honor to lay before the House of Representatives the contest for a seat in the House of Representatives from the Fourth Congressional District of the State of Iowa, Steven V. Carter against Karl M. LeCompte, notice of which has been filed in the office of the Clerk of the House; and also transmit herewith original testimony, papers, and documents relating thereto.*

LEAVE OF ABSENCE

By unanimous consent, leave of absence was granted to:

Mr. CONYERS (at the request of Mr. HOYER) for today on account of personal business.

Mr. ENGEL (at the request of Mr. HOYER) for today on account of a codel flight delay.

Mr. GENE GREEN of Texas (at the request of Mr. HOYER) for today on account of a doctor's appointment.

SPECIAL ORDERS GRANTED

By unanimous consent, permission to address the House, following the legislative program and any special orders heretofore entered, was granted to:

(The following Members (at the request of Ms. WOOLSEY) to revise and extend their remarks and include extraneous material:)

Ms. WOOLSEY, for 5 minutes, today.
Mr. DeFAZIO, for 5 minutes, today.
Ms. KAPTUR, for 5 minutes, today.
Mr. SPRATT, for 5 minutes, today.

(The following Members (at the request of Mr. SMITH of Nebraska) to revise and extend their remarks and include extraneous material:)

Mr. POE, for 5 minutes, June 20, 23 and 24.

Mr. JONES of North Carolina, for 5 minutes, June 20, 23 and 24.

Mr. BISHOP of Utah, for 5 minutes, today and June 18.

Mr. McCOTTER, for 5 minutes, June 19.

ADJOURNMENT

Mr. FORBES. Mr. Speaker, I move that the House do now adjourn.

The motion was agreed to; accordingly (at 9 o'clock and 56 minutes p.m.), under its previous order, the House adjourned until tomorrow, Wednesday, June 18, 2008, at 9:30 a.m.

RECESS

The SPEAKER pro tempore. Pursuant to clause 12(a) of rule I, the Chair declares the House in recess until 2 p.m. today.

Accordingly (at 12 o'clock and 50 minutes p.m.), the House stood in recess until 2 p.m.

□ 1400

AFTER RECESS

The recess having expired, the House was called to order by the Speaker pro tempore (Mr. LARSEN of Washington) at 2 p.m.

[Follow manuscript as to expressing time of adjournment as 6 o'clock and 25 minutes p.m., or 6:25 p.m.]

MOTION TO DISCHARGE COMMITTEE

MARCH 17, 2008.

TO THE CLERK OF THE HOUSE OF REPRESENTATIVES:

Pursuant to clause 4 of rule XXVII, I, PERCY J. PRIEST, move to discharge the Committee on Banking and Currency from the consideration of the bill (H.R. 2887) entitled "A bill transferring certain functions of the Price Administrator, with respect to petroleum and petroleum products, to the petroleum Administrator for War," which was referred to said committee March 7, 2008, in support of which motion the undersigned Members of the House of Representatives affix their signatures, to wit:

1. Percy J. Priest.
2. Oren Harris. . . .
217. William E. Hess.
218. James G. Polk.

This motion was entered upon the Journal, entered in the CONGRESSIOAL RECORD with signatures thereto, and referred to the Calendar of Motions To Discharge Committees, February 29, 2008.

House briefs

[The briefs follow at end of day's proceedings, heads and dashes to be used as shown here. This data is supplied from the House and is printed as submitted.]

EXECUTIVE COMMUNICATIONS, ETC.

Under clause 8 of rule XII, executive communications were taken from the Speaker's table and referred as follows:

7144. A letter from the Congressional Review Coordinator, Department of Agriculture, transmitting the Department's final rule—Consolidation of the Fruit Fly Regulations [Docket No. APHIS–2007–0084] (RIN: 0579–AC57) received June 9, 2008, pursuant to 5 U.S.C. 801(a)(1)(A); to the Committee on Agriculture.

7145. A letter from the Director, Regulatory Management Division, Environmental Protection Agency, transmitting the Agency's final rule—Bifenthrin; Pesticide Tolerances [EPA–HQ–OPP–2007–0535; FRL–8366–4] received June 9, 2008, pursuant to 5 U.S.C. 801(a)(1)(A); to the Committee on Agriculture.

7146. A letter from the Director, Regulatory Management Division, Environmental Protection Agency, transmitting the Agency's final rule—1,3-Dichloropropene and metabolites; Pesticide Tolerance [EPA–HQ–OPP–2007–0637; FRL–8345–1] received April 30, 2008, pursuant to 5 U.S.C. 801(a)(1)(A); to the Committee on Agriculture.

[Use the following form if only one communication is submitted—8 point:]

7147. Under clause 8 of rule XII, a letter from the Director, Regulatory Management Division, Environmental Protection Agency, transmitting the Agency's final rule—(Z)-7,8-epoxy-2-methyloctadecane (Disparlure); Exemption from the Requirement of a Tolerance [EPA–HQ–OPP–2007–0596; FRL–8367–7] received June 9, 2008, pursuant to 5 U.S.C. 801(a)(1)(A), was taken from the Speaker's table, referred to the Committee on Agriculture, and ordered to be printed.

REPORTS OF COMMITTEES ON PUBLIC BILLS AND RESOLUTIONS

Under clause 2 of rule XIII, reports of committees were delivered to the Clerk for printing and reference to the proper calendar, as follows:

Mr. WAXMAN: Committee on Oversight and Government Reform. Supplemental report on H.R. 5781. A bill to provide that 8 of the 12 weeks of parental leave made available to a Federal employee shall be paid leave, and for other purposes. (Rept. 110–624 Pt. 2).

REPORTS OF COMMITTEES ON PUBLIC BILLS AND RESOLUTIONS

Under clause 2 of rule XIII, reports of committees were delivered to the

Clerk for printing and reference to the proper calendar, as follows:

Mr. RAHALL: Committee on Natural Resources. H.R. 2964. A bill to amend the Lacey Act Amendments of 1981 to treat nonhuman primates as prohibited wildlife species under that Act, to make corrections in the provisions relating to captive wildlife offenses under that Act, and for other purposes, with an amendment (Rept. 110–712). Referred to the Committee of the Whole House on the State of the Union.

Mr. RAHALL: Committee on Natural Resources. H.R. 3702. A bill to direct the Secretary of Agriculture to convey certain land in the Beaverhead-Deerlodge National Forest, Montana, to Jefferson County, Montana, for use as a cemetery (Rept. 110–713). Referred to the Committee of the Whole House on the State of the Union.

Mr. RAHALL: Committee on Natural Resources. H.R. 5511. A bill to direct the Secretary of the Interior, acting through the Bureau of Reclamation, to remedy problems caused by a collapsed drainage tunnel in Leadville, Colorado, and for other purposes (Rept. 110–715). Referred to the Committee of the Whole House on the State of the Union.

Mr. THOMPSON of Mississippi: Committee on Homeland Security. House Resolution 1150. Resolution expressing the sense of the House of Representatives that the Transportation Security Administration should, in accordance with the congressional mandate provided for in the Implementing Recommendations of the 9/11 Commission Act of 2007, enhance security against terrorist attack and other security threats to our Nation's rail and mass transit lines, with amendments (Rept. 110–716). Referred to the House Calendar.

[Use above form also when only one report is submitted.]

_____

PUBLIC BILLS AND RESOLUTIONS

Under clause 2 of rule XII, public bills and resolutions were introduced and severally referred, as follows:

By Mr. SHADEGG:

H.R. 6274. A bill to provide an equivalent to habeas corpus protection for persons held under military authority under that part of Cuba leased to the United States; to the Committee on the Judiciary, and in addition to the Committee on Armed Services, for a period to be subsequently

determined by the Speaker, in each case for consideration of such provisions as fall within the jurisdiction of the committee concerned.

By Mr. RANGEL (for himself, Mr. MCDERMOTT, Mr. LEWIS of Georgia, Mr. NEAL of Massachusetts, Mr. POMEROY, Mrs. JONES of Ohio, Mr. BLUMENAUER, Ms. BERKLEY, Mr. CROWLEY, Mr. VAN HOLLEN, Mr. MEEK of Florida, Mr. LEVIN, and Mr. LARSON of Connecticut):

H.R. 6275. A bill to amend the Internal Revenue Code of 1986 to provide individuals temporary relief from the alternative minimum tax, and for other purposes; to the Committee on Ways and Means.

[Use the following form when only one bill or resolution is submitted:]

Under clause 2 of rule XII:

Mr. CAZAYOUX (for himself, Mr. CHILDERS, Ms. WATERS, Mr. THOMPSON of Mississippi, Mr. FRANK of Massachusetts, Mr. CUELLAR, and Mrs. CAPITO) introduced a bill (H.R. 6276) to repeal section 9(k) of the United States Housing Act of 1937; to the Committee on Financial Services.

_____

MEMORIALS

Under clause 3 of rule XII, memorials were presented and referred as follows:

[Use the following form when submitted by the Speaker if *By the Speaker* is not in manuscript:]

327. By the SPEAKER: Memorial of the Legislature of the State of Louisiana, relative to Senate Concurrent Resolution No. 76 memorializing the Congress of the United States to take such actions as are necessary to expedite the reopening of the Arabi branch of the United States Postal Service located in St. Bernard Parish; to the Committee on Oversight and Government Reform.

328. Also, a memorial of the Legislature of the State of Idaho, relative to Senate Joint Memorial No. 114 expressing opposition to S. 40 and H.R. 3200; jointly to the Committees on Financial Services and the Judiciary.

_____

MEMORIALS

Under clause 3 of rule XII,

[Use the following form when only one memorial is submitted:]

326. The SPEAKER presented a memorial of the Legislature of the State of Louisiana, relative to Senate Concurrent Resolution No. 51 memorializing the Congress of the United States to establish a grant program to assist the seafood industry in St. Tammany, St. Bernard, Orleans, and Plaque-mines parishes; to the Committee on Financial Services.

PRIVATE BILLS AND RESOLUTIONS

Under clause 1 of rule XXII, private bills and resolutions were introduced and severally referred as follows:

By Mr. ATKINSON:
H.R. 6583. A bill for the relief of Mohamed Tejpar and Nargis Tejpar; to the Committee on the Judiciary.

By Mr. AuCOIN:
H.R. 6584. A bill for the relief of Celia Maarit Halle; to the Committee of the Judiciary.

[Use the following form when only one bill or resolution is submitted:]

Under clause 1 of rule XXII,

Mr. LANTOS introduced a bill (H.R. 6766) for the relief of Shanna Teresa Millich; which was referred to the Committee on the Judiciary.

ADDITIONAL SPONSORS

Under clause 7 of rule XII, sponsors were added to public bills and resolutions as follows:

H.R. 78: Mr. GARRETT of New Jersey.
H.R. 96: Mr. RANGEL.
H.R. 154: Mr. TOWNS, Mr. FRELINGHUYSEN, Mr. DOYLE, Mr. SPACE, and Mr. LARSON of Connecticut.

[Note.—Set sponsors caps and Members caps and lower case.]

DISCHARGE PETITIONS

Under clause 2 of rule XV, the following discharge petitions were filed:

Petition 10, June 24, 2008, by Mr. JOHN R. "RANDY" KUHL, Jr. on H.R. 5656, was signed by the following Members: John R. "Randy" Kuhl Jr., Doug Lamborn, David Davis, Robert E. Latta, Joseph R. Pitts, Charles W. Boustany, Jr., Ron Paul, Michael T. McCaul, John Kline, Randy Neugebauer, Lynn A. Westmoreland, and Wally Herger.

Petition 11, June 24, 2008, by Mr. THOMAS G. TANCREDO on House Resolution 1240, was signed by the following Members: Thomas G. Tancredo and Jean Schmidt.

DISCHARGE PETITIONS— ADDITIONS OR DELETIONS

The following Members added their names to the following discharge petitions:

Petition 3 by Mr. PENCE on House Resolution 694: Timothy V. Johnson.
Petition 4 by Mr. ADERHOLT on H.R. 3584: Trent Franks.
Petition 5 by Mrs. DRAKE on H.R. 4088: Timothy V. Johnson.

PETITIONS, ETC.

Under clause 3 of rule XII, petitions and papers were laid on the clerk's desk and referred as follows:

283. The SPEAKER presented a petition of the City Council of Compton, CA, relative to Resolution No. 22,564 supporting the Homeowners and Bank Protection Act of 2007; to the Committee on Financial Services.

284. Also, a petition of the California State Lands Commission, relative to a Resolution regarding the taking of marine mammals and sea turtles incidental to power plant operations of once-through cooling power plants in California; to the Committee on Natural Resources.

[Use the following form when only one petition is submitted:]

Under clause 1 of rule XXII,

139. The SPEAKER presented a petition of the Council of the District of Columbia, relative to the Council-adopted resolution entitled, "National Park Service-Georgetown Branch Rail Right-of-Way Acquisition Resolution of 1990"; which was referred to the Committee on the District of Columbia.

AMENDMENTS

Under clause 8 of rule XVIII, proposed amendments were submitted as follows:

H.R. 1328

OFFERED BY: MR. COLE OF OKLAHOMA

AMENDMENT No. 4: Page 341, line 11, after "title." insert the following: "The Federal Government shall not withhold funding.".

CONGRESSIONAL RECORD INDEX

General instructions

Set in 7 point on 8 point, Record measure (168 points, 14 picas).

Cap lines and italic lines are set flush left.

Entries are indented 1 em, with overs 2 ems.

Bill introductions are to be identified as to sponsor or cosponsor.

Bullet following page number in index identifies unspoken material.

Pages are identified as S (Senate), H (House), and E (Extensions).

Pages in bound Record index are entered numerically, without S, H, or E prefixes.

Abbreviations and acronyms—
(for use on notation of content line)

Abbreviations

Streets: St.; Ave.; Ct.; Dr.; Blvd.; Rd.; Sq.; Ter.

Names: Jr.; Sr.; II (etc.)

Businesses: Co.; Corp. (includes all Federal corporations); Inc.; Ltd.; Bros.

States: See rule 9.13.

Dept. of Agriculture	Sec. of Agriculture.
Dept. of Commerce	Sec. of Commerce.
Dept. of Defense	Sec. of Defense.
Dept. of Education	Sec. of Education.
Dept. of Energy	Sec. of Energy.
Dept. of Health and Human Services	Sec. of Health and . . .
Dept. of Homeland Security	Sec. of Homeland Security
Dept. of Housing and Urban Development	Sec. of Housing and . . .
Dept. of the Interior	Sec. of the Interior.
Dept. of Justice	Attorney General.
Dept. of Labor	Sec. of Labor.
Dept. of State	Sec. of State.
Dept. of Transportation	Sec. of Transportation.
Dept. of the Treasury	Sec. of the Treasury.
Dept. of Veterans Affairs	Sec. of Veterans Affairs.

Acronyms

Agency for International Development .... AID
Acquired Immunodeficiency Syndrome .... AIDS
American Association of Retired Persons .... AARP
American Bar Association .... ABA
American Civil Liberties Union .... ACLU
American Federation of Labor and Congress of Industrial Organizations .... AFL–CIO
American Medical Association .... AMA
British Broadcasting Corp .... BBC
Bureau of Alcohol, Tobacco, Firearms and Explosives .... ATF
Bureau of Indian Affairs .... BIA
Bureau of Land Management .... BLM
Bureau of Labor Statistics .... BLS
Cable News Network .... CNN
Cable Satellite Public Affairs Network .... C–SPAN
Central Intelligence Agency .... CIA
Civil Service Retirement System .... CSRS
Civilian Health and Medical Program of the Uniformed Services .... CHAMPUS
Commodity Credit Corp CCC
Commodity Futures Trading Commission .... CFTC
Comprehensive Environmental Response, Compensation and Liability Act ..... CERCLA
Congressional Budget Office .... CBO
Consolidated Omnibus Budget Reconciliation Act .... COBRA
Consumer Product Safety Commission .... CPSC
Daughters of the American Revolution .... DAR
Deoxyribonucleic acid .... DNA
Disabled American Veterans .... DAV
Drug Enforcement Administration .... DEA
Employee Retirement Income Security Act .... ERISA
Environmental Protection Agency .... EPA
Equal Employment Opportunity Commission .... EEOC
Export-Import Bank .... Eximbank
Federal Aviation Administration .... FAA
Federal Bureau of Investigation .... FBI
Federal Communications Commission .... FCC
Federal Crop Insurance Corp .... FCIC
Federal Deposit Insurance Corp .... FDIC
Federal Election Commission .... FEC
Federal Emergency Management Agency .... FEMA
Federal Employee Retirement System .... FERS

Federal Energy Regulatory Commission..FERC
Federal Housing Administration ....FHA
Federal Insurance Contribution Act...FICA
Federal National Mortgage Association...Fannie Mae
Federal Reserve System...FRS
Federal Trade Commission..FTC
Food and Drug Administration..FDA
General Agreement on Tariffs and Trade ....GATT
General Services Administration...GSA
Government Accountability Office...GAO
Government Printing Office..GPO
Gross national product ....GNP
Health maintenance organization(s) ....HMO(s)
Human immunodeficiency virus ....HIV
Internal Revenue Service..IRS
International Business Machines Corp...IBM
International Monetary Fund...IMF
International Trade Commission...ITC
Legal Services Corp...LSC
Low-Income Home Energy Assistance Program..LIHEAP
Missing in action...MIA(s)
National Aeronautics and Space Administration ....NASA
National Association for the Advancement of Colored People......................NAACP
National Broadcasting Co..NBC
National Collegiate Athletic Association..NCAA
National Institute of Standards and Technology ....NIST
National Institutes of Health...NIH
National Labor Relations Board ....NLRB
National Oceanic and Atmospheric Administration..NOAA
National Railroad Passenger Corp..Amtrak
National Rifle Association ....NRA
National Security Council..NSC
National Science Foundation ....NSF
National Transportation Safety Board ....NTSB
North American Free Trade Agreement..NAFTA
North Atlantic Treaty Organization...NATO
Nuclear Regulatory Commission ....NRC
Occupational Safety and Health Administration ....OSHA
Office of Management and Budget..OMB
Office of Personnel Management...OPM
Office of Thrift Supervision ....OTS
Organization of American States ....OAS
Organization of Petroleum Exporting Countries..OPEC

Spacing

Biweekly Record index folioed in upper right and left corner; no extra spacing.

Bound Record index folioed in upper right and left corner; no extra spacing.

History of Bills folioed in upper right and left corner using H.B. numbers; no extra spacing.

Bound History of Bills folioed in lower right and left corner, first folio numerically higher than the last folio of index; no extra spacing.

Capitalization

Capitalize principal words after these formats:

Addresses

Analyses

Appendices

Articles and editorials

Biographies

Book reviews

Booklets

Brochures

Conference reports

Descriptions

Documents	Prayers by visitors
Essays	Prefaces
Essays: Voice of Democracy	Press releases
Eulogies	Proclamations
Explanations	Reports
Factsheets	Report filed
Forewords	Resolutions of ratification
Histories	Résumés
Homilies	Sermons
Hymns	Sngs
Memorandums	Statements
Messages	Studies
Oaths of office	Summaries
Pamphlets	Surveys
Papers	Synopses
Platforms	Testimonies
Poems	Transcripts
Prayers	Treaties

Lowercase after these formats:

Advertisements	Commentaries
Affidavits	Comments
Agenda	Communications from
Agreements	Communiques
Amendments	Comparisons
Announcements	Cost estimates
Appointments	Court decisions
Awards	Court documents
Bills and resolutions	Declarations
Bills and resolutions cosponsored	Dedications
Bills and resolutions introduced	Definitions
Bills and resolutions relative to	Descriptions
Briefs	Designated acting Presidents pro tempore
Briefings	Designated acting Speaker pro tempore
Broadcasts	Digests
Bulletins	Dispatches
Certificates of election	Examples
Chronologies	Excerpts
Citations	Executive orders
Civilian	Financial statements
Cloture motions	Granted
Colloquies	Granted in the House

Granted in the Senate
Guidelines
Hearings
Inscriptions
Interviews
Introductions
Invocations
Journals
Letters
Lists
Meetings
Military
Motions
Newsletters
Notices
Obituaries
Opinion polls
Orders
Outlines
Petitions
Petitions and memorials
Press conferences
Privilege of the floor
Programs
Projects
Proposals
Questionnaires
Questions
Questions and answers
Quotations
Recorded
Regulations
Remarks
Remarks in House
Remarks in House relative to
Remarks in Senate
Remarks in Senate relative to
Resignations
Resolutions by organizations
Results
Reviews
Rollcalls
Rosters
Rules
Rulings of the chair
Schedules
Subpoena notices
Subpoenas
Tables
Tests
Texts of
Transmittals
Tributes
Voting record

Punctuation

Comma precedes folio figures.

If numbers of several bills are given, use this form: (see S. 24, 25); (see H.R. 217, 218), etc.; that is, do not repeat S. or H.R. with each number.

In consecutive numbers (more than two) use an en dash to connect first with last: S46–S48, 518–520.

Quotes are used for book titles.

A 3-em dash is used as a ditto for word or words leading up to colon:

Taxation: capital gains rates
————earned income tax credit
————rates

Roman and italic

Use italic for Members of Congress descriptive data:

CARDIN, BENJAMIN L. *(a Senator from Maryland)*;
EMANUEL, RAHM *(a Representative from Illinois).*

Names of vessels in italic:

Brooklyn (U.S.S.);
Savannah (vessel);
Columbia (space shuttle).

Flush cap lines

All cap lines are separate entries. They are set flush with overs indented 2 ems:

CARDIN, BENJAMIN *(a Senator from Maryland)*

EMANUEL, RAHM *(a Representative from Illinois)*

PRESIDENT OF THE UNITED STATES (George W. Bush)

VICE PRESIDENT OF THE UNITED STATES (Richard B. Cheney)

COMMITTEE ON FOREIGN AFFAIRS (House)

COMMITTEE ON FOREIGN RELATIONS (Senate)

FARMERS *see* AGRICULTURE

SENATE *related term(s)* COMMITTEES OF THE SENATE; LEGISLATIVE
    BRANCH OF THE GOVERNMENT; MEMBERS OF CONGRESS; VOTES
    IN SENATE

DEPARTMENT OF THE INTERIOR *related term(s)* BUREAU OF LAND
    MANAGEMENT, BUREAU OF RECLAMATION

PRESIDENTIAL APPOINTMENTS

VOTES IN HOUSE

VOTES IN SENATE

No. XII

Congressional Record Index

PROCEEDINGS AND DEBATES OF THE 107th CONGRESS, SECOND SESSION

Vol. 154   JULY 21 TO AUGUST 8, 2008   *Nos. 119 to 132*

NOTE.—For debate and action on bills and resolutions see "History of Bills and Resolutions" at end of Index, under numbers referred to in Index entry.

NOTE: Elements in brackets which follow page numbers in the Index refer to the dates of the Congressional Record in which those pages may be found. Unspoken material is indicated by a bullet (•).

AARP (ORGANIZATION)

Letters
Evaluate and extend the basic pilot program for employment eligibility confirmation and ensure protection of Social Security beneficiaries, H7592 [30JY]

Press releases
Medicare Trigger Ignores Real Problem-Skyrocketing Health Care Costs, H7125 [24JY]

ABERCROMBIE, NEIL (*a Representative from Hawaii*)

Bills and resolutions cosponsored
Armed Forces: tribute to the 28th Infantry Division (see H. Con. Res. 390), H7308 [29JY]
Bulgaria: independence anniversary (see H. Res. 1383), H7630 [30JY]
Bureau of Prisons: provide stab-resistant personal body armor to all correctional officers and require such officers to wear such armor while on duty (see H.R. 6462), H6734 [21JY]
Diseases: improve and enhance research and programs on cancer survivorship (see H.R. 4450), H7308 [29JY]
Education: strengthen communities through English literacy, civic education, and immigrant integration programs (see H.R. 6617), H7164 [24JY]
Medicare: ensure more timely access to home health services for beneficiaries (see H.R. 6826), H7808 [1AU]
——replace the prescription drug benefit with a revised and simplified program for all beneficiaries (see H.R. 6800), H7807 [1AU]
Motor vehicles: encourage increased production of

natural gas vehicles and provide tax incentives for natural gas vehicle infrastructure (see H.R. 6570), H7630 [30JY]
Palladio, Andrea: anniversary of birth (see H. Con. Res. 407), H7788 [31JY]
Power resources: open Outer Continental shelf areas to oil and gas leasing, curb excessive energy speculation, and require Strategic Petroleum Reserve sale and acquisitions of certain fuels (see H.R. 6670), H7628 [30JY]
——provide a comprehensive plan for greater energy independence (see H.R. 6709), H7785 [31JY]
U.S. Public Service Academy: establish (see H.R. 1671), H7789 [31JY]
Yunus, Muhammad: award Congressional Gold Medal (see H.R. 1801), H7629 [30JY]

Remarks
Pearl Harbor, HI: anniversary of the Pearl Harbor Naval Shipyard (H. Res. 1139), H6773, H6774 [22JY]

ABORTION

Remarks in House
China, People's Republic of: mandatory abortion and sterilization policies, H7344, H7345 [30JY]
Supreme Court: anniversary of Roe v. Wade decision, H7283 [29JY], H7611 [30JY], H7776 [31JY], E1545 [23JY], E1701 [1AU]
U.S. Leadership Against HIV/AIDS, Tuberculosis, and Malaria Act: prohibit use of funds for any organization or program which supports or participates in the management of coerced abortions or involuntary sterilization, H7116 [24JY]

Remarks in Senate
Dept. of HHS: proposed regulation to change the definition of abortion, S7141 [23JY]

ACCESS, COMPARISON, CARE, AND ETHICS FOR SERIOUSLY ILL PATIENTS (ACCESS) ACT
Remarks in Senate
Enact (S. 3046), S7620 [29JY], S8021 [1AU]

ACCESS FOR ALL AMERICA ACT
Bills and resolutions
Enact (see S. 3412, 3413), S7905 [31JY]
Remarks in Senate
Enact (S. 3413), S7971–S7973 [31JY]

ACHIEVING OUR IDEA ACT
Remarks in House
Enact (H.R. 1896), E1701 [1AU]

ACKERMAN, GARY L. (*a Representative from New York*)
Bills and resolutions cosponsored
Bangladesh: elections (see H. Res. 1402), H7788 [31JY]
China, People's Republic of: call for end to human rights abuses of citizens, cease repression of Tibetan and Uyghur people, and end support for Governments of Sudan and Burma (see H. Res. 1370), H7309 [29JY]
Dept. of the Treasury: establish a commemorative quarter dollar coin program emblematic of prominent civil rights leaders and important events advancing civil rights (see H.R. 6701), H7809 [1AU]
Great Lakes-St. Lawrence River Basin Water Resources Compact: grant congressional consent and approval (see H.R. 6577), H7165 [24JY]
Human rights: defeat campaign by some members of the Organization of the Islamic Conference to divert the U.N. Durban Review Conference from a review of problems in their own and other countries (see H. Res. 1361), H7059 [23JY]
Immigration: modify certain requirements with respect to H–1B nonimmigrants (see H.R. 5630), H7629 [30JY]
New York, NY: extend and improve protections and services to individuals directly impacted by the terrorist attack (see H.R. 6594), H7630 [30JY]
Palladio, Andrea: anniversary of birth (see H. Con. Res. 407), H7809 [1AU]
Religion: support spirit of peace and desire for unity displayed in the letter from leading Muslim scholars, and in the Pope Benedict XVI response (see H. Con. Res. 374), H7165 [24JY]
Bills and resolutions introduced
Syria: express concern regarding continued violations of political, civil, and human rights and call for release of prisoners of conscience and other political prisoners (see H. Res. 1398), H7788 [31JY]

ADAMS, MICHAEL F.
Letters
Higher Education Opportunity Act, S7854 [31JY]

ADERHOLT, ROBERT B. (*a Representative from Alabama*)
Bills and resolutions cosponsored
Crime: provide for the use of information in the

National Directory of New Hires in enforcing sex offender registration laws (see H.R. 6539), H7165 [24JY]
Dept. of the Interior: establish oil and gas leasing program for public lands within the Coastal Plain of Alaska (see H.R. 6758), H7787 [31JY]
House of Representatives: prohibit adjournment until approval of a bill to establish a comprehensive national energy plan addressing energy conservation and expansion of renewable and conventional energy sources (see H. Res. 1391), H7629 [30JY]
National Prostate Cancer Awareness Month: support goals and ideals (see H. Res. 672), H7790 [31JY]
Power resources: expedite exploration and development of oil and gas from Federal lands (see H.R. 6379), H7629 [30JY]
——promote alternative and renewable fuels, domestic energy production, conservation, and efficiency, and increase energy independence (see H.R. 6566), H6824 [22JY]
——provide a comprehensive plan for greater energy independence (see H.R. 6709), H7809 [1AU]
Schools: withhold Federal funds from schools that permit or require the recitation of the Pledge of Allegiance or the National Anthem in a language other than English (see H.R. 6783), H7806 [1AU]
Social Security: extend funding for the State Children's Health Insurance Program (see H.R. 6788), H7806 [1AU]
Bills and resolutions introduced
Power resources: enhance energy independence through the usage of existing resources and technology (see H. Con. Res. 401), H7787 [31JY]

ADMINISTRATIVE OFFICE, U.S. COURTS *see* **COURTS**

ADOPTION *see* **FAMILIES AND DOMESTIC RELATIONS**

ADRIAN, MI
Remarks in House
Sand Creek Telephone Co.: anniversary, E1703 [1AU]

ADVANCING AMERICA'S PRIORITIES ACT
Bills and resolutions
Enact (see S. 3297), S7030 [22JY]
Cloture motions
Enact (S. 3297): motion to proceed, S7509 [26JY], S7551 [28JY]
Letters
Provisions: Lynne Zeitlin Hale, Nature Conservancy (organization), S7548 [28JY]
——Molly McCammon, National Federation of Regional Associations for Coastal and Ocean Observing, S7547 [28JY]
——Peter R. Orszag, CBO, S7510 [26JY], S7543 [28JY]
——several ocean and coastal research, education, and conservation organizations, S7547 [28JY]
Motions
Enact (S. 3297), S7509 [26JY]
Remarks in Senate
Appalachian Regional Development Act: reauthorize and improve, S7545 [28JY], S7888 [31JY]
Chesapeake Bay Initiative Act: provide for continuing authorization of the Chesapeake Bay Gateways.

In history of bills, sequence is: Senate bills, Senate joint resolutions, Senate concurrent resolutions, and Senate resolutions; then House bills, House joint resolutions, House concurrent resolutions, and House resolutions: S. 14, S.J. Res. 7, S. Con. Res. 26, S. Res. 5, H. 980, H.J. Res. 9, H. Con. Res. 16, and H. Res. 50.

History of Bills and Resolutions

DATES, ISSUE NUMBERS AND BILLS INTRODUCED IN INDEX VIII

May 12	No. 77	S.	3001–3009	S. Con. Res. 82	S. Res. 558–560
		H.R.	6021–6024		
May 13	No. 78	S.	3010–3014	S.J. Res. 32	S. Res. 561–563
		H.R.	6025–6046	H. Con. Res. 348	H. Res. 1187–1193
May 19	No. 82	S.	3030–3034		S. Res. 569–570
		H.R.	6083–6084	H. Con. Res. 354	H. Res. 1208–1209
May 21	No. 84	S.	3045–3047	S.J. Res. 33 S. Con. Res. 83	S. Res. 572–573
		H.R.	6104–6122	H.J. Res. 86–87 H. Con. Res. 360	H. Res. 1217–1219
May 22	No. 85	S.	3048–3073	S.J. Res. 34–36 S. Con. Res. 84–85	S. Res. 574–579
		H.R.	6123–6166	H.J. Res. 88–89 H. Con. Res. 361–365	H. Res. 1220–1232

Bills receiving legislative action during this Index period numerically precede new bills introduced.

SENATE BILLS

S. 11—A bill to provide liability protection to volunteer pilot nonprofit organizations that fly for public benefit and to the pilots and staff of such nonprofit organizations, and for other purposes; to the Committee on the Judiciary.
Cosponsors added, S4621 [21MY]

S. 2062—A bill to amend the Native American Housing Assistance and Self-Determination Act of 1996 to reauthorize that Act, and for other purposes; to the Committee on Indian Affairs.
Committee on Banking, Housing, and Urban Affairs discharged, S814 [8FE]
Amendments, S850 [11FE], S4836, S4839, S4844 [22MY]
Passed Senate amended, S4839 [22MY]

SENATE JOINT RESOLUTIONS

S.J. Res. 17—A joint resolution directing the United States to initiate international discussions and take necessary steps with other Nations to negotiate an agreement for managing migratory and transboundary fish stocks in the Arctic Ocean; to the Committee on Foreign Relations.
Debated, H4067 [19MY]
Text, H4067 [19MY]
Rules suspended. Passed House, H4402 [21MY]
Message from the House, S4790 [22MY]

S.J. Res. 28—A joint resolution disapproving the rule submitted by the Federal Communications Commission with respect to broadcast media ownership; to the Committee on Commerce, Science, and Transportation.
By Mr. DORGAN (for himself, Ms. Snowe, Mr. Kerry, Ms. Collins, Mr. Dodd, Mr. Obama, Mr. Harkin, Mrs. Clinton, Ms. Cantwell, Mr. Biden, Mr. Reed, Mrs. Feinstein, Mr. Sanders, Mr. Tester, and Mr. Stevens), S1597 [5MR]
Cosponsors added, S1704 [6MR], S1878 [11MR], S2136 [13MR], S2233 [31MR], S2348 [2AP], S2947 [10AP], S3081 [16AP], S3700 [1MY]
Reported (S. Rept. 110–334), S3975 [8MY]
Passed Senate amended, S4267 [15MY]
Text, S4270 [15MY]
Message from the Senate, H4065 [19MY]
Held at the desk, H4065 [19MY]

SENATE CONCURRENT RESOLUTIONS

S. Con. Res. 82—A concurrent resolution supporting the Local Radio Freedom Act; to the Committee on Commerce, Science, and Transportation.
By Mrs. LINCOLN (for herself, Mr. Wicker, Mr. Brownback, Mr. Allard, Mr. Nelson of Nebraska, Ms. Murkowski, and Mr. Webb), S4029 [12MY]

S. Con. Res. 85—A concurrent resolution authorizing the use of the rotunda of the Capitol to honor Frank W. Buckles, the last surviving United States veteran of the First World War.
By Mr. SPECTER (for himself, Mr. Byrd, Mrs. Dole, Mr. McCain, Mr. Warner, Mr. Lieberman, Mr. Rockefeller, and Mr. Burr), S4793 [22MY]

S. Con. Res. 85—Continued
Text, S4810, S4848 [22MY]
Agreed to in the Senate, S4848 [22MY]

SENATE RESOLUTIONS

S. Res. 496—A resolution honoring the 60th anniversary of the commencement of the carving of the Crazy Horse Memorial; to the Committee on the Judiciary.
By Mr. THUNE (for himself and Mr. Johnson), S2346 [2AP]
Text, S2362 [2AP], S4427 [20MY]
Committee discharged. Agreed to in the Senate, S4427 [20MY]

S. Res. 562—A resolution honoring Concerns of Police Survivors as the organization begins its 25th year of service to family members of law enforcement officers killed in the line of duty.
By Ms. MURKOWSKI (for herself, Mr. Biden, Mr. Brown, Mr. Menendez, Ms. Mikulski, Mr. Craig, Mr. Whitehouse, Mr. Baucus, Mr. Dodd, Mrs. Feinstein, Mr. Inouye, Mr. Lautenberg, Mrs. Lincoln, Mr. Nelson of Florida, Mr. Pryor, Mr. Smith, Ms. Stabenow, Mr. Stevens, Mr. Tester, and Mr. Thune), S4106 [13MY]
Text, S4114, S4121 [13MY]
Agreed to in the Senate, S4120 [13MY]

HOUSE BILLS

H.R. 158—A bill to direct the Secretary of the Treasury to mint coins in commemoration of the battlefields of the Revolutionary War and the War of 1812, and for other purposes; to the Committee on Financial Services.
Cosponsors added, H3108 [6MY], H4061 [15MY]

H.R. 503—A bill to amend the Horse Protection Act to prohibit the shipping, transporting, moving, delivering, receiving, possessing, purchasing, selling, or donation of horses and other equines to be slaughtered for human consumption, and for other purposes; to the Committees on Energy and Commerce; Agriculture.
By Ms. SCHAKOWSKY (for herself, Mr. Whitfield, Mr. Rahall, Mr. Spratt, Mr. Gallegly, Mr. Markey, Mr. Pallone, Mr. Nadler, Mr. Van Hollen, Ms. McCollum of Minnesota, Ms. Bordallo, Ms. Schwartz, Mr. Ackerman, Mr. Doyle, Ms. Lee, Mr. Cleaver, Mr. Serrano, Ms. Berkley, Mr. Shays, Mr. Jones of North Carolina, Mr. McCotter, Mr. Cummings, Ms. DeLauro, Mr. George Miller of California, Mr. Grijalva, Mrs. Capps, Ms. Bean, Ms. Matsui, Mr. King of New York, Mr. Burton of Indiana, Mr. Kildee, Ms. Kaptur, Mr. Dicks, Mr. Berman, Ms. Hirono, Mr. Chandler, Mr. Gerlach, Mr. Tierney, Mr. Bishop of New York, Mr. Frank of Massachusetts, Mr. Lynch, Mr. Kirk, Mr. Campbell of California, Mr. Wilson of South Carolina, Ms. Jackson-Lee of Texas, Mr. Sherman,

Mr. LaTourette, Mr. Larson of Connecticut, Mr. Israel, Ms. Woolsey, Mr. Brown of South Carolina, Ms. Eddie Bernice Johnson of Texas, Mr. Moore of Kansas, Mr. Moran of Virginia, Mr. McNulty, Mrs. Maloney of New York, Mr. Inslee, Mr. Wolf, Ms. Carson, Mr. Weiner, Mr. Ruppersberger, Mr. Smith of New Jersey, and Mr. Linder), H670 [17JA]
Cosponsors added, H1055 [30JA], H1153 [31JA], H1565 [13FE], H1668 [14FE], H1896 [16FE], H2165 [5MR], H2621 [15MR], H2821 [21MR], H3279 [28MR], H3363 [29MR], H3476 [17AP], H3724 [20AP], H4553 [7MY], H5054 [15MY], H5927 [24MY], H6181 [7JN], H6439, H6476 [14JN], H6828 [20JN], H7202 [26JN], H8121 [18JY], H8821 [27JY], H9656 [2AU], H10696 [20SE], H11028 [27SE]

H.R. 4841—A bill to approve, ratify, and confirm the settlement agreement entered into to resolve claims by the Soboba Band of Luiseno Indians relating to alleged interences with the water resources of the Tribe, to authorize and direct the Secretary of the Interior to execute and perform the Settlement Agreement and related waivers, and for other purposes; to the Committee on Natural Resources.
Cosponsors added, H390 [22JA], H480 [28JA], H558 [29JA]
Reported with amendment (H. Rept. 110–649), H4059 [15MY]
Debated, H4075 [19MY]
Text, H4075 [19MY]
Rules suspended. Passed House amended, H4401 [21MY]
Message from the House, S4790 [22MY]
Passed Senate, S7197 [23JY]

H.R. 6081—A bill to amend the Internal Revenue Code of 1986 to provide benefits for military personnel, and for other purposes; to the Committee on Ways and Means.
By Mr. RANGEL (for himself, Mr. Stark, Mr. McDermott, Mr. Lewis of Georgia, Mr. Neal of Massachusetts, Mr. Pomeroy, Mrs. Jones of Ohio, Mr. Larson of Connecticut, Mr. Emanuel, Mr. Blumenauer, Mr. Kind, Ms. Berkley, Mr. Crowley, Mr. Van Hollen, Mr. Meek of Florida, Mr. Altmire, Mrs. Boyda of Kansas, Mr. Cohen, Ms. DeLauro, Mr. Ellsworth, Mr. Loebsack, Ms. Tsongas, Mr. Welch of Vermont, Mr. Walz of Minnesota, Mr. Arcuri, Ms. Shea-Porter, Mr. Becerra, Mrs. Davis of California, and Mr. Doggett), H4064 [16MY]
Cosponsors added, H4151 [19MY]
Debated, H4160 [20MY]
Text, H4160 [20MY]
Rules suspended. Passed House amended, H4187 [20MY]
Message from the House, S4617 [21MY]
Passed Senate, S4772 [22MY]
Message from the Senate, H4821 [22MY]

H.R. 6166—A bill to impose certain limitations on the receipt of out-of-State municipal solid waste, and for other purposes; to the Committee on Energy and Commerce.
By Mr. WITTMAN of Virginia (for himself, Mr. Wolf, Mr. Moran of Virginia, and Mr. Donnelly),

20. Reports and Hearings

The data for these publications arrives at GPO from many different sources. Congressional committee staff members are responsible for gathering the information printed in these publications.

Report language is compiled and submitted along with the bill language to the clerks of the respective Houses. The clerks assign the report numbers, etc., and forward this information to GPO for typesetting and printing. In many instances the reports are camera ready copy, needing only insertion of the assigned report number.

Likewise, hearings are also compiled by committee staff members. The data or captured keystrokes as submitted by the various reporting services are forwarded to GPO where the element identifier codes are programmatically inserted and galley or page output is accomplished without manual intervention. It is not cost effective to prepare the manuscript as per the GPO STYLE MANUAL as it is too time-consuming to update and change the data once it is already in type form. Therefore, these publications are to be FIC & punc., unless specifically requested otherwise by the committee. It is not necessary to stamp the copy. However, style as stated in the following rules will be followed.

Style and format of congressional reports

Below are rules that should be followed for the makeup of congressional numbered reports. In either Senate or House reports, follow bill style in extracts from bills. Report numbers run consecutively from first to second session:

1. All excerpts to be set in 10-point type, cut in 2 ems on each side, except as noted in paragraph 3 below. For ellipses in cut-in matter, lines of five stars are used.

2. Contempt proceedings to be considered as excerpts.

3. The following are to be set in 10-point type, but not cut in:

(a) Letters which are readily identified as such by salutation and signature.

(b) Appendixes and/or exhibits which have a heading readily identifying them as such; and

(c) Matter printed in compliance with the Ramseyer rule.[1]

4. All leaderwork and lists of more than six items to be set in 8-point type.

5. All tabular work to be set in 7-point gothic type.

6. An amendment in the nature of a substitute to be set in 8-point type, but quotations from such amendment later in the report to be treated as excerpts, but set full measure (see paragraph 10 below).

7. Any committee print having a report head indicated on original copy to be set in report type and style.

8. Committee prints not having a report head indicated on original copy to be set in committee print style; that is, excerpts to be set in 8 point, full measure.

9. If a committee print set as indicated in paragraph 8 is later submitted as a report or included in a report, and the type is available for pickup, such type shall be picked up and used as is in the report.

10. On matter that is cut in on the left only for purposes of breakdown, no space is used above and below, but on all matter that is cut in on both sides, 4 points are used above and below. If a bill is submitted as an excerpt, it will not be squeezed because of the indentions and the limited number of element identifiers.

11. On reports of immigration cases, set memorandums full measure unless preceded or followed directly by committee language. Memorandums are indented on both sides if followed by such language. Preparers should indicate the proper indention on copy.

12. Order of printing (Senate reports only): (1) Report, (2) minority or additional views, (3) Cordon rule[2] (last unless an appendix is used), (4) appendix (if any).

---

[1] Ramseyer rule.—House: If report has "Changes in Existing Law" use caps and small caps for heads, except for breakdown within a cap and small cap head.

[2] Cordon rule.—Senate: If report has "Changes in Existing Law" use small cap heads, except for breakdown within a cap and small cap head.

13. Minority or additional views will begin a new page with 10-point cap heading. In Senate reports, "Changes in Existing Law" begins a new page if following "views." In conference reports, "Joint Explanatory Statement" begins a new odd page.

14. Minority or additional views are only printed if they have been signed by the authoring congressperson.

[Sample of excerpt]

In *Palmer v. Mass.*, decided in 1939, which involved the reorganization of the New Haven Railroad, the Supreme Court said:

> The judicial processes in bankruptcy proceedings under section 77 are, as it were, brigaded with the administrative processes of the Commission.

[Sample of an excerpt with an added excerpt]

The Interstate Commerce Commission in its report dated February 29, 1956, which is attached hereto and made a part hereof, states that it has no objection to the enactment of S. 3025, and states, in part, as follows:

> The proposed amendment, however, should be considered together with the provisions of section 959(b), title 28, United States Code, which reads as follows:
>
> "A trustee, receiver, or manager appointed in any cause pending in any court of the United States," etc.

[Sample of amendment]

On page 6, line 3, strike the words "and the service", strike all of lines 4, 5, and 6, and insert in lieu thereof the following:

> and, notwithstanding any other provision of law, the service credit authorized by this clause 3 of rule XIII of the Rule of the House of Representatives, change shall not—

(A) be included in establishing eligibility for voluntary or involuntary retirement or separation from the service, under any provision of law;

[Sample of amendment]

The amendments are indicated in the bill as reported and are as follows:
On page 2, line 15, change the period to a colon and add the following:

Provided, That such approaches shall include only those necessary portions of streets, avenues, and boulevards, etc.

On page 3, line 12, after "operated", insert "free of tolls".

[Sample of amendment in the nature of a substitute]

The amendment is as follows:
Strike all after the enacting clause and insert the following:

That the second paragraph under the heading "National Park Service" in the Act of July 31, 1953 (67 Stat. 261, 271), is amended to read as follows: "The Secretary of the Interior shall hereafter report in detail all proposed awards of concessions leases and contracts involving a gross annual business of $100,000 or more, or of more than five years in duration, including renewals thereof, sixty days before such awards are made, to the President of the Senate and Speaker of the House of Representatives for transmission to the appropriate committees."

[Sample of letter inserted in report]

The Department of Defense recommends enactment of the proposed legislation and the Office of Management and Budget interposes no objection as indicated by the following attached letter, which is hereby made a part of this report:

MARCH 21, 2008.

Hon. NANCY PELOSI,
Speaker of the House of Representatives,
Washington, DC.

MY DEAR MADAM SPEAKER: There is forwarded herewith a draft of legislation to amend section 303 of the Career Compensation Act.

  *   *   *   *   *   *   *

Sincerely yours,

> DOUGLAS A. BROOK, ☐☐☐☐☐
> *Assistant Secretary of the Navy* ☐☐☐
> *(Financial Management).* ☐

[Sample of cut-in for purposes of breakdown; no spacing above or below]

Under uniform regulations prescribed by the Secretaries concerned, a member of the uniformed services who—

  (1) is retired for physical disability or placed upon the temporary disability retired list; or

  (2) is retired with pay for any other reason, or is discharged with severance pay, immediately following at least eight years of continuous active duty (no single break therein of more than ninety days);

may select his home for the purposes of the travel and transportation allowances payable under this subsection, etc.

[Sample of leaderwork]

Among the 73 vessels mentioned above, 42 are classified as major combatant ships (aircraft carriers through escort vessels), in the following types:

Forrestal-class aircraft carriers	4
Destroyers	10
* * * * * * *	
Guided-missile submarine	1
Total	42

[Sample of sectional analysis]

SECTIONAL ANALYSIS

Section 1. Increase of 1 year in constructive service for promotion purposes

The principal purpose of the various subsections of section 1 is to provide a 1-year increase for medical and dental officers in * * *

*   *   *   *   *   *   *

Subsection 101(a) is in effect a restatement of the existing law

This subsection authorizes the President to make regular appointments in the grade of first lieutenant through * * *

*   *   *   *   *   *   *

―――――――――

[Sample of amendment under Ramseyer rule]

CHANGES IN EXISTING LAW

In compliance with clause 3 of rule XII of the Rules of the House of Representatives, changes in existing law made by the bill, as introduced, are shown as follows (existing law proposed to be omitted is enclosed in black brackets, new matter is printed in italic, existing law in which no change is proposed is shown in roman):

EXPORT CONTROL ACT OF 1949

*   *   *   *   *   *   *

TERMINATION DATE

SEC. 12. The authority granted herein shall terminate on June 30, [1956] *1959,* or upon any prior date which the Congress by concurrent resolution or the President may designate.

[The following examples are for sample purposes only]
[Sample of "Report" Skeleton]

| 110TH CONGRESS 2d Session | HOUSE OF REPRESENTATIVES | REPT. 110–542 Part 1 |

PROVIDING FOR AND APPROVE THE SETTLEMENT OF CERTAIN LAND CLAIMS OF THE SAULT STE. MARIE TRIBE OF CHIPPEWA INDIANS [1]

MARCH 6, 2008.—Ordered to be printed [2]

Mr. RAHALL, from the Committee on Natural Resources, submitted the following

R E P O R T

together with

DISSENTING VIEWS

[To accompany H.R. 4115]

[Including cost estimate of the Congressional Budget Office]

The Committee on Natural Resources, to whom was referred the bill (H.R. 4115) to provide for and approve the settlement of certain land claims of the Sault Ste. Marie Tribe of Chippewa Indians, having considered the same, report favorably thereon with an amendment and recommend that the bill as amended do pass. [3]

PURPOSE OF THE BILL [4]

The purpose of H.R. 4115 is to provide for and approve the settlement of certain land claims of the Sault Ste. Marie Tribe of Chippewa Indians.

---

[1] If title makes more than three lines in 10-point caps, set in 8-point caps.
[2] Must be set as indicated in copy. If illustrations accompany copy and are not ordered to be printed, do not add *with illustrations*. Return copy to Production Manager.
[3] If the wording in this paragraph is prepared in the singular form, follow.
[4] For *Senate Committee on Finance* and *House Committee on Ways and Means*, heads are set in bold caps.

[Sample of "Report" Skeleton]

| 110TH CONGRESS
2d Session | SENATE | Calendar No. 652 [1]
REPORT
110–300 |

CIVIL WAR BATTLEFIELD PRESERVATION ACT OF 2008

APRIL 10, 2008.—Ordered to be printed

Filed under authority of the order of the Senate of April 10
(legislative day, April 9), 2008 [2]

Mr. BINGAMAN, from the Committee on Energy and Natural
Resources, submitted the following

R E P O R T

together with

ADDITIONAL VIEWS

[To accompany S. 1921]

The Committee on Energy and Natural Resources, to which was
referred the bill (S. 1921) to amend the American Battlefield Protection Act of 1996 to extend the authorization for that Act, and for
other purposes, having considered the same, reports favorably
thereon with an amendment and recommends that the bill, as
amended, do pass.

PURPOSE

The purpose of S. 1921 is to reauthorize the American Battlefield
Protection Act for an additional five years, from 2008 until 2013.

BACKGROUND AND NEED

The American Battlefield Protection Program was authorized in
1996 to provide funding for preservation of threatened Civil War
battlefields. The program leverages Federal appropriations by requiring matching non-Federal funds. The battlefield protection

---

[1] Use this type and form only on Senate reports. There is only one calendar in the Senate.
[2] Style for filed line, if present.

[Sample of "Report" Skeleton]

110TH CONGRESS } HOUSE OF REPRESENTATIVES { REPORT
2d Session 110–590

PROVIDING[1] FOR CONSIDERATION OF THE BILL (H.R. 5715) TO ENSURE CONTINUED AVAILABILITY OF ACCESS TO THE FEDERAL STUDENT LOAN PROGRAM FOR STUDENTS AND FAMILIES[2]

APRIL 15, 2008.—Referred to the House Calendar and ordered to be printed

Ms. CASTOR, from the Committee on Rules,
submitted the following

R E P O R T

[To accompany H. Res. 1107]

The Committee on Rules, having had under consideration House Resolution 1107, by a record vote of 8–4, report the same to the House with the recommendation that the resolution be adopted.

SUMMARY OF PROVISIONS OF THE RESOLUTION

The resolution provides for consideration of H.R. 5715, the Ensuring Continued Access to Student Loans Act of 2008, under a structured rule. The rule provides one hour of general debate equally divided and controlled by the chairman and ranking minority member of the Committee on Education and Labor. The rule waives all points of order against consideration of the bill except clauses 9 and 10 of rule XXI. The rule provides that the amendment printed in Part A of the Rules Committee report accompanying the resolution shall be considered as adopted and that the bill, as amended, shall be considered as read. The rule waives all points of order against provisions of the bill, as amended. (This waiver does not affect the point of order available under clause 9 of rule XXI (regarding earmark disclosure).

The rule provides that no further amendments to the bill, as amended, shall be in order except those amendments printed in Part B of this report. The further amendments made in order may be offered only in the order printed in this report, may be offered only by a Member designated in this report, shall be considered as read, shall be debatable for the time specified in this report equally divided and controlled by the proponent and an opponent, shall not

---

[1] If copy reads "To make" change to "Making", "To provide" change to "Providing", "To amend" change to "Amending".
[2] Sample of 8-point head.

110TH CONGRESS ⎫   ⎧   REPORT
  1st Session ⎬   HOUSE OF REPRESENTATIVES   ⎨   110–317

COLLEGE COST REDUCTION AND ACCESS ACT

SEPTEMBER 6, 2007.—Ordered to be printed

Mr. GEORGE MILLER of California, from the committee of
conference, submitted the following

CONFERENCE REPORT

[To accompany H.R. 2669]

The committee of conference on the disagreeing votes of the two
Houses on the amendment of the Senate to the bill (H.R. 2669), to
provide for reconciliation pursuant to section 601 of the concurrent
resolution on the budget for fiscal year 2008, having met, after full
and free conference, have agreed to recommend and do recommend
to their respective Houses as follows:

That the House recede from its disagreement to the amendment of the Senate and agree to the same with an amendment as
follows:

In lieu of the matter proposed to be inserted by the Senate
amendment, insert the following:

SECTION 1. SHORT TITLE; REFERENCES.

(a) SHORT TITLE.—*This Act may be cited as the "College Cost
Reduction and Access Act".*

(b) REFERENCES.—*Except as otherwise expressly provided,
whenever in this Act an amendment or repeal is expressed in terms
of an amendment to, or repeal of, a section or other provision, the
reference shall be considered to be made to a section or other provision of the Higher Education Act of 1965 (20 U.S.C. 1001 et seq.).*

(c) EFFECTIVE DATE.—*Except as otherwise expressly provided,
the amendments made by this Act shall be effective on October 1,
2007.*

59–006

JOINT EXPLANATORY STATEMENT OF THE COMMITTEE OF CONFERENCE

The managers on the part of the House and the Senate at the conference on the disagreeing votes of the two Houses on the amendment of the Senate to the bill (H.R. 2669), to provide for reconciliation pursuant to section 601 of the concurrent resolution on the budget for fiscal year 2008, submit the following joint statement to the House and the Senate in explanation of the effect of the action agreed upon by the managers and recommended in the accompanying conference report:

The Senate amendment struck all of the House bill after the enacting clause and inserted a substitute text.

The House recedes from its disagreement to the amendment of the Senate with an amendment that is a substitute for the House bill and the Senate amendment. The differences between the House bill, the Senate amendment, and the substitute agreed to in conference are noted below, except for clerical corrections, conforming changes made necessary by agreements reached by the conferees, and minor drafting and clarifying changes.

SECTION 1. SHORT TITLE

The House bill's short title is the "College Cost Reduction Act."

The Senate amendment provides that the Act may be cited as the "Higher Education Access Act of 2007" and that, unless otherwise indicated, references in the bill are made to the Higher Education Act of 1965.

The House recedes with an amendment to provide a new short title of the "College Cost Reduction and Access Act." The Conferees adopt the Senate amendment as amended by the House.

TITLE I—GRANTS TO STUDENTS IN ATTENDANCE AT INSTITUTIONS OF HIGHER EDUCATION

SECTION 101. TUITION SENSITIVITY

The House bill (Sec. 101) eliminates the Pell grant "tuition sensitivity" provision that prevents low-income students attending low-cost institutions, such as community colleges, to benefit fully from the Pell Grant. Authorizes and appropriates $5,000,000 for fiscal year 2008.

The Senate amendment (Sec. 101) also eliminates the Pell grant "tuition sensitivity" provision and authorizes and appropriates $5,000,000 for fiscal year 2008.

The House and the Senate recede with an amendment to authorize and appropriate $11,000,000 for fiscal year 2008 to ensure that all eligible students in award year 2007–2008 receive funding. The Conferees concur and adopt the amendment.

54

COMPLIANCE WITH HOUSE RULE XXI

Pursuant to clause 9 of rule XXI of the Rules of the House of Representatives, this conference report contains no congressional earmarks, limited tax benefits, or limited tariff benefits as defined in clause 9(d), 9(e), or 9(f) of rule XXI.

GEORGE MILLER,
ROBERT E. ANDREWS,
BOBBY SCOTT,
RUBÉN HINOJOSA,
JOHN F. TIERNEY,
DAVID WU,
SUSAN A. DAVIS,
DANNY K. DAVIS,
TIMOTHY BISHOP,
MAZIE K. HIRONO,
JASON ALTMIRE,
JOHN YARMUTH,
JOE COURTNEY,
Managers on the Part of the House.

TED KENNEDY,
CHRIS DODD,
TOM HARKIN,
BARBARA A. MIKULSKI,
JEFF BINGAMAN,
PATTY MURRAY,
JACK REED,
HILLARY RODHAM CLINTON,
BARACK OBAMA,
BERNARD SANDERS,
SHERROD BROWN,
MICHAEL B. ENZI,
LAMAR ALEXANDER,
ORRIN G. HATCH,
Managers on the Part of the Senate.

O

FINANCIAL SERVICES AND GENERAL GOVERNMENT APPROPRIATIONS FOR 2009

HEARINGS

BEFORE A

SUBCOMMITTEE OF THE

COMMITTEE ON APPROPRIATIONS

HOUSE OF REPRESENTATIVES

ONE HUNDRED TENTH CONGRESS

SECOND SESSION

SUBCOMMITTEE ON FINANCIAL SERVICES AND GENERAL GOVERNMENT
APPROPRIATIONS

JOSÉ E. SERRANO, New York, *Chairman*

CAROLYN C. KILPATRICK, Michigan
C.A. "DUTCH" RUPPERSBERGER, Maryland
DEBBIE WASSERMAN SCHULTZ, Florida
PETER J. VISCLOSKY, Indiana
ROBERT E. "BUD" CRAMER, JR., Alabama
MAURICE D. HINCHEY, New York
ADAM SCHIFF, California

RALPH REGULA, Ohio
MARK STEVEN KIRK, Illinois
RODNEY ALEXANDER, Louisiana
VIRGIL H. GOODE, JR., Virginia
JO BONNER, Alabama

NOTE: Under Committee Rules, Mr. Obey, as Chairman of the Full Committee, and Mr. Lewis, as Ranking
Minority Member of the Full Committee, are authorized to sit as Members of all Subcommittees.

DALE OAK, BOB BONNER, KARYN KENDALL, and FRANCISCO CARRILLO,
Subcommittee Staff

PART 7

U.S. GOVERNMENT PRINTING OFFICE

WASHINGTON : 2008

42–831

COMMITTEE ON APPROPRIATIONS
DAVID R. OBEY, Wisconsin, *Chairman*

JOHN P. MURTHA, Pennsylvania
NORMAN D. DICKS, Washington
ALAN B. MOLLOHAN, West Virginia
MARCY KAPTUR, Ohio
PETER J. VISCLOSKY, Indiana
NITA M. LOWEY, New York
JOSÉ E. SERRANO, New York
ROSA L. DeLAURO, Connecticut
JAMES P. MORAN, Virginia
JOHN W. OLVER, Massachusetts
ED PASTOR, Arizona
DAVID E. PRICE, North Carolina
CHET EDWARDS, Texas
ROBERT E. "BUD" CRAMER, JR., Alabama
PATRICK J. KENNEDY, Rhode Island
MAURICE D. HINCHEY, New York
LUCILLE ROYBAL-ALLARD, California
SAM FARR, California
JESSE L. JACKSON, JR., Illinois
CAROLYN C. KILPATRICK, Michigan
ALLEN BOYD, Florida
CHAKA FATTAH, Pennsylvania
STEVEN R. ROTHMAN, New Jersey
SANFORD D. BISHOP, JR., Georgia
MARION BERRY, Arkansas
BARBARA LEE, California
TOM UDALL, New Mexico
ADAM SCHIFF, California
MICHAEL HONDA, California
BETTY McCOLLUM, Minnesota
STEVE ISRAEL, New York
TIM RYAN, Ohio
C.A. "DUTCH" RUPPERSBERGER, Maryland
BEN CHANDLER, Kentucky
DEBBIE WASSERMAN SCHULTZ, Florida
CIRO RODRIGUEZ, Texas

JERRY LEWIS, California
C. W. BILL YOUNG, Florida
RALPH REGULA, Ohio
HAROLD ROGERS, Kentucky
FRANK R. WOLF, Virginia
JAMES T. WALSH, New York
DAVID L. HOBSON, Ohio
JOE KNOLLENBERG, Michigan
JACK KINGSTON, Georgia
RODNEY P. FRELINGHUYSEN, New Jersey
TODD TIAHRT, Kansas
ZACH WAMP, Tennessee
TOM LATHAM, Iowa
ROBERT B. ADERHOLT, Alabama
JO ANN EMERSON, Missouri
KAY GRANGER, Texas
JOHN E. PETERSON, Pennsylvania
VIRGIL H. GOODE, JR., Virginia
RAY LAHOOD, Illinois
DAVE WELDON, Florida
MICHAEL K. SIMPSON, Idaho
JOHN ABNEY CULBERSON, Texas
MARK STEVEN KIRK, Illinois
ANDER CRENSHAW, Florida
DENNIS R. REHBERG, Montana
JOHN R. CARTER, Texas
RODNEY ALEXANDER, Louisiana
KEN CALVERT, California
JO BONNER, Alabama

ROB NABORS, *Clerk and Staff Director*

(II)

[House Appropriation Hearing sample]

DEPARTMENT OF HOMELAND SECURITY APPROPRIATIONS FOR 2009

TUESDAY, FEBRUARY 26, 2008.

IMMIGRATION ENFORCEMENT: IDENTIFICATION AND REMOVAL OF CRIMINAL ALIENS, STUDENT AND EXCHANGE VISITOR PROGRAM FEE INCREASES

WITNESSES

CATHERYN COTTEN, DIRECTOR, INTERNATIONAL OFFICE, DUKE UNIVERSITY

JULIE L. MYERS, ASSISTANT SECRETARY, U.S. IMMIGRATION AND CUSTOMS ENFORCEMENT [ICE], DEPARTMENT OF HOMELAND SECURITY

Mr. PRICE. Subcommittee will come to order. Good morning, everyone. Today we will be discussing the wide variety of activities carried out by Immigration and Customs Enforcement, or ICE, and we will first focus on the Agency's Student and Exchange Visitor Program.

BALANCING SECURITY AND STUDENT NEEDS

Mr. PRICE. Thank you very much. We will put your entire statement in the record, which of course elaborates on the points you made and goes beyond them. Let me ask you first a rather broad question, and then I will zero in somewhat on the fee increases and the benefits that might accrue from an increased flow of fee revenue.

[Note style for questions and answers]

Question. What percentage of cases presented to prosecutors along the Southwest border are prosecuted? Provide by sector and/or state. What was the prosecution rate of criminals picked up off the street? (Culberson)

Answer. ICE does not track prosecutions, however, ICE works closely with U.S. Attorneys and state and local prosecutors nationwide on a wide variety of cases.

FY2007 SAC office	Criminal arrests	Indictments	Convictions*
El Paso, TX	2,435	1,882	1,704
Phoenix, AZ	1,641	623	770
San Antonio, TX	1,588	1,172	1,155
San Diego, CA	2,318	1,147	1,842
Fiscal Year Total	7,982	4,824	5,471

*Indictments and convictions may be comprised of arrests from previous years.

Mr. CULBERSON. Okay.

[Standard Hearing sample]

ORGANIZATIONAL MEETING ON ADOPTION OF COMMITTEE RULES; CONSIDERATION OF INTERIM REPORT; AND HEARING ON VOTING IN THE HOUSE OF REPRESENTATIVES

THURSDAY, SEPTEMBER 27, 2007

HOUSE OF REPRESENTATIVES,☐☐☐☐☐☐☐
SELECT COMMITTEE TO INVESTIGATE THE VOTING☐☐☐☐☐
IRREGULARITIES OF AUGUST 2, 2007,☐☐☐
Washington, DC.☐

The committee met, pursuant to call, at 9:11 a.m., in Room H–313, The Capitol, Hon. William D. Delahunt (Chairman of the committee) presiding.

Present: Representatives Delahunt, Davis, Herseth Sandlin, Pence, LaTourette and Hulshof.

The CHAIRMAN. A quorum being present, the select committee will come to order.

Today we are meeting to do three tasks: adopt our committee rules, adopt the internal report, and to hear for the first time—of what we expect to be multiple occasions—from the Office of the House Clerk. We will wait for the gentlelady from South Dakota, who was at her other select committee.

I now recognize myself for 5 minutes to make an opening statement, but before I do, let me note I will then go to Congressman Pence as the Ranking Member. And in subsequent hearings, it would be our hope that just he and I would make opening statements. But on this initial hearing, any member of the panel that wishes to make an opening statement is most welcome.

I would be remiss not to begin by thanking the Chair of the House Rules Committee, Louise Slaughter, and the Ranking Member, David Dreier, for making their hearing room available to the select committee.

I also want to welcome everyone to this initial meeting of the select committee that has been mandated by the House to review roll call No. 814. I would note that none of the Members sought this particular assignment, but each of us appreciates the role and the significance of the House in our unique constitutional order, and recognize that the integrity of the system by which we cast our votes on the House floor is essential to the confidence that the American people have in this institution, aptly described as the people's House.

Index